Law, Governance and Technology Series

Volume 59

The *Law, Governance and Technology Series* is intended to attract manuscripts arising from an interdisciplinary approach in law, artificial intelligence and information technologies. The idea is to bridge the gap between research in IT law and IT-applications for lawyers developing a unifying techno-legal perspective. The series will welcome proposals that have a fairly specific focus on problems or projects that will lead to innovative research charting the course for new interdisciplinary developments in law, legal theory, and law and society research as well as in computer technologies, artificial intelligence and cognitive sciences. In broad strokes, manuscripts for this series may be mainly located in the fields of the Internet law (data protection, intellectual property, Internet rights, etc.), Computational models of the legal contents and legal reasoning, Legal Information Retrieval, Electronic Data Discovery, Collaborative Tools (e.g. Online Dispute Resolution platforms), Metadata and XML Technologies (for Semantic Web Services), Technologies in Courtrooms and Judicial Offices (E-Court), Technologies for Governments and Administrations (E-Government), Legal Multimedia, and Legal Electronic Institutions (Multi-Agent Systems and Artificial Societies).

Angelos Kornilakis • Georgios Nouskalis •
Vassilis Pergantis • Themistoklis Tzimas
Editors

Artificial Intelligence and Normative Challenges

International and Comparative Legal Perspectives

Springer

Editors
Angelos Kornilakis
Faculty of Law
Aristotle University of Thessaloniki
Thessaloniki, Greece

Georgios Nouskalis
Faculty of Law
Aristotle University of Thessaloniki
Thessaloniki, Greece

Vassilis Pergantis
Faculty of Law
Aristotle University of Thessaloniki
Thessaloniki, Greece

Themistoklis Tzimas
School of Economics and Political Sciences
Aristotle University of Thessaloniki
Thessaloniki, Greece

ISSN 2352-1902 ISSN 2352-1910 (electronic)
Law, Governance and Technology Series
ISBN 978-3-031-41080-2 ISBN 978-3-031-41081-9 (eBook)
https://doi.org/10.1007/978-3-031-41081-9

This Springer imprint is published by the registered company Springer Nature Switzerland AG
The registered company address is: Gewerbestrasse 11, 6330 Cham, Switzerland

Paper in this product is recyclable.

Preface

This edited volume is the outcome of an international online conference on "Artificial Intelligence and Normative Challenges" organized on 1–2 April 2021 by the *Law Faculty of the Aristotle University of Thessaloniki* and the *Kalliopi Koufa Foundation for the Promotion of International and Human Rights Law*, with the support of the European Society of International Law and the Research Committee of the Aristotle University of Thessaloniki.

The editors would like to thank all conference participants for fruitful discussion. Special thanks go to Christos Zois and Fotini Zarogianni for their editorial assistance and to the Springer team for streamlining the project.

The editors

Thessaloniki, Greece

Angelos Kornilakis
Georgios Nouskalis
Vassilis Pergantis
Themistoklis Tzimas

Contents

Introduction

Angelos Kornilakis, Georgios Nouskalis, Vassilis Pergantis, and Themistoklis Tzimas

Artificial Intelligence (AI)—both in its current narrow form and even more in its potential future forms (such as General and Super Intelligence)—has raised concerns as well as expectations. Its actual and potential consequences are ever-expanding and apply to almost every facet of human life at the collective and individual levels. From the use of mobile phones and social media to autonomous weapons, from digitalization of knowledge and information to patent-eligibility for AI innovations, unexpected, until recently, philosophical, ontological, political, and legal issues arise.

AI constitutes an ambiguous concept; "[I]n spite of what I regard as AI's significant achievements. . .the not so well-kept secret is that AI is internally in a paradigmatic mess. There is really no broad agreement on the essential nature or formal basis of intelligence and the proper theoretical framework for it", Chandrasekaran comments.[1] Hence, AI, despite the prevalent approach of "we

[1] Chandrasekaran (1990), p. 14.

A. Kornilakis
Faculty of Law, Aristotle University of Thessaloniki, Thessaloniki, Greece
e-mail: akornil@law.auth.gr

G. Nouskalis
Criminal Law, Aristotle University of Thessaloniki, Thessaloniki, Greece
e-mail: gnouskal@law.auth.gr

V. Pergantis
Public International Law, Aristotle University of Thessaloniki, Thessaloniki, Greece
e-mail: vpergantis@law.auth.gr

T. Tzimas (✉)
School of Economics and Political Sciences, Aristotle University of Thessaloniki, Thessaloniki, Greece
e-mail: thtzimas@polsci.auth.gr

A. Kornilakis et al. (eds.), *Artificial Intelligence and Normative Challenges*, Law, Governance and Technology Series 59,
https://doi.org/10.1007/978-3-031-41081-9_1

know it when we see it", can be quite controversial regarding its definition, especially in light of the distinctions between automation and autonomy, as well as the different levels of its evolution.[2] In addition, the fact that AI at large attempts to replicate human intelligence means that ambivalences around human intelligence emerge with AI as well.

A rather generic, anthropomorphic definition argues that AI refers to "[m]achines that are capable of performing tasks that, if performed by a human, would be said to require intelligence".[3] Therefore, AI is expected to be able to replicate and emulate a variety of human intelligence characteristics such as "consciousness, self-awareness, language use, the ability to learn, the ability to abstract, the ability to adapt, and the ability to reason".[4]

AI is distinguished between weak and strong, with the latter yet to come. Weak AI, which is described as Artificial Narrow Intelligence (ANI) is the existing form of AI. While it may exceed specific, human intelligence capacities and while it can still demonstrate significant levels of autonomy,[5] it does so only in a pre-determined, narrow area and not at the level of general intelligence. Strong AI is distinguished between Artificial General Intelligence (AGI) and Artificial Super Intelligence (ASI).[6] AGI describes a future situation, when AI will be able to demonstrate intellectual capacities, equal to these of the human mind, at a general level. Therefore, AGI will be adaptable to novel environments, in a manner unforeseen by its software-writer and capable of multiple missions. ASI, on its part, describes a level of intelligence, superior to human intelligence in general.[7] ASI may take different forms. While we can guess some of these missions, our speculations may be surpassed by future reality. One potential scenario is that ASI will exercise functions of the human mind, although exponentially faster.[8] A second potential outcome of superintelligence may be collective intelligence.[9] Until now we have experienced cooperative types of intelligence, namely, in academia, in social media, social networks of various types, in political parties etc. ASI could be able to perform as a single mind.[10] In such a sense, it may reach qualities that are different compared to human ones.[11] Last but not least, AI could possibly merge with human intelligence producing the era of trans- or post-humanism. A new form of existence or species, different but not completely alien to existing humanity.

---

[2] Russell and Norvig (2010), p. 2; Winograd (1990), p. 167.

[3] Scherer (2016), p. 362.

[4] Ibid., p. 360.

[5] Bekey (2005).

[6] Urban (2015).

[7] Bostrom (2006).

[8] Bostrom (2014), pp. 40–60.

[9] Tzimas (2021), pp. 51–64.

[10] Shanahan (2010).

[11] Bostrom (2014), pp. 40–60.

Central to the above is the concept of singularity,[12] namely, the emergence of such technological developments which might result in unpredictable phenomena with infinite intelligence and speed, capable of reproducing themselves.[13] Obviously, such an expectation—or threat—constitutes a highly speculatory idea, involving techno-ideological elements. Still, it is a potential evolution that we need to keep in mind, when discussing about the possible impact of AI.

Closer to the current evolution of AI, its benefits cannot be overstated[14]: AI makes outcomes on the evolution of environmental degradation or of a human's health more predictable; it optimizes the operation of various activities, such as the administration of justice, reducing costs and the duration; it allows for a faster allocation of resources by rendering quasi-automatic the relevant processes; it customizes service delivery according to the personal needs and preferences of every user; it improves healthcare services, by making diagnosis more accurate and helping to better prevent various diseases; it improves farming productivity; it can help maintain household appliances in better shape by predicting possible malfunctions; it increases human security through new systems of crime control, identifying rapidly online terrorist propaganda or alerting about illicit substances hidden in products; it can make transportation cleaner and safer. Especially in the field of environmental protection, apart from its predictive strengths, AI can help achieve the sustainability development goals set by the United Nations.

In the juridical realm, AI has a series of unique features that challenge the constants of our legal culture. For example, AI entities can write music, articles, take part in hostilities, solve mathematical theorems, proceed to facial recognition, drive, choose products for us and order them, manage our assets, evaluate humans professionally but also legally, coordinate factories, conduct medical and political research and, possibly, in the future enhance humanity or subdue it.

This complex technological evolution poses serious challenges to the existing legal rules, raises uncertainties in various fields and warrants law to foresee potential developments regarding AI so as to establish a pre-emptive regulatory framework. This is, all the more so, for international law due to the borderless nature of AI and its frequent use in transnational contexts. Hence, law has a significant role to play in delimiting AI uses on the basis of current norms or in conjuring new concepts, principles and rules conveying new transnational, "plurispace" and agile normative forms.

A first, comprehensive response to the challenges posed by AI system can be found in EU's legislative proposals concerning AI. The *2021 AI Act*, for instance, introduces three categories of AI systems, namely prohibited, high-risk and low-risk ones. It imposes various mandatory requirements related to human oversight, transparency, fundamental rights conformity assessment and AI registration in public

[12] Vinge (1993); Kurzweil (2005); Yudkowsky (2007).

[13] Chalmers (2010), p. 9.

[14] European Commission, White Paper on AI – A European approach to excellence and trust, Com (2020) 65 final, pp. 1–2.

databases for high-risk systems, while allowing relevant codes of conduct for low-risk AI.[15] Moreover, the proposed *2022 AI Liability Directive*[16] imposes a reversal of the burden of proof concerning the discrimination and the damages caused to the claimant, as well as a rebuttable presumption of causality between the defendant's fault and the AI system's outcome. Furthermore, a normative framework of strict liability is enacted for high-risk activities. These normative responses constitute an effort to normatively adapt the current regulatory framework to the employment of AI systems.

The goal of this book is to explore the impact of AI on various areas of human conduct and the response of law generally thereto, including the questions of AI and legal personhood; responsibility, liability and culpability in the age of AI; the challenges posed by AI to intellectual property regimes; human rights challenges raised by AI; and the impact of AI on *jus ad bellum* and *jus in bello*.

The first thematic cluster explores from a historical and theoretical perspective the phenomenon of Artificial Intelligence. It focuses on ways for the legal recognition of intelligent entities and their acquisition of legal personhood in various contexts taking into account their unique, ontological characteristics. Legal orders—national, transnational and international ones—are state- or human-centered and accommodating AI entities within the current normative framework concerning subject and the construction of legal personality encounters serious challenges and must be subject to specific conditions. Both chapters of this thematic cluster explore what conditions should underpin the legal recognition of personhood to AI entities and whether a different approach should be adopted with regard to AGI and ASI, if they ever come to exist. Further questions concern the spatial and temporal scope of such AI personhood and limitations thereto, as well as differences that might exist across the normative spectrum between private/civil law, criminal law and public international law in tackling the challenge of legal recognition of intelligent machines.

Marco Rizzuti draws a provocative analogy between the status of slaves in ancient Rome and artificial intelligence in today's legal orders. He highlights both the linguistic affinities, as well as the sociological effects of both phenomena in the context of an evolution towards a jobless society. He then explores the similarities between the legal institution of *peculium*, where a slave was granted the task to administer part of the master's patrimony, to the current discussions on the personhood of artificial intelligence and the consequences thereof. He pursues a functional, rather than an ontological, perspective in pinpointing the civil liability issues that the use of artificial intelligence can raise and solutions that can be inspired by the *peculium*, and he extends his analysis to non-patrimonial relationships too, such as the conclusion of contracts and the construction of family relations, particularly in the field of succession. Throughout his analysis, he warns about the impact that new

[15] European Commission, COM (2021), 206 final.

[16] Proposal of the EU Commission for a Directive of the European Parliament and of the Council adapting the rules on non-contractual civil liability in artificial intelligence (AIL-D), 28.9.2022, COM(2022) 496 final.

distinctions and categorizations may have in an ontological and axiological sense, marginalizing, for instance, those humans that cannot compete in intelligence "overbidding".

Angelos Kornilakis further details the practical consequences of legal personhood of autonomous AI in private law, with an emphasis on identification, right to personality, capacity to hold property rights and to contract, as well as issues of liability. The AI's uncertainty permeates his analysis, while analogies are drawn between AI and corporations, where functional limitations in normatively admissible actions are placed, but equally between AI and humans, where a principal/agent model is explored in order to fill gaps in the action and liability of intelligent machines in connection to their users. Of course, AI agents do not act for their benefit and cannot operate outside their *modus operandi,* elements that lead him to conclude that AI can only have a restricted legal personhood and enjoy limited autonomy, as they will always need a guardian. Such legal personhood, he concludes allows for the implementation of a model of strict agency and vicarious, strict liability.

Vasiliki Papadouli introduces the ethical and legal dilemmas that AI poses in modern societies. She highlights how AI's ability of machine learning is coupled with the black box effect, namely the inability to understand how an AI system operates and the latter's difficult to provide a relevant explanation. This is due, according to the author, to the complexity of the system, the lack of visibility of training data and methods of date selection (so-called intentional concealment), the limited understanding concerning the inherent bias of data sets and technological illiteracy and cognitive mismatch of the wider public and the experts, respectively, regarding AI systems. Using a series of real-world AI applications in job recruitment/dismissal, loan risk assessment by banks, health status review for insurance purposes, criminal recidivism prediction tools, contract-conclusion and artwork suggestion by AI systems, AI and intellectual property rights, and, last but not least, accidents by self-driving vehicles, she showcases the practical ramifications of the black box problem and puts forward a series of normative solutions. These include, particularly, the shifting of the burden of proof from those complaining injury by the use of AI systems to the defendant, and the application of a rebuttable presumption of causal link between the AI's employment and the injury caused, as well as the strict liability of the defendant, as suggested by the *Artificial Intelligence Act* of the European Commission. Finally, she proposes three measures for counteracting the black-box effect, namely the creation of ethical systems, or more precisely, of an ethical code by inscribing specific rules (tort liability, prohibition of racial or sexual discrimination, respect for human dignity) to it; increased transparency through the employment of explainable AI; and, finally, provisions for human oversight on AI systems, particularly in the form of *human-on-the-loop* or *human-in-command* mechanisms.

The second thematic cluster delves more systematically into the questions of wrongfulness, attribution, and liability in the field of civil law. Two contributions shed light to the issue of liability in contract-making, as well as the issue of risk as a cornerstone of sound liability regulation. Private law liability is very much affected by the employment of AI agents. For instance, it is not always clear whether a wrongful conduct should be attributed to the software designer, the manufacturer, the user, or those feeding the machine with data. More fundamentally, can AI be held directly liable? What are the challenges raised in contract and tort law regarding civil liability for AI applications? How does the merging of the human and AI impacts on the liability question? How do notions of attribution and risk play out in the case of AI agents? What kind of remedies exist in case of wrongfulness in the field of private (civil) law? Those and other elements are covered by these two contributions.

More specifically, *Vasiliki Papadouli*, explores the role of autonomous machines on the conclusion of contracts, as well as the question of contractual liability in case of breach of such contracts. She highlights the advantages and weaknesses of the two main approaches thereto, namely, the approach that treats autonomous machines as mere communication tools that cannot generate their own declaration of intent and the approach of disclosed agency, which recognises the fact that the AI forms an autonomous declaration of intent but the latter is attributed to its user. Having rejected both of them and while admitting that private law as it stands does not recognize legal personhood to intelligent machines, she proposes a combined solution in the form of *de facto* contracts and *reliance* liability in order to embed the liability of an AI user. Both solutions, developed in the context of the mass transactions of the late twentieth century, mark a turning point in the doctrine of contract law, where conduct and reliance are deemed sufficient for a contractual relationship and the establishment of contractual or quasi-contractual liability. Such theories, however, encounter serious challenges in case of mistake and rescission of contract, where the risk should be shared between the AI user and the counter party. In contrasting the hardship of the rules on mistake with those of non-contractual liability and commenting on the special rules of law regarding proof in favor of the user and the rebuttable presumption of causality introduced by Art. 4 of the EU Proposal for a Directive on non-contractual liability, she explores how could these solutions be implemented *mutatis mutandis* in a contractual setting.

Risk as a crucial element of liability is exhaustively explored by *Nasir Muftic*. In his contribution and after having examined the contribution of adjudication in regulating AI technology, he opts for an increased role of the legislation in shaping liability regimes. He focuses on risk as the crucial factor, since the characteristics of AI technology, namely autonomy, opacity and vulnerability constitute extraordinary challenges that prevent us from fully employing the traditional liability regimes. Thus, after having examined and dismissed the application of strict liability, fault liability and product liability and having stressed the difficulties from the involvement of various actors in AI, which renders establishing a causal link almost impossible, he turns towards a risk-based approach to liability. There, he expounds various methods for incorporating risk in liability regimes and ultimately advocates for a technology-specific approach to regulate risk, where different AI technologies will be subject to varied liability regimes. This view takes into account the recent EU proposals for an Artificial Intelligence Liability Directive and for a revised Product Liability Directive and their interplay, as well as the relation with the Artificial Intelligence Act. This technology-specific approach is preferred to technology-neutral or sectorial approaches to liability, the latter encompassing all emerging digital technologies together.

The third thematic cluster approaches the questions of wrongfulness and its consequences from a criminal and international law perspective. For instance, are the notions of attribution or causality modified in the face of the AI phenomenon? How should criminal responsibility be conceptualized in the face of AI evolution and on the basis of the different levels of AI autonomy? How can we distinguish between human and AI responsibility, in case of human and AI merging? How is the subjective element of responsibility (*animus*) modified in the context of AI? How does AI impact justice and particularly criminal justice? Is autonomous decision-making with regard to liability and sentencing acceptable on the basis of the proper administration of justice and the procedural rights of the parties to a judicial procedure?

From an international law perspective, *Samuli Haataja* explores the resilience of international law norms on state responsibility *vis-à-vis* the practice of using autonomous software agents (ASAs) with separate legal personality for the performance of cyber security functions. Since such agents have the capacity to react and make autonomous decisions within their environment without direct/real-time human control, a recognition of a form of legal status is advocated so as to shift liability for their actions from human to the ASAs themselves, as they are capable of learning, adapting and acting in unpredictable ways. This evolution must be confronted, however, with the rules on state responsibility, which apply a model of attribution of acts to State. The author argues that despite some conceptual and practical difficulties, the articles on state responsibility can accommodate the above entities/organs. Firstly, acts of ASAs, which, while having a separate legal status, are completely dependent on State control or are empowered to perform governmental functions, such as defence or security tasks, should be attributed to the State. The same applies, according to the author, with regard to private (but registered to a specific State) ASAs, which receive instructions and directions by the State in the form of the latter's involvement in their design and development and in setting the goals that they must pursue, and the same applies for the notion of effective control, since *per* the author ASAs' autonomy is a form of control exercised in advance and any unpredictable behaviour is covered by ASR, which establishes a no-fault model of state responsibility.

Turning towards the challenges that AI creates when used in judicial proceedings, *Athina Sachoulidou* introduces us to the debate regarding the use of algorithms in criminal justice, primarily for different types of sentencing, whether in the form of pre-trial detention or post-trial sanctioning. More particularly, she sheds light to the benefits of using algorithms in criminal justice, such as saving time, reducing costs, enhancing impartiality and independency and systematizing new knowledge; but she also warns about its drawbacks, spanning from risks on data accuracy to the reproduction and expansion of biases—now coated on a film of scientific objectivism. Moreover, she aptly showcases that the individualized assessment of each criminal case, pertaining not only to individualized liability but equally to the specific human values and social perceptions that should be balanced in each specific case, cannot be fully ensured through the model algorithmic criminal justice. Furthermore, the lack of transparency on how the algorithm works makes it difficult for both the judge and the affected individual to counter its outcome, a fact that undermines due process. More generally, the idea that AI engineers can shape the values and create uniform and universal algorithms for criminal justice replacing the choices made in the legislative process is, according to her, deeply disconcerting. She finally raises further questions concerning judicial independence, accountability for judicial outcomes and trust to such algorithmic tools, which, if absent, might undermine trust to the whole judicial system.

The fourth thematic cluster delves into the complex relationship between AI and human rights. There are two different aspects to this question. On the one hand, there is a developing debate over whether AI can be a holder of human rights, which is inextricably linked to both recognizing legal personality for AI and conceptualizing human rights in specific ways. In this framework, if the human-centric conceptualization of our legal orders is overcome, a right of existence or of survival could be envisaged for AI. Inversely, the risks represented by AI for human rights are a burgeoning part of the debate on AI. Human rights can be both an enabler of AI—if AI is used to enhance their protection, as well as an obstacle, setting limitations to AI and barring its evolution towards general or super intelligence. The most important element in the latter part of the discussion revolves around the discriminatory biases that might be reproduced in algorithmic tools. It is this aspect that had been subject to extensive debate and elaboration in the framework of international organizations. Nevertheless, another, equally decisive aspect of the interaction between human rights and AI relates to the role of social rights in the development of AI. Both these aspects are analyzed in the two contributions of this thematic cluster.

A first aspect of AI's interaction with human rights is presented by *Joanna Mazur*, who delves into the safeguards concerning data protection that should be introduced in AI systems developed through the processing of personal data. The author focuses on the relevant provisions of the General Data Protection Regulation with an emphasis on the obligation to conduct a Data Protection Impact Assessment (DPIA) in case of use of AI technology for the processing of data. She highlights how different strategies have been pursued, especially at national levels, with regard to the subjection of AI-driven data processing into a DPIA requirement, whether through the assessment of such practice as high-risk for the rights and freedoms of persons or *via* national blacklists. She, then, turns into how lessons drawn from GDPR's encounter with AI tools can be employed in the EU legislative initiatives for regulating AI technology and stresses the importance of risk therein, with special reference to the EU proposals on AI risk regulation. She concludes by comparing the experience with regard to precautionary measures introduced into the GDPR's system and analogous proposals, for instances, of human oversight that are present in the *AI Act*, as well as the limited publicity to which high-risk AI uses will be subjected. This final insistence on transparency is a leitmotiv permeating various contributions to this volume.

Furthermore, *Themistoklis Tzimas* explores the risk of a widening, ontological, inequality that might be caused by AI technology in the future and how the incorporation of social rights in AI development can limit such a dystopic future. More specifically, he highlights the direction of AI towards post-humanism, namely, a non-human-centered world, where man and machine are merged leading to an overcoming of biological limitations. If such evolution is not shared by all, it might lead to a level of inequality never seen before, where the non-privileged ones might be dehumanized—a development that surprisingly returns to some of the themes tackled in the first chapter. The solution, according to the author, is a greater focus on social rights, particularly the rights to science and health, which can ensure the sharing of the advances of AI technology by the whole of humanity. He identifies various obstacles towards the full realization of those rights and their iterations (i.e. right of access to science and its applications; right to the highest attainable standard of health), such as the economic interests of our market-oriented world as represented, for instance, by intellectual property rights or the privatization of health provision. Finally, he examines how social rights can be incorporated into AI technologies by insisting on centralized international governance model for AI.

The fifth thematic cluster approaches the question of intellectual property in the era of AI autonomy. Artificial intelligence constitutes both the programming of machines using a specific code, as well as, more crucially, machine learning, where the system assesses itself how to respond to external reaction through data training. This individual judgment and production of its own products creates challenges on how to subject AI to current intellectual property rules and renders patents probably a more suitable means for the protection of AI and its applications. Thus, a series of questions arise concerning the adaptability of patent eligibility to AI autonomy, even more so to AI of higher intelligence. Can analogies be drawn from the third Industrial Revolution and the era of computers and the internet or from the way patenting has developed in other fields, such as pharmaceuticals? Are there limits to patenting material contributing to AI technologies or the outcomes of AI workings, that is, AI inventions? Those issues are examined by the two following contributions.

Eleni Tzoulia's contribution addresses the question whether and how AI can be patented. She firstly highlights the insufficient protection that intellectual property regimes (copyrights, trade secrets etc) offer to AI and then turns towards patents as the appropriate way for protection AI-related subject matter, particularly on the basis of the European Patent Convention. She explains the various obstacles that AI-related software must overcome in order to be deemed patent-eligible and shows how automated and machine-learning systems are not as such patent-eligible, since what is crucial is that the software resolve technical problems through purely technical means. On a final part, she examines challenges related to inventions contributing to—or generated by—AI, particularly in the fields of morality/*ordre public* considerations, novelty and non-obviousness, and disclosure. On the one hand, the self-improving aspects of AI, the opaque (non-explainable) nature of it, and the level of disclosure of the data and the training process, particularly for unsupervised machine learning, are aspects that render more difficult the patenting process. On the other hand, inventions generated by AI run counter to the broad conception that inventions are human-generated. While at the current stage of AI development, such inventions can always be traced back to a specific human, issues arise both with regard to secondary inventions and to future types of AI that will generate in a fully autonomous way their own inventions.

David Tilt, on his part, examines how AI regulation can be achieved through patenting by drawing analogies to earlier patenting challenges regarding software and pharmaceuticals and by comparing three different approaches to AI in the EU, Japan and the USA. The author highlights how patents simultaneously encourage technological innovation and economic growth, but also might prevent the acceptance of egregious forms of AI that run afoul of *ordre public* or morality. He also stresses the important transparency function of patenting regulation through the disclosure requirements. Furthermore, and turning to pharmaceuticals, he explains how patenting might influence the accessibility of AI technology by everyone and additionally, he explores the role played by data protection systems and private industry initiatives, as well as self-auditing proposals (as means of self-regulation) for controlling AI systems. Ultimately, while much of the above proposals intervene *ex post facto*, after the AI system has been in operation and produced its results, the author concludes by recommending a system of self-regulation that is supported by robust data protection as the best way forward.

This sixth thematic cluster aims at examining the consequences of AI use in international humanitarian law and the law on the use of force. AI Weapons Systems (AIWSs) are oftentimes employed in conflicts taking places in spaces where there is no territorial sovereignty, such as the cyberspace or outer space. Moreover, very often such AIWSs might be used as a response or to counter similar weapons, which makes equally daunting the assertion of an armed attack by a state that might give rise to self-defence. Additionally, the use of AIWSs further blurs the line between use of force and low-intensity operations. As a result, such weapon systems might be endangering the collective security system and the prohibition of the use of force, taking also into account that they might act autonomously. Even more concerning is the picture drawn by the use of AIWSs with regard to international humanitarian law (IHL). AI challenges basic principles of IHL, such as humanity/humane treatment, distinction, necessity, proportionality or the taking of precautions. On the one hand, operations using AI weapons are allegedly more precise and refrain from unnecessary loss of life. Such systems act without the emotional burden that influences the decision-making of humans and thus can allegedly make rational choices that ensure better compliance with IHL norms. On the other hand, the data fed into such systems might not be adequate for operations, where AI weapon systems are employed by both sides. Furthermore, human control and predictability might be undermined by the use of AI, where the learning process is opaque and cannot be easily explained. Last but not least, different generations of AIWSs, from unmanned machines reaching kinetic decisions to fully autonomous weapons require different adaptations from the rules of IHL and pose totally different challenges to such rules.

Anthi Koskina, explores one of the most interesting aspects concerning AI weapons, namely their use in outer space. After outlining the unique aspects of outer space, such as the absence of territorial sovereignty, which impact on the rules regarding the use of force (*jus ad bellum*) in outer space, she focuses on the relationship between Art. IV of the *Outer Space Treaty* and international humanitarian law, on the one side, and AI weapon systems (AWS), on the other side. She raises a series of issues related to the complex and highly digitalized environment of outer space, which include the difficulty to provide sufficient data for the AI learning process and the fact that AI's capacity to make the right calls with regard to targeting and IHL principles, such as distinction, necessity and proportionality, are complicated by the dual-use nature of many space appliances and the fact that AI systems might be used also from the side of the targets. The result is that distinction in the era of automated decision-making by AI systems becomes inherently risky, as many times threats might be understood by AI systems as programming errors and *vice versa*. The author concludes by highlighting that while such AWS might reduce destruction and thus cannot be considered as inherently unlawful under the OST and IHL, the ultimate decisions concerning their use should be taken by humans.

The performance of AI weapon systems *vis-à-vis* explainability of machine-learning techniques are at the heart of the next chapter by *Jonathan Kwik* and *Tom van Engers*. The two authors analyze how AI weapon systems must be both performant and transparent in their working to allow humans to understand how and why a decision was reached by such a system. This so-called explainability feature is important for weapons review, error mitigation and holding someone accountable in case something goes wrong. Such requirements are crucial both at the adoption and the operational phase. Yet, as the authors skilfully prove, increased explainability comes at the cost of weapons' performance, as complexity allows for higher predictive power while simplicity reduces a weapon's accuracy. Under these circumstances and taking into account that both principles are incorporated into the normative body of IHL, the authors present a balanced approach on the trade-off between explainability and performance, which will help decision-makers and commanders in prioritizing those traits (and the relevant AI weapon systems) that would allow an increased performance while still respecting the requisite precautions in the context of an armed conflict.

References

Bekey GA (2005) Autonomous robots: from biological inspiration to implementation and control. MIT Press, Cambridge

Bostrom N (2006) How long before superintelligence? Linguist Philos Investig 5:11–30. https://nickbostrom.com/superintelligence.html

Bostrom N (2014) Superintelligence paths, dangers, strategies. Oxford University Press, Oxford

Chalmers DJ (2010) The singularity, a philosophical analysis. J Conscious Stud 17:7–65

Chandrasekaran B (1990) What kind of information processing is intelligence? In: Partridge D, Wilks Y (eds) The foundations of artificial intelligence: a sourcebook. Cambridge University Press, Cambridge, pp 14–46

European Commission (2020) White paper on artificial intelligence – a European approach to excellence and trust, COM (2020) 65 final

Kurzweil R (2005) The singularity is near: when humans transcend biology. Viking, New York

Russell SJ, Norvig P (2010) Artificial intelligence: a modern approach, 3rd edn. Pearson Education Limited, New Jersey

Scherer MU (2016) Regulating artificial intelligent systems: risks, challenges, competences, and strategies. Harv J Law Technol 29:353–400

Shanahan M (2010) Embodiment and the inner life: cognition and consciousness in the space of possible minds. Oxford University Press, New York

Tzimas T (2021) Legal and ethical challenges of artificial intelligence from an international law perspective. Springer, Cham

Urban T (2015) The AI revolution: the road to superintelligence. Available via WAIT BUT WHY. https://waitbutwhy.com/2015/01/artificial-intelligence-revolution-1.html

Vinge V (1993) The coming technological singularity: how to survive in the post-human era. In: Vis 21: interdisciplinary science and engineering in the era of cyberspace. NASA Lewis Research Center, pp 11–22

Winograd T (1990) Thinking machines: can there be? Are we? In: Partridge D, Wilks Y (eds) The foundations of artificial intelligence: a sourcebook. Cambridge University Press, Cambridge, pp 167–189

Yudkowsky E (2007) Three major singularity schools. https://intelligence.org/2007/09/30/three-major-singularity-schools/

Part I
AI and Questions of Personhood and Ethics

The *Peculium* of the *Robot*: Artificial Intelligence and Slave Law

Marco Rizzuti

Abstract The chapter discusses the analogy between the status of contemporary types of artificial intelligence and that of ancient slaves under Roman law, in order to evaluate the theorical as well as applied perspectives of the recognition of some degree of juridical subjectivity to artificial intelligences in the field of patrimonial, but also non-patrimonial, legal relationships.

1 The Intriguing Analogy

When reading the growing legal literature on Artificial Intelligence, one could be surprised in noticing that it is not unusual to find references to the ancient Roman Law institution of *peculium*. In fact, prominent authors are proposing to construe the legal patrimonial relationships of a *robot* by analogy with those of an ancient slave.[1]

As said, it is a quite surprising analogy that links the paradigms of the remote past to those of the forthcoming future. And this is not just a merely technical use of some Roman Law categories, because the reference to an historically so controversial institution such as slavery, which is in evident contrast with the fundamental values of our liberal-democratic societies, implies something more. This is precisely what makes the analogy so interesting and challenging, not only from a strictly legal point of view.

Indeed, it is possible to find some similarities among these two, seemingly, so distant worlds. First of all, we can consider how the ancient and modern linguistic usages reflect a certain degree of connection among them.

---

[1]See, further, Pagallo (2013), pp. 102–106 and pp. 132–134; Katz (2008); Franchini (2020); Ruffolo (2020). However, the discussed analogy is not so recent, but can be found also in Wiener (1950) and Wein (1992) pp. 103 et seq.

M. Rizzuti (✉)
Department of Legal Sciences of the University of Florence, Florence, Italy
e-mail: marco.rizzuti@unifi.it

A. Kornilakis et al. (eds.), *Artificial Intelligence and Normative Challenges*, Law, Governance and Technology Series 59,
https://doi.org/10.1007/978-3-031-41081-9_2

In fact, from the one hand, ancient Greeks considered the slave as a "*κτῆμά τι ἔμψυχον*",[2] i.e. an animated object, while ancient Romans defined the slave as an "*instrumentum vocale*",[3] i.e. a speaking instrument. Indeed, both these two particular expressions meant something that is quite near to "intelligent machine". On the other hand, the modern word "*robot*", today commonly used to indicate artificial intelligences, is derived from a Slavic term that was originally referred precisely to the serfs.[4]

From a different perspective, we can consider a possible connection between the concerned paradigms from a more general societal viewpoint. In fact, today the widespread use of Artificial Intelligence is posing the problem of the so-called jobless society, i.e. of a (desired and/or feared—depending on the different viewpoints) society where every kind of human work could be surrogated by machines.[5]

---

[2]This is a reference is to Aristotle's Politics (1252b–1253b). As is well known, Aristotle defended slavery as a natural institution and confuted the arguments of certain anonymous abolitionists, but he also hypothesized that a possible alternative to slave work could be represented by automata, as depicted by some Homeric mythological accounts. See Bodei (2019); Mayor (2020). Indeed, later in Hellenistic Alexandria a sort of automation technology was effectively developed (*cf.* Heron of Alexandria's *Automata*) and, as a consequence, the social and economic importance of slavery underwent a relative decline; see, Russo (2001), pp. 286–287. We lack information about ancient abolitionists and in the most part of the case also the great slave rebellions were not meant to abolish the institution but just to reconquer personal freedom and, if possible, to enslave the former masters, even if at least in some particular cases the idea of a different society could be elaborated; see Africa (1961), pp. 110–124. It needs to be reminded that slavery did not disappear with the end of the ancient world, given that both Christianity and Islam just introduced the rule that, respectively, a Christian or a Muslim could not be enslaved (indeed not so different from the ancient rule prohibiting the enslavement of a Roman citizen). Therefore, slaves had to be imported from heathen countries and, as is well known, such trade underwent an enormous growth in early modern times after the discovery of the Americas. Slavery was finally abolished only when the modern Industrial Revolution made it antieconomic, in times when the living conditions of the new working class could be considered even worse than those of the slaves; see Calhoun (1837).

[3]According to the famous classification provided by Varro in its work *Rerum Rusticarum libri tres* (3.17), an instrument could be *vocale* (slaves) *semi-vocale* (animals), *non vocale* (other things). Indeed, Roman jurists considered the distinction between freemen and slaves as the most fundamental one (see Gaius, *Institutiones*, 1.9: '*omnes homines aut liberi sunt aut servi*'), even if they did not consider slavery as natural but as product of the civil law (see Ulpianus, *Liber primus Institutionum*, in *D.1.1.4*: '*iure naturali omnes liberi nascerentur... sed posteaquam iure gentium servitus invasit...*'). Nevertheless, it must be clear that such a conceptual assumption never led them to criticize the institution of slavery at all.

[4]As is well known, the word "robot" has been introduced in modern languages around the world by the 1920 science-fiction play of Čapek entitled *Rossumovi univerzální roboti*, and it derives from the Czech language, where it was traditionally used for referring to the forced labor of medieval and early modern serfs.

[5]Such a fear is ancient too: according to Suetonius' *Vita Divi Vespasiani* (18) a Roman emperor refused the use of Hellenistic technologies in order to avoid the spread of unemployment among the plebs, while during the first modern Industrial Revolution in England the Luddites were used to destroy textile machineries in the attempt to defend their jobs. On the other hand, for centuries, the use of automation was mostly limited to spectacular or recreational, and therefore quite harmless, purposes; see, Standage (2002). In more recent times, the perspective of a technological liberation

Accordingly, in the last years many countries all over the world have introduced some form of universal basic income or of guaranteed minimum income, in order to face the growth of unemployment due to the increasing recourse to automation. More recently, the necessity to face the severe social and economic consequences of the covid-19 pandemic has even strengthened such a trend.

Therefore, while in modern world's Constitutions the dignity of the citizen was grounded above all in his/her status as a worker and a producer, now he/she could be turned into the mere recipient of a basic income substantially deriving from the work of *robots*. Such an outcome would be indeed quite similar to the condition of the ancient *civis* (citizen in Latin language), whose dignity was precisely based on the fact that he was not a worker, but the recipient of rents produced by slave work.

2 A Patrimony for the *Robot*

In light of such a framework, we have to go back to a more technically legal viewpoint on the analogy between ancient slaves' *peculium* and the hypothesis of a *robot*'s patrimony. On the one hand, in Roman times slaves were not legally considered as persons, but, according to a common practice, the most educated, and therefore also economically valuable, slaves could be charged with the relatively free administration of a part of the master's patrimony,[6] the so-called *peculium*, in order to run an enterprise in his interest. A *peculium* could encompass any kind of properties, including other slaves, and above all could produce an effect of legal segregation inside the master's patrimony with specific relevance towards third parties.

On the other hand, today the core of our problem is to understand if and how it is possible to refer legal patrimonial relationships to an artificial intelligence. Indeed, if we consider the concept of legal personhood from an ontological perspective and, accordingly, we look for substantial similarities in order to extend it beyond human beings, we are unable to establish useful connections because the gap between humans and machines remains anyway enormous. Moreover, to argue that machines can be even more intelligent than many humans, and hence they must have their legal subjectivity recognized, may lead to a dangerous slippery slope, implying the risk of a denial of legal subjectivity to those humans (e.g., infants and/or severely disabled persons) who are not intelligent enough.

But if we look at the same issue from a merely functionalist perspective, we can of course accept that legal entities may be totally different from natural persons, and

of mankind from the burden of work was also discussed by Keynes (1930), pp. 358–373. But in our times of rising artificial intelligence, the issue is much more relevant; see, further, Ford (2015); Danaher (2017), pp. 41–64; Kaplan (2017); Baldwin (2019).

[6]The classical definition of *peculium*, elaborated by Tubero and reported by Ulpianus, is: '*quod servus domini permissu separatum o rationibus dominicis habet*' (*D.15.1.5.4*).

also that we can have different and relative degrees of legal subjectivity,[7] so that we have just to answer an easier question: is it useful to refer patrimonial relationships to an artificial intelligence? Indeed, it can be useful, just like in the past it was useful to refer patrimonial relationships to the *peculium* of a slave, who was not considered as a person in legal terms.

The issue has been discussed, first of all, having regard to civil liability problems. With the development of artificial intelligences in many fields that pose such problems (e.g., robotic surgery, self-driving vehicles, algorithmic finance, and so on), it is becoming progressively more difficult to consider anyone legally liable for the actions of an autonomous and self-learning machine, if considered as a mere object, in accordance with the ordinary rules of tort law on causal link. In fact, such artificial systems make their own decisions irrespective of any previous guidelines, so that the final outcomes of the actions of such systems could be totally uncontrollable and unpredictable for humans.[8]

Therefore, the resulting responsibility gap, which seems to be morally unacceptable and unjustified, can be filled by the reference of a patrimony not to a human agent, but directly to the intelligent machine itself, in order to allow the damaged party to sue an artificial respondent endowed with adequate assets.[9]

On the other hand, the same legal mechanism could be seen as an instrument to produce a patrimonial segregation,[10] and therefore a kind of liability limitation quite similar to the ancient liability "*dumtaxat de peculio*" of the master with regard to the

[7]The issue of the historically variable boundaries of legal subjectivity and of its possible graduations is widely debated in all legal orders around the world and with regard to very different specific entities, from embryos to trusts, and from corporations to pets. Of course, here we cannot further engage with the specific analysis, but we will just recall the pioneering contribution of Taddei Elmi (1990), pp. 685 et seq., on the possibilities of shaping subjective rights for the artificial intelligences.

[8]See, also for further references: Krausová and Hazan (2017), pp. 162–172; Tjong Tjin Tai (2018); Michalski (2018), pp. 1022 et seq.; Passinhas (2018); Patti (2019), pp. 136 et seq.; Monterossi (2020), pp. 20190054 et seq.; Salanitro (2020), pp. 1246 et seq.; Santoni de Sio and Mecacci (2021). Issues of civil liability and artificial intelligence are discussed in greater depth also in other chapters included in the present volume.

[9]This is precisely the reason why the well-known, and widely debated, Resolution issued by the European Parliament on February 16, 2017, with recommendations to the Commission on Civil Law Rules on Robotics, has even provided in paragraph 59 letter f, for the creation of "a specific legal status for robots in the long run, so that at least the most sophisticated autonomous robots could be established as having the status of electronic persons responsible for making good any damage they may cause, and possibly applying electronic personality to cases where robots make autonomous decisions or otherwise interact with third parties independently". Indeed, in the present chapter we are not discussing a whole recognition of the so-called "electronic personhood", that is just a future, and probably quite remote, perspective, but we are considering mechanisms to refer legal relationships to non-subjects, as the slaves were in the past and as the artificial intelligences are today.

[10]See the open letter to the European Commission published by a group of Artificial Intelligence and Robotics Experts on http://www.robotics-openletter.eu/. Among the Italian legal scholars see also, for a critical perspective: Passagnoli (2019), pp. 79 et seq.; Astone (2020), pp. 253–264; Palmerini (2020), pp. 445–474.

part of his patrimony freely administered by the slave charged to manage an enterprise, a legal device that was indeed very useful in times when modern corporate law was still to come.[11]

Today, the level of automation and self-learning is not always the same,[12] so that there will be cases where the legal construction of a *robot*'s patrimony fills, as said, a responsibility gap, given that no human respondents could be found, but also other cases where such a construction may indeed shield an otherwise liable human agent.

Of course, not all these possible uses of *peculium* in the field of artificial intelligence have the same value; moreover, *peculium* could sometimes be substituted by other legal instruments that we can, at least in some cases, perceive as its functional equivalents, such as a mandatory insurance and/or a public compensation scheme to fill responsibility gaps,[13] as well as the corporate law mechanisms to shield human agents.

In any case, we should not exclude on an ontological basis the possibility of referring patrimonial relationships to a *robot* but, following as we said a functionalist approach, we can accept that legislative interventions and the elaboration of judicial case-law or of private autonomy may give a legal basis to such kind of responsibility mechanisms, that are, generally speaking, comparable to the ancient *peculium*. But, on the other hand, we should also carefully evaluate if and when such mechanisms can be considered as consistent with the moral values and the political objectives (e.g., to fill or not fill certain gaps, and to shield or not to shield certain human agents, *etc.*) of each specific legal order, to be ascertained primarily by having regard to the axiological principles enshrined in the national Constitutions as well as in the supranational Charters of Fundamental Rights.

---

[11] According to Roman law such a situation gave origin to the system of the so-called "*actiones adiecticiae qualitatis ex causa peculiari*", i.e., more specifically: "*actio institoria*", "*actio exercitoria*", "*actio tributoria*", "*actio de peculio*", "*actio de in rem verso*" and "*actio quod iussu*". Moreover, sharing a common slave, endowed with a *peculium* encompassing an enterprise, was a sort of functional equivalent of a modern company; see Stolfi (2009). In some cases, it was even possible for a slave to use the gains acquired to his *peculium* through his commercial activities in order to buy his personal freedom from the master.

[12] The most recent studies underline the importance of shaping differentiated regimes of liability for the different aspects of artificial intelligence systems. See, also for further references Becker and Teubner (2022). With specific regard to autonomous vehicles and their differentiated levels of automation see also Zornoza Somolinos (2021), who pays particular attention to the impact on insurance law.

[13] Such possibilities are considered also in the European Parliament's Resolution of October 20, 2020, with recommendations to the Commission on a civil liability regime for artificial intelligence. For further information about these recent developments see Zornoza Somolinos (2020), p. 95 et seq.

3 Further Perspectives: Towards the *Contubernium* of the *Robots*?

Many different possible scenarios can be hypothesized if we consider other legal aspects too, going beyond the specific field of civil liability. Of course, at the moment we just have to pose questions and to hypothesize scenarios, without pretending to have all the final answers, but simply trying to elaborate some possible lines of argumentation.

Today, intelligent agents may, once again like ancient slaves, conclude contracts on behalf of their "masters" after a complex negotiation involving also humans or even involving only other *robots*[14]*:* in legal terms they are not representatives, because they are non-persons; however their role cannot be reduced to that of the so-called *nuncius*, that has just to transmit an already elaborated decision, but could be compared precisely to that of the above-mentioned Roman slaves charged as *institores* to manage a master's enterprise.

From a different point of view, according to some proposals, a *robot*'s patrimony should have to be taxed: e.g., precisely, in order to retrieve the financial resources that are needed to grant a basic income for the persons who have lost their jobs because of automation.[15] Or, conversely, a self-learning machine's patrimony may encompass the patent for an invention created by the same machine.[16]

Moreover, nowadays empathic artificial intelligences[17] are utilized also in order to provide relational and affective,[18] or even sexual assistance.[19] Therefore, we could hypothesize the relevance of such entities also from a person's, family's, and succession's law point of view, maybe in analogy with other recent legal

---

[14] Indeed, contracts concluded by a human with a machine (e.g., a vending machine) are not so new, and they were studied from a legal point of view more than a century ago by Cicu (1901), p. 561 et seq. But today contract can be formed between two, or more, intelligent machines, as in the case regulated by Section 14 of the US Uniform Electronic Transactions Act of 1999 (UETA): "A contract may be formed by the interaction of electronic agents of the parties, even if no individual was aware of or reviewed the electronic agents' actions or the resulting terms and agreements". For a recent study about contractual negotiations among robots, and also for further references, see Azara (2020), p. 361 et seq.

[15] See, also for further references regarding the different legal orders: Varoufakis (2017); Oberson (2017), pp. 232–239; Cordeiro Guerra (2020), p. 921 et seq.

[16] A case has already been reported by the media regarding the patent granted in South Africa to the artificial intelligence system called DABUS for the invention of a food container based on fractal geometry.

[17] See Fong et al. (2003), pp. 143 ss.; Darling (2016) pp. 213 ss.; Dumouchel and Damiano (2019); O'Gieblyn (2021).

[18] A recent example reported by the media is Ami-Chan, the doll with artificial intelligence that accompanies the elderly in confinement. Ami, in fact, is designed to create her own personality, learn grandparents' names, and even remember their birthdays and the seasons of the year. For a wider survey see also: Robinson et al. (2014); Broekens et al. (2009), pp. 94 ss.

[19] See at these regards: Danaher and MacArthur (2017); Balistreri (2018); Kleeman (2020).

developments regarding pets, today often considered as a sort of "non-human persons".

The media have already reported the case of Sophia, a *robot* designed to be a companion for elderly people and explicitly awarded with a status of citizenship in Saudi Arabia.[20] But we could also imagine, precisely in analogy with some developments concerning pets, that maybe a judge will have to decide about the joint custody of an empathic *robot* in the context of a family breakdown, or that a notary will be asked to draft a will benefiting such a *robot*. Accordingly, also in these cases the idea of a *robot*'s patrimony could be useful, for instance, to construe the acquisition of the bequeathed legacy, but we will have to consider even the relevance of non-patrimonial legal relationship regarding artificial intelligences.

Indeed, in the last decades family law has been deeply transformed, from the traditional defense of one legally recognized family model, i.e. heterosexual patriarchal monogamous indissoluble marriage with natural procreation, towards a new approach that opens the door to the recognition of a plurality of different models of family relationships (from same-sex couples to polyamory, from open adoptions to medically assisted procreation), including the mentioned relationships with pets that, as said, can be regulated in family breakdowns with judicial provisions of joint custody, not based on the mere consideration of property titles but quite similar to those regarding children.[21] Then, within this pluralistic postmodern concept of family, it could be also possible to speak of family relationships between humans and artificial intelligences.

Moreover, it could be even possible to imagine the development of some relevant family relationships among empathic *robots* themselves. Of course, *robots*, once again like ancient slaves, lack marital capacity, but in light of the aforementioned pluralistic framework we could speak in a broader sense of family relationships. Therefore, in this case the most suitable Roman Law analogy could perhaps be not *peculium* but *contubernium*, i.e. the quasi-marital *de facto* relationships among slaves.[22]

In fact, under Roman law both *peculium* and *contubernium* were specific legal institutions elaborated in order to give some degree of relevance to the legal relationships of non-subjects in the patrimonial and in the familial sphere respectively. Accordingly, also some kind of modern equivalents of such institutions could play a similar role with regard to intelligent agents that are qualified as non-subjects but

[20]The case has been reported in Maza (2017). For some critical remarks at these regards see also Pagallo (2018), pp. 230 et seq.

[21]For some references to the Italian judicial case-law regarding pets' custody, and the possible analogy with artificial intelligences, see Rizzuti (2020), pp. 453 et seq. For a wider comparison between the status of animals and robots with specific reference to the Spanish legal order see also Cerdeira Bravo de Mansilla (2021) pp. 14–53.

[22]The legal relevance of *contubernium* was indeed very limited in the classical period of Roman law, but the situation changed in the postclassical period when specific provisions were enacted at these regards, possibly also due to Christian influences, in order to, e.g., impede the forced separation of slave families: see also for further references Melluso (2000).

that, for the said both functional and axiological reasons, have to be endowed with a relative level of legal relevance, somehow different from the one of mere objects.

4 Some Concluding Remarks

In order to complete our short discussion, we have also to summarize some of the reasons why the possible analogy between artificial intelligence and slave law could be useful under different points of view.

First of all, in the starting paragraph of the present chapter we considered how this analogy may help to reflect about some more general trends of the developments of our societies and legal orders. The relationships, and possible comparisons, between slave work and machine work are, in fact, relevant in order to understand some characteristics of our world in an historically deeper perspective.

Then, in the second paragraph we took into consideration some more technically legal aspects of our analogy, with particular regard to the specific comparison between the Roman law institution of the slave's *peculium* and the possible construction of a robot's patrimony. This is indeed a well-known analogy, discussed by many authors in order to shape some patrimonial relationship for artificial intelligences. The final objectives of such interpretative elaborations, as mentioned in the said paragraph, could be very different and even opposite: e.g., from filling unacceptable responsibility gaps to shield otherwise responsible human agents with mechanisms of patrimonial segregation.

Of course, such an analogy is not a necessity, given that similar results can be achieved also through totally different legal instruments as, e.g., a mandatory insurance scheme to fill responsibility gaps. However, it remains one of the possible instruments of the legal reasoning, if we follow a functionalist approach: therefore, we cannot exclude on an ontological basis the possibility of referring legal relationships to a *robot,* but we should carefully evaluate if and when such mechanisms can be considered as consistent with the ethical values and the political objectives of our legal orders.

Finally, in the third paragraph, we discussed also other perspectives that involve not only patrimonial but also non-patrimonial relationships. We tried, in fact, to elaborate a possible relevance of artificial intelligences not only with regard to contract and tort law but also in the realms of family and succession law. Whilst the analogy with *peculium* has a quite long history in our legal scholarship, here we propose a different, and more innovative, analogy with another Roman law institution, the so-called *contubernium,* in order to hypothesize some degrees of legal recognition to family relationships between humans and artificial intelligences, as well as between artificial intelligences themselves.

References

Africa TW (1961) Aristonicus, Blossius, and the city of the sun. Int Rev Soc Hist 6:110–124

Aristotle (1252a–1342b) Politics. In: Bekker AI (1831–1870) Aristotelis Opera edidit Academia Regia Borussica

Astone A (2020) La persona elettronica: verso un tertium genus di soggetto? In: Bilotta F, Raimondi F (eds) Il soggetto di diritto. Storia ed evoluzione di un concetto nel diritto privato. Jovene, Naples

Azara A (2020) La trattativa robotica. In: Perlingieri P, Giova S, Prisco I (eds) Rapporti civilistici e intelligenze artificiali: attività e responsabilità. Edizioni Scientifiche Italiane, Naples, pp 361–379

Baldwin R (2019) The globotics upheaval: globalization, robotics, and the future of work. Oxford University Press, Oxford

Balistreri M (2018) Sex robot. L'amore al tempo delle macchine. Fandango, Rome

Becker A, Teubner G (2022) Three liability regimes for artificial intelligence. Algorithmic actants, hybrids, crowds. Bloomsbury, London

Bodei R (2019) Dominio e sottomissione. Schiavi, animali, macchine, Intelligenza Artificiale. Il Mulino, Bologna

Broekens J, Heerink M, Rosendal H (2009) Assistive social robots in elderly care: a review. Gerontechnology 8:94–103

Calhoun JC (1837) Speech in the U.S. Senate. The positive good of slavery. In: Calhoun JC (ed) Speeches of John C. Calhoun: delivered in the Congress of the United States from 1811 to the present time. Harper & Brothers, New York

Čapek K (1920) Rossumovi univerzální roboti. Aventinum, Prague

Cerdeira Bravo de Mansilla G (2021) Entre personas y cosas: animales y robots. Actual Juríd Iberoam 14:14–53

Cicu A (1901) Gli automi nel diritto privato. Il Filangieri 26:561. et seq

Cordeiro Guerra R (2020) L'intelligenza artificiale nel prisma del diritto tributario. Diritto e pratica tributaria 3:921–935

Danaher J (2017) Will life be worth living in a world without work? Technological unemployment and the meaning of life. Sci Eng Ethics 1:41–64

Danaher J, MacArthur N (2017) Robot sex: social and ethical implications. The MIT Press, Cambridge

Darling K (2016) Extending legal protection to social robots: the effects of anthropomorphism, empathy, and violent behaviour towards robotic objects. In: Calo R, Froomkin AM, Kerr I (eds) Robot law. Elgar, Cheltenham, pp 213–232

Dumouchel P, Damiano L (2019) Vivere con i robot. Saggio sull'empatia artificiale. Raffaello Cortina Editore, Milan

Fong T, Nourbakhsh I, Dautenhahn K (2003) A survey of socially interactive robots. Robot Auton Syst 42:143–166

Ford M (2015) Rise of the robots: technology and the threat of a jobless future. Basic Books, New York

Franchini L (2020) Disciplina romana della schiavitù ed intelligenza artificiale odierna. Spunti di comparazione. Available via Diritto mercato tecnologia. https://www.dimt.it/la-rivista/articoli/disciplina-romana-della-schiavitu-ed-intelligenza-artificiale-odierna-spunti-di-comparazione/

Gaius, Institutiones. In: Seckel E, Kuebler B (1903) Gai Institutionum commentarii quattuor separatim ex iurisprudentiae anteiustinianae reliquiis a Ph. Eduardo Huschke compositis. Teubner, Leipzig, p 1.9

Heron, Automata. In: Grillo F (2019) Hero of Alexandria's Automata: a critical edition and translation, including a commentary on Book One. PhD thesis, University of Glasgow. https://theses.gla.ac.uk/76774/1/2019GrilloPhD.pdf

Kaplan J (2017) Humans need not apply: a guide to wealth and work in the age of artificial intelligence. Yale University Press, New Haven

Katz A (2008) Intelligent agents and internet commerce in Ancient Rome. Available via Society for Computer and Law. https://www.scl.org/articles/1095-intelligent-agents-and-internet-commerce-in-ancient-rome
Keynes JM (1930) Economic possibilities for our grandchildren. In: Essays in Persuasion (1932). Harcourt Brace & Co., New York, pp 358–373
Kleeman J (2020) Sex robots & vegan meat: adventures at the frontier of birth, food, sex, and death. Pan Macmillan, New York
Krausová A, Hazan H (2017) Robots with biological brains: autonomy and liability of a semi-artificial life form. Lawyer Q 7:162–172
Mayor A (2020) Gods and robots: myths, machines, and ancient dreams of technology. Princeton University Press, Princeton
Maza C (2017) Saudi Arabia Gives Citizenship to a Non-Muslim, English-Speaking Robot, in Newsweek. Available via Newsweek. https://www.newsweek.com/saudi-arabia-robot-sophia-muslim-694152
Melluso M (2000) La schiavitù nell'età giustinianea. Disciplina giuridica e rilevanza sociale. Presses Universitaires de Franche-Comté, Besançon
Michalski R (2018) How to sue a robot? Utah Law Rev 5:1021–1071
Monterossi MW (2020) Liability for the fact of autonomous artificial intelligence agents. Things, agencies and legal actors. Global Jurist 3:20190054 et seq
O'Gieblyn M (2021) God, human, animal, machine. Technology, metaphor, and the search for meaning. Doubleday Books, New York
Oberson X (2017) Taxer les robots? L'émergence d'une capacité contributive électronique. Pratique juridique actuelle 2:232–239
Pagallo U (2013) The laws of robots. crimes, contracts, and torts. Springer, Berlin
Pagallo U (2018) Vital, Sophia, and Co.—the quest for the legal personhood of robots. Information 9:230. https://doi.org/10.3390/info9090230
Palmerini E (2020) Soggettività e agenti artificiali: una soluzione in cerca di un problema? Osservatorio del diritto civile e commerciale 2:445–474
Passagnoli G (2019) Regolamento giuridico e tutele nell'intelligenza artificiale. Persona e mercato 3:79–85
Passinhas S (2018) Robotics and law: a survey. In: Proceedings of the workshop on social interaction and multimodal expression for socially intelligent robots. http://ceur-ws.org/Vol-2059/
Patti FP (2019) The European Road to autonomous vehicles. Fordham Int Law J 43:125–162
Rizzuti M (2020) Il peculium e il robot: nuovi spunti su soggettività e intelligenza artificiale. In: Perlingieri P, Giova S, Prisco I (eds) Rapporti civilistici e intelligenze artificiali: attività e responsabilità. Edizioni Scientifiche Italiane, Naples, p 453 et seq
Robinson H, McDonald B, Broadbent E (2014) The role of healthcare robots for older people at home: a review. Int J Soc Robot 6:575–591
Ruffolo U (2020) Il problema della "personalità elettronica". J Ethics Leg Technol 2:76–88
Russo L (2001) La rivoluzione dimenticata, Il pensiero scientifico greco e la scienza moderna. Feltrinelli, Milan
Salanitro U (2020) Intelligenza artificiale e responsabilità: la strategia della Commissione europea. Rivista di diritto civile 66:1246–1276
Santoni de Sio F, Mecacci G (2021) Four responsibility gaps with artificial intelligence: why they matter and how to address them. Philos Technol 34:1057–1084
Standage T (2002) The Turk: the life and times of the famous 18th century chess playing machine. Walker & Co., New York
Stolfi E (2009) La soggettività commerciale dello schiavo nel mondo antico: soluzioni greche e romane. Teoria e Storia del Diritto Privato 2:1–59
Suetonius, Vita Divi Vespasiani. In: Ihm M (1907) De Vita XII Caesarum C. Suetonii Tranquilli. Teubner, Leipzig, p 18

Taddei Elmi G (1990) I diritti dell' "intelligenza artificiale" tra soggettività e valore. Fantadiritto o ius condendum? In: Lombardi Vallauri L (ed) Il meritevole di tutela. Giuffrè, Milan, pp 685–711

Tjong Tjin Tai E (2018) Liability for (semi)autonomous systems: robots and algorithms. In: Tilburg Law School Research Paper No. 2018–19. https://papers.ssrn.com/sol3/papers.cfm?abstract_id=3161962#

Ulpianus, liber primus Institutionum. In: Mommsen T (1870) Digesta Iustiniani Augusti. Weidmann, Berlin, p D.1.1.4

Varoufakis Y (2017) A tax on robots? Available via Project Syndicate. https://www.project-syndicate.org/commentary/bill-gates-tax-on-robots-by-yanis-varoufakis-2017-02

Varro, Rerum Rusticarum libri tres. In: Keil H (1889) M. Terenti Varronis Rerum rusticarum libri tres. Teubner, Leipzig, p 3.17

Wein L (1992) The responsibility of intelligent artifacts. Harv J Law Technol 6:103–154

Wiener N (1950) The human use of human beings. Houghton Mifflin, Boston

Zornoza Somolinos A (2020) Breves apuntes a la Propuesta de Reglamento del Parlamento Europeo sobre responsabilidad civil en materia de inteligencia artificial. Revista de Derecho, Empresa y Sociedad 17:95–101

Zornoza Somolinos A (2021) Vehículos automatizados y seguro obligatorio de automóviles. Dykinson, Madrid

Legal Personhood for Autonomous AI: Practical Consequences in Private Law

Angelos Kornilakis

Abstract The chapter examines the option of recognizing legal personality to autonomous AI machines from the perspective of private law, focusing on practical challenges. In particular, the chapter shall examine the scope and practical implications of recognizing legal personality to autonomous AI systems regarding: (a) the estate and the liability of the AI (including vicarious liability), (b) the right of personality and its protection, (c) the capacity to conclude binding and legally enforceable contracts as a contractual party and the application of contract law including the law of mistake and agency, (d) the question of identification and legal residence. Furthermore, it shall try to point out the interdependence between the legal status of AI and that of its user and the complexities arising from it.

1 Introduction

The question about the recognition of legal personhood for autonomous AI agents is a much debated and highly controversial one.[1] This chapter will not address the ethical, philosophical and legal, mainly constitutional, questions concerning the recognition of legal personhood for autonomous AI agents, but rather focus on the practical implications of such a recognition for private law.

Autonomy means in our context the ability to make a decision under uncertainty that would be not only *ex ante* deterministically unpredictable, but also *ex post* unexplainable, hence the *black box* phenomenon of autonomous AI agents.[2] As *Teubner* pointed out, the personification of non-human agents is, from a practical

[1] Cf. Solum (1992); Karnow (1994); Teubner (2007, 2018); Pagallo (2013), pp. 152 et seq; Kersten (2015), pp. 6 et seq; Koch (2020), p. 130; Mühlböck and Taupitz (2021), pp. 213 et seq.

[2] Bathaee (2018); cf. also Koch (2020), p. 120; Karanasiou and Pinotsis (2017), pp. 3 and 7; Müller-Hengstenberg and Kirn (2014), p. 312.

A. Kornilakis (✉)
Faculty of Law, Aristotle University of Thessaloniki, Thessaloniki, Greece
e-mail: akornil@law.auth.gr

A. Kornilakis et al. (eds.), *Artificial Intelligence and Normative Challenges*, Law, Governance and Technology Series 59,
https://doi.org/10.1007/978-3-031-41081-9_3

point of view, a strategy to deal with uncertainty and causal indeterminacy.[3] By recognizing legal personhood to a non-human structure, the Subject-Object relationship is transformed to an intersubjective relationship and accordingly the objective, causal risks linked to the subject-object structure and its functions are transformed to decision risks of the personified structure.[4]

It is quite clear that legal personhood does not mean legally equating human beings and machines. The legal personhood of autonomous AI machines will be restricted in comparison with the legal personhood of human beings. Accordingly, the tricky question is not solely, whether machines should have legal personhood, but also to what extent.[5]

AIs as legal persons would share characteristics of both humans and corporations. Like corporations, the legal existence of AI agents would depend on their scope of activity. Their legal capacity would not be limitless but should extend to cover the needs of their function. For example, like corporations, there is no reason for economic AI agents to have family rights. Furthermore, for an AI agent whose function is solely to operate in an industrial environment participating in the material production and which will never be asked to conclude a contract, capacity to enter contracts would be useless. It follows that not all AI agents should necessarily share the same aspects of legal personhood.

On the other hand, unlike corporations, the actions of an autonomous AI machine are not directly traceable back to the actions of a human agent. AI agents as legal persons do not need "members" or "organs" since they do not lack the ability to decide autonomously and interact directly with their environment. An AI agent can directly form and express its will and perform itself the actions needed for its function. This means that the actions or declarations of AI agents could be directly attributed to them. Nevertheless, caution is advised, since AI agents will be able to personally perform only the tasks for which they are designed. An AI agent who has the technical capacity to decide whether to enter into a specific contract or not will not necessarily (and most probably) have also the technical capacity to decide whether to sue or take some other legal action in case some of its rights are infringed. It follows that although AI agents don't need human agents to form their will and make the decisions and actions they are designed to perform autonomously, they would most probably need a human agent as some kind of legal guardian to manage all legally relevant operations that do not fall under the technical competencies of the AI agents.

A last point of interest would be that AI agents do not act for their personal benefit and do not have personal interests, but act for the benefit and in order to promote the interests of their users. Hence, their utilization would give rise to a principal-agent

[3]Cf. Teubner (2007), pp. 6 et seq. More abstract but along this line Kersten (2017), pp. 9 and 12.

[4]Teubner (2007), pp. 6 et seq.

[5]Cf. Solum (1992), p. 1239; Schirmer (2016), pp. 662 et seq; Kersten (2017), p. 9; Teubner (2018), pp. 163 and 177.

relationship.[6] In that sense, the relationship between the AI agent and its user should also be taken into consideration when evaluating the legal personhood of the former. This is closely related to the aforementioned fact that AI agents would most probably not have the technical capacity to evaluate a legal situation, be it a breach of contract, a tort or any other infringement, if not closely and directly related to their *modus operandi*. In that sense there will be a point, after which the intervention of the user will be necessary. Not only because of technical reasons but also because, after all, it is the user's interests that are at play. In relation to this it should also be pointed out that, AI agents will be (at least for the near future) owned by some other legal person (human or corporation) and will be utilized either directly by their owner or indirectly through contractual arrangements, predominantly some kind of lease agreement between the owner and the user.

2 Identification/Domicile

Legal persons must be personally identifiable. Like corporations, the most obvious way to achieve this would be through registration[7] which could allow AI agents to also acquire a personal signature contributing to their identification in all sorts of transactions. Apart from that, the registry could offer information on the characteristics of each AI agent and most importantly determine their owner and/or user.

AI agents as legal persons should also have a domicile. The choice of the exact location is not of interest for our enquiry. From a practical point of view, domicile is important in three aspects: jurisdiction, service of legal documents and especially service of process, and place of performance. Regarding jurisdiction and service, the question is intertwined with the user-AI relationship and the ability—or most probably inability—of AI agents to cope on their own with a legal dispute in its entirety. Accordingly, it would make sense to accept as domicile, at least as a rule of thumb, the domicile of the registered user, since almost all actions against the AI agent would ultimately interfere with their own interests.

The place of performance would be relevant only if no specific stipulations are made in the contractual agreement. Most jurisdictions follow the general rule (save especially for money debts) that the creditor has to collect the debt from the residence of the debtor.[8] The solution proposed above aligning the domicile of the AI agent with the one of its user seems to make *prima facie* sense also in this case, since the performance would be in the interest of the user.

---

[6] Teubner (2018), p. 162.

[7] Cf. Allen and Widdison (1996), p. 42; Beck (2012), p. 129.

[8] Cf. for Germany §269 BGB; Austria §905 ABGB; Switzerland Art. 74 OR; France Art. 1247 C. civ.; Italy Art. 1182 c.c.; Spain 1171 CC; for England cf. Beatson et al. (2020), p. 441.

3 Right to Personality

Legal personhood for AI agents means also a restricted right to personality. This is no novelty since corporations have also a restricted right to personality in comparison with humans.[9] Again, the exact extent of the right to personality shall depend on the function of the AI agent. An industrial AI agent who makes no transactions has no interest in protecting its fame, in contrast to an AI agent whose main operation would be to conclude contracts.

Two aspects of personality would seem indispensable for almost all AI agents: existence and function.[10] These would not only render any external (that is not from their user and/or owner) interference with the existence and function of the AI agents illegal, but would also include the right to communicate on line or more generally the right to have access to the digital environment.[11] It should, nevertheless, be kept in mind that any interference with the existence and operation of the AI agents would also be an infringement of the property rights of the owner and/or the contractual rights of the user, whatever the case may be. Since, as already mentioned, the AI agents would most probably not be able to enforce their rights personally, the recognition of a right to personality for them, although for many jurisdictions a necessary consequence of legal personhood, would have little if any practical effect. Nevertheless, at least theoretically, the infringement of the property rights of the owner and of the right to personality of the AI agent could depict two distinct damages, which could lead to an increased liability of the perpetrator, especially considering the possibility to raise a claim for non-pecuniary losses (as in the case of defamation).

The fact that AI agents are owned by some other legal person means that the right to personality cannot expand to a right not to be arbitrarily deleted, as proposed by *Karnow*.[12] Such an extension would make sense only if AI agents could demonstrate a totally autonomous existence, independent from their user. The dependence of AI agents as legal persons from their users is manifested also in that respect, just like in the case of corporations, which of course have no right not to be dissolved by their owners.

[9]Cf. Wolf and Neuner (2016), p. 165, §16 Rn. 6; BGH NJW 2016, p. 1584.

[10]Kersten (2015), p. 7.

[11]Karnow (1994), p. 13.

[12]Karnow (1994), p. 12.

4 Legal Capacity/Property

Legal capacity is the capacity to hold rights and duties. It does not determine what right and duties the person really holds or is able to hold. Like corporations, the legal capacity of AI agents will be restricted to the rights or duties compatible with their nature as technical artifacts (e.g. no family rights or duties).

The most important practical consequence of the legal capacity of AI agents will be that they will be able to hold property rights. This includes property rights in tangible and intangible assets as well as personal claims.[13] The main practical problem that arises in this context is the protection of these rights. Property rights, real or personal, can in some cases be lost or rendered "unenforceable", if the holder of the right does not take legal measures against infringements or merely refrains from any kind of action. The typical cases would be adverse possession and limitation of actions (prescription) for real and personal rights respectively. We face again the question of the ability of AI agents to evaluate a legal situation, which may not fall directly under their technical specifications. Since an infringement of the property rights of the AI agent would not constitute, like in the case of the right to personality, an infringement of the property right of the owner, at least not directly, the only way to overcome this problem *de lege lata* would be *via* an indirect action (*action oblique*),[14] provided that the user could be deemed a creditor of the AI agent. However, it should be noted that not all jurisdictions recognize this feature.[15] This problem is part of the larger problem of the ability of AI agents to initiate judicial proceedings, since legal capacity usually corresponds with the procedural capacity to appear as applicant or respondent in a relevant case. When, on the other hand, the AI agent is the defendant, it should be possible for the user to be involved in the proceedings as a joint litigant or as intervening party in support of the defendant.

5 Capacity to Contract

The question of capacity to contract of autonomous AI agents boils down, for the purposes of our research, to the issue of agency.[16] Agency law presumes agents that are persons. The authority could be conferred to the AI agent solely by the act of registration and should include all contracts that fall under the technical

[13] Cf. first Additional Protocol to the European Convention on Human Rights (ECHR), Art. 1; Kaiser (2012), Art. 1 ZP I, Rn. 17, with further references especially to the case law of the European Court of Human Rights (ECtHR). On the differences between common and civil law jurisdictions regarding the concept of property and property rights cf. Graziadei (2017), pp. 71 et seq.

[14] Cf. Art. 1341-1 C.civ (France).

[15] Most notably Germany and Switzerland.

[16] Obviously, the discussion does not include the cases of undisclosed principals.

configurations of the agent. This is a crucial point, since it eliminates for all practical reasons the problem of *falsus procurator* and the corresponding problem of the liability of the latter towards the principal and/or any third party.[17] It is the responsibility of the user to configure the AI agent according to their needs and to describe accurately the predetermined objectives and constraints delimitating the scope of authority.[18] It should be kept in mind that the cases we are discussing are cases of non-supervised agents, to whom the user has delegated the formation and conclusion of contracts on their behalf. As *Sartor* points out:

"...neither the user nor the programmer are in such a condition to fully anticipate the contractual behaviour of the SA (*software agent*) in all possible circumstances, and therefore to "want" the contracts which the SA will conclude. Even when the user is in the condition of making such a forecast, he cannot be required to do so, since, as observed above, this would contradict the very reason for using an SA: delegating cognitive tasks, as the acquisition of knowledge and its use in deliberation. Therefore, the fact that the effects of a contract made by an SA fall upon the user is not explained by the fact that the user foresaw the behaviour of its SA, or could have foreseen it, or even ought to have foreseen it".[19]

Since in most cases it will be not the user herself but some programmer or maybe the producer or seller of the AI agent the one who performs the configuration, the user would be able to claim from the latter any damages arising due to unwanted contracts, on the basis of their contractual relationship.

The other major problem, apart from the liability of the *falsus procurator*, arising in this context, is the case of the rescission of contract due to mistake, fraud and duress. Duress is rather unthinkable for machines, since it involves psychological interactions. Misrepresentation, on the other hand, is possible. The most common case should be the manipulation of the database used by the AI agent in order to collect the necessary information for the decision. In the same sense, a mistake[20] is possible, when a relevant database is temporarily offline for technical reasons, thus not allowing the AI agent to identify a better offer, or when a database used by the AI agent has misclassified a relevant entry (e.g. a golden ring as silver).[21]

The general rule is that the principal can rescind the contract for defective knowledge of the agent due to misrepresentation or mistake, provided that the principal did not have herself knowledge of the real situation.[22] It follows that the user should be able to rescind the contract made by the AI agent due to mistake or

[17] For these problems, cf. Teubner (2018), p. 184.

[18] Cf. along this line Schirmer (2016), p. 664; also, see the remarks of *Gsell*, reported by Rentsch (2018), p. 209.

[19] Sartor (2009), p. 278.

[20] The concept of mistake differs substantially between the European jurisdictions, especially between Anglo-Saxon and continental ones, cf. Sefton-Green (2005), p. 5, with further references.

[21] Cf. the examples in Lerouge (2000), pp. 426 et seq; Sartor (2009), p. 279.

[22] Cf. for Germany §166 BGB; for Switzerland Schwenzer (2009), pp. 310 et seq; for France Malaurie et al. (2017), p. 445.

misrepresentation. The protection of the third party (the contractual counterparty of the principal) will follow the general rules in each jurisdiction. Most commonly, in the case of rescission due to mistake, the third party may have a right to sue for the damages incurred by the rescission.[23]

6 Liability

The liability for decisions made by autonomous AI agents is perhaps the major problem concerning the use of such agents under current law. The core of the problem is causation and more specifically the total lack of foreseeability regarding the course of action to be chosen by the AI agent in each case due to the *black-box* phenomenon already discussed.[24] Consequently, the determination of causation is practically impossible,[25] regardless of the specific regime of causation that each jurisdiction applies, since all causation regimes are based at least to some extent on the concept of foreseeability. Moreover, foreseeability is also an element of negligence, both as a tort[26] (i.e. illegal behavior) and as a form of fault (*Verschulden*). Consequently, the lack of foreseeability negates both causation and fault as elements of liability, as well as illegality (negligence as tort), should this be the case.

More specifically, an unpredictable decision means that the damaging behavior cannot be avoided in advance.[27] According to the current legal status, where AI agents do not possess legal personhood, the breach of duty leading to liability, be it contractual or in tort, should be attributed to the user. Yet, there can be no duty to avoid the unpredictable and because of the inherent unpredictability of the choices of the autonomous AI agents, no causal link between the deployment of the autonomous agent and the resulting damage and no fault of the user can be established. Hence, the user could hardly be found liable for decisions—and actions that followed according to these decisions—that were objectively unpredictable. The user who simply uses an autonomous AI agent is hardly in breach of any duty contractual or in tort and hence cannot be found liable for any damages accruing from the actions of the autonomous AI agent.[28]

---

[23] Cf. §122 BGB (Germany), Art. 26 OR (Switzerland).

[24] Cf. supra note 2

[25] Cf. Karnow (1996), pp. 181 et seq; Pagallo (2013), pp. 73 et seq.

[26] The tort of negligence is also known to the continental jurisdictions, for the Germanic family commonly under the name of *Verkehrssicherungspflichten* cf. Fikentscher and Heinemann (2017), pp. 852 et seq and 948 et seq, directly comparing them to the "duty of care"; Tortious liability in Romanic jurisdictions is in any case based on fault (along with damages and causation), cf. Bénabent (2017), pp. 410 et seq.

[27] Teubner (2018), p. 175.

[28] Cf. Koch (2020), p. 126; Teubner (2018), pp. 158 et seq, 185 and 189, on contractual and tortious liability.

Recognizing legal personhood to the autonomous AI agent is a most promising way to overcome the abovementioned obstacles. It is exactly in this case, where the remark of *Teubner* on the practical value of personification, mentioned above, deserves the outmost attention. By transforming the AI agent from a tool to a person, the whole structure changes. Liability will be judged according to the decisions and actions of the AI agent and not of the user, moving the link of predictability from the couple *user's action (that is the deployment of the AI agent)—resulting damage,* to the couple *AI agent's action—resulting damage.* The unpredictability of the AI agent's choice becomes legally irrelevant in the same sense that the unpredictability of a human agent's choice is legally irrelevant.[29] The question will not be whether it was predictable that the deployment of an AI agent could lead to the resulting damage, which begs the question on the predictability of the AI agent's choice. On the contrary, the question will be whether a certain action (the choice of the AI agent) could foreseeably lead to the resulting damage. The answer to this question does not change, whether the acting agent is a human or a machine.

Establishing liability is just the first piece of the puzzle. Of course, as legal persons, AI agents shall have the ability to hold property and hence be able to compensate the victims of their actions—though, not necessarily so, since the ability to hold property rights does not mean that one actually has property. Regardless of the patrimonial status of the AI agent, it should be kept in mind that these agents do not act on their own behalf and for their benefit but on behalf and for the benefit of their users. As in the case of contracting, also in the case of liability there is a principal—auxiliary relationship between the user and the AI agent, rendering the AI agent a vicarious agent.[30] Vicarious liability (*respondeat superior* doctrine) would focus on the breach of duty[31] of the machine not of the human person.[32] Should the liability of the AI agent be established, like in any other case of human vicarious agents, the principal would be held responsible for the damages caused by the actions of their vicarious agents. It becomes clear that as far as liability is concerned, the importance of rendering legal personhood to autonomous AI agents is not that the AI agent itself could compensate the victim, but that it would be possible to establish liability in the person of the user as principal of a vicarious agent.[33] In this

[29] Cf. Karanasiou and Pinotsis (2017), p. 9, pointing also out that rationalizing intelligence as cornerstone of AI personhood shall help overcome the problem of unpredictability.

[30] The term is used for both tortious and contractual settings cf. Erfüllungs- and Verrichtungsgehilfe according to §§278 and 831 BGB respectively.

[31] Teubner suggests that it would be possible to establish a higher duty of care for AI agents, Teubner (2018), p. 189.

[32] Schirmer (2016), p. 665; Expert Group on Liability and New Technologies (2019), p. 25.

[33] This solution is not applicable to German law due to the infamous *Entlastungsbeweis* of § 831 Abs. I S. 2 BGB according to which:

"*Liability in damages does not apply if the principal exercises reasonable care when selecting the person deployed and, to the extent that he is to procure devices or equipment or to manage the business activity, in the procurement or management, or if the damage would have occurred even if this care had been exercised*"; cf. Teubner (2018), p. 190; generally on the *Entlastungsbeweis*

context, it should be kept in mind that the user will be liable only for the typical risks arising from the deployment of the vicarious agent.

7 Conclusion

Autonomous AI agents can make autonomous, and thus unpredictable, decisions. The main problem arising from this feature is the attribution of the actions of the AI agent to its user. Legal personhood can help, since AI agents as persons can be deemed contractual as well as vicarious agents of the user.

The recognition of legal personhood can only be restricted, dependent on their scope and their technical configuration. Moreover, restricted autonomy of actions is not equal to a fully autonomous existence. *Firstly*, AI agents operate always for the benefit and in order to promote the interests of their principal. *Secondly*, they cannot cope with legal interactions that fall outside their *modus operandi*. Hence, they shall need a legal guardian, in order to protect their rights. It follows that recognizing legal personhood to autonomous AI agents should go hand in hand with the establishment of a direct legal link between the AI agent and its user and/or owner. This is a weak version of the hybrid construct proposed by *Teubner*,[34] since according to this version solely the AI agent is the legal person.

Furthermore, it is clear that the solution of legal personhood, as elaborated here, poses at least two further questions. The first question concerns the entanglement of the legal positions of the owner of the AI agent and the AI agent itself, since an infringement of the rights of the latter could also, at least in some cases, be deemed an infringement of the rights of the owner. The second question concerns the case of self-replicating AI agents and their relationship with the principal-user, an issue that becomes more difficult in the case of Distributed Autonomous Organizations (DAOs).

It seems that the solution provided by recognizing legal personhood to autonomous AI agents carries with it a new set of problems, concerning mainly the need for legal guardianship and the assessment of the user-AI agent legal relationship. An introduction of strict agency and strict liability for AI agents user could solve the problem of the attribution of the actions of the AI agent to its user in a simpler way.[35]

---

cf. Fikentscher and Heinemann (2017), pp. 986 et seq. In Swiss law, a similar exception can be found in Art. 55 OR. The rule is strongly criticized and the judiciary tends to pose high standards for the principal, cf. Schwenzer (2009), pp. 158 et seq. In Austria it is questionable whether the principal will be found liable due to their knowledge of the risk according to § 1315 ABGB.

[34] Cf. Teubner (2018), pp. 196 et seq; Teubner (2007), pp. 14 et seq.

[35] Along this lines Koch (2020), p. 130; for agency Bellia (2001), pp. 1061 et seq.

References

Allen T, Widdison R (1996) Can computers make contracts? Harvard J Law Technol 9:25–52

Bathaee Y (2018) The artificial intelligence black box and the failure of intent and causation. Harvard J Law Technol 31:889–938

Beatson J, Burrows A, Cartwright J (2020) Anson's law of contract, 31st edn. Oxford University Press, Oxford

Beck S (2012) Brauchen wir ein Roboterrecht? Ausgewählte Fragen zum Zusammenleben von Mensch und Robotern. In: Japanisch-Deutsches Z (ed) Mensch-Roboter-Interaktionen aus interkultureller Perspektive. Japan und Deutschland im Vergleich JDZB, Berlin, pp 124–146

Bellia A (2001) Contracting with electronic agents. Emory Law J 50:1047–1092

Bénabent A (2017) Droits des obligations, 16th edn. LGDJ, Paris

Expert Group on Liability and New Technologies (2019) Liability for artificial intelligence and other emerging digital technologies. Available via EU Publications Office. https://op.europa.eu/en/publication-detail/-/publication/1c5e30be-1197-11ea-8c1f-01aa75ed71a1/language-en

Fikentscher W, Heinemann A (2017) Schuldrecht: Allgemeiner und Besonderer Teil, 11th edn. De Gruyter, Berlin

Graziadei M (2017) The structure of property ownership and the common law/civil law divide. In: Graziadei M, Smith L (eds) Comparative property law: global perspectives. Elgar, Northampton, pp 71–99

Kaiser K (2012) Art. 1 ZP EMRK. In: Karpenstein U, Mayer F (eds) EMRK: Konvention zum Schutz der Menschenrechte und Grundfreiheiten: Kommentar. C.H. Beck, Munich

Karanasiou A, Pinotsis D (2017) Towards a legal definition of machine learning. Paper presented at the 2017 international conference on artificial intelligence & law (ICAIL), London, 12–16 June 2017. https://doi.org/10.1145/3086512.3086524

Karnow C (1994) The encrypted self: fleshing out the rights of electronic personalities. John Marshall J Comput Inf Law 13:1–16

Karnow C (1996) Liability for distributed artificial intelligences. Berkley Technol Law Rev 11: 147–204

Kersten J (2015) Menschen und Maschinen. JuristenZeitung 70:1–8

Kersten J (2017) Relative Rechtssubjektivität: Über autonome Automaten und emergente Schwärme. Zeitschrift für Rechtssoziologie 37:8–25

Koch B (2020) Liability for emerging digital technologies: an overview. J Eur Tort Law 11:115–136

Lerouge J-F (2000) The use of electronic agents questioned under contractual law: suggested solutions on a European American level. John Marchall J Comput Inf Law 18:403–434

Malaurie P, Aynès L, Stoffel-Munck P (2017) Droit des obligations, 9th edn. LGDJ, Paris

Mühlböck L, Taupitz J (2021) Haftung für Schäden durch KI in der Medizin. AcP 221:179–218

Müller-Hengstenberg C, Kirn S (2014) Intelligente (Software-)Agenten: Eine neue Herausforderung unseres Rechtssystems. MMR 2014:307–313

Pagallo U (2013) The laws of robots: crimes, contracts, and torts. Springer, Dordrecht

Rentsch B (2018) Diskussionsbericht zum Referat von Gunther Teubner. AcP 218:206–212

Sartor G (2009) Cognitive automata and the law: electronic contracting and the intentionality of software agents. Artif Intell Law 17:253–290

Schirmer J-E (2016) Rechtsfähige Roboter? JuristenZeitung 71:660–666

Schwenzer I (2009) Schweizerisches Obligationenrecht: Allgemeiner Teil, 5th edn. Stämpfli Verlag, Bern

Sefton-Green R (2005) General introduction. In: Sefton-Green R (ed) Mistake, fraud and duties to inform in European Contract Law. Cambridge University Press, Cambridge, pp 1–38

Solum L (1992) Legal personhood for AI. North Carolina Law Rev 70:1231–1287

Teubner G (2007) Elektronische Agenten und grosse Menschenaffen: Zur Ausweitung des Akteursstatus in Recht und Politik. In: Becchi P, Graber CB, Luminati M (eds) Interdisziplinäre Wege in der juristischen Grundlagenforschung. Schulthess, Zurich, pp 1–30
Teubner G (2018) Digitale Rechtssubjekte? Zum privatrechtlichen Status autonomer Softwareagenten. AcP 218:155–205
Wolf M, Neuner J (2016) Allgemeiner Teil des Bürgerlichen Rechts, 11th edn. C.H. Beck, Munich

Artificial Intelligence's Black Box: Posing New Ethical and Legal Challenges on Modern Societies

Vasiliki Papadouli

Abstract Artificial Intelligence has been proven to be one of the most influential scientific fields in today's business world since its technological breakthroughs play an ever-increasing role in various sectors of modern life and transactions. Nonetheless, concerns are raised about the possible adverse effects they may have on individuals and society, given that various incidents of human rights violations, during—and due to—the operation of the so-called *autonomous AI systems,* have already been noticed. This 'negative' aspect of AI systems is attributed to the so-called "*black box problem*" or "*black-box effect*", which constitutes an inherent limitation of AI challenging AI's further evolution and public acceptance and sparking a lively debate in scientific community about the potential tools for counteracting it. The present paper aims at shedding light on the "new" legal and ethical challenges that AI poses for modern societies. First, the paper introduces the concept of AI "opacity" and examines certain reasons for it. Subsequently, it presents several incidents of violation of human rights taken place due to AI systems in various sectors, including the job market, the banking sector, (private) insurances, justice, transactions, art, and transportations. The paper concludes with some of the most important recommended guiding principles for counteracting the black box effect of AI and defying the new legal and ethical challenges posed by AI.

V. Papadouli (✉)
Faculty of Law & Criminology, Vrije Universiteit Brussel, Brussels, Belgium

Research team "Digital Economy and Private Law", School of Law, Aristotle University of Thessaloniki, Brussels, Belgium
e-mail: vasiliki.papadouli@vub.be; https://digec.law.auth.gr/en/home

A. Kornilakis et al. (eds.), *Artificial Intelligence and Normative Challenges*, Law, Governance and Technology Series 59,
https://doi.org/10.1007/978-3-031-41081-9_4

1 Introduction

Although quite 'new', Artificial Intelligence (henceforth *AI*) has become one of the most influential scientific fields, altering for good our lives. In today's business world the AI systems play an ever-increasing role in various sectors,[1] from finance and banking, other transactions, and the job market to medicine, justice and the entertainment industry.

However, despite the great achievements of AI systems, concerns are raised about the possible adverse effects they may have on individuals and society in general. Indeed, multiple incidents of human rights violations, during—and due to—the operation of the so-called *autonomous AI systems,* have already been noticed. These incidents show that, apart from astonishing successes, AI systems can also have severe negative effects. This constitutes an inherent limitation that challenges AI's further evolution and public acceptance, sparking a lively debate in scientific community about the potential tools for counteracting these effects.

Surprisingly, the main reason AI systems demonstrate such astonishing accomplishments equally induces their adverse effects: this is their inherent *ability of learning.* This ability is accompanied by an *opacity* regarding how AI systems internally operate and why they reache certain outcomes. This opacity constitutes the so-called *black box problem* or *black box effect* from which all modern AI systems, i.e. the so-called autonomous ones, suffer.

The present chapter aims at shedding light on the potential negative impact AI black box may have on human rights. At the introductory part, the concept and the operation of the autonomous AI systems are presented (Sect. 2). In Sect. 3, the concept of 'black box' as well as its reasons are investigated. In Sect. 4, the chapter presents incidents of human rights violations already caused by AI systems, while in Sect. 5, guiding principles for facing the black box effect are recommended.

2 What is an Autonomous AI System?

The most significant AI breakthrough of the last decades are undoubtedly the *autonomous systems* (or *autonomous machines*). These are advanced and highly 'sophisticated' AI systems, which can have extended usage in various sectors of modern life, performing optimally in any sector they are used.

As explained, their basic characteristic is their *ability of learning*, namely the systems' ability of conducting any assigned task, without having been explicitly

[1] See more about AI applications in our lives: European Commission, White Paper on AI—A European approach to excellence and trust, Com (2020) 65 final, p. 1; European Commission, Communication-Building trust in Human-Centric Artificial Intelligence, Com (2019) 168 final, p. 1; Kemper and Kolkman (2019), p. 2082, who argues about an 'algorithmic life'.

programmed to do so. This ability, called *machine learning,*[2] takes place without any human intervention and supervision,[3] thanks to sophisticated 'superpower' algorithms, which are trained to learn through observation.[4] The more they are 'exposed' to new 'experiences', the better are their outcomes, which, for this reason, are not determined in advance, rather are increasingly unpredictable, as the systems gain more and more 'experiences'.

Thanks to their ability of machine learning, autonomous AI systems perform better than their 'ancestors', i.e. the so-called *expert* or *knowledge systems,*[5] as well as human cognition. Nonetheless, machine learning renders AI systems' operation *opaque*, whist inhibiting their explicability about how and why they reached certain decisions.[6] But if the autonomous AI systems cannot justify their results (*black box problem* or *black box effect*), then AI sustainability is endangered.[7]

3 What is the Black Box Problem or Black Box Effect?

The *black box problem* or *black box effect*[8] is described in literature as the incomprehensible by humans way an autonomous AI system operates.[9] The problem has three basic aspects: first, the term is used to describe the complex and opaque way an autonomous AI system operates from a technical perspective; second, the term is linked with the autonomous system's difficulty in providing a suitable explanation about how and why it reached a specific decision, using a comprehensible for human beings language;[10] third, the concept refers to the overall incapacity to explain the AI system's outcomes *a posteriori*, even if we go back to the system's designers and programmers.

There are several reasons for the black box problem, the most prevailing of which are the following ones.[11]

[2] Denicola (2016), pp. 254–255; Yanski-Ravid (2017), p. 676.

[3] European Commission, Annexes, SWD (2021) 84 final, p. 35.

[4] Russell and Norvig (2020), p. 39; Wettig and Zehendner (2004), pp. 111–135.

[5] Karnow (1996), pp. 155 ff.; Yanski-Ravid (2017), pp. 674–675· Adadi and Berrada (2018), p. 52144.

[6] Felzmann et al. (2019), p. 1.

[7] Cf. Licht and Licht (2020), p. 918.

[8] McCarthy and Hayes (1969).

[9] Wulf and Seizov (2020), p. 619.

[10] Burrel (2016), p. 1; Adadi and Berrada (2018), p. 52141; Zednik (2019); European Commission, Com (2020) 65 final, p. 12; European Commission, Annexes, SWD (2021) 84 final, p. 34.

[11] Schmelzer (2020). See also Lepri et al. (2018), pp. 611 ff.; Thelissone et al. (2017).

3.1 *Complexity*[12]

Autonomous AI systems are complicated models whose operation is based on interactions among hundreds or thousands of parameters. How these parameters are combined with each other, how AI systems edit the received information and how they 'transform' it to a certain output are processes partially (or, sometimes, totally) unknown even for their designers, let alone for simple users. Nonetheless, the AI systems' complexity may vary.[13] The problem is more intensive with specific kind of autonomous AI systems, like the *artificial neural networks* (ANN),[14] which are considered the most complex autonomous AI systems yet, but at the same time the most accurate ones.[15] ANN are AI systems inspired by biological neural networks. They consist of several artificial "neurons", like the biological ones, that are aggregated into different layers (especially in case of deep learning).[16] They are trained by processing examples, based on several learning paradigms, such as supervised learning, unsupervised learning and the, much-discussed, reinforcement learning. On the contrary, other autonomous AI systems, like the ones using *decisions trees,* are considered less opaque for humans,[17] although less accurate.[18] Decisions trees are AI systems used for regression and classification tasks. Their "instruction" is based on supervised machine learning algorithms that solve the assigned tasks with graphs (trees) using a branching method to illustrate every possible output for a specific input.[19]

3.2 *Lack of Visibility into Training Data Sets or into Methods of Data Selection*[20]

An autonomous AI system's instruction is based on given data; the system receives data from several sources, such as the internet or public registries, edits the received data, stores them, and based on the stored data, produces a certain outcome. But how the AI system edits certain data and which of them may play a more significant role for the AI system's rendered outcome, is not always known. Furthermore, there is always the risk that companies and governments do not reveal the actual source of

[12] Burrel (2016), p. 5; Carabantes (2020), p. 310. See also European Commission, Annexes, SWD (2021) 84 final, p. 34.

[13] Lipton (2017), p. 13· Carabantes (2020), p. 310.

[14] Russell and Norvig (2020), p. 727; Bathaee (2018), pp. 901–902.

[15] Hacker et al. (2020), pp. 433–435; Wulf and Seizov (2020), pp. 617–618.

[16] Russell and Norvig (2020); Bathaee (2018), pp. 901–902.

[17] See also European Commission, Annexes, SWD (2021) 84 final, p. 34.

[18] Hacker et al. (2020), pp. 429–430.

[19] Russell and Norvig (2020); Kotsiantis (2013).

[20] Burrel (2016), p. 1.

the data an 'employed' AI system uses, or the methods of the data's selection. Their basic argument for such a concealment is that they must protect the relevant system from possible malicious attacks or that they must maintain their competitiveness, trade secrets,[21] or, regarding administrative authorities, that they must keep state secrets. Although their argumentation carries an element of truth, doubts are raised about possible illegal or immoral circumstances behind the accumulation and use of said datasets. In this case, the opacity of AI does not constitute a system's property, but is rather due to an *intentional concealment*[22] of the data or of the methods for their selection.

3.3 *Limited Understanding of the* Inherent Biases *in Training Data Sets*

Sometimes, although the origin of the training data and their selection process are known (e.g. they are derived from a specific registry), the AI system may reach wrong and incomprehensible decisions because of the *inherent biases* underpinning the data fed to the system.[23] As it is already mentioned above, the autonomous AI systems' ability of learning is based on the use of (terabyte of) data through which the system 'trains' its algorithms, thus, gaining experience and knowledge. But should these data be based on previous prejudiced human decisions, the AI system's decisions are expected to be also biased.[24] This constitutes a significant drawback of AI systems, given that these biases could have a much more significant effect on society in comparison to similar individual decisions, mainly for two reasons: first, because the use of AI systems can massively affect and discriminate people worldwide, as the examples in Sect. 4 will reveal; second, because there are no social control mechanisms for governing the AI systems' behavior, as in the case of humans.[25]

---

[21] Smith (2016).

[22] Diakopoulos (2014), p. 1; Burrel (2016), p. 3; Carabantes (2020), p. 311.

[23] Goodman and Flaxman (2017), p. 54; Opinion of the European Economic and Social Committee on "White paper on Artificial Intelligence — A European approach to excellence and trust", COM (2020) 65 final 364/12), Recital 2.6.

[24] Zerilli et al. (2018); Kemper and Kolkman (2019), p. 2082.

[25] European Commission, COM (2020) 65 final, p. 11.

3.4 Technological Illiteracy *and* Cognitive Mismatch *Between Human and Artificial Intelligence*[26]

Understanding an algorithm code is a highly specialized skill absent not only in the vast majority of the population, but also in a great number of computer engineers, who are not specialized in this field. As it is aptly pointed out, even engineers involved in the development and maintenance of autonomous AI systems do not have detailed information about the ongoing process.[27] Therefore, if an expert cannot decode any given information originated by the AI system regarding its operation, then it is certain that the user cannot do it. This is not only a matter of *technological illiteracy*,[28] but also a problem of *cognitive mismatch*;[29] that is, a mismatch between mathematical optimization of machine learning algorithms and the humans' semantic interpretation: the autonomous AI systems are, in fact, software programs and the only thing they recognize is electrical signals. They receive data through electrical signals and they 'train' their algorithm to be able to transform the received input to an output. This procedure takes place without words, sentences, or arguments. This constitutes a great difference between human intelligence and artificial one. For this reason, it is claimed that any attempt to understand the function of autonomous AI systems is doomed to fail because of the already existing cognitive mismatch between the systems' and the human's way of 'thinking'.[30]

4 Applications of Autonomous AI Systems with Potential Adverse Effects on Human Rights

In today's business world there is a great number of autonomous AI systems imperceptibly used in various sectors.[31] Facial recognition, drafting of legal documents, recommending medical treatment, inventory forecasting, robots in deep sea and space exploration, weapon systems, software agents, self-driving vehicles are only some examples of such use.[32] Despite their astonishing accomplishments, their inherent black box can have several adverse effects on individuals and society, as well as on business. The following paradigms illustrate this.[33]

---

[26] Burrel (2016), p. 2; Carabantes (2020), pp. 312–313.

[27] Hacker et al. (2020), p. 430.

[28] Burrel (2016), p. 4; Carabantes (2020), pp. 312–313.

[29] Burrel (2016), pp. 4–5; Carabantes (2020), p. 313.

[30] Carabantes (2020), p. 316. Cf. Hacker et al. (2020), p. 435.

[31] Kemper and Kolkman (2019), p. 2082; Carabantes (2020), p. 310; Lipton (2017), p. 2.

[32] See European Commission, Statement on Artificial Intelligence, Robotics and 'Autonomous Systems' (2018).

[33] See Uni global Union, Top 10 Principles for ethical artificial intelligence.

4.1 Decision-Making at Recruitment, Dismissal, or Promotion Procedures in the Job Market[34]

Autonomous AI systems have already been 'employed' in the job market at recruitment processes for assessment of the candidates' qualifications and profile before hiring, or similarly, before promotions or dismissals. To execute this task batches of data from the enterprise are usually provided to the AI system. But should these data suffer from inherent biases, i.e. they are based on previous prejudiced human decisions (e.g. against specific group of people), the AI system's decisions will be also biased.

This has already happened with a prominent company in international trade some years ago: *Amazon*.[35] The famous company used AI systems at recruitment processes. The AI system was trained to assess applicants' qualifications, *inter alia*, by observing patterns in CVs submitted to the company over the past 10 years. After a period of usage, it was discovered that the system gave preference to white male candidates. The most probable reason for this choice was that the system was 'taught' itself that male candidates were preferable than women, or Afro-American males, because it encountered more white male's images at the company's past files of employees.

Although the problem was quickly found and the company took measures to eliminate the 'bug' at its AI system's code, the incident reveals the potentially adverse effects AI systems may have on human dignity and personality of candidates, or employees accordingly, including their future career prospects and livelihoods. Moreover, such bias may crucially impact on candidates' or employees' privacy and personal data. Ultimately, this practice if left unchecked, contravenes the general principle of non-discrimination and equality, which constitutes one of the most basic principles of international human rights law, enshrined, *inter alia*, in Article 14 of the European Convention on Human Rights (ECHR) and Protocol No. 12 to the ECHR, as well as in a series of European Union Directives directly applied to the job market.[36]

Further, the biased AI systems' outcomes result in wrong business decisions since they, first, deprive employers of valuable human capital, and second, expose companies to compensation claims.

Indeed, any violation of the right to personality as well as of the principle of equal treatment raises, *inter alia*, compensation claims in favor of the victims against

[34] European Economic and Social Committee, COM (2020) 65 final 364/12, Recital 2.24; European Commission, Annexes, SWD (2021) 84 final, pp. 36–37.

[35] See Dastin (2018).

[36] *Council Directive 2000/43/EC* about implementing the principle of equal treatment between persons irrespective of racial or ethnic origin; the *Council Directive 2000/78/EC* about establishing a general framework for equal treatment in employment and occupation; *Council Directive 2006/54/EC* on the implementation of the principle of equal opportunities and equal treatment of men and women in matters of employment and occupation.

employers. The substantiation of these claims is quite difficult for the victims/claimants, but recently they have been significantly facilitated by the aforementioned Directives. More specifically, these Directives reverse the burden of proof as far as the causal link between the illegal/discriminatory treatment and the complainant's injury is concerned.[37] In the same line, the recent European Commission Proposal of Directive on adapting non-contractual (on fault-based) civil liability rules to artificial intelligence (*AI liability Directive*)[38] provides a rebuttable presumption of causal link in favor of the person who suffered damages by AI systems,[39] while according to the European Court of Justice (henceforth *ECJ*), in case of illegal discrimination the claimant does not need to prove any fault of the defendant to claim compensation, because liability arising therefrom must be strict.[40]

The potentially adverse impact these AI systems may have on human rights in the context of the job market has led to their categorization as '*high-risk AI systems*', according to the recent Proposal for a Regulation (*Artificial Intelligence Act)* of the European Commission about AI, which is going to be (amended and) enacted soon.[41] According to this Act, supplementary measures must be taken before the use of such kind of AI systems in the job market.[42]

4.2 Loan Risk Assessment Systems in the Banking Sector[43]

Autonomous AI systems are also 'employed' in the banking sector for several tasks, including loan risk assessment. That means that the approval or rejection of a loan application depends on a prior decision of autonomous AI systems about the applicant's creditworthiness.

Here too the AI systems are 'instructed' with specific data usually originating from the bank's archives, or with data stored on public registries (such as criminal or creditworthiness[44] records), as well as with data from the web, derived even from social media.[45] Any inherent biases against specific groups of people (e.g. against women, Afro-Americans, etc.) in the training datasets can lead to biased AI systems' decisions, accordingly.

---

[37] Art. 8 of the Council Directive 2000/43/EC; Art. 10 of the Council Directive 2000/78/EC; Art. 19 of the Council Directive 2006/54/EC.

[38] European Commission, COM (2022) 496 final.

[39] Art. 4.

[40] C-177/88 of 8 November 1990 (Dekker); C-180/95 of 22 April 1997 (Draehmpaehl).

[41] European Commission, COM (2021), 206 final, Art. 6 par. 2 and Annex III, n. 4.

[42] European Commission, COM (2021) 206 final, Art. 16–29.

[43] Wulf and Seizov (2020), pp. 637–638.

[44] For instance, in Spain the "Central de Informatcion des Reisigos" (CIR); in Greece the "Teiresias registry"; in UK the ""behavioural" account data".

[45] Langenbucher (2020), pp. 1–2.

This has already been noticed in case of a credit card launched some years ago by the prominent American bank *Goldman Sachs* in cooperation with the famous tech-giant company *Apple*:[46] their "employed" AI system was blamed for discriminating against women and the most prevalent reason was found to be the 'intrusion' of inherent biases in its training datasets.

As in the previous paradigm, such kind of an AI system's decisions infringe on the right of personality since they deprive specific groups of people of financial resources or other essential services, such as housing, thus restricting their participation in economic life. Indeed, the exclusion seems to be much more intensive in this case compared to the previous paradigm due to the specific role and oligopolistic dominance credit institutions have in modern societies.

Further, any discriminatory AI systems' decision violates the principle of equality regarding access in goods and services provided by a series of European Union Directives, especially by the Council Directive 2000/43/EEC, which applies also regarding the access to and supply of goods and services available to the public, including housing,[47] and by the Council Directive 2004/113/EC.[48]

Therefore, compensation claims can also be raised from anyone deprived of financial services due to an opaque and discriminatory AI system's decision. This person will enjoy the same advantages as the employees or the candidates in the previous paradigm: (a) a rebuttable presumption regarding the causal link between the illegal-discriminatory treatment and the caused damaged,[49] as well as regarding the causal link between the fault of the defendant (at the fault-based liability) and the output produced by the AI system (or the failure of the AI system to produce an output),[50] while (b) one could also claim that the bank's arising liability should be strict, according to the ECJ decisions applied in this case mutatis mutandis.[51]

Further, any AI system's discriminatory decision regarding creditworthiness not only constitutes a wrong business decision[52] but its possible adverse effects can be even more intensive for the companies, compared to the previous ones, given that credit institutions must adhere to the *principle of responsible lending*. The latter is enacted in EU law *via* Art. 8 of *Directive 2008/48/EC on credit agreements for consumers*, as well as Art. 18 of *Directive 2014/17/EC on credit agreements for consumers relating to residential immovable property*. According to this principle, the credit institutions must assess the creditworthiness of credit/loan applicants

[46] Burt (2019), p. 2; see Vigdor (2019).

[47] Art. 3 par. 1h.

[48] Art. 3 par. 1.

[49] See Art. 9 of the Directive 2004/113/EC.

[50] See Art. 4 Com (2022) 496 final.

[51] See previous footnote n. 41. The EuCJ has reached a similar conclusion three decades ago at *Danfoss* case (C-109/88 of 17 October 1989), where it was stated that in case of a payment system that totally lacks transparency, it is not the claimant, rather the defendant-user of the opaque system, who must bear the burden of proof that a discrimination has not been taken place.

[52] Langenbucher (2020), passim.

before the conclusion of the credit agreement, or prior to any significant increase in the total amount of credit, otherwise sanctions against them can be imposed. Therefore, any wrong decisions of an AI system adopted by the credit institution, may result in administrative sanctions, or loss of significant profit for the latter.

This kind of AI systems are placed equally in the category of '*high-risk AI systems*', according to the recent proposal for an *Artificial Intelligence Act* of the European Commission.[53]

4.3 *Health Status Assessment for Insurance Purposes*[54]

Another sector where autonomous AI systems are successfully used is the private insurance industry. With the aid of autonomous AI systems, this industry can, *inter alia*,[55] assess the health status of a client, predict one's future vulnerabilities, and subsequently, efficiently estimate the insurance premium rate for every client.

This assessment is based on data analyzed by the AI system pertaining to personal information (e.g. place of residence, marital and family status, educational background, income), as well as customer traits (e.g. driving habits, vehicle maintenance history). The data can be gathered either by registries (public or private) or by sensors (e.g. from connected devices in case of the Internet of Things), but equally by social networks, including *Facebook*, *LinkedIn*, or *Instagram*.[56]

For instance, *Deloitte*, a renowned private insurance company worldwide, has already announced that it has 'employed' a software system which can use thousands of non-traditional third-party data sources to predict the health status of a life insurance applicant with accuracy comparable to a medical exam.[57] The assessment takes place thanks to machine learning algorithms that are able to discover correlations between phenomena as causally distant as the consumer's buying history (e.g. based on the postal code) and his/her health status.[58]

Thanks to this technological evolution the private insurance industry is finally able to face information asymmetry and tackle the so-called *adverse selection problem*,[59] as well as to identify fraud incidents. However, the number of someone's appearances in online platforms, such as in the Amazon site, is not directly relevant

[53] See Annex III, Art. 5b.

[54] European Insurance and Occupational Pensions Authority (2021); Kancevičienė (2019).

[55] European Insurance and Occupational Pensions Authority (2021), p. 9.

[56] Langenbucher (2020), pp. 1–2.

[57] See https://www2.deloitte.com/content/dam/Deloitte/xe/Documents/financial-services/Artificial-Intelligence-in-Insurance.pdf.

[58] Carabantes (2020), p. 314. Cf. Langenbucher (2020), pp. 1–2.

[59] The *adverse selection problem* refers generally to a situation in which sellers have information that buyers do not have, or vice versa, about some aspect of product quality. In the health insurance field, this manifests itself through healthy people choosing managed care and less healthy people choosing more generous plans. To fight adverse selection, insurance companies reduce exposure to

to someone's health status. In addition, there is always the risk that the data is missing, incomplete, corrupted, or inconsistent. Based on such information, the AI system may reach inaccurate assessments leading to discriminatory (e.g. higher premiums for minorities) and wrong business decisions.

Further, the present paradigm raises several concerns about privacy. Indeed, the fact that an AI system may have access to one's personal data (e.g. because the data have been made available on the web), does not mean that the data subject consents to their use for purposes that are incompatible with the purpose(s) for the initial data collection.[60] In other words, the data subject must give their prior consent to the processing of their personal data for insurance purposes (especially for profiling), otherwise a violation of privacy and personal data may has taken place.[61]

The person that suffered damage because of such an opaque and discriminatory AI system decision can claim compensation against the insurance company based on Directive 2000/43/EC,[62] which is applicable regarding access to and supply of services that are available to the public, as well as on Directive 2004/113/EC[63] that is directly applicable to private insurances. The advantages regarding the burden of proof provided in these Directives,[64] in conjunction with the rebuttable presumption of proof provided in the recent Proposal of the European Commission regarding AI non-contractual liability, can also apply in this case.

Further, one can claim compensation based on Art. 82 of the *Regulation 2016/679 on the protection of natural persons with regard to the processing of personal data and on the free movement of such data*, for any material or non-material damage in case of infringement of their persona data.

Despite the risks these systems entail, they are not deemed '*high-risk AI systems*', according to the recent Proposal for an *Artificial Intelligence Act* of the European Commission. This raises even more concerns about the future adverse effects such AI systems may induce on privacy and personal data, as well on the principle of equal treatment in the relevant field.

---

large claims by limiting coverage or raising premiums. See for more Furubotn and Richter (2005), p. 222; Veljanovski (2007), pp. 40, 117.

[60] See Articles 5 and 6 of the Regulation of the European Parliament and of the Council 2016/679 (General Data Protection Regulation).

[61] The same concern is also raised in case of AI system in medical sector, like the famous IBM's AI system 'Watson' accused of incorrect medical treatment, see Ross and Swetlitz (2018).

[62] Art. 3 par. 3h.

[63] Art. 5 par. 1 and Recital Nr. 15, 18 and 20.

[64] Art. 8 of Directive 2000/43/EC and Art. 9 of Directive 2004/113/EC.

4.4 Criminal Recidivism Prediction[65]

AI systems could be adopted by judicial authorities for several tasks, such as anonymization of court decisions, speech-to-text conversion and transcription, machine translation, providing chatbots for supporting access to justice, and robot process automation.[66] But apart from these usages, AI systems can fulfil much more sophisticated activities in the judicial sector, such as rendering court decisions by themselves. This is about the so-called *robot-judges*, which seem to be able even to (fully) replace human judges throughout the juridical process.

The most typical example of such a robot-judge already exists in the U.S.A., where autonomous AI systems have been 'employed' in criminal justice for predicting the criminal recidivism of offenders.[67] These systems (whose function constitutes a trade secret) are able to estimate the risk of recidivism based on interviews with the offenders, information originating from public registries, and publicly available data, such as the age, sex/gender, family status, education, income and/or antisocial behavior of the offender.[68]

But given the black box effect, these systems can display gender and racial biases, namely demonstrate a differentiated recidivism prediction probability for specific groups of people (e.g. women, non-nationals, minorities), also in relation to the specific country employing them (e.g. higher probability against Afro-Americans in the U.S.A., or against women in countries of Middle East).[69] This way they can result in infringing human rights, such as the right to fair justice, human dignity, the right to personality and the principle of equality.

This has already been noticed in the U.S.A. in 2016, where it was found that thousands of AI algorithms used in criminal justice are biased against Afro-Americans.[70] After the disclosure, a lot of motions have been filed against state juridical authorities by offenders arguing that the use of algorithms in criminal justice violates their right to due process and the right of individual sentence based on accurate information,[71] while the use of data related to gender and race should be deemed unconstitutional.[72] However, the *Wisconsin Supreme Court of Justice* rejected in

[65] Zerilli et al. (2018); European Commission, White Paper on AI, COM (2020) 65 final, p. 14; European Commission, Proposal on Artificial Intelligence Act, COM (2022) 206 final, Recital Nr. 40.

[66] European Commission, COM (2021) 710 final, 3.2, pp. 12–13; Freeman (2016), pp. 76–77.

[67] The most prevalent one is the risk assessment system COMPAS (Correctional Offender Management Profiling for Alternative Sanctions).

[68] Eaglin (2021), p. 364.

[69] European Commission, COM (2021), 710 final, p. 11.

[70] Angwin et al. (2016).

[71] Already established in Wisconsin criminal justice jurisprudence at State v. Skaff, 447 N.W.2d 84, 85 (Wis. Ct. App. 1989) regarding accuracy of sentencing (based on the previous case Gardner v. Florida, 430 U.S. 349, 351–52 (1977), and at State v. Gallion, 678 N.W.2d 197, 209 (Wis. 2004) regarding individual sentencing.

[72] Loomis v. Wisconsin, 881 N.W.2d 749 (Wisc. 2016).

2016 such a motion claiming that the applicant did not provide sufficient evidence for their racial discrimination. It is also argued that the court decision was not based solely on the algorithm' s outcomes, but also on other elements that explained the sentence imposed (*Loomis v. State*).[73] The *Indiana Supreme Court* had previously reached the same conclusion (*Malenchic v. State*)[74] by overturning an earlier decision of the *Indiana Court of Appeal* at Rhodes case (*Rhodes v. State*),[75] where the infringement on the right to individual sentence because of algorithm's use was accepted. Subsequently, the *Court of Appeal of Michigan,* aligning with the *Loomis* and *Malenchic* court decisions, rejected a motion in 2019, claiming a lack of evidence for any discriminatory treatment of the claimants by the algorithm (*People v. Younglove case*).[76]

However, this standpoint seems to be overly restrictive for the claimants' rights, since it does not take into account the black box effect from which all autonomous AI systems suffer.[77] In addition, it underestimates the importance of data's quality and their complex editing process,[78] ignores the factual and objective inability of evidence from the claimants' side, while it endorses the extended use of AI systems from judges[79] that do not have the appropriate knowledge to explain judicial reasoning influenced by algorithmic predictions.[80]

These concerns have been taken into consideration in other jurisdictions, as the paradigm of Australian courts reveals. In contrast to U.S.A. courts' approach, the *Supreme Court of Western Australia* has promptly pointed out that "*the research data and methods underlying the assessment tools are assumed to be correct, but this has not been established by the evidence*".[81] Similarly, the recent Proposal of the European Commission for a Directive on AI non-contractual liability takes into account, *inter alia*, the inability of claimants, who suffered damage due to AI systems, to prove the causal link between the fault of the defendant (for fault-based liability) and the output produced by the AI system (or the failure of the AI system to produce an output). On that basis, the Proposal also provides a rebuttable presumption of proof in favor of the claimants (Article 4). Accordingly, the recent Proposal for a Regulation on Artificial Intelligence of the European Commission considers the AI systems intended to assist a judicial authority and to apply the law to a concrete set of facts as '*high-risk*'.[82]

---

[73] Loomis v. Wisconsin, 881 N.W.2d 749 (Wisc. 2016). See also Han-Wei et al. (2019).

[74] Malenchik v. State 928 N.E. 2d 564 (Ind. 2010).

[75] Rhodes v. State 896 N.E. 2d 1193 (Ind. Ct. Appeal 2008).

[76] People v. Younglove, N. 341901, 2019 WL 846117 (Mich. Ct. Appeal Feb. 21, 2019).

[77] See also Washington (2018).

[78] Freeman (2016), p. 93; Washington (2018), pp. 134, 146–147.

[79] See also Freeman (2016), p. 99.

[80] Id., p. 104.

[81] Director of Public Prosecutions for Western Australia v. Mangolamara (2007) 169 A. Crim. R. 379[2007] WASC 71, [165].

[82] See Annex III, Art. 8a.

4.5 *Contract-Conclusion Through AI Systems and Artwork Recommendations by AI Systems*

AI systems are extensively used at modern transactions. Smart devices, such as smart fridges or intelligent personal assistants, like *Amazon's Alexa* or *Apple's Siri*,[83] can negotiate, form, and finally, conclude a contract without, or with little, human intervention. Their employment facilitates contractual procedures since they can eliminate the time of negotiations and thus rapidly lead to the conclusion of a contract that meets the desires/needs of the interested parties.

However, their use raises several concerns regarding how these AI systems choose the counterparty among those with the same characteristics. For example, how and why an intelligent agent installed in a smart fridge decides to buy products from certain suppliers (e.g. from a big supermarket), while there are plenty of suppliers providing the same goods at the same price? An operational malfunction, a hack-bug in the AI system's code, or any inherent biases intruded at its training datasets can eliminate the access to economic life for certain groups of merchants, whilst causing *unfair competition.*

The same happens also in case of artworks recommended by AI systems.[84] Online entertainment platforms, like the famous media streaming companies *Netflix* and *Spotify*, not only offer artworks (like songs, series, or movies) to their subscribers, but also recommend artworks to them for their enjoyment. These recommendations can be based on previous decisions of AI systems, whose internal operation and training data are usually unknown. This means that the AI systems may privilege certain creators and put aside their peers. This way the AI systems significantly restrict the right of creators to actively participate in cultural (and economic) life, as well as the audience's access to diverse cultural expressions,[85] while they also cause *unfair competition* between the artists worldwide. None of that is perceived by the subscribers most of the times. For instance, due to AI's discriminatory recommendations the subscribers are unconsciously familiarized only with 'west' type artefacts, such as *Hollywood* films, rather with the 'east' ones. In addition, these discriminatory recommendations may violate the principle of equal treatment, if the creators put aside belong to specific social groups (e.g. minorities) in certain societies.

Contrary to the previous examples, in this case it is uncertain whether the person that suffered damage from the AI system's discriminatory decisions (merchant or artist, accordingly) can efficiently claim compensation, since most of the times the person incurring liability will be unknown. Indeed, the beneficiary competitors may

[83] Both Alexa and Siri are voice-controlled digital or virtual assistant programs based on AI that accept voice commands to create to-do lists, order items online, set reminders and answer questions (via internet searches), see for more https://en.wikipedia.org/wiki/Amazon_Alexa, https://en.wikipedia.org/wiki/Siri.

[84] UNESCO (2019), p. 16.

[85] Id.

have no liability for the biased AI system's results, at least under antitrust law *stricto sensu* since they may be fully unaware of the AI system's discriminatory decision favoring them and, besides, almost always they are not the ones choosing to 'employ' the discriminatory AI systems and install it into the entrainment platform.

At this point the potential platforms' liability against merchants or artists, as well as against consumers, should be investigated. Appropriate legal bases in the juridically advanced EU context could be, *inter alia*, the *Directive 31/2000/EC on electronic commerce*, as recently amended by the Re*gulation 2022/2065 on a Single Market of Digital Service Act (DSA)*[86] and the *Regulation 2022/1925 on contestable and fair markets in the digital sector—Digital Market Act (DMA),* accordingly, as well as the *Directive 2014/104/EC on certain rules governing actions for damages under national law for infringements of the competition law,* and the *Regulation 1/2003/EC on the implementation of the rules on competition.*

4.6 AI Artifacts and Intellectual Property Rights

Similarly, AI systems are able to produce artworks, like songs, poems or paintings, by themselves perfectly 'imitating' the work of famous artists. The paradigm of '*The Next Rembrandt*' project as well as the recent achievement of the '*Huawei Mate 20 Pro*' are apocalyptic.[87]

At '*The Next Rembrandt*' project, the tech-giant company *Microsoft* in cooperation with the bank *ING*, and the *Delf University of Technology*, created an algorithm which was exposed to the paintings of the famous Dutch painter *Rembrandt.* After having 'studied' his genre, and elements like the light or the shape and distance of forms in his paintings, the algorithm created a totally new painting based on *Rembrandt's* technique, which was printed with the aid of 3D-printers.[88] Similarly, the tech-giant company *Huawei* has recently constructed an artificial neural network which was able to complete the unfinished eighth symphony of *Schubert* after being 'exposed' to the songs of the great compositor.[89]

These capabilities of AI systems constitute a real 'revolution' in the field of art. However, they raise several concerns about whether these 'artifacts' created by AI systems constitute new pieces of art, or infringement of works already being granted with copyrights.[90] Should the answer to this question be that they constitute new pieces of art, then another one is raised: who shall be deemed the creator of an AI

[86] See, inter allia, the provisions of Art. 26 'Advertising on Online Platforms', and Art. 27 'Recommender System Transparency'.

[87] See more paradigms at Iglesias et al. (2019), pp. 12 ff.

[88] Yanski-Ravid (2017), p. 676.

[89] See Kennedy (2019).

[90] European Parliament resolution of 20 October 2020 on intellectual property rights for the development of artificial intelligence technologies (2020/2015(INI)), Recital D.

artifact, the AI user or the AI system itself? Subsequently, shall these 'artifacts' created by AI systems deserve legal protection similar (or even identical) to the human artifacts'?

In the European Union as well as in the U.S.A. the idea that "there is no authorship without humanness" remains prevalent even today;[91] that is, the law as it now stands does not recognize any copyright to artifacts created by AI systems. Therefore, only the persons using the AI systems could be deemed 'authors'. Nonetheless, other legal orders have already started to move towards a different direction. Indeed, the United Kingdom is elaborating a bill[92] about granting copyrights not only to artists using AI systems in their work, but also to '*computer-generated works*', i.e. works generated by a computer without any human factor being involved. In the latter case, the 'author' is deemed "*the person by whom the arrangements necessary for the creation of the work are undertaken*". The legal protection will last for 50 years from the date the work is made, namely 20 years less compared to the 70 years of protection granted to the rest copyright-protected works.

The recent creations of AI linguistic models like the '*ChatGPT*', designed by *OpenAI* and launched for the first time in November 2022, as well as the '*New Bing*', designed by *Microsoft* and launched in February 2023, confirm the necessity of new legal enactments regarding intellectual property. These 'sophisticated' systems are deep neural networks which are able not only to conduct discussions with their user (thus, passing the famous *Turing-test*),[93] but also to write computer codes, poems, or essays,[94] thus, posing new legal challenges to (industrial and) intellectual property law.

4.7 *Damage Caused by Self-Driving Vehicles*

Self-driving vehicles, in particular cars, are autonomous AI systems, capable of sensing their environment and moving in it with little or no human involvement. Their extended use in roads is expected to significantly reduce car accidents, thus, decrease important property losses, severe injuries, and deaths. However, were they to be widely adopted,[95] they would soon face ethical dilemmas, and consequently be asked to explain their decisions. For instance, in case of an inevitable collision, the self-driving car should be able to explain, why it chose to harm a specific person and not another (e.g. a passenger and not its driver, an elder passenger and not a child, a

[91] Id., pp. 13–15.

[92] See https://www.gov.uk/government/consultations/artificial-intelligence-and-ip-copyright-and-patents/artificial-intelligence-and-intellectual-property-copyright-and-patents#copyright.

[93] Turing (1950).

[94] See Varadi (2023).

[95] Self-driving cars have already involved in car-accidents in America, see for more O'kane (2018); Wulf and Seizov (2020), p. 631.

woman passenger and not a man one, an Afro-American and not a white person, and *vice versa*). But the black box problem does not allow such a justification, while any inherent biases 'intruded' in the AI systems' training datasets leave reasonable doubts for the answer's 'correctness', if any.

Like in the previous cases, this is not a science-fiction story, rather a concern already raised in real life, as the example of an *Uber self-driving* car accident in 2018 reveals:[96] although the self-driving car had detected a woman who crossed the road in front of it, it decided not to take an evasive action. The accident was inevitable and led to the 49-old woman's death.

This example poses the most difficult ethical challenges for AI, not only because it leads to a human's death or severe injury, but also because there may not be a right/ethical answer or course of action. Indeed, even a human cannot explain their decisions in cases of ethical dilemmas. Nonetheless, human judgment may be affected by defects that are inherent in human nature, such as the lack of composure, attention and experience, or by external factors, such as reduced visibility, bad weather conditions, or a bad road network, which may restrict, or even eliminate, the human driver's liability. But in the case of AI systems their only inherent defect is their black box, fed by terabytes of data on a constant basis; should any bias intervene to the AI system's training datasets, the AI system's decision will be biased accordingly.

But in contrast to the previous paradigms, where the AI user (e.g. the employer, the credit institution or the insurance company) has the potential to overrule the AI system's decisions by choosing not to adopt them, if they are conscious of any biases, in case of self-driving cars there is no such alternative. The reason is that very often the AI user-driver does not have enough time to assess the AI system's decision and opt for a different handling, in case the AI system allows the user-driver to take the wheel, even at the very last moment. On that sense, self-driving cars constitute a clear departure from AI systems used in other sectors, thus requiring a consistent legal framework to be enacted before the extended use of self-driving cars is allowed.

Considering that there is no concrete legal regulation applicable for damages caused by self-driving cars up today (in the European Union, at least), any person that suffered material and non-material damage due to a self-driving car can claim compensation based on the general provisions of tort law. However, in the European Union claimants will soon be able to invoke the special rules of burden of proof (the rebuttable presumption) provided in the recent Proposal of Directive on AI non-contractual liability. Further, they will be able to claim compensation against the AI designer, according to the recent Proposal of Directive of the European Commission on liability of defected products,[97] in conjunction with the recent Proposal of the European Commission for a Regulation on machinery products.[98]

[96] See O'kane (2018).

[97] European Commission, COM (2022) 495 final.

[98] European Commission, COM (2021) 202 final.

5 Guiding Principles for Counteracting the Black-Box Effect

The aforementioned paradigms reveal the astonishing potential the autonomous AI systems can have in today's business world, but also the new ethical and legal challenges they may pose for modern societies. As the technology goes rapidly forward, any attempt to inhibit the AI's further evolution seems to be out of discussion. On the contrary, the point is that the scientific community must try to 'see' inside the AI black box, i.e. understand the autonomous AI systems' technical operation and explain their decisions reached. This way the AI systems' inherent opacity can be eliminated, or at least decrease, whilst their high 'performance' rates be maintained.

How this goal could be achieved is hotly debated in scholarship. Worldwide the scientific community has put emphasis, *inter alia*, mainly to the following elements/concepts: (1) creation and implementation of an *ethical box* in the autonomous AI systems; (2) *transparency*, either *ex ante* or *ex post*; and (3) *human oversight* over autonomous AI systems.

5.1 Creation and Implementation of an Ethical Box in Autonomous AI Systems

The creation of ethical AI systems is one of the recent, much-discussed ideas for counteracting the black box problem.[99] But what means creating ethical AI systems remains 'vague' in so far as there is no specific definition about it.

According to one opinion, systems with an ethical box are *moral AI systems*, namely AI systems which can *display an acceptable behavior*, not causing any harm either to the people or to themselves;[100] or, according to a more progressive approach, *moral systems* are the systems that can select the best action in case of ethical dilemmas.[101] Nonetheless, any attempt to construct such kind of AI systems seems doomed to fail for several reasons,[102] the most important of which is that there is no worldwide acceptable global ethical theory; actually, there never was and maybe there will never be. Although scientific research has exhibited quite interesting ideas on this field (e.g. the proposal of creating AI systems that will follow Kant's *categorical imperative* or Aristotle's theory on *ethics* or the principles of

---

[99] Cf. Allen et al. (2000), p. 257; Anderson and Anderson (2007), p. 18; Hagendorff (2020), p. 111.

[100] See Assaro (2006), p. 10.

[101] Id.

[102] Papadouli (2022), p. 34.

utilitarianism),[103] it cannot be ascertained that AI systems capable of rendering ethical decisions will be ever constructed.[104]

Therefore, creating ethical AI systems should rather mean designing autonomous AI systems that are able to follow specific rules encoded in their interior code.[105] It is the latter which should be ethical, namely in accordance with the current legal social values, which—in turn—are reflected in the current legal framework.

From a practical point of view, this task demands that rules of law be 'translated' from a human language in a computer one and, subsequently, be implemented in the AI systems' code. Although some years earlier this task was extremely difficult,[106] significant progress has been recently made. According to recent surveys,[107] several rules of law, like the provisions of tort liability,[108] can be 'embedded' in a computer code. Thus, the prohibited criteria of racial or sexual discrimination, as described in the aforementioned EU Directives for equal treatment, could be 'translated' and 'embedded'. This remains difficult, however, for abstract legal concepts, like fairness or human dignity.[109] Nonetheless, as the AI scientific field rapidly evolves, even these concepts may soon be mathematically operationalized.[110]

5.2 *Transparency*

In order to eliminate the black box effect, a specific subfield of AI called *explainable AI* (also known as *XAI*) has recently emerged.[111] This subfield aims at creating the appropriate techniques that will allow autonomous AI systems to be self-explicable, whilst maintaining high levels of autonomy.[112] To that aim, XAI fosters the request of embedding transparency in AI systems.[113]

Transparency is a multidisciplinary concept since it can be found in various scientific fields. Particularly in the field of AI, transparency entails: (a) the autonomous AI system's capacity to show its inner working processes and the origin of its

[103] See Allen et al. (2000), p. 251; Anderson and Anderson (2007), p. 15.

[104] Carabantes (2020), p. 316; Papadouli (2022), pp. 34 ff.

[105] Papadouli (2022), p. 35. Cf. also Assaro (2006), p. 11; Anderson and Anderson (2007), p. 15.

[106] See Rissland (1988).

[107] See Spyropoulos et al. (2022).

[108] Id.

[109] See Floridi et al. (2018); European Commission, Com (2019), 168 final, p. 2; European Commission, COM (2020), 65 final, p. 3.

[110] See Rissland (1990).

[111] Van Lent et al. (2004), p. 900. See also Adadi and Berrada (2018), p. 52139; Zednik (2019), p. 2; Licht and Licht (2020), p. 919; Carabantes (2020), p. 314; Wulf and Seizov (2020), pp. 621–622.

[112] Adadi and Berrada (2018), p. 52138.

[113] Id., p. 52142. See also European Parliament, Civil Law Rule on Robotics, (2018/C 252/25), Ethical Principles, Recital Nr. 12.

training data; and (b) the requirement that the AI system be able to provide comprehensible explanations regarding its decisions.[114] The first type of transparency applies *ex ante*, while the latter *ex post*: namely, the fist type allows for human technical control over the system, while the second facilitates the AI system's accountability and, further, its user's or its designers' liability. Both types result in enhancing the public's confidence[115] in the AI inner procedures and in the aptness of their outcomes.

In this direction, many legal orders have started to ask for more transparent AI systems. The European Commission has often pointed out the significance of AI transparency for enhancing public trust, and respect of the fundamental rights across the Union.[116] Nonetheless, the transparency standards may vary among AI systems, based on their nature as 'high-risk' or 'low-risk', according to the recent Proposal of Regulation on Artificial Intelligence. Indeed, Article 13 of the Proposal imposes transparency requirements only on high-risk AI systems as defined in Article 6 of the Proposal. However, even in these systems the information[117] about them provided to the AI user seems in essence to be rather technical and ordinary rather than illuminating.[118]

5.3 Human Oversight over the Autonomous AI System

The aforementioned concepts (ethical AI box and transparency) should always be coupled with a human right to both oversee the whole AI system's operation and appeal its rendered outcomes,[119] if needed. According to this aspect, apart from encoding ethical-legal rules in the AI systems' code, decoding its internal operation, and asking for its provided justifications,[120] it is likewise important that human interference in the decision-making process be ensured, either prior to being made (override) or after that (recall).[121]

This last aspect is of primary importance for AI's public acceptance, given that the inherent black box effect hampers the system's inner visibility, and can negatively affect its explainability.[122] This aspect is also aligned with the prevalent attempts within the EU towards a *human-on-the-loop (HOTL)* and a *human-in-*

[114] Papadouli (2022), p. 28.
[115] See also Lipton (2017), pp. 7 ff.
[116] See European Commission, COM (2021) 206 final, Recital Nr. 38, 39.
[117] See Art. 13 par. 3 COM (2021) 206 final.
[118] Papadouli (2022), p. 33.
[119] Cf. Floridi et al. (2018), pp. 697–698.
[120] Lipton (2017), pp. 15 ff.
[121] See Woodstra (2020), p. 3.
[122] Felzmann et al. (2019), p. 4.

command (HIC) approach rather than a *human-in-the-loop (HITL)* AI system.[123] The first refers to the human capability to interfere during the design cycle of the AI system and to the monitoring of the system's operation, while the second regards the human capability to oversee the overall activity of the AI system and ability of humans to decide when and how to use the system in any particular situation including their ability to override a decision made by the system. On the contrary, the last approach refers to human intervention in every decision cycle of the system, which in many cases is neither possible nor desirable.

But a human oversight over an autonomous AI system demands that AI users be trained on AI to be able to understand the AI system's outcomes, detect for any mistake and decide whether to appeal them. Therefore, the cooperation between any professionals specialized in any field where the AI is used (e.g. judges) and the AI engineers is vital for AI's future, thus, confirming the AI's interdisciplinary character as a scientific field.

6 Conclusions

The present chapter sought to present some of the most significant and repeatedly encountered ethical challenges that the AI poses in the context of modern societies, as well as the new legal concerns these challenges raise in turn. All the aforementioned examples of AI use indicated at Sect. 4 show that AI can have adverse effects on several human rights and freedoms, in particular on the right to personality, human dignity, privacy, the right to personal data, the right to fair trial, the principle of non-discrimination, the fair competition, while it can also negatively affect business.

The concerns raised cannot be addressed only by existing legal norms, but rather demand the enactment of new and systematic rules of law. A legislative reform has already begun worldwide. The European Union, in particular, has elaborated a consistent legal framework regarding AI that will apply soon. This framework, along with traditional rules of law, such as the rules of contract, tort or competition law, can counter more efficiently the challenges that the AI's black box poses on modern societies.

But apart from these legislative initiatives, it is highly important that any interdisciplinary cooperation between any professionals, using AI in any field (e.g. judges), with the AI designers/developers and engineers be enhanced. Only through an interdisciplinary approach the construction of an ethical/legal box, as described above, will be realized, the much-discussed transparency will be achieved and the user oversight over AI will be feasible, thus, enhancing AI sustainability and its public acceptance.

---

[123] See European Commission, COM (2019), 168 final, p. 4 (Reference 13)·Opinion of the European Economic and Social Committee, COM (2020) 65 final, Recital Nr. 2.3.

References

Adadi A, Berrada M (2018) Peeking inside the black-box: a survey of explainable artificial intelligence (XAI). IEEE Access 6:52138–52160

Allen C, Varner G, Zinser J (2000) Prolegomena to any further artificial moral agent. J Exp Theor Artif Intell 12:251–261

Anderson M, Anderson SL (2007) Machine ethics: creating an ethical intelligent agent. AI Mag 4: 15–26

Angwin J, Larson J, Mattu S & Kirchner L 2016 Machine bias: there's software used across the country to predict future criminals. And it's biased against blacks, PROPUBLICA (May 23, 2016). Available online at https://www.propublica.org/article/machine-bias-risk-assessments-in-criminal-sentencing

Assaro P (2006) What should we want from a robot ethic? Int Rev Inf Ethics 6:9–16

Bathaee Y (2018) The artificial intelligence black box and the failure of intent and causation. Harv Law Rev 31:890–934

Burrel J (2016) How the machine "thinks": understanding opacity in machine learning algorithms. Big Data Soc 2016:1–12

Burt A (2019) The AI transparency paradox. Available online at Accessed 02 Sept 2023

Carabantes M (2020) Black-box artificial intelligence: an epistemological and critical analysis. AI Soc 35:309–317

Dastin J (2018) Amazon scraps secret AI recruiting tool that showed bias against women. Available online at https://www.reuters.com/article/us-amazon-com-jobs-automation-insight-idUSKCN1MK08G

Denicola R (2016) Ex machina: copyright protection for computer-generated works. Rutgers Univ Law Rev 69:251–287

Diakopoulos N (2014) Algorithmic accountability reporting: on the investigation of black boxes Columbia Journalism School-Tow Center for Digital Journalism. Available online https://academiccommons.columbia.edu/doi/10.7916/D8ZK5TW2

Eaglin J (2021) Population-based sentencing. Cornell Law Rev 106:353–408

European Commission (2018) Statement on artificial intelligence, robotics and autonomous systems. Available online at http://earthnet.ntua.gr/wp-content/uploads/2018/07/Artificial-inteligence-robotics-and-autonomous-systems.pdf

European Commission (2020) White Paper on AI, COM (2020) 65 final

European Commission (2021) Impact assessment accompanying the proposal for a regulation of the European Parliament and of the Council Laying down harmonized rules on Artificial Intelligence and Amending Certain Union Legislative Acts SWD (2021) 84 final

European Economic and Social Committee (2020) Opinion on "White paper on artificial intelligence — A European approach to excellence and trust", COM (2020) 65 final (2020/C 364/12)

European Insurance and Occupational Pensions Authority (2021) Artificial intelligence governance principles: towards ethical and trustworthy artificial intelligence in the European Insurance Sector. Available online at https://www.eiopa.europa.eu/document-library/report/artificial-intelligence-governance-principles-towards-ethical-and_en

European Parliament, Civil Law Rule on Robotics (2018/C 252/25)

European Parliament Resolution of 20 October 2020 on intellectual property rights for the development of artificial intelligence technologies (2020/2015(INI))

Felzmann H, Villaronga EF, Lutz C, Tamò-Larrieux A (2019) Transparency you can trust: transparency requirements for artificial intelligence between legal norms and contextual concerns. Big Data Soc 2019:1–19

Floridi L, Cowls J, Beltrametti M, Chatila R, Chazerand P, Dignum V, Luetge C, Madelin R, Pagallo U, Rossi F, Schafer B, Valcke P, Vayena E (2018) AI4People: an ethical framework for a good ai society: opportunities, risks, principles, and recommendations. Mind Mach 28:689–707

Freeman K (2016) Algorithmic injustice: how the Wisconsin supreme court failed to protect due process rights in state v. Loomis. NC J Law Technol 75:76–105

Furubotn E, Richter R (2005) Institutions & economic theory, 2nd edn. University of Michigan Press, Michigan

Goodman B, Flaxman S (2017) European Union regulations on algorithmic decision making and a "right to explanation". AI Mag 2017:50–57

Hacker P, Krestel R, Grundmann S, Naumann F (2020) Explainable AI under contract and tort law: legal incentives and technical challenges. Artif Intell Law 28:415–439

Hagendorff T (2020) The ethics ff AI ethics: an evaluation of guidelines. Mind Mach 30:99–120

Han-Wei L, Ching-Fu L, Yu-Jie C (2019) Beyond State v. Loomis: artificial intelligence, government algorithmization, and accountability. Int J Law Inf Technol 27:122–141

Iglesias M, Shamuilia S & Anderberg A (2019) Intellectual property and artificial intelligence publication office of the European Union

Kancevičienė N (2019) Insurance, smart information systems and ethics. ORBIT J 2(2) Available online at https://doi.org/10.29297/orbit.v2i2.106

Karnow C (1996) Liability for distributed artificial intelligences. Berkley Technol Law Rev 11: 147–204

Kemper J, Kolkman D (2019) Transparent to whom? No algorithmic accountability without a critical audience. Inf Commun Soc 22:2081–2096

Kennedy J (2019) How AI completed Schubert's Unfinished Symphony No 8. Available online at https://www.siliconrepublic.com/machines/unfinished-symphony-no-8-ai-huawei

Kotsiantis SB (2013) Decision trees: a recent overview. Artif Intell Rev 39:261–283

Langenbucher K (2020) Responsible A.I. credit scoring-a legal framework. Eur Bus Law Rev 31:1–5

Lepri B, Oliver N, Letouze E, Pentland A, Vinck P (2018) Fair, transparent and accountable algorithmic decision-making processes. Philos Technol 31:611–627

Licht K, Licht J (2020) Artificial intelligence, transparency, and public decision-making. AI Soc 35: 915–926

Lipton Z (2017) The mythos of model interpretability. Acmqeue 2017:1–27

McCarthy J, Hayes P (1969) Some philosophical problems from the standpoint of artificial intelligence. Available online http://jmc.stanford.edu/articles/mcchay69/mcchay69.pdf

O'kane S (2018) Uber reportedly thinks its self-driving car killed someone because it decided not to swere. Available online at https://www.theverge.com/2018/5/7/17327682/uber-self-driving-car-decision-kill-swerve

Papadouli V (2022) Transparency in artificial intelligence: a legal perspective. J Ethics Leg Technol 4:25–40

Rissland E (1988) Artificial intelligence and legal reasoning, a discussion of the field and Gardner's Book. AI Mag 9(3):45–55

Rissland E (1990) artificial intelligence and law: stepping stone to a model of legal reasoning. Yale Law J 99:1957–1981

Ross C, Swetlitz I (2018) IBM's Watson supercomputer recommended 'unsafe and incorrect' cancer treatments, internal documents show. Available online at https://www.statnews.com/2018/07/25/ibm-watson-recommended-unsafe-incorrect-treatments

Russell S, Norvig P (2020) Artificial intelligence: a modern approach, 4th edn. Pearson Series for AI, Hoboken

Schmelzer R (2020) Towards a more transparent AI. Journal of Decision Systems 2020. Available online https://www.forbes.com/sites/cognitiveworld/2020/05/23/towards-a-more-transparent-ai/?sh=29a5f52d3d93

Smith M (2016) In Wisconsin, a backlash against using data to foretell defendants' futures, N.Y. Times (June 22, 2016). Available online at https://www.nytimes.com/2016/06/23/us/backlash-in-wisconsin-against-using-data-to-foretell-defendants-futures.html

Spyropoulos A, Kornilakis A, Makris G, Bratsas C, Tsiantos V, Antoniou I (2022) Semantic representation of the intersection of Criminal Law and Civil Tort. Data 7(12):1–15

Thelissone E, Padh K, Celis LE (2017) Regulatory mechanism and algorithms towards trust in AI/ML. Available online at https://www.researchgate.net/profile/Eva-Thelisson/publication/318913104_Regulatory_Mechanisms_and_Algorithms_towards_Trust_in_AIML/links/5984d9ef458515605844ef66/Regulatory-Mechanisms-and-Algorithms-towards-Trust-in-AI-ML.pdf

Turing A (1950) Computing machinery and intelligence. Mind 59(236):433–460

Uni global Union, Top 10 Principles for ethical artificial intelligence. Available online at http://www.thefutureworldofwork.org/media/35420/uni_ethical_ai.pdf

UNESCO (2019) Preliminary study on the ethics of AI. Available online at https://unesdoc.unesco.org/ark:/48223/pf0000367823. Accessed 02 Sept 2023

Van Lent M, Fisher W, Mancuso M (2004) An explainable artificial intelligence system for small-unit tactical behavior. IAAI Emerg Appl 2004:900–907

Varadi P (2023) Can ChatGBT write a Book? Available online at https://medium.com/@umfpeti/can-chat-gpt-write-a-book-3cca3d00e4e4; https://www.theatlantic.com/books/archive/2023/02/chatgpt-ai-technology-writing-poetry/673035/

Veljanovski C (2007) Economic principles of Law. Cambridge University Press, Cambridge

Vigdor N (2019) Apple card investigated after gender discrimination complaints. Available online at also https://www.nytimes.com/2019/11/10/business/Apple-credit-card-investigation.html

Washington A (2018) How to argue with an algorithm: Lessons from the COMPAS-Propublica Debate. Colo Technol Law J 17(2018):133–159

Wettig S, Zehendner E (2004) A legal analysis of human and electronic agents. Artif Intell Law 12: 111–135

Woodstra F (2020) What does transparent AI mean?. AI Police Exchange 2020. Available online https://aipolicyexchange.org/2020/05/09/what-does-transparent-ai-mean/

Wulf A, Seizov O (2020) Artificial intelligence and transparency: a blueprint for improving the regulation of AI applications in the EU. Eur Bus Law Rev 31:611–640

Yanski-Ravid S (2017) Generating rebrandt, artificial intelligence, copyright, and accountability in the 3A era-the human-like authors are already here- a new model. Mich State Law Rev 2017: 659–726

Zednik C (2019) Solving the black box problem. Available online https://arxiv.org/ftp/arxiv/papers/1903/1903.04361.pdf

Zerilli J, Knott A, Maclaurin J, Gavaghan C (2018) Transparency in algorithmic and human decision-making: is there a double standard? Philos Technol 32:1–24

Part II
AI and Civil Liability

The Role of the Autonomous Machines at the Conclusion of a Contract: Contractual Responsibility According to Current Rules of Private Law and Prospects

Vasiliki Papadouli

Abstract Nowadays, one of the most important applications of autonomous AI systems is the conclusion of contracts. Nonetheless, concerns are raised about the validity of the contracts concluded by autonomous machines and, subsequently, about the contractual responsibility in case of non-performance. Various theories have already been expounded in legal doctrine, with the view to tackling thereon. Some of them suggest that autonomous AI systems are mere communication tools or agents that render their user liable, whilst other legal scholars suggest that autonomous AI systems themselves—not their user—should be held liable. After presenting the arguments of these theories, the chapter concludes that the legal community should absolutely accept the validity of the contracts concluded by intelligent agents, considering their users legally bound to their performance. Users' liability could be based on the theory of de facto contracts (faktische Verträge) or, alternatively, on the doctrine of reliance liability (Vertrauenshaftung). In both cases, users' right to invalidate the contract in case of mistake must be guaranteed and the mistake shall be assigned to the intelligent agent.

V. Papadouli (✉)
Vrije Universiteit Brussel, Faculty of Law & Criminology, Brussels, Belgium

Research Team "Digital Economy and Private Law", School of Law, Aristotle University of Thessaloniki, Thessaloniki, Greece
https://digec.law.auth.gr/en

A. Kornilakis et al. (eds.), *Artificial Intelligence and Normative Challenges*, Law, Governance and Technology Series 59,
https://doi.org/10.1007/978-3-031-41081-9_5

1 Introduction

Over the past decades, Artificial Intelligence (AI) has become a scientific field of primary importance on a global scale.[1] Since its establishment in 1956 at the Dartmouth College Conference, until today, it has been constantly contributing to various fields of modern life through several scientific achievements.

Autonomous systems are undoubtedly among those. Their application is increasingly widespread in many fields of modern life, such as medicine, finance, banking, programming, and transactions.[2] But their ever-expanding application triggers several concerns about the very real benefits and dangers they may induce. Regarding transactions, concerns are raised, among others, about the role of the autonomous machines at the stage of the conclusion of a contract, that is, about the validity of the contract concluded fully or partially through autonomous machines and, subsequently, about the contractual responsibility in case of non-performance.

The present chapter aims to shed light on the current doctrinal debate over the applicable rules of private law. The first part describes the traits of the autonomous machines and their function in the contractual procedure via specific examples ("case studies") (2). The next part focuses on the theories supported in legal doctrine about the legal role of autonomous machines in the contractual procedure, according to current legal framework (3). The chapter concludes by pointing out the much discussed *de lege ferenda* alternative theories thereon, aiming to introduce a new prospect based on *de lege lata* arguments (4).

2 Definitions: Case Studies

2.1 Definitions

The *autonomous systems* or *autonomous machines* are deemed the most characteristic technological achievement of the fourth Industrial Revolution[3] and the main representative of the fourth evolutionary stage of AI.[4] Their basic characteristic is their *ability of learning*. That is the system's ability of improving itself in the execution of any assigned task, without being explicitly programmed. This ability,

[1] Although the term "*Artificial Intelligence*" is widely accepted, the scientific community does not fully agree about its specific content. See Rissland (1990), pp. 1957–1961; Ertel (2017), p. 1 ff.; UNESCO (2019), p. 7–9; Stanford Encyclopedia of Philosophy (2020), pp. 2–3.

[2] Eidenmüller (2017), pp. 2–4; Karanasiou and Pinotsis (2017), p. 1; Keßler (2017), pp. 589–590; UNESCO (2019), passim.

[3] See more about the fourth Industrial Revolution Braütigam and Klindt (2015), p. 1137.

[4] See about the "ages" of Artificial Intelligence as scientific field Smith and Ting (2006), p. 6; Bostrom (2014), para 1.

called *machine learning*,[5] takes place without any human intervention and supervision, thanks to sophisticated "superpower" algorithms, whose construction is mainly based on the concept of reward and punishment (*reinforcement learning*[6]). In this context, autonomous system behavior is determined by its own experience/knowledge.[7] Therefore, its produced results cannot be determined in advance; instead, they are *unpredictable* and *uncontrollable* by the user or by another system, even by its programmer. This characteristic leads to the dominant attribute of *autonomy* that distinguishes this kind of AI systems from all the previous ones and basically from the so-called *knowledge* or *expert* systems,[8] such as *Deep Blue*[9] and *Deep Mind.*[10]

The *intelligent agent*[11] is considered the most prevalent autonomous AI system.[12] According to the prevailing definition,[13] an *intelligent agent* is an entity capable of perceiving its environment through specific sensors, editing the external information and reacting to the received stimuli through specific mechanisms (actuators),[14] in order to attain a specific goal. Additionally, this entity is able to collaborate with other intelligent agents, building along with them a network of intelligent agents, called *multi-agent system* (MAS) or *distributed AI (DAI)*,[15] with the aim to achieve more complicated tasks or to maximize the utility.[16]

The intelligent agent is considered a "strong" AI system, since it is capable of exhibiting the following features:[17]

---

[5] Russell and Norvig (2020), p. 651 ff.; Wettig and Zehendner (2004), pp. 111–135; Denicola (2016), pp. 254–255.

[6] Russell and Norvig (2020), p. 789 ff.; Panait and Luke (2005), pp. 387–434.

[7] Wettig and Zehendner (2004), pp. 111–135; Borges (2018), p. 978.

[8] Karnow (1996), pp. 152 and 155 ff.; Huang (2006), p. 12; UNESCO (2019), pp. 10–11.

[9] Susskind and Susskind (2018), p. 125.

[10] Karanasiou and Pinotsis (2017), p. 1.

[11] The word is derived from the latin word "agere" that meant "act" or "work". See more about the etymological root of the word Wettig and Zehendner (2004), p. 111.

[12] One can also encounter it as *digital agent, autonomous agent, softbot* (software robots), *knowbot* (knowledge robot), etc. See Weitzenboeck (2001), p. 207; Wettig and Zehendner (2004), pp. 111–135.

[13] Although the notion of the "Intelligent Agent" is widely used, there is no single universally accepted definition for it. The most prevalent definition is the one mentioned in the text, attributed to Russell and Norvig (2020), p. 37 (see next footnote).

[14] Russell and Norvig (2020), p. 37; Panait and Luke (2005), p. 2; Ertel (2017), p. 17; Eidenmüller (2017), pp. 4–5.

[15] Wooldridge and Jennings (1995), pp. 41–42; Ertel (2017), pp. 10–11. Cf. on the difference between DAI and MAS Panait and Luke (2005), p. 1.

[16] Karnow (1996), p. 165; Panait and Luke (2005), p. 1.

[17] Wooldridge and Jennings (1995), p. 4; Kerr (1999), p. 195; Weitzenboeck (2001), p. 5; Wettig and Zehendner (2004), p. 2; van Haentijens (2002); Cornelius (2002), p. 353; Balke (2010), pp. 3–4. See also UNESCO (2019), pp. 11–12.

1. *Autonomy,* as the notion has already been mentioned above.
2. *Reactivity.* The system's ability to perceive the stimuli stemming from its environment, which can be the physical or the digital world or both, and its ability to respond in time, by changing its internal situation.
3. *Social ability.* This is the system's ability to interact with other systems, mainly autonomous ones or with humans, through a specific communication language.[18]
4. *Proactivity.* The system's ability to take the initiative in order to achieve a concrete goal, beyond reacting to the stimuli stemming from its environment.

   In addition to these traits, it is claimed that some intelligent agents feature some other (supplementary) traits thanks to which they can be categorized as "strong" AI autonomous machines.[19] These are:
5. *Mobility.* The agent's ability to move in its environment.
6. *Veracity.* The assumption that the system does not provide intentionally wrong information.
7. *Benevolence.* The assumption that the system does not serve conflicted goals.
8. *Rationality.* The assumption that the system never acts against its goals.

2.2 Case Studies

Thanks to the aforementioned features, the intelligent agent can actively participate in the contractual procedure, fully replacing, sometimes, the human beings. Typical examples are the following ones:

Case study 1:[20] A Professor of Law wants to participate in an international conference abroad. For this reason, she needs to buy an airline ticket to the specific destination where the conference is going to take place. Instead of performing a search on the Internet, she assigns this task to her *personal electronic assistant.*[21] She instructs it to find the most affordable ticket for the given date and destination at the most convenient time for her (e.g. 10:00–20:00). She also points out that she wants a direct flight and a seat with leg extension in order to be more comfortable. The personal assistant, which is a software intelligent agent, starts to execute the assigned task by surfing on the internet, while the Professor works on her upcoming presentation. In a short period of time the agent comes up with a ticket that meets Professor's given requirements, having, of course, already charged her connected bank account.

---

[18] See also about "communication" Panait and Luke (2005), p. 13.

[19] See the above-mentioned authors (footnote 17).

[20] See also Karnow (1996), pp. 152–153; Kerr (1999), pp. 196–197; Pagallo (2013), p. 57.

[21] It can be located either in her PC or in an external server rum by a provider; see van Haentijens (2002), p. 2.

Case study 2:[22] Our Professor is rather overloaded with the preparation of her presentation and does not have enough free time to go to the supermarket and buy the necessary products for her nutrition. For this reason, she has bought a "smart fridge"; this is a fridge with an installed intelligent agent capable of "concluding" sales contracts on behalf of its user and according to her instructions. But even though the Professor has not provided the system with specific instructions, the system is capable of defining on its own the quantity and the quality of the products, because it is programmed to do so.[23] The system searches the Internet and orders the products after charging the Professor's connected bank account.

In the above-mentioned examples, the intelligent agent "concluded" a contract without any intervention from the side of its user (Professor). More specifically, thanks to its ability of *proactivity* the agent was able to start negotiations on the Internet, which is its "physical" environment. During this process, the agent moves in its environment, "migrating" from site to site, until it finds the best offer *(mobility)*.[24] In that case, it comes in contact with several potential contractual partners thanks to its *social ability*.[25] These potential contractual partners can be either humans or intelligent agents, both acting on behalf of the airline companies/ supermarkets.

In case study 1 the system declines the offers that do not meet the user's specific requirements and classifies the ones which meet them in descending order, aiming to select the most cost-effective one. In case there are no offers meeting the specific requirements, the assistant can wait until such an offer comes up, thanks to its ability of *reactivity*. But if there are two or more offers that meet the requirements with the same cost, the assistant can choose which one wants without any explanation, because it acts in an *autonomous* way (*autonomy*). Furthermore, since the assistant successfully attained the assigned task, it is ready to repeat it faster at any time in the future thanks to its previously gained experience (*machine learning*).

In light of these examples, it is shown that intelligent agents are playing an increasingly active role in negotiations, as well as in the formation and conclusion of a contract, *selecting the contractual partner*, while in case study 2 the system was also capable of *defining the content of the contract*.[26] But since the selection of the contractual partner and the formation of the contract are considered the two basic pillars of the *freedom of contract*, it seems that the application of the intelligent agents can lead to a total replacement of the human beings throughout the contractual procedure.[27]

---

[22] See also Allen and Widdison (1996), p. 29; Kerr (1999), p. 197–198; Kerr (2001), pp. 185–187; Grundmann and Hacker (2017), pp. 20–21.

[23] See also Cornelius (2002), p. 355.

[24] Nevertheless, there are also stationary intelligent agents which are agents not able to leave their original environment; nonetheless, they are called "robots" as well; see Wettig and Zehendner (2004), p. 112.

[25] See Balke (2010), p. 7.

[26] Balke (2010), p. 2; Grundmann and Hacker (2017), pp. 16–17.

[27] Lerouge (2000), p. 406; Kerr (2001), p. 185.

The advantages of the application of intelligent agents in the contractual procedure are obvious. In both examples the intelligent agents eliminate the cost and the time for negotiations,[28] leading rapidly to the conclusion of a contract that meets the contractual partners' specific needs.[29]

Yet the application of intelligent agents triggers several concerns about the validity of the contract they conclude. More particularly, the main legal question in case of concluding a contract through intelligent agents is, who the person considered to be legally bound from this contact and, subsequently, responsible in case of non-performance, is. For instance, if in case study 1 there was a malfunction and the personal assistant did not ultimately book the most cost-effective ticket, can its user (Professor) deny fulfilling her obligations stemming from the concluded contract?[30] In case study 2, if the user does not want one of the bought products, does she have the right to withdraw from the contract or nullify it because of mistake?[31] These questions are of primary importance for the transactions' security and, subsequently, for the acceptance of AI autonomous systems by the legal community and their "sustainability" in society.

3 The Legal Role of Intelligent Agents at the Stage of Conclusion of a Contract

Various theories have already been expounded in legal doctrine, with the view to tackling the above-mentioned issues. According to one of them, the intelligent agent is not capable of "generating" its own *declaration of intent* (DOI); the "constructed" DOI belongs to the user, who "employed" the agent (3.1). On the other hand, it is widely claimed that the intelligent agent can "develop" its own DOI, which should, however, always be attributed to its user (3.2). Both theories result in the same conclusion: the concluded contract is *valid* and legally binding upon the *user,* who is deemed the only person responsible for its performance.

[28] Köhler (1982), p. 129; Allen and Widdison (1996), p. 29; Lerouge (2000), pp. 404–434; Kerr (2001), p. 184. A reason why an intelligent agent can act so rapidly in comparison with other kinds of software systems lies in the fact that its function is not based on an inter-server connection, in order to collect the necessary information. Instead, the intelligent agent can "migrate" from site to site, working even though the user's PC is offline. Therefore, it is able to select faster the necessary information, leading to reduction of "network traffic", see Karnow (1996), p. 164; Kotz and Gray (1999); van Haentijens (2002), p. 3; Wettig and Zehendner (2004), p. 112.

[29] See Cornelius (2002), p. 353. See for more advantages (and disadvantages) arising by the application of intelligent (shopping) agents in the transactions van Haentijens (2002), p. 1.

[30] See also Katz (2008), p. 2.

[31] See Mehrings (1998), p. 31; Balke (2010), p. 2.

3.1 The Autonomous Machines as Mere Communication Tools

According to the so-called "traditional" or "conservative" approach,[32] the law cannot consider an autonomous machine liable for the execution of a contract.[33] The reason lies in its lack of *legal capacity* and, as a consequence, in its lack of *capacity of contract*. Since it has no free will and consciousness, it cannot form its own DOI. Therefore, the demonstrated "DOI" belongs to the person using it;[34] the latter should be the only person legally bound by the contract concluded by her "employed" intelligent agent.

According to this approach, in the eyes of the law as it stands the intelligent agents are *mere communication tools*. Like any other software systems (e.g. email) or electronic devices (e.g. telephone, fax machine), the role of the intelligent agent in the contractual procedure is merely to convey the DOI (offer or acceptance) of its user to the other contractual partner. In essence, this approach adopts a *legal fiction* that anything issued by an intelligent agent is actually issued by its user.[35] Even though the user does not know either the context of the DOI generated by the agent or the person to whom this DOI is addressed, she should be held legally bound just because she has "employed" the agent.[36] The situation is similar (but not identical) to that of a person who signs a contract without reading it first.[37] As a consequence, the DOI "produced" by an intelligent agent is, in fact, a DOI of its user.

Furthermore, the following arguments support this approach. *First*, the application of intelligent agents in the contractual procedure closely resembles the application of vending machines in transactions.[38] According to legal doctrine, installing a vending machine in a public place means that its owner addresses an invitation of proposal *(invitatio ad offerendum)* or a declaration *ad incertas personas*[39] (the latter meaning a DOI to anyone who wants to be the contractual counterparty). The counterparty expresses her intention to conclude the contract just by putting the coins in the slot of the vending machine. The contract is considered to be concluded between the owner and the person who puts the coins in the vending machine.

---

[32] See also the classification of approaches according to Pagallo (2013), p. 49.

[33] Allen and Widdison (1996), p. 44; Mehrings (1998), p. 31; Kerr (2001), p. 232; Cornelius (2002), p. 355; Boden et al. (2017), passim.

[34] Mehrings (1998), p. 31; Allen and Widdison (1996), p. 43 ff.; Brożek and Jakubiec (2017), pp. 293 and 303.

[35] Allen and Widdison (1996), p. 46. See also Kerr (2001), pp. 219 and 232; Weitzenboeck (2001), p. 207; Chopra and White (2009), p. 372; Balke (2010), p. 5.

[36] Mehrings (1998), p. 31; Balke (2010), p. 5.

[37] Allen and Widdison (1996), p. 45; Kerr (2001), p. 232.

[38] Köhler (1982), p. 132; Kerr (2001), p. 188; Cornelius (2002), p. 354; Wettig and Zehendner (2004), p. 121; Chopra and White (2009), pp. 372–373.

[39] Wolf and Neuner (2016), p. 437; Bork (2016), p. 282; Brox and Walker (2018), p. 85. Cf. also Medicus and Petersen (2016), p. 159.

Second, it is argued that the user by using an intelligent agent in transactions expresses, in fact, a *white declaration of intent*, that is, a user's DOI which content is intentionally not defined by her and has to be fulfilled by the intelligent agent at a next stage.[40] For example, in case study 2 the user assigns to the "smart fridge" the task to buy products from the supermarket without providing the system with any further detailed description (e.g. quantity and quality of the products). It is considered that the user addresses on purpose a DOI with an undefined context which is going to be fulfilled by the system according to its programming.

Third, it is suggested that the role of an intelligent agent in the contractual procedure is similar to those of a *messenger* (*nuntius*).[41] A *messenger* is a natural person who transmits a third person's DOI, called "*principal*"; that is the "beneficiary", the person who "employs" the messenger. According to contract law, it is not necessary that the messenger has contractual capacity in order to convey the DOI of her "principal", but solely legal capacity; thus, she can be even a minor.[42] The messenger is not considered legally bound by the contract and, therefore, she is not responsible in case of non-performance. The contract is deemed to be binding only upon the principal. Even if the messenger did not transmit the DOI correctly, the principal is still considered legally bound by the contract and the only way to be released is by invoking the doctrine of mistake.[43]

The basic advantages of this approach are twofold. *First,* it boosts the *transactions' security*, since it clarifies that a contract fully or partially concluded by intelligent agents is valid, defining at the same time the person who is responsible in case of non-execution, namely, the *user*. *Second*, it provides the user with a strong incentive to ensure that the "employed" intelligent agent operates properly and, thus, it will not conclude contracts that the user does not actually want. Indeed, had the user not be considered legally bound regarding the contract concluded by her "employed" intelligent system, she would not have been cautious enough about the system's proper function. Moreover, she could rely on the system's alleged malfunction or *opaque function* (the so-called *AI black box problem* or *black box effect*[44]) in order to avoid her engagement in the contract. In such a case, the other contractual partner would bear the risk of the system's (mal)function, without having any power over it and, most of the times, without even knowing that she transacts with an intelligent agent and not with a human.

[40] Cf. Köhler (1982), p. 134, regarding the automated DOI; Wettig and Zehendner (2004), pp. 121–122.

[41] Wettig and Zehendner (2004), p. 125; Keßler (2017), p. 592.

[42] Wolf and Neuner (2016), p. 602; Medicus and Petersen (2016), pp. 385–386.

[43] See about §120 BGB Wolf and Neuner (2016), p. 379; Medicus and Petersen (2016), p. 328.

[44] See more about the so-called b*lack box problem* or *black box effect* Zednik (2019); Adadi and Berrada (2018).

This is a characteristic situation of *information asymmetry* between the contractual parties, which typically causes the so-called *moral hazard problem.*[45] This problem appears when a person, whose behavior cannot be fully monitored, has an incentive to increase her exposure to risk because another person (the contractual partner) will bear the cost in case of loss.[46] Actually, in case of intelligent agents it could be argued that the other contractual party is not affected by asymmetric information, but—due to the *black box problem* or *black box effect*—by a *complete lack of information* regarding the risk of transacting with an intelligent agent and, thus, of being engaged in an invalid contract, where there is no option to opt out. The aforementioned "conservative" approach diminishes such risk by decreasing the *moral hazard* of the user, hence it protects more efficiently the other contractual party.

Third, this approach provides a certain *element of justice*, since the user is the one who opts to employ an intelligent agent and to involve it in trading. Thus, the assumption that the user bears the cost of the (mal)function of her intelligent agent sounds logical.[47] Moreover, it is a well-known principle of Civil Law's liability regime that a person to whose *sphere* a risk can be assigned, is supposed to be liable for it.[48] The intelligent agent's (mal)function is a risk, which lies in the user's sphere; should any malfunction appear, resulting in the conclusion of a contract that does not meet the user's needs/desires, the latter shall bear the risk. Moreover, in common law the contractual parties are held liable in case of damage irrespective of fault. Therefore, the AI user must be sure about the right function of her "employed" AI system, prior to using it in a transaction.

Nevertheless, this theory ignores the prevalent concept of the *autonomy* that distinguishes intelligent agents from all the previous AI systems.[49] As mentioned above, their results are most of the time unpredictable and uncontrollable by their users or other systems. Therefore, it cannot be accepted that the autonomous AI systems just convey the DOI of their user. Instead, they "create"—and further convey—user's DOI,[50] entering dynamically in the contractual procedure by selecting the contractual partner (see case study 1 and 2) and forming the contractual context (see case study 2).

Furthermore, in response to the aforementioned arguments in favor of the "conservative" approach, one could argue that:

---

[45] See more about this problem Furubotn and Richter (2005), pp. 206–222; Veljanovski (2007), pp. 40–41; Cooter and Ulen (2008), p. 53; Voigt (2009), pp. 84–85.

[46] Firstly, the concept of moral hazard appeared in assurances, but today one can encounter it in many other fields as well, see Dembe and Boden (2000), p. 257; Bannier (2005), pp. 69–71.

[47] Allen and Widdison (1996), p. 46. See also Cornelius (2002), p. 355.

[48] Andrade et al. (2007b), p. 219.

[49] Kerr (2001), p. 188.

[50] Allen and Widdison (1996), p. 25; Andrade et al. (2007a), p. 369; Chopra and White (2009), p. 371.

1. There is no similarity between autonomous machines and vending machines because the latter do not actually participate in the contractual procedure, not even by transmitting a DOI; they just accept the DOI of the other contractual party and execute the performance of the contractual agreement.
2. In case of a white DOI, one party authorizes a third person to fill in at a next stage an intentionally undefined DOI (usually offer) addressed to the other contractual partner. The exact way in which this task is completed is not discretionary but follows certain contractual rules or at least some general principles of law, such as good faith (*bona fides*). However, this line of reasoning is contradictory to the other two arguments suggested by the "conservative approach" (vending machines, *nuntius*), which presuppose a DOI already formed by the principal. It is also noteworthy, that German scholarship suggests in these cases the *mutatis mutandis* application of the rules of agency, which will be examined later.
3. We cannot equate the role of the messenger with the role of the intelligent agent at the contractual procedure. Although both are "autonomous" and intervene between the principal and the other contractual partner, the intelligent agent has no legal capacity which is a prerequisite for someone to be a messenger.[51]

Moreover, according to current rules of law, the principal is considered liable in case of a DOI wrongfully *transmitted* by the messenger, not in case of a DOI wrongfully "*generated*" by her. Since their role in the contractual procedure is not the same, the body of rule on messengers is not directly applicable to the intelligent agents. For this reason, it is supported that they can apply *mutatis mutandis.*[52] However, in this case one actually needs a double analogy: firstly, an analogy about legal and contractual capacity of the intelligent agents and secondly, an analogy about the user's liability in case of wrong "creation"—not just in case of wrong transmission—of her DOI by the "employed" intelligent agent.[53] But such a *mutatis mutandis* application seems to exceed the *ratio legis* of the current rules of law about the role of the messenger in the contractual procedure, according to which the principal is held liable only in case of wrong transmission of her DOI by the messenger, not in case of its false "creation". The latter could happen only in case of *representation,* as discussed below.

For the above-mentioned reasons, it is questionable whether autonomous AI systems should be treated as mere communication tools in the framework of private law as it now stands.[54]

[51] See van Haentijens (2002), p. 5.

[52] Wettig and Zehendner (2004), pp. 125–126.

[53] Cornelius (2002), p. 355.

[54] Wettig and Zehendner (2004), p. 123; Chopra and White (2009), p. 372; Braütigam and Klindt (2015), p. 1137; Karanasiou and Pinotsis (2017), p. 4.

3.2 *The Autonomous Machines as Agents Under the Law of Disclosed Agency*

Since the "conservative" theory about the role of the autonomous machines at the stage of the conclusion of a contract as mere communication tools is questionable, another opinion suggests that they should be legally treated as representatives under the analogous application of the law of disclosed agency.[55]

According to the law of agency, a person (agent)—who, in civil law jurisdictions, must have legal and contractual capacity, that is, must be a natural or legal person—is assigned the task to conclude a contract in the name and on behalf of her principal. The agent forms and expresses her own DOI (offer or acceptance) to the other contractual partner, but the legal effects of the concluded contract are attributed directly to the principal.[56] Regarding the agent's legal and contractual capacity in civil law jurisdictions, the agent has to have legal capacity and contractual capacity—even a restricted one; in other words, the agent must be a *natural or a legal person.*[57]

In case the human agent acts without the principal's authority or exceeding it, the principal is not deemed legally bound. The other contractual partner has the right to ask the principal to confirm the contract within a concrete period of time.[58] If the principal denies confirming the transaction, the contract is definitely not legally binding upon the principal. Instead, it is binding upon the agent who is considered liable in case of non-performance *(falsus procurator).*[59] Moreover, the agent is liable against the principal for all breaches concerning their internal contractual relationship.[60]

By invoking the legal rules on agency, this approach tries to avoid the rigid implications of the previous "conservative" theory, by "releasing" the user of any obligations in case the intelligent agent acts against her will. Moreover, this approach pays attention to the fact that the DOI is not formed by the principal but by another agent, thus a *mutatis mutandis* application of the legal rules of agency is not, at least *prima facie*, so farfetched as in the above described "conservative" approach.

The basic advantage of this approach is that it takes into account the characteristic features of the fourth evolutionary stage of AI systems. Especially it acknowledges

---

[55] Fisher (1997), p. 545; Chopra and White (2009), pp. 369–370 and 384.

[56] See in German law Wolf and Neuner (2016), p. 599; Bork (2016), pp. 513 and 649. See in common law Beatson et al. (2020), p. 680.

[57] Cf. for the Romanic jurisdictions, where authority is conferred by contract, Bénabent (2017), p. 61. In Germanic jurisdictions it suffices for the agent to have restricted contractual capacity (e.g. the agent can be a minor), cf. on §165 BGB Wolf and Neuner (2016), p. 601; Bork (2016), p. 539; for Switzerland cf. Watter (2011), Art. 32, N. 21; for Austria cf. Bydlinski (2005), Art. 1018, Rn. 1.

[58] See about §177 I BGB Wolf and Neuner (2016), p. 653; Medicus and Petersen (2016), p. 426.

[59] Wolf and Neuner (2016), p. 652 ff.; Bork (2016), p. 627 ff.

[60] Wolf and Neuner (2016), p. 620; Bork (2016), p. 615.

that, *firstly*, the intelligent agents act *autonomously*, like human agents, who can exceed principal's authority or even act against their principal's benefit, although it is widely accepted that the intelligent agents do not act against their goals. *Secondly*, this approach conforms to the principle that a party enjoying the benefits of an activity must also bear the inconvenience caused by this activity, which is prevalent in private law.[61]

Nevertheless, implementation of the law of disclosed agency in case of the intelligent agents causes a series of drawbacks. First of all, this approach "overestimates" the element of "rationality", not taking into consideration the fact that the autonomous system may demonstrate unpredictable malfunctions,[62] while at the same time it cannot provide specific explanations about its autonomously reached decisions because of its inherent *black box effect* that "combats" system's *rationality*.

More importantly, there are several problems regarding the construction of disclosed agency, as a matter of legal doctrine:

(a) First, the intelligent agent lacks legal capacity and, consequently, contractual capacity. Therefore, the legal role of the intelligent agents is not similar to those of human agents.[63] The only way for the rules on disclosed agency to apply here is again by a *double analogy*, acknowledging a fictitious legal *and*, accordingly, contractual capacity.[64]

(b) Secondly, in contract law, disclosed agency is based on the *principle of transparent authority*.[65] According to this principle, in case of disclosed agency it must be clear to the other contractual partner that she is going to make an agreement with an agent who acts in the name and on behalf of another person, the principal. The aim of this principle is to protect the *private autonomy* since the other contractual partner has the right to choose not to conclude a contract with a person (principal) that she does not know. For this reason, in case the principle of transparency is violated, the contract is considered as not concluded with the principal, but with the agent herself.[66]

    There are two exceptions to this rule.[67] Firstly, when the face of the principal is actually irrelevant to the other contractual partner, so she would conclude the contract in each case. Secondly, when the agent discloses that it acts in the name and on behalf of another person but does not reveal the latter's exact identity.

---

[61] Pagallo (2013), p. 58.

[62] Kerr (2001), pp. 243–244; Bellia (2001), pp. 1060–1061.

[63] Cornelius (2002), p. 355. For the same reason it cannot be held that it is similar to the legal role of children. Contra Chopra and White (2009), p. 378.

[64] Wettig and Zehendner (2004), 124.

[65] For §164 Abs. 1 BGB (*Offenlegungsgrundsatz*) see, Wolf and Neuner (2016), p. 608; Bork (2016), p. 543. See about common law Beatson et al. (2020), p. 685.

[66] Wolf and Neuner (2016), p. 609 ff.; Bork (2016), p. 543.

[67] Medicus and Petersen (2016), p. 402 ff.; Bork (2016), p. 548 ff. See also about common law Beatson et al. (2020), p. 683.

However, these exceptions are not applicable in the case of intelligent agents, where it is not always clear to the other contractual partner that she, in fact, transacts with an autonomous machine and not with a person. Besides, in *multi-agent systems* the contract can be fully concluded through "employed" intelligent agents. As a result, it can be said that the principle of transparency is not being respected in all cases.[68]

(c) Thirdly, according to civil law, disclosed agency is established through a contract or a unilateral juridical act. In order to establish the agency, the principal must address her relative DOI, conferring the authority, either directly to the agent or alternatively to the eventual contractual counter partner.[69] However, in the case of intelligent agents, only the second alternative is feasible, since the intelligent agent has no juridical standing in the eyes of the law and, as a result, it cannot receive any DOI.[70] The main practical problem is that at the time when an intelligent agent is "employed", the user does not know her eventual counterparty (see case study 1), in order to address the DOI, conferring the authority to the AI, directly to her. As a consequence, it seems that the contract is finally concluded without the required authority and for this reason it cannot be held legally bound upon the principal.[71] The same problem appears also in common law, where the agency is usually based on an express agreement, whether contractual or not, between the principal and the agent.[72] It follows that since the intelligent agent has no juridical standing in the eyes of the law, no authority can be transferred to it. As a result, in both jurisdictions the law of agency can apply only *mutatis mutandis*, the authority being conferred to the agent implicitly.

Furthermore, the implementation of the rules of agency seems to be troublesome and unsatisfactory in practice, because:

(d) In case of *multi-agent systems* it can be extremely difficult for the other contractual partner to identify the person of the user-principal, in order to ask her to ratify the contract concluded by the intelligent agent without the required authority.[73]

(e) In case the user-principal does not confirm the transaction, the contractual counterparty cannot ask the intelligent agent to perform the contract itself, because the intelligent agent has no juridical standing in the eyes of the law.[74] Therefore, in this case the contractual counterparty is the one who shall bear the

[68] See also *Kerr's* approach (2001), pp. 197–198.

[69] Wolf and Neuner (2016), pp. 606 and 630; Bork (2016), p. 564.

[70] Bellia (2001), p. 1060; Andrade et al. (2007b), p. 360.

[71] However, it is argued that in these cases there is an *apparent authority* since the user has already expressed her will to conclude a contract through an intelligent agent by "employing" it. See Kerr (2001), pp. 241–243; Bellia (2001), pp. 1059.

[72] See Beatson et al. (2020), p. 681.

[73] Weitzenboeck (2001), p. 18.

[74] Lerouge (2000), pp. 408–409; Wettig and Zehendner (2004), p. 125; Cornelius (2002), p. 355.

risk.[75] This is very important, because it shows that the legal rules on *falsus procurator,* aiming at protecting the contractual counterparty, cannot apply in the case of intelligent agents.

(f) It remains unanswered, whether the user should be held legally bound, in case her "employed" intelligent agent delegates its tasks to other intelligent agents (sub-agency), especially in the framework of a *multi-agent system.*[76]

For all these reasons, the implementation of the law of disclosed agency seems quite problematic, finally leading to *transaction insecurity*. Since a contract concluded by the intelligent agent may not be legally binding upon the user and the latter has the right not to ratify the transaction, this theory questions, in fact, the validity of contracts concluded through intelligent agents, while at the same time it does not protect the contractual counter partner's interests. To avoid this adverse effects, proponents of this theory support that only the "external" elements of agency (those dealing with the relationship between principal and third party) should apply *mutatis mutandis.*[77] Nonetheless, a great number of legal concerns remains, not allowing even such an implementation.[78]

4 Prospects

The approaches described above try to deal with the legal issue of the validity of a contract concluded by intelligent agents based on the current legal framework. Since the acceptance of any of these theories is not uncontroversial, many legal scholars have already tried to cope with that problem by invoking *de lege ferenda* arguments. The most widely discussed are the following ones:

1. The attribution of *legal personhood* to the autonomous machines, in order to acquire legal and, thus, contractual capacity, like legal persons.[79]
2. The legal treatment of intelligent agents as contemporary *electronic "slaves"*[80] that will not bear full legal capacity but will have a restricted capacity of contracting and will be capable of acquiring a certain amount of property (*peculium*), like the ancient roman slaves. According to this approach, intelligent agents' actions should be binding upon their principals, whose liability is limited to the value of the "*digital peculium*".[81]

[75] Braütigam and Klindt (2015), p. 1138.

[76] Kerr (2001), p. 244; Bellia (2001), p. 1061.

[77] Fisher (1997), pp. 558 and 561; Kerr (2001), p. 239.

[78] Lerouge (2000), pp. 408–409; Bellia (2001), p. 1063; van Haentijens (2002), p. 5; Balke (2010), p. 12.

[79] Solum (1992), passim.

[80] Kerr (2001), pp. 236–238.

[81] Katz (2008), p. 5; Pagallo (2011), pp. 5–6; Pagallo (2013), pp. 59–60.

3. The acceptance of *electronic person* or *hybrid-electronic person*;[82] that is a business registry for up-to-date certificated autonomous machines[83] that will possess a bare minimum of property deposited by their owners,[84] whose liability in case of damages is limited accordingly.

Both the second and the third approaches presuppose the creation of a registry for intelligent agents and can be combined with a compulsory insurance.[85]

Despite the fact that those approaches are highly interesting, they are not applicable, since they "exceed" the current legal framework: the current rules of private law have not (yet) attributed legal personhood to the intelligent agents,[86] while it cannot be held that they could have contractual capacity, even a restricted one, without legal capacity. Besides, in practice no registry or insurance about intelligent agents has been established yet.[87]

Legal doctrine should deal with the legal role of the intelligent agents in contractual procedure on the basis of the current rules of law, proposing solutions *de lege lata* that will be sound and satisfactory from both a doctrinal and a practical point of view.

Within this framework, we should absolutely accept the validity of a contract concluded fully or partially through intelligent agents, considering the user legally bound for its execution.[88] In civil law jurisdictions, the agents' contractual liability can be based on the theory of *de facto* contracts (*faktische Verträge*[89]). These are contracts concluded without explicit DOIs (offer and acceptance), based only on the actual behavior of the contractual partners. Alternatively, one could argue that the AI user's liability for non-perfomance can be based on the doctrine of *reliance liability* (*Vertrauenshaftung*).[90] This theory has been heavily criticized in German scholarship mainly because most of the problems it addresses can be solved by the acceptance of an implied DOI.[91] Nevertheless, this concept can be useful in order to establish a legal relationship between the user and the contractual counterparty.

---

[82] Wettig and Zehendner (2004), p. 128 ff.; Wettig and Zehendner (2003), p. 9; Andrade et al. (2007b), p. 371.

[83] Karnow (1996), p. 193 ff. ("*Turing Register*"). See also Weitzenboeck (2001), pp. 36–37; Balke (2010), pp. 18–19.

[84] Bellia (2001), p. 1067. Contra Lerouge (2000), p. 411.

[85] Karnow (1996), pp. 193–194; Wettig and Zehendner (2004), pp. 127–129; Pagallo (2011), p. 6.

[86] See also the recent proposal of the *European Financial and Social Commission* Com (2020) 65 final, which strongly recommends that no legal personhood should be attributed to AI.

[87] It is noteworthy that according to Art. 60 of Proposal of European Commission for a Regulation of the European Parliament and of the Council regarding harmonized rules on AI (COM (2021) 206 final), a database for *stand-alone high-risk AI systems* is to be established.

[88] See also Cornelius (2002), p. 355.

[89] Wolf (1999), Bd. 2, Vor para 145 Rn. 106; Fikentscher and Heinemann (2017), pp. 58–62.

[90] Canaris (1971), p. 411 ff.; Fikentscher and Heinemann (2017), p. 57.

[91] Cf. Busche (2021), Vor para 145, Rn. 40.

Moreover, a person could be held liable, when creating, by words or conduct, the impression that she is responsible for the performance of a contract, so that any reasonable person could *trust* this "*inference" (Rechtschein)*; if this latter person acts in good faith, her reliance (*Vertrauen*) should be protected.[92]

In the case of AI, the "employment" of an electronic agent can create such an *appearance*. The situation is similar (but not identical) with that of the human agent who acts without actual authority (*Anscheinsvollmact/Recthscheinsvollmacht* in German law; *apparent authority* in Anglosaxon law[93]),[94] since the counter party reasonably believes that the electronic agent "acts" in the name and on behalf of its user, who chose to "employ" it in a transaction. Although there is no actual authority, the counter party's interests must be protected, unless she knew or could have known that the user would have never concluded this contract.

However, should one accept the conclusion of the contract between the AI user and the third counter party on the basis of one of the above-mentioned theories, then she must also accept the right of the AI user to challenge its validity in case of *mistake*. However, in case of agency, a contract can be invalidated, only when the mistake is attributed to the agent—not to the principal—provided that the agent didn't follow the principal's instructions.[95] *Mutatis mutandis* it could be argued that the AI user can rescind the contract concluded through her "employed" intelligent agent, if there is a mistake *about its declaration of intention*[96] or *about the object's or other party's properties*,[97] provided that the AI user's instructions were right and she did not know or, more to the point, invoked the mistake of her "employed" intelligent agent. For instance, the AI user can rescind the contract when her e-assistant concluded it without any order by the principal herself[98] or because it did not hear the given order correctly *(mistake about the DOI)* or when the intelligent agent did not adhere to the given order, e.g. when it didn't booked a fly seat with leg-extension, against the user's order (*mistake about object's properties*). In any case, the intelligent agent's mistake should be so important, that the user would have never entered the contract, had she known the true situation. In case of mistake the user must prove that there is a mistake attributed to her "employed" e-assistant, i.e. that her order was different and that the intelligent agent "has perceived" and conveyed it incorrectly, that is, that there is a causal link between intelligent agent's "misunderstanding" and the conclusion of the contract, as well that the mistake was

[92] See Schubert (2021), para 167 Rn. 122 ff.

[93] Wolf and Neuner (2016), p. 641 ff.; Bork (2016), p. 601 ff.; Schubert (2021), para 167 Rn. 112 ff. See also about *ostensible/apparent authority* in common law Beatson et al. (2020), pp. 685–687.

[94] See also Kerr (2001), pp. 241–243; Bellia (2001), p. 1059.

[95] See about §166 BGB Bork (2016), p. 540.

[96] See about §119 Abs. 1 Alt. 1, 2 BGB (*Inhaltsirrtum, Erklärungsirrtümer*) Bork (2016), pp. 324–325 and 329–330.

[97] See Wolf and Neuner (2016), p. 484 *et seq.*

[98] This happened in case of Amazon's electronic assistant *Alexa*, which ordered a dollhouse and tons of cookies because it heart this order on TV. See Wulf and Seizov (2020), p. 632.

so crucial that she would never enter a contract with such a content. However, the evidence will be difficult for the user, because of the features of the intelligent agent (autonomy, complexity, opacity). In contrary to non-contractual liability, where special rules of law regarding proof in favor of the user are going to be enacted soon in the European Union,[99] there are no such rules for mistake as well as for contractual liability. In these cases, one could argue only for *mutatis mutandis* application of a rebuttable presumption of causality, such as this provided in Article 4 of the recent EU proposal for non-contractual civil liability rules to AI.

If the contract is finally rescinded due to mistake, in civil law jurisdictions the rescinding party must compensate the other contractual party for the caused damage.[100] In this way a fair balance between the two contractual parties is achieved: on the one hand, the user can avoid the performance of a contract that does not meet her needs/desires, while on the other hand the other contractual partner shall not bear the full risk, since her loss can be compensated.

5 Conclusion

The provision of the aforementioned prospect could eliminate the negative effects of the AI autonomy at the stage of the conclusion of a contract, highly contributing to the transactions' security, while on the other hand it conforms to the existing legal framework.[101] Until new legislative initiatives are taken, the legal doctrine can tackle the issue regarding the validity of contracts concluded fully or partially through AI systems, based on the above-described prospect.

References

Adadi A, Berrada M (2018) Peeking inside the black-box: a survey on explainable artificial intelligence (XAI). IEEE Access 6:52138–52160

Allen T, Widdison R (1996) Can computers make contracts. Harvard Law Rev 9:26–52

Andrade F, Novais P, Machado J, Neves J (2007a) Contracting agents: legal responsibility and representation. Artif Intell Law 15:357–373

Andrade F, Novais P, Machado J, Intelligent NJ (2007b) Contracting, software agents, corporate bodies and virtual organizations. In: Camarinha-Matos L, Afsarmanesh H, Novais P, Analide C (eds) Establishing the foundations of collaborative networks. Springer, New York, pp 217–224

Balke T (2010) "Entity" and "autonomy"-the conclusion of contracts by software agents in the eyes of the law. Rev Intell Artif 24:391–413

[99] European Commission, Proposal of Directive of the European Parliament and of the Council on adapting non-contractual civil liability rules to artificial intelligence (COM (2022) 496 final).

[100] See about §122 BGB Wolf and Neuner (2016), p. 507 ff.; Medicus and Petersen (2016), p. 340 ff.

[101] Uni global union (2017), p. 7.

Bannier C (2005) Vertragstheorie. Eine Einführung mit finanzökonomischen Beispielen und Anwendungen. Physica-Verlag, Heidelberg

Beatson J, Burrows A, Cartwright J (2020) Anson's law of contract, 31st edn. Oxford University Press, Oxford

Bellia A (2001) Contracting with electronic agents. Emory Law J 50:1047–1092

Bénabent A (2017) Droits des obligations, 16th edn. LGDJ, Paris

Boden M, Bryson J et al (2017) Principle of robotics: regulating robots in the real world. Connect Sci 29:124–129

Borges G (2018) Rechtliche Rahmenbedingungen für autonome Systeme. NJW 2018:977–982

Bork R (2016) Allgemeiner Teil des Bürgerlichen Gesetzbuchs, 4th edn. Mohr Siebeck, Tübingen

Bostrom N (2014) Superintelligence: paths, dangers, strategies. Oxford University Press, Oxford

Braütigam P, Klindt T (2015) Industrie 4.0, das Internet der Dinge und das Recht. NHW 2015: 1137–1142

Brox H, Walker W-D (2018) Allgemeiner Teil des BGB, 42th edn. Franz Vahlen, Munich

Brożek B, Jakubiec M (2017) On the legal responsibility of autonomous machines. Artif Intell Law 25:293–304

Busche J (2021) Kommentar der §§139-157 BGB. In: Säcker F, Rixecher R, Oetker H, Limperg B (eds) Münchener Kommentar BGB, 9th edn. C.H. Beck, Munich

Bydlinski P (2005) Zweiundzwanzigstes Hauptstück. Von der Bevollmächtigung und andern Arten der Geschäftsführung. §§1002-1044. In: Koziol H, Bydlinski P, Bollenberg R (eds) Allgemeines Bürgerliches Gesetzbuch: Kurzkommentar, 1st edn. Springer, Vienna, pp 978–1049

Canaris C-W (1971) Die Vertrauenshaftung im deutschen Privatrecht. C.H. Beck, Munich

Chopra S, White L (2009) Artificial intelligence and the contracting problem. Univ Ill J Law Tech Policy, pp 363–403

Cooter R, Ulen T (2008) Law and economics, 5th edn. Pearson, Harlow

Cornelius K (2002) Vertragsabschluss durch autonome elektronische Agenten. MMR 2002:353–258

Dembe A, Boden L (2000) Moral hazzard: a question of morality? New Solut 10:257–279

Denicola R (2016) Ex machina: copyright protection for computer-generated works. Rutgers Univ Law Rev 69:251–287

Eidenmüller H (2017) The rise of robots and the law of humans. Oxford Legal Studies Research Paper, No. 27/2017

Ertel W (2017) Introduction to artificial intelligence, 2nd edn. Springer, Cham

Fikentscher W, Heinemann A (2017) Schuldrecht: Allgemeiner und Besonderer Teil, 11th edn. De Gruyter, Berlin

Fisher J (1997) Computer as agents: a proposed approach to revised U.C.C. Article 2. Indiana Law J 72:545–570

Furubotn E, Richter R (2005) Institutions & economic theory, 2nd edn. University of Michigan Press, Michigan

Grundmann S, Hacker P (2017) Digital technology as a challenge to european contract law-from the existing to the future architecture. Eur Rev Contract Law 13:255–293

Huang T (2006) The history of artificial intelligence. https://courses.cs.washington.edu/courses/csep590/06au/projects/history-ai.pdf

Karanasiou A, Pinotsis D (2017) Towards a legal definition of machine learning. Paper presented at the 2017 international conference on artificial intelligence & law (ICAIL), London, 12–16 June 2017. https://doi.org/10.1145/3086512.3086524

Karnow C (1996) Liability for distributed artificial intelligences. Berkley Tech Law Rev 11:147–204

Katz A (2008) Intelligent agents and internet commerce in ancient Rome. Available via Society for Computers and Law. https://www.scl.org/articles/1095-intelligent-agents-and-internet-commerce-in-ancient-rome

Kerr I (1999) Spirits in the material world: intelligent agents as intermediaries in electronic commerce. Dalhousie Law J 22:189–249

Kerr I (2001) Ensuring the success of contract formation in agent-mediated electronic commerce. Electron Commer Rev 1:183–202

Keßler O (2017) Intelligente Roboter-neue Technologie im Einsatz. MMR 2017:589–594

Köhler H (1982) Die Problematik automatisierter Rechtsvorgänge, insbesondere von Willenserklärungen. AcP 182:126–171

Kotz D, Gray R (1999) Mobile agents and the future of the internet. ACM SIGOPS Oper Syst Rev 33:7–13

Lerouge J-F (2000) The use of electronic agents questioned under contractual law: suggested solutions on a European American level. J Marchall J Comput Info Law 18:403–434

Medicus D, Petersen J (2016) Allgemeiner Teil des BGB, 11th edn. C.F. Müller, Heidelberg

Mehrings J (1998) Vertragsabschluss im Internet. Eine neue Herausforderung für das "alte" BGB. MMR 1998:30–34

Pagallo U (2011) Killers, fridges, and slaves: a legal journey in robotics. AI Soc 26:347–354

Pagallo U (2013) What robots want: autonomous machines, codes and new frontiers of legal responsibility. In: Hildebrandt M, Gaakeer J (eds) Human law and computer law: comparative perspectives. Springer, Dordrecht, pp 47–65

Panait L, Luke S (2005) Cooperative multi-agent learning: the state of the art. Auton Agent Multi-Agent Syst 11:387–434

Rissland E (1990) Artificial intelligence and law: stepping stones to a model of legal reasoning. Yale Law Rev 99:1957–1981

Russell S, Norvig P (2020) Artificial intelligence: a modern approach, 4th edn. Pearson Series for AI, Hoboken

Schubert M (2021) §167 Erteilung der Vollmacht. In: Säcker F, Rixecher R, Oetker H, Limperg B (eds) Münchener Kommentar BGB, 9th edn. C.H. Beck, Munich

Smith C, Ting H (2006) The history of artificial Intelligence. https://courses.cs.washington.edu/courses/csep590/06au/projects/history-ai.pdf

Solum L (1992) Legal personhood for AI. North Carolina Law Rev 70:1231–1287

Stanford Encyclopedia of Philosophy (2020) Ethics on AI and robotics. https://plato.stanford.edu/entries/ethics-ai/

Susskind D, Susskind R (2018) The future of the professions. Proc Am Philos Soc 162:125–138

UNESCO (2019) Preliminary study on the ethics of AI. https://unesdoc.unesco.org/ark:/48223/pf0000367823

Uni Global Union (2017) Top 10 principles for ethical AI. Available via The Future World of Work. http://www.thefutureworldofwork.org/media/35420/uni_ethical_ai.pdf

van Haentijens O (2002) Shopping agents and their legal implications regarding Austrian Law. In: Papers of the LEA 2002 workshop on law of electronic agents. http://citeseerx.ist.psu.edu/viewdoc/download?doi=10.1.1.201.9341&rep=rep1&type=pdf

Veljanovski C (2007) Economic principles of law. Cambridge University Press, Cambridge

Voigt S (2009) Institutionenökonomik: Neue Ökonomische Bibliothek. Fink (Wilhelm) UTB, Stuttgart

Watter R (2011) Art. 32-40. In: Honsell H, Vogt N, Wiegand W (eds) Basler Kommentar: Obligationenrecht I, 5th edn. Helbing & Lichtenhahn, Basel

Weitzenboeck E (2001) Electronic agents and the formation of contracts. Int J Law Inform Technol 9:204–234

Wettig S, Zehendner E (2003) The electronic agent: a legal personality under German Law. Proceedings of the law and electronic agents workshop, 97–112. http://citeseerx.ist.psu.edu/viewdoc/download?doi=10.1.1.99.81&rep=rep1&type=pdf

Wettig S, Zehendner E (2004) A legal analysis of human and electronic agents. Artif Intell Law 12: 111–135

Wolf M (1999) Bd. 2, para 145. In: Soergel HT (ed.) Bürgerliches Gesetzbuch, Allgemeiner Teil 2 §§104–240, 13 Auflage. W. Kohlhammer, Stuttgart

Wolf M, Neuner J (2016) Allgemeiner Teil des Bürgerlichen Rechts, 11th edn. C.H. Beck, Munich, pp 32–40
Wooldridge M, Jennings N (1995) Intelligent agents: theory and practice. Knowl Eng Rev 10:115–152
Wulf A, Seizov O (2020) Artificial intelligence and transparency: a blueprint for improving the regulation of AI applications in the EU. Eur Bus Law Rev 31:611–640
Zednik C (2019) Solving the black box problem: a normative framework for explainable artificial intelligence. Philos Technol 34:265–288

Understanding the Risks of Artificial Intelligence as a Precondition for Sound Liability Regulation

Nasir Muftic

Abstract Not all AI risks are new. Risk of traffic accidents that self-driving cars generate is already reality in today's traffic. Physical injuries a patient may suffer during a medical treatment occur regardless of whether the damage is caused by an autonomous agent or a human doctor. Modern societies are already familiar with the aforementioned risks. This chapter explores whether liability regimes, traditionally designed to deter physical risks and compensate an injured person when they occur, have rules apt for tackling the social risks that AI represents. In the European Union, the European Parliament has adopted a text of a Regulation on AI liability. The text is a clear step forward in adjusting liability rules to the challenges of AI. It sets out a position on who should be responsible and on what basis and provides injured persons with procedural devices in order to enhance their position and tackle the black-box issue. It, thus, for better or worse, deals with well-known fundamental issues surrounding AI liability. However, while social risks have been previously recognized by the European Commission in the White Paper and by some scholars, the adopted text omits to address them specifically. This chapter presents the nature of AI risks that liability rules should regulate. It seeks to address whether the traditional liability concepts are apt for regulating the novel types of risks. Just like in the case of safety regulation, this chapter attempts to demonstrate that a proper understanding of AI risks is a basis for sound regulation of liability.

1 Introduction

Regulation of artificial intelligence (hereinafter: AI) and other emerging digital technologies is a widely discussed topic today. There is a consensus about the tremendous opportunities offered by these new technologies but also about their great disruptive potential. Regulators worldwide are deliberating on the appropriate

N. Muftic (✉)
University of Sarajevo, Faculty of Law, Sarajevo, Bosnia and Herzegovina
e-mail: n.muftic@pfsa.unsa.ba

A. Kornilakis et al. (eds.), *Artificial Intelligence and Normative Challenges*, Law, Governance and Technology Series 59,
https://doi.org/10.1007/978-3-031-41081-9_6

approach to be pursued and many, sometimes opposed to, proposals have been made.

This chapter discusses the relationship between the risks of AI and the regulatory response thereto. The first part concerns the regulation of new technologies with a focus on a risk-based approach. It places the rules of liability in a broader context of mechanisms that are available to the regulator. In the second part, some of the main characteristics of AI that bear a potential for disruption have been outlined. They are coupled with the challenges they generate for current liability concepts. The third part deals with a risk-based approach to liability for AI. It presents various projects regarding the classification of AI risks, as well as highlights sectors in which those risks raise significant challenges. Lastly, it elaborates on the extension of current liability regimes where it is viable.

2 The Risk-Based Approach to Regulation and the Role of Liability

Whether AI or any other new technology should be applied in society and the conditions under which that is allowed, are a matter of public policy. Regulatory law is a manifestation of public policy, whereby the actors set the rules and the methods for successful enforcement. Regulation focused on the risks of AI, like other 'risk-based' approaches to governance, should employ various mechanisms to control and mitigate harms and not be limited to liability or any single available device. Moreover, the purpose of regulation is not to eliminate risks at any cost. Rather, "in an adaption of Paracelsus' maxim—the *likely* dose makes the poison—'-risk-based' approaches pay attention to both the *probability* and *impact* of potential adverse outcomes".[1]

Liability is part of a legal framework surrounding AI and new technologies, whose role is to find a balance between risks and benefits.[2] Apart from liability, other mechanisms to be considered for AI regulation are insurance, development of ethical and safety standards, requirements of transparency, compensation funds, etc. The joint application of various mechanisms ensures that risks are dealt with both *ex-ante* and *ex-post*, effectively guaranteeing the corrective function of liability.

The role of liability as the main *ex-post* mechanism in the regulation of risk is disputed.[3] A traditional understanding of the tort law system focuses on allocation of responsibilities between parties involved in a dispute based on their behavior and accompanying risks. However, some argue that adjudication is a form of risk regulation made by the courts, since their decisions have an impact that transcends the interests of parties in a specific case. De Jong claims that tort cases have

[1] Rothstein et al. (2013), p. 16.

[2] Zech (2021), p. 4.

[3] See de Jong et al. (2018), pp. 6–13.

regulatory implications since the courts are setting and enforcing standards in tort law that are applicable beyond a specific case.[4] Information made public during the proceedings and the decisions of the courts provide directions that shape the behavior of private actors and public authorities. Apart from the straightforward setting of standards, they can spark public debate about certain issues. Moreover, court decisions might have an impact on "the availability and costs of insurance, the availability of public funding for achieving policy objectives in case of public authority liability, or the willingness of actors to bring new products to the market and the implications of court rulings for product prices".[5] Of course, the aforementioned function of courts as risk regulators should be mitigated. In jurisdictions where the national court decisions are not considered precedents, the regulatory power of courts is limited. For instance, in the EU, where the law is harmonized and unified through the *acquis*, as well as in its Member states that mostly embrace the civil law tradition, legislative acts are the main source of law. Even so, the role of the courts in establishing a liability regime should not be neglected. Unlike other branches of government, provided there are no procedural constraints, a court has to address the merits of the claim presented before it. Furthermore, the parties to a case are in a position to scrutinize otherwise unreachable state actors. Kysar suggests that discovery rights in the hands of a plaintiff are powerful too so as "to uncover risk information, including information that may not have been disclosed to regulators".[6] An incentivized individual committed to the utilization of discovery rights could create an impact beyond this case. The public might receive information that scrutinizes the work of wrongdoers, which might be particularly interesting if a defendant is a person who provides products or services on a large scale. If access to the court is allowed to a broad group of plaintiffs, the level of scrutiny increases proportionally. This could be even more impactful if attorneys are incentivized to foster the process via means such as contingency fees and collective redress.

Consequently, until AI is fully developed and understood, the role of the courts might be even more important. Legislators cannot predict the risks of AI with certainty, since technology is still in an infantile stage. Although the lack of information can be mitigated by a sectoral and risk-oriented approach to a certain extent, only *ex-post* measures such as court decisions allow for a complete assessment. The courts are, thereby, able to extend the time window for legislators to deliberate on the appropriate approach in the form of legislation.

Nevertheless, the role of the courts is limited. They do not possess relevant knowledge to make policy choices about highly sophisticated matters nor do they have democratic legitimacy. Furthermore, other problems limit their regulatory function in practice. For instance, if the number of wrongdoers is high and their contribution to the harm cannot be calculated precisely, court rulings hardly impact on the control of the risk of private individuals. In environmental law, for instance,

[4] Rodríguez de las Heras Ballell (2019), pp. 308 et seq.

[5] de Jong et al. (2018), pp. 6–13.

[6] Kysar (2018), p. 54.

where similar challenges on risk regulation arise, "any individual harm will be seen as the result of greenhouse gas emissions by literally billions of alleged wrongdoers, likely including the plaintiff herself. Such problems of defendant numerosity are at the very heart of the public policy challenges posed by climate change. Tort seems to offer only meager resources to overcome them".[7] In the same vein, AI can be developed by many actors who may contribute to its development in various stages of the process. There could also be many deployers. The full potential of this technology can be achieved if it is a part of a broader ecosystem where it interacts with other software. Since many actors contribute to the output of the technology, it might be very hard to determine which of them should be liable. The situation could be even more complex since there could be many actors involved in the process of development and deployment of each part of a digital ecosystem. The number of potentially liable parties is high and there might not be an easy way to attribute liability. Last but not least, the court could also be limited by procedural constraints such as the statute of limitation or a remuneration cap.

Therefore, the role of liability is to act as a piece of a greater puzzle that holistically addresses the risks of new technology. The courts as regulators have an important but limited role. Public policy choices should be in the hands of legislators.

3 Understanding AI

As a multi-purpose technology based on various different techniques, AI is understood differently by the general and expert public. General public does, most likely due to the influence of popular culture, see it only as humanoid robots with or without human consciousness vested in it. This technology however has a broader potential field application and can appear in other forms.

There is not a single universally accepted definition of AI. Nilsson defines it as an "activity devoted to making machines intelligent, and intelligence is that quality that enables an entity to function appropriately and with foresight in its environment".[8] Calo argues that it is "a set of techniques aimed at approximating some aspect of human or animal cognition using machines".[9] In the definition used by the EU Commission, AI "refers to systems that display intelligent behaviour by analysing their environment and taking actions—with some degree of autonomy—to achieve specific goals". AI-based systems can be purely software-based, acting in the virtual world (e.g., voice assistants, image analysis software, search engines, speech and

[7] Ibid, p. 53.

[8] Nilsson (2010).

[9] Calo (2017), pp. 399–435.

face recognition systems) or AI can be embedded in hardware devices (e.g., advanced robots, autonomous cars, drones, or Internet of Things applications)".[10]

The common denominator of the majority of definitions include the term intelligence or cognition as a characteristic of this technology. Intelligence itself can be understood very differently as it is a notion employed in various scientific fields. Even with several definitions of AI, no one is generally accepted, thus it is hard to capture the essence of AI since it is prone to great and unpredictable improvements.[11] For the purposes of this work, a system can be considered intelligent if it has a capacity to make rational decisions based on inputs from the environment. Rationality has been recognized as a word which depicts the intelligence this technology yields.[12] Intelligence, thus, does not mean the presence of cognition which expands into other fields from the ones the system is suppose to express. In that sense, AI does not need to have a universal rationality in order to be perceived as intelligent. Rather, its role can be constrained to a limited set of tasks or even a single task where it behaves rationally. For instance, the fact that some AI systems might outperform humans in translating words does not mean their ability to understand the context behind the speech is supreme. Also, intelligence does not mean consciousness. Again, consciousness is very hard to define and usually entails moral, ethical or philosophical considerations. It requires the understanding of an entity as possessing subjectivity, which can be based on different grounds, and the ability of humans to create relationships with it.[13] Notwithstanding the lack of consensus on this issue in the available research,[14] this question is not essential for determining legal liability. It might appear so when examining the question whether it is appropriate to hold AI itself liable, but, as it will be demonstrated, other considerations such as AI's ability to compensate the injured party are more important, or at least have a more direct and tangible impact.

Moreover, AI can perceive the environment, process the inputs, make a decision on how to act accordingly, and execute it. However, the ability to perform tasks is not what makes it different from other human inventions. Such an understanding would not separate a traditional cuckoo clock from the Tesla self-driving car as each, arguably, performs their allocated actions. The main potential of AI lies in the ways in which it perceives and performs those tasks, separating it from traditional technologies. As it will be demonstrated below, there are various techniques, systems and methods used with a view to making the algorithms behave intelligently. The number of differences within AI, as mentioned above, do not allow one to easily provide for a definition of this technology. The lack of clarity has caused occasional

[10]Communication from the Commission to the European Parliament, the European Council, the Council, the European Economic and Social Committee and the Committee of the Regions on Artificial Intelligence for Europe, Brussels, 25.4.2018 COM(2018) 237 final.

[11]Turner (2019), p. 7.

[12]Russell and Norvig (2009).

[13]Hildt (2019).

[14]For instance: Reggia et al. (2015).

failures of optimism in technology, backed by the lack of funding, usually referred to as AI winter.[15] Yet, it is exactly this diversity of approaches that was one of the reasons for the flourishment of AI, as the failed expectations for a single, universally accepted definition, have not curtailed researchers. As one of the commentators put it: "Curiously, the lack of a precise, universally accepted definition of AI probably has helped the field to grow, blossom, and advance at an ever-accelerating pace. Practitioners, researchers, and developers of AI are instead guided by a rough sense of direction and an imperative to "get on with it".[16]

4 Characteristics of AI

The absence of a universally accepted definition allowed AI to be perceived in a broader way. Rather than trying to define it, we started to see a shift towards addressing its main characteristics. Furthermore, AI often does not operate in isolation. It is interconnected with other digital technologies and they can create impact jointly. For this reasons, some authorities focus on a broader term than AI, described as "emerging digital technologies". The Expert Group on Liability and New Technologies—New Technologies Formation Complexity (The Expert Group), a body established by the European Commission for purposes of providing an opinion on the suitability of the current liability framework in light of the challenges of new technologies, does not focus on AI in its *Report on Liability for Artificial Intelligence and other emerging technologies* (hereinafter: Report).[17] Rather, it provides an assessment of digital emerging technologies that "have extraordinary potential to transform products, services, and activities, procedures and practices, in a multitude of economic sectors and in relation to many aspects of society".[18] AI is mentioned only as one of the technologies under this umbrella term, with the likes of the Internet of Things and of Services (IoT/IoS), or distributed ledger technologies (DLT). Such a subject matter definition made by the Expert Group is in line with the previous approach of the European Commission, which used the notion of "emerging digital technologies" to encompass AI and related technologies.[19] It seems that such an approach recognizes the close connection of digital technologies and/or their impact. In other words, the approach of the Expert Group means that particular characteristics of emerging digital technologies with a

[15] Open Philanthropy (2016).

[16] Stone et al. (2016).

[17] European Commission Directorate-General for Justice and Consumers (2019).

[18] Ibid, 11.

[19] In general, an attempt to provide a legal definition of AI seems to be a troubling task. It is hard to encompass main characteristics of this technology in an operable definition. Rather unsatisfying attempt has been made by the European Parliament in the Resolution 2020/2014(INL) on a Civil Liability Regime for Artificial Intelligence.

potential to influence current liability regimes had been addressed, without attempts to precisely define the technologies. The Report mentions characteristics of emerging digital technologies that require consideration since they bear the potential to cause disruption. Those characteristics are complexity, opacity, openness, autonomy, predictability, data-drivenness, and vulnerability. The Report does not distinguish between digital technologies and does not attribute the abovementioned characteristics specifically to AI. However, the Expert Group's explanations and relevant scholarship concerning AI liability have recognized the appropriateness of those traits.

Autonomy, opacity and vulnerability will be addressed below, as they are those characteristics that are most closely related to AI and, simultaneously, most relevant for the assessment of the liability regime. Other characteristics mentioned in the Report might be of relevance as well, but they will be either elaborated within the autonomy, opacity and vulnerability triptych, or they are more relevant for other emerging digital technologies.

4.1 Autonomy

The first characteristic that is brought up in a discussion about AI is usually autonomy. It is often seen as a supreme, hitherto unmatched characteristic of technology. AI is understood as autonomous in the sense of bearing the capacity to conduct the process of decision-making on its own. So far, human creations have acted as instructed by their manufacturers or operators, regardless of the level of sophistication of instructions that is required. AI is peculiar in that it does not strictly follow the instructions of humans, especially in scenarios that have not occurred before. The term autonomy might not be the most appropriate as it suggests the existence of free will, which has not been confirmed in the case of AI. Rather, it should convey the idea that AI does not strictly follow the rules (especially when they are not provided for new situations), but it obeys the principles set by humans. This process has been described in the Report as an ability of AI to alter "the initial algorithms due to self-learning capabilities that process external data collected in the course of the operation".[20]

4.2 Opacity

Opacity is closely connected with autonomy, since jointly they create a challenge to current liability regimes. It is related to a lack of understanding of the decision-making process of AI. The process of learning from its previous experiences is

[20] European Commission Directorate-General for Justice and Consumers (2019), p. 33.

conducted in a fashion that might not be discernable to people. It does not mean that the outcome of the decisions is wrong or harmful. Moreover, opacity does not simply express the unpredictability that can be attributed to technology, as traditional software can behave unpredictably too.[21] This characteristic refers to a "black-box", a concept closely related to the complexity of AI that renders its decision-making process often untransparent and hardly explainable. It might, thus, be hard to unveil the cause of a decision. The first reason for opacity lies in the application of various self-learning techniques. Although a programmer can set the goal an AI has to reach and provide it with data, very often she cannot understand the patterns that the AI recognized. Put it differently, AI has a supreme computational power which allows it to recognize what humans cannot. The lack of explainability of AI is "particularly likely in the case of connectionist AI that learns from data".[22] Opacity can also be attributed to the complexity of AI. Not only robots which consist of various parts, but also stand-alone AI are increasingly sophisticated. In both cases, there are various components of either hardware or an algorithm which might contribute to the harm.[23] Moreover, as AI requires vast amounts of data in order to operate and improve, the data itself can lead to harmful actions. For instance, data-sets might be corrupted or there might be errors in labelling in the process of training data.[24]

4.3 *Vulnerability*

Vulnerability reflects the potential risks generated by the exposure to external data. The data might arrive from various parts within a specific AI or other components of a digital ecosystem, as well as from the data AI processes in its environment.

As mentioned above, more than one actor might participate in the production of an AI as they might contribute to different parts of the production process. For instance, in case of a robot, some producers can provide sensors and other receptors used for data collection, while others might provide algorithms for processing the data in order for a robot to act. A different scenario would exist in case of a variety of interconnected components of a digital ecosystem which interact but each constitutes a separate unit. For instance, an example would be a smart fridge and other related devices which interact within a household. In both situations, a number of different actors who produce or maintain digital devices come into play. Such complexity is additionally enhanced by the openness of parts of components or components of an ecosystem. Today, AI and other digital products are often produced even after they leave the factory as the manufactures are able to enhance their impact through

[21] Wendehorst (2020), p. 152.
[22] Abbott (2020), p. 33.
[23] Koch (2020), p. 120.
[24] Wendehorst (2020), p. 152.

updates. The openness refers to the fact that such components "are not static but dynamic and are subject to frequent or even continuous change. It is in particular through the provision of over-the-air (OTA) updates for embedded or accessory software as well as through a variety of different data feeds and cloud-based digital services that products change their safety-relevant features after the product has been put into circulation".[25]

As it has already been mentioned, AI is a so-called data-intensive technology. Its prime potential can be achieved only if it is provided with data that can be analyzed. Its decision-making process is being improved depending on the availability of data that enables it to "learn" from it. Due to the need for constant interaction with outside information, there is increased exposure to external threats. The availability and quality of data is not only relevant for the advancement of AI, but also for the accuracy of the results. "Even the smartest algorithm does not deliver usable results, if the underlying data (structure) quality is poor".[26] AI is, therefore, vulnerable as it depends on the externally provided data.

Cybersecurity breaches are a potential threat too. As modern technologies typically operate in an interconnected fashion, potential breaches to any component of a digital ecosystem might generate a threat to others, including AI. This increases the magnitude of AI's exposure to external threats.[27]

5 Risks Relevant for Liability Regulation

The aforementioned characteristics attest to the disruptive potential of AI. This section will roughly outline the main risks those characteristics generate for the liability regime.[28] If a liability regime is understood as a system that aims at providing compensation to the suffering person, as well as ensuring deterrence against future harmful behavior of the liable party, several risks are generated by AI.

First of all, it is hard to determine a responsible party as many potential actors come into play. Manufacturers, operators, holders, users, or AI itself could be held liable for a harmful event, and there are arguments to support each of the choices. For instance, control of the risk might be a criterion (manufacturers and operators), benefits of use (manufacturers, operators, and users) another, or autonomy of the technology (AI itself) a third one. The most striking choice discussed in this respect would be to hold the AI liable, either as a separate legal person,[29] or as an entity that holds a certain amount of property for purposes of compensation.[30] The idea of

[25] Ibid, p. 153.

[26] Steinrötter (2020), pp. 270–271.

[27] Rodríguez de las Heras Ballell (2019), pp. 308 et al.

[28] The full list of risks identified by the Expert Group is included in the Report.

[29] Schirmer (2019), p. 131.

[30] van den Hoven van Genderen (2018), p. 21.

holding an AI liable was apparently not favoured both in the legislative process[31] and in scholarly analysis.[32] However, as AI possesses a degree of autonomy and a significant cognitive apparatus, the problem of allocation of liability puts into perspective a liability of technology itself, an unusual position for human creations. Apart from the conceptual problems, the complexity and opacity of AI might create difficulties for the tortfeasors at the redress level.[33] The solution should aim to hold liable the ones who can impact future behavior of AI, as they are the cheapest cost avoiders.[34]

Another unsettled issue is the proper basis of liability. Due to the information asymmetry between developers and the rest of the population, developers can be held liable on a basis of strict liability, which incentivizes them to be more careful as they constitute the only involved parties who have sufficient information so as to mitigate AI risks. The problem with strict liability, however, is related to its severity that might disincentivize technological improvement. On the other hand, fault liability and product liability require rethinking as well. Fault liability relies on the anthropocentric conception that is incompatible with the autonomous behavior of AI.[35] Fault, conduct, intention, and similar concepts are not designed to cope with non-human actors. Product liability, on its part, also requires attention, as the appropriateness of the current Product Liability Directive[36] seems to be questionable for digital technologies.[37] For instance, it is unclear whether it covers intangible objects,[38] what is the standard of safety which a person is entitled to expect,[39] and how to deal with situations where there has not been human error or failure and the wrongful event has been caused solely by the autonomous decision-making process.

[31] EU Parliament had mentioned it before in the Resolution on Civil Law Rules on Robotics from 2017, but the idea has been abandoned in the Resolution on a Civil Liability Regime for Artificial Intelligence from 2020.

[32] For example: Eidenmüller (2019), p. 109; van den Hoven van Genderen (2018), p. 21.

[33] European Commission Directorate-General for Justice and Consumers (2019), p. 32.

[34] In order to recognize a multitude of actors who might be involved in the process of development of AI, a distinction between backend and frontend operators had been suggested by the Expert Group. The EU Parliament's Resolution of 2020 accepted it. See European Commission Directorate-General for Justice and Consumers (2019), pp. 39–42.

[35] Supra note 12, p. 312.

[36] Council Directive 85/374/EEC of 25 July 1985 on the approximation of the laws, regulations and administrative provisions of the Member States concerning liability for defective products.

[37] See: European Law Institute (n.d.).

[38] Wagner (2019), p. 42.

[39] Defect under Product Liability Directive is defined as a standard of safety one is entitled to expect. See Borghetti (2019), p. 67. He notes that traditional methods of establishing defect employed by the courts are incompatible with characteristics of AI. He elaborates that the courts establish the defect in one of the following ways and elaborates why none of them are appropriate: proof that the product malfunctioned, proof of the violation of safety standards, balancing the product's risks and benefits, and comparing the product with other products.

Furthermore, AI requires reconceptualization of causation. Even if the liability of AI itself is not taken into consideration, many actors are involved as tortfeasors. As a result, it might be hard to determine their contribution to the harm. AI's interconnectedness and complexity provide that the impact of some actors might be unknown or unassessable. Accordingly, the corresponding problem vis-à-vis the position of the injured party arises. Complex relationships between the multitude of actors involved on the side of tortfeasor are impeding with a choice of the defendant. Additionally, due to the high technological complexity and opacity of AI, the victim may be required to prove facts in a sophisticated and costly process. For all those reasons, rules should provide an one-stop shop for an injured party by holding involved actors jointly and severally liable. Moreover, the standard of proof and access to compensation should be favorable to the injured party, corresponding to the hardship it faces.

Apart from challenges related to classic concepts of legal liability, determining an appropriate liability regime is a sensitive task from a constitutional and political perspective. Tort law, along with the majority of civil law, is, in general, subject to the national law of each Member State in the EU. Exceptionally, only a few issues, such as product liability, are harmonized at the EU level. Features of AI, such as complexity, data-dependency, and interconnectedness, entail a size of a market to be fully utilized. The availability of data used by AI and the free flow of information within the digital ecosystem and between digital ecosystems determine the quality of technology and the pace of its development. Although there is a reason for the adoption of rules at the level of the EU, the question is far greater. It concerns reaching a political consensus that might not be determined by the features of technology only. Furthermore, a political argument in favor of the adoption of rules at the EU level stems from the current geopolitical landscape related to the development of new technologies. As a technology bearing transformative potential, it should not be treated as any other innovation. In a geopolitical race regarding the development and deployment of AI, the US and China are currently leading the way, while the EU is lagging.[40] Given the importance of this technology, the EU does not want fragmentation of a market that means an impairment of innovation.

6 The Risk-Based Approach to Liability

The above discussion mainly concerned peculiar characteristics of AI. However, AI does have many characteristics that mirror or highly resemble classic sources of harm, and the corresponding risks they generate are likewise. Recognition of similarities could be useful as current liability regimes have been designed to address them. Provided that traditional risks can, to a certain degree, be isolated from other, disruptive characteristics of AI, current concepts can be applied. They should be

[40] Craglia (2018), p. 12.

applied since the liability regimes that are in force today are well-oiled systems that have passed the test of time.

"Risk-based regulation is commonly taken to mean that regulators operate decision-making frameworks and procedures to prioritize regulatory activities and the deployment of resources according to an assessment of the risks that regulated firms pose to the regulator's objectives."[41] The application of risk-based regulation entails assessment of the risk, a process which involves various methodologies and processes.[42] The underlying principle of this approach is the following: "the greater the potential for harm, the more stringent the requirements and the more far-reaching the intervention by means of regulatory instruments".[43] However, even within the EU, the risk-based approach does not materialize in the same way. Rather, it depends on the field of application and desired goals set by the lawmaker, as exemplified in both the GDPR and the Digital Services Act.[44] This regulatory technique is an expression of a technocratic approach to governance, which aims at avoiding "over-regulation, legalistic and prescriptive rules, and the high costs of regulation".[45] Although the EU has been a champion of this approach recently, the risk-based approach has not been a hallmark of its regulation. Rather, national lawmakers have also employed it in the regulation of technology.[46]

Regulation of risk, however, has to impose a specific set of duties to a person to be effective. At a certain point, understanding of risk has to be embedded into traditional legal proceedings.

> When regulators seek to take formal enforcement action such as impose fines or institute prosecutions, they will then have to reconfigure the risk according to a legal framework. As Hawkins's research illustrates, what field officers may see as the relevant set of risks, and the correct data to support their claim, may not be the same as is recognized in law: events have to be reconstructed from the language of risk into one of duties and liabilities.[47]

Risk-based regulation of AI does not mean that all legal instruments regulating AI are supposed to recognize and treat the same risks. By analogy, legal instruments adopted by the EU in the area of data privacy do not recognize and regulate the same risks in a uniform fashion. De Gregorio and Dunn noted that different legal instruments might tackle different risks stemming even from the same technologies.[48] Similarly, a risk-based approach to AI does not mean that the same risks of AI will be regulated by different legal instruments. The risks might be different. Also, they

[41] Baldwin and Black (2016), p. 567.

[42] Hutter (2006); Alemanno (2013).

[43] Dataethikommision (2019).

[44] Proposal for a Regulation of the European Parliament and of the Council on a Single Market for Digital Services (Digital Services Act) and amending Directive 2000/31/EC (COM/2020/825 final).

[45] Macenaite (2017), p. 509.

[46] Black (2005), p. 510.

[47] Craglia (2018), p. 588.

[48] de Gregorio and Dunn (2021), p. 11.

might be the same but approached from different perspectives. However, legal instruments must not contradict each other and thereby impose either too heavy a regulatory burden or vague and confusing duties.

The risk-based regulation of liability is reflecting this approach as well. In the Parliament Resolution from 2020, there is a different treatment of AI depending on two criteria. First, the sector in which the system is employed (healthcare, transport, energy, and parts of the public sector) and second, whether there is a risk of significant and unavoidable harm to the affected persons (uses with a significant impact on the affected persons). For instance, strict liability will be applicable, if a particular AI system meets the requirements, namely, it is considered high-risk and, thus, merits different treatment. As has been pertinently observed, "(...) an AI-system that entails an inherent high risk and acts autonomously potentially endangers the general public to a much higher degree; (...) based on the legal challenges that AI-systems pose to the existing civil liability regimes, it seems reasonable to set up a common strict liability regime for those high-risk autonomous AI-systems".[49] Conversely, if the above criteria are not fulfilled, fault-based liability remains the default rule. Overall, the Resolution has been the subject of criticism.[50] However, this is only an invitation to the Commission to propose a text of a legally binding instrument and does not represent a final position of the EU Parliament. Moreover, the choice of specific categories of risk being linked to different rules of liability can be modified. Nevertheless, the Resolution is a signal of the acceptable approach to the EU Parliament as the final decision-maker in the legislative process and depicts what might be expected to become binding law.

Understanding different risks and the ability to isolate them would foster a proper regulatory response. The European Law Institute's *"Response to the public consultation on the White Paper: On Artificial Intelligence"*[51] advocates a targeted approach, whereby traditional physical risks would be tackled with current liability regimes, while social risks would require the use of more sophisticated regulatory techniques, or rather a combination of existing techniques that would target specific risks and sectors where they appear.[52] This proposal isolates risks that cannot be dealt with by present liability rules. Thereafter, it further curtails the target by isolating areas where the risk is materialized. Such an approach aims at shrinking the application of new and unreliable liability rules only to such situations that are strictly necessary. A final elaboration of the risk-based approach to liability regulation has been made by Christiane Wendehorst.[53] In order to determine a proper regulatory response, this author created a taxonomy of risks generated by AI. It consists of several classifications of risks that aid in determining a proper basis of

---

[49] Recital 3 of the Proposal.

[50] Antunes (2021); European Law Institute (2020).

[51] Ibid.

[52] The advocated approach includes a combination of a set of fully horizontal principles, a list of blacklisted AI practices, and a creation of a regulatory framework for defined high-risk applications.

[53] Dataethikommision (2019).

liability and addressees of liability. This author stresses the importance of differentiation between risks based on the type of harm, namely whether they are generated freely or under the influence of technology, whether they can harm an individual or an entire system, and whether a risk is a characteristic of the specific intended function.

The first attempt of the Commission to deal with the issue of AI regulation was in 2021 when it introduced the so-called AI Act.[54] This is a rather product-safety instrument that attempts at unifying standards for the development, marketing, and use of AI in the EU. In its essence, it operates with different categories of AI based on the risk they generate—it differentiates between four levels of risks: (i) unacceptable risks (Title II); (ii) high risks (Title III); (iii) limited risks (Title IV); (iv) minimal risks (Title IX). For each, it prescribes a different set of rules, with the exception of unacceptable risks that are prohibited. While it mainly deals with *ex ante* measures for risk regulation, AI Act plays an important role in the regulation of liability. In September 2022, the Commission issued two proposals—Proposal for an Artificial Intelligence Liability Directive[55] (hereinafter: AI Liability Directive) and a proposal for revised Product Liability Directive[56] (hereinafter: PLD Proposal). Both proposals should be addressed as a part of a single framework as they aim to be complementary. This is primarily evident through the question of addressees of liability—roughly speaking, AI Liability Directive regulates the liability of non-manufacturers while the PLD Proposal deals with those of manufacturers. Also, while AI Liability Directive is focused on fault-based liability, the PLD Proposal regulates strict liability. Analyzed individually, the former instrument embodies a risk-based approach more than the latter. However, this can be understood as they have different aims. As it will be explained in the next section, unlike the AI Liability Directive, the PLD Proposal does not have a limited goal of dealing exclusively with harms caused by AI.

AI Liability Directive is a completely new instrument with rather modest ambitions. As Wagner notes, "The provisions of the AI Liability Directive themselves remain rudimentary in another sense, as they are deeply interwoven with the provisions and definitions of the proposal for the AI Regulation, the so-called Artificial Intelligence Act."[57] For instance, AI Liability Directive adopts definitions of AI, high-risk AI, operators, and users by providing reference to the AI Act. If the aim was to follow the line of the reason of the EU Parliament expressed in the 2020 Resolution, it has not been done so as it fails to adopt strict liability and it does not

[54] Official title is: Proposal of the EU Commission for a Regulation of the European Parliament and of the Council laying down harmonised rules on Artificial Intelligence (Artificial Intelligence Act) and amending certain acts of the Union (AI Act), 21.4.2021, COM(2021) 206 final.

[55] Proposal of the EU Commission for a Directive of the European Parliament and of the Council adapting the rules on non-contractual civil liability in artificial intelligence (AIL-D), 28.9.2022, COM(2022) 496 final.

[56] Proposal of the EU Commission for a Directive of the European Parliament and of the Council on Liability for Defective Products (PL-D), 28.9.2022, COM(2022) 495 final.

[57] Wagner (2023), p. 11.

use notions of operators/backend operators. It is rather focused on the problem of information asymmetry caused by the use of AI.[58] This instrument does not apply to contractual liability and a couple of other fields of law.[59] A central part of the AI Liability Directive is the disclosure of information. It prescribes the defendant's duty to disclose evidence but limits this duty to high-risk AI systems. If it fails to comply, a national court shall presume the defendant's non-compliance with a relevant duty of care. It further lists rules under which courts should presume causality between a defendant's behavior and harm. It applies only to the operators of high-risk AI systems who breached duties under chapters 2 and 3 of Title III of the AI Act. "The AIL-D wants to include the measures according to the risk management system according to Art. 9 of the AI-Act in the consideration, although the concrete weight of the respective measures apart from the mentioned obligations remains unclear".[60] In the case of non-high-risk AI systems, the presumption of causality only applies where the national court considers it excessively difficult for the claimant to prove the causal link.[61]

The PLD Proposal aims at fixing errors and inconsistencies identified throughout decades of implementation in the Member States, as well as modernizing the framework to render it fit for emerging digital technologies. It expands the notion of a product to include software, extends liability to "components" of a product or services that are connected to the product, expands recognised damage (most notably to cover loss or corruption of data), adapts tests for defectiveness to digital technologies, deals with the effects of updates and machine learning to product liability, amends lists of addressees to include so-called "fulfillment providers", and includes online marketplaces as an addressee under certain circumstances. Further, it deals with the problem of information asymmetry and deteriorated position of an injured party by setting out disclosure obligations for potential tortfeasors and the rebuttable presumption of defectiveness of the product if the defendant does not submit any documents. It also introduces the rebuttable presumption of causality between the defectiveness of the product and the damage that has occurred, if the defectiveness has been proven beforehand and it is a typical course of events. Lastly, the PLD Proposal removes the 500 EUR liability cap that exists in the current instrument.[62]

A targeted approach to establishing a liability regime for AI might be an apt avenue. However, it does not solve the question of whether we need to demarcate AI from other technologies it interacts with. If we accept the answer to be affirmative, than we need to determine criteria for such demarcation.

---

[58] Spindler (2023), p. 30.

[59] Ibid, p. 33 et al.

[60] Ibid, p. 39.

[61] See Hacker (2022).

[62] Ibid.

7 AI-Specific or Technology-Neutral Approach

Regulation of liability is concerned with the detrimental consequences of a certain activity or phenomenon. We previously expounded on why AI deserves to be singled out for various reasons from a general liability regime. If that stipulation is accepted, the question is how can we determine specific consequences of AI that are relevant for liability law. As an emerging digital technology, AI is highly sophisticated and opaque, as we have seen. In some situations, we might not be able to fathom whether it caused harm or not. This question is not novel, however. Highly sophisticated human inventions had previously caused harm and tort law had dealt with it through adaptation or adoption of various doctrines, such as strict liability, a lowered burden of proof etc. A more complex question concerns the interaction of AI with other emerging technologies and their joint impact.

Emerging digital technologies are increasingly interconnected. Harm might occur when they act in concert. If we establish that AI deserves specific liability rules, one might wonder whether the same approach should be applied to all emerging digital technologies. This question is closely related to the one mentioned in part 3 where we discussed briefly how to define AI for purposes of civil liability. The task of defining AI in a legal document is hard due to the lack of overall consensus on the meaning of this term, as well as due to its changing (evolving) nature. From the perspective of civil liability, defining harmful consequences of this technology is hard as the differences compared to other sources of harm might be hard to differentiate. Similarly, even if we manage to overcome this impediment, it would be very hard to differentiate between AI and other emerging digital technologies with which it acts in concert. If, for example, the harm is caused by joint action of various components of a digital ecosystem, of which AI is only a part, it might be very hard to attribute liability to only one of them. The struggle might be even harder if different liability regimes would apply to different components of a digital ecosystem.

This dilemma is broader than a simple binary choice between technology-neutral and technology-specific approaches to liability. The former approach would treat harm via liability rules irrespective of its source. It would be blind to the specific characteristics of AI or its role in society. The latter approach would entail specific liability rules which would be applied strictly to AI. This approach, while being at first glance the preferred strategy, might entail equally a series of challenges, as we have seen. A third approach would be to treat AI, all other connected emerging technologies, as well as all activities surrounding a single AI, with the same liability rules. In the words of the German *Dataethikommision*, "the sociotechnical system as a whole must be considered, or in other words all the components of an algorithmic application, including all the people involved, from the development phase—for example, the training data used—right through to its implementation in an application environment and any evaluation and adjustment measures".[63,64]

On its part, the Expert group uses in its Report the umbrella term "emerging digital technologies" to assess challenges to current rules of liability. This can be understood as a materialization of the third approach. However, as the Report also recognizes, "[i]t is, therefore, necessary to consider adaptations and amendments to existing liability regimes, bearing in mind that, given the diversity of emerging digital technologies and the correspondingly diverse range of risks these may pose, it is impossible to come up with a single solution suitable for the entire spectrum of risks."[65] While there might be concerns to liability law caused by the joint impact of AI and other related technologies, a single set of rules which would govern them all might not be possible to achieve. Specific definitions can be provided for technologies recognized as emerging and digital, and which merit to be defined in the first place. Liability rules for emerging digital technologies might not be technology-neutral as the task is too difficult. Specifying rules for AI and each technology incrementally allows for flexibility to lawmakers as new rules can be attributed once the risks are familiar enough. Risks which stem from the joint impact of more technologies should be assessed jointly, but also only when they are familiar enough. At the same time, the addressees of the new rules would not be perplexed by the uncertainty of the terminology used, as specific rules are to be used for specific technologies, provided there is coherence between them. Finally, victims who suffered harm should be provided with clarity as their chances of obtaining compensation in a reasonable time should not deteriorate due to the complexity of AI and related technologies. A technology-specific approach to regulation of liability for AI is thus desirable. It should take into account specific risks of this technology as well as its joint impact with other emerging digital technologies.

The Commission proposals (AI Act, the AI Liability Directive, and the PLD Proposal) mutually differ. AI Act and the AI Liability Directive are devoted to AI as a technology. As mentioned above, the AI Liability Directive directly refers to the definition of AI contained in the AI Act. The main problem with such an approach is a lack of an appropriate definition of AI. This is one of the main criticisms of the AI Act ever since its introduction.[66] On the other hand, the PLD Proposal is technology-neutral as it does not use the definition of AI but rather expands the scope of the instrument to cover software as well as related services. As such, it has further reach and attempts to cover not only AI but other digital technologies. The PLD Proposal, if it remains in its current form, is likely to have more significant effects on the

[63] European Commission Directorate-General for Justice and Consumers (2019).

[64] Notably, the Dataethikommision uses the term algorithm instead of AI, but it does so arguably as the focus of its work is on the algorithmic impact on data in general, and not only on the impact of AI.

[65] European Commission Directorate-General for Justice and Consumers (2019), p. 5.

[66] For example: https://www.euractiv.com/section/digital/news/leading-meps-raise-the-curtain-on-draft-ai-rules/.

development of AI and other emerging digital technologies. This proposal mentions digital templates and versions of movable property, which aims to clarify that files for 3D printing are also covered.[67] It can be argued that the PLD Proposal is more significant also for other reasons, such as the inclusion of data, regulation of online marketplaces liability, and removal of the 500 EUR liability cap. Due to its ambitions, this instrument has the potential to trigger the Brussels effect, a soft power of the EU that may influence the development of product liability way beyond the EU.

8 Conclusion

Risk-oriented regulation of AI should be understood as a mosaic of many mechanisms that jointly seek to provide a balance between risks and benefits of this technology. Some mechanisms are designed to operate *ex-ante*, while others operate *ex-post*. The liability regime is only a part of the legal framework. Its main goal is to provide compensation to the injured party that is affordable and timely. However, liability and tort adjudication have broader policy impacts and should not be treated merely as dispute resolution mechanisms that settle the interests between the involved individuals.

AI is a technology that is often described as bearing transformative potential. It currently receives attention from regulators worldwide, due to the belief that it might influence today's settings of economy and life in general. This technology is transformative from a legal perspective as well. It requires rethinking legal concepts that have been in force for a long time. The most important characteristics of AI which disrupt current liability concepts are autonomy, opacity, and vulnerability. Autonomy is the ability of AI to conduct a decision-making process without or with a low degree of human assistance. Opacity refers to the complexity of AI that causes inexplicability of the decision-making process. Vulnerability means a high level of exposure of AI to cyberattacks, as well as the potential to malfunction due to the erroneous data it might process. These characteristics generate risks that require a rethinking of some of the long-lasting concepts of liability law. Some of the main risks concern the questions of an addressee of liability, the basis of liability, and of causation. A pool of potential parties to be held responsible consists of manufacturers, operators, users, keepers, and AI itself. Determining the appropriate basis of liability is a sensitive task that requires the regulator to choose between strict liability, fault-based liability, and product liability. There is also a possibility of combination in different scenarios. The problem of causation arises from the opacity of AI's decision-making. A multitude of actors, as well as the inexplicability of the decision-making process generate a hardship for traditional concepts surrounding provability. Moreover, an injured party might be worse off and the compensation might be hard and costly to receive.

[67] Wagner (2023), p. 14.

Understanding AI risks allows for the application of familiar liability concepts, provided they can be treated in isolation. Furthermore, the classification of risks allows for regulation that would be designed to meet the exact challenges they bring, while the general liability regime would remain untouched. In that respect, it is very important to understand that certain risks where AI is present are materialized when it acts in concert with other "emerging digital technologies". AI-specific regulation is connected with the broader problem of defining AI. The negotiations around AI Act attest to this problem. It seems that it is very hard to define AI in a legal document. By deciding to provide reference to the AI Act in the AI Liability Directive, the Commission bets that it can be done. While technology-specific liability instruments have the potential to be tailor-made, their potential is limited. The ambitions of the Commission in that respect are limited too, as the AI Liability Directive only mildly tweaks the liability rules. However, different levels of risk that AI generates are decisive for the application of these rules. On the other hand, the PLD Proposal has greater ambitions as it attempts to deal with product liability for modern digital technologies in general, rather than only AI. It does not differentiate between the duties and standards based on the level of risk the product generates. The two liability instruments, along with the AI Act, are still the subject of debate within the EU. It is hard to predict their final form and whether they will become law. As it seems today, the EU may decide to regulate liability for AI through its product liability framework, to pass on the adoption of other liability rules to the Member States with some exceptions, and to marry the final form of the harmonized liability rules for AI on the EU level to the AI Act.

References

Abbott R (2020) Reasonable Robot. Cambridge University Press

Alemanno A (2013) Regulating the European Risk Society. In: Alemanno A et al (eds) Better business regulation in a risk society. Springer

Antunes HS (2021) Civil liability applicable to artificial intelligence: a preliminary critique of the European Parliament Resolution of 2020. https://papers.ssrn.com/sol3/papers.cfm?abstract_id=3743242

Baldwin R, Black J (2016) Driving priorities in risk-based regulation: what's the problem? J Law Soc 43(4):565–595

Black J (2005) The emergence of risk-based regulation and the new public risk management in the United Kingdom. Public Law Autumn:512–549

Borghetti JS (2019) How can artificial intelligence be defective? In: Lohsee S, Schulze R, Staudenmayer D (eds) Liability for Artificial Intelligence and the Internet of Things: Münster Colloquia on EU Law and the Digital Economy IV. Nomos

Calo R (2017) Artificial intelligence policy: a primer and roadmap. UC Davis Law Rev 51:399–435

Craglia M (ed) (2018) Artificial intelligence: a European perspective. Publications Office of the European Union

Dataethikommision (2019) Opinion. https://www.bmj.de/DE/Themen/FokusThemen/Datenethikkommission/Datenethikkommission_EN_node.html

De Gregorio G, Dunn P (2021) Profiling under Risk-based Regulation: Bringing together the GDPR and the DSA. https://assets.ctfassets.net/iapmw8ie3ije/5EuxLPaUIsgGt7R6PgeuFK/c9269e55e10bb2a7a0b392624c08f4d0/De_Gregorio_Dunn_My_Data_is_Mine__1_.pdf

de Jong ER et al (2018) Judge-made risk regulation and tort law: an introduction. Eur J Risk Regul 9:6–13
Eidenmüller H (2019) Machine performance and human failure: how shall we regulate autonomous machines? J Bus Tech L 15(1):109–133
European Commission Directorate-General for Justice and Consumers (2019) Liability for artificial intelligence and other emerging digital technologies. Publications Office. https://data.europa.eu/doi/10.2838/25362
European Law Institute (2020) Response to the public consultation on the White Paper: on Artificial Intelligence – a European approach to excellence and trust. COM(2020) 65 final. https://www.europeanlawinstitute.eu/fileadmin/user_upload/p_eli/News_page/2020/ELI_Response_AI_White_Paper.pdf
European Law Institute (n.d.) Guiding principles for updating the product liability directive for the digital age. ELI innovation paper series. https://europeanlawinstitute.eu/fileadmin/user_upload/p_eli/Publications/ELI_Guiding_Principles_for_Updating_the_PLD_for_the_Digital_Age.pdf
Hacker P (2022) The European AI Liability Directives – critique of a half-hearted approach and lessons for the future. https://ssrn.com/abstract=4279796
Hildt E (2019) Artificial intelligence: does consciousness matter? Available via Frontiers in Psychology. https://www.frontiersin.org/articles/10.3389/fpsyg.2019.01535/full
Hutter BM (2006) Risk, regulation, and management. In: Taylor-Gooby P, Zinn J (eds) Risk in social science. Oxford University Press
Koch BA (2020) Liability for emerging digital technologies: an overview. JETL 11(2):115–136
Kysar D (2018) The public life of private law: tort law as a risk regulation mechanism. Eur J Risk Regul 9(1):48–65
Macenaite M (2017) The "riskification" of European data protection law through a two-fold shift. Eur J Risk Regul 8(3):506–540
Nilsson JN (2010) The quest for artificial intelligence: a history of ideas and achievements. Cambridge University Press
Open Philanthropy (2016) What should we learn from past AI forecasts? Available via Open Philanthropy. https://www.openphilanthropy.org/focus/global-catastrophic-risks/potential-risks-advanced-artificial-intelligence/what-should-we-learn-past-ai-forecasts
Reggia JA, Huang DW, Katz G (2015) Beliefs Concerning the Nature of Consciousness. J Conscious Stud 22:146–171
Rodríguez de las Heras Ballell T (2019) Legal challenges of artificial intelligence: modelling the disruptive features of emerging technologies and assessing their possible legal impact. Uniform Law Rev 24(2):302–314
Rothstein H et al (2013) Risk and the limits of governance: exploring varied patterns of risk-based governance across Europe. Regul Gov 7(2):212–235
Russell S, Norvig P (2009) Artificial intelligence: a modern approach, 3rd edn. Prentice Hall
Schirmer JE (2019) Artificial intelligence and legal personality: introducing "Teilrechtsfähigkeit": a partial legal status made in Germany. In: Wischmeyer T, Rademacher T (eds) Regulating artificial intelligence. Springer
Spindler G (2023) Different approaches for liability of artificial intelligence – pros and cons – the new proposal of the EU Commission on Liability for Defective Products and AI Systems. https://ssrn.com/abstract=4354468
Steinrötter B (2020) The (envisaged) legal framework for commercialisation of digital data within the EU: data protection law and data economic law as a conflicted basis for algorithm-based products and services. In: Ebers M, Navas S (eds) Algorithms and law. Cambridge University Press, Cambridge
Stone P et al (2016) Defining AI. In: Stone P et al (eds) Artificial intelligence and life in 2030. One hundred year study on artificial intelligence: report of the 2015–2016 study panel. Stanford University, Stanford California. http://ai100.stanford.edu/2016-report
Turner J (2019) Robot rules: regulating artificial intelligence. Palgrave Macmillan

van den Hoven van Genderen R (2018) Do we need new legal personhood in the age of robots and AI? In: Corrales M, Fenwick M, Forgó N (eds) Robotics, AI and the future of law. Springer
Wagner G (2019) Robot liability. In: Lohsee S, Schulze R, Staudenmayer D (eds) Liability for artificial intelligence and the Internet of Things: Münster Colloquia on EU Law and the Digital Economy IV. Nomos
Wagner G (2023) Liability rules for the digital age - aiming for the Brussels effect. https://ssrn.com/abstract=4320285
Wendehorst C (2020) Strict liability for AI and other emerging technologies. JETL 11(2):150–180
Zech H (2021) Liability for AI: public policy considerations. ERA Forum 22:147–158

Part III
AI and Issues of Responsibility and Adjudication

Attributing Conduct of Autonomous Software Agents with Legal Personality under International Law on State Responsibility

Samuli Haataja

Abstract This chapter considers attribution under international law on state responsibility in relation to the conduct of autonomous software agents (ASAs) with legal personality that are used to perform a state's cyber security functions. It examines the extent to which existing international law is applicable to wrongful conduct by ASAs, and the extent to which the technical autonomy and separate legal status of these entities problematizes the application of the law. Overall, it is argued that ASAs as legal entities are conceptually compatible with existing law, and that even where these entities are legally distinct from the human agents of the state, the link between these entities and the human beings responsible for their creation is sufficient to establish attribution under the law on state responsibility.

1 Introduction

This chapter considers responsibility for the conduct of autonomous software agents (ASAs) with legal personality, with a focus on attribution in international law on state responsibility. Its analysis is premised on a possible future scenario in which states have given a degree of legal personality to ASAs that are used to perform cyber security functions. In light of this future, this chapter explores the extent to which the law at present is capable of attributing internationally wrongful conduct by these agents to the state. The chapter is divided into two sections. The first section provides an overview of ASAs and autonomy in the cyber context, and examines the notion of legal personality for artificial agents. The second section outlines the rules on state responsibility and attribution as detailed in the International Law Commission's Articles on the Responsibility of States for Internationally Wrongful Acts, and

Part of this chapter appears in Haataja (2021).

S. Haataja (✉)
Griffith Law School, Griffith University, Gold Coast, Australia
e-mail: s.haataja@griffith.edu

A. Kornilakis et al. (eds.), *Artificial Intelligence and Normative Challenges*, Law, Governance and Technology Series 59,
https://doi.org/10.1007/978-3-031-41081-9_7

in the *Tallinn Manual 2.0 on the International Law Applicable to Cyber Operations*. It then examines the application of the rules surrounding attribution to wrongful conduct by ASAs, and the extent to which the technical autonomy and prospective separate legal status of these entities problematizes these rules. Overall, this chapter concludes that ASAs as legal entities are conceptually compatible with existing law, and that even where these entities are legally distinct from the human agents of the state, the link between these entities and the human beings responsible for their creation is sufficient to establish attribution under the law on state responsibility.

2 Autonomous Software Agents and Legal Personality?

2.1 Autonomous Software Agents

The legal issues surrounding the potential development and use of (electromechanical) autonomous weapons systems has been subject to high level international discussions in recent years.[1] Less attention, however, has been given to the issues surrounding ASAs capable of being used as 'autonomous cyber weapons.'[2]

An autonomous agent is defined in this chapter in technical terms as 'a system situated within and a part of an environment that senses that environment and acts on it, over time, in pursuit of its own agenda and so as to effect what it senses in the future.'[3] Software agents operate in computer systems, networks, databases and so on. An ASA is a software agent which has the ability to act within an environment in pursuit of its goal without direct or real-time human control. This broad technical definition and approach to autonomy means that a software agent has autonomy whether it uses artificial intelligence (AI) techniques like machine learning, or whether it simply follows pre-determined instructions in its coding.[4] Autonomy in this context is not to be conflated with self-governance or self-regulation in the way the term is used in the social sciences.

A useful example of the technical capabilities of an ASA comes from Stuxnet—the malicious software that was discovered in 2010 which was designed to undermine Iran's uranium enrichment program.[5] Stuxnet infected computers within Iran's Natanz enrichment facility and adjusted the frequency setting that determines the

---

[1] See *'Meeting of the High Contracting Parties to the Convention on Prohibitions or Restrictions on the Use of Certain Conventional Weapons which may be deemed to be Excessively Injurious or to have Indiscriminate Effects'* (Final Report, 13 December 2019) UN Doc CCW/MSP/2019/9.

[2] See, however, United Nations Institute for Disarmament Research (UNIDIR) (2017); Tsagourias and Buchan (2018), p. 203; Liivoja et al. (2019); Väljataga and Liivoja (2021). See also Tyugu (2012); Guarino (2013); Heinl (2014); Stuard and McGhee (2015).

[3] Franklin and Graesser (1997), p. 25.

[4] I rely on the account about the legally relevant features of autonomous systems by Tim McFarland. See McFarland (2020), pp. 28–51.

[5] Halliday and Borger (2010); Sanger (2012).

speed at which nuclear centrifuges are spun.[6] It used a number of features to prevent anti-virus and other security mechanisms from detecting it, and also made it appear to the human operators of the facility that the infected computers were operating normally.[7] Stuxnet is believed to have been responsible for causing physical damage to approximately 1000 centrifuges at Iran's uranium enrichment facility in Natanz.[8] While Stuxnet's authors had the technical ability to control Stuxnet through its command-and-control servers, given the non-networked nature of the Natanz facility it operated in, all of its functions were embedded within its code enabling it to operate autonomously.[9] Therefore, once activated, Stuxnet was capable of propagating, identifying the particular systems it targeted, and delivering its payload without any direct or real-time human control.

An illustration of the possible ways in which ASAs can be used in cyber operations comes from Mayhem—the system that won the 2016 Defense Advanced Research Projects Agency (DARPA) 'Cyber Grand Challenge' competition. For teams participating in the DARPA competition, the objective was to score points and avoid losing them by protecting the team's software from adversaries by finding and patching vulnerabilities and keeping the software available, functional and efficient, while exploiting vulnerabilities in adversary software.[10] However, all of this was to be done autonomously so that, once activated, each team's cyber reasoning system would perform its cyber security functions without any real-time human intervention. As such, Mayhem had the capacity to autonomously discover and patch software vulnerabilities, as well as to discover and exploit vulnerabilities in its adversaries' software.[11] It also had the ability to adapt so as to make strategic decisions about which vulnerabilities to patch or leave unpatched, which patches to use, which teams to attack and with what exploits, and how to allocate its resources in performing these functions.[12]

Stuxnet and Mayhem therefore had a significant degree of technical autonomy as they were able to act within their environment in pursuit of their goals without direct or real-time human control.[13] Developments in AI are expected to enable even higher degrees of autonomy, with experts predicting developments in reinforcement machine learning to be particularly significant in cyber operations.[14] For example, this may enable the development of ASAs that are assigned a particular goal without the specific ways in which the goal are achieved being predetermined. The ASA can then experiment and develop the strategies through which to achieve the goal

[6] Falliere et al. (2011), pp. 41–43.

[7] Ibid pp. 14, 48–9.

[8] Warrick (2011).

[9] Falliere et al. (n 6), p. 3.

[10] Avgerinos et al. (2018), pp. 52–53. See also Lohr (2016).

[11] Avgerinos et al. (n 10).

[12] Ibid, pp. 56–57.

[13] This definition is based on McFarland (n 4), p. 35. See also McFarland (2021).

[14] See Buchanan et al. (2020), p. 25.

itself.[15] Given the broad approach to autonomy adopted in this chapter, however, these systems are also captured within the definition of an ASA.

2.2 Artificial Agents and Legal Personality

As a means of addressing concerns about the accountability and responsibility of sophisticated autonomous systems, the possibility that artificial agents of this kind are given a special legal status has been raised. For example, in its 2016 Report on Robotics, the European Union Parliament outlined a range of issues relating to robots that need to be considered in the future when legislating around the use of autonomous systems such as autonomous vehicles and health care robots.[16] The report highlighted that robots with larger amounts of autonomy will require us to consider whether existing rules around liability are sufficient or whether new principles are required to provide clarity on the legal liability for the actions of robots causing harm.[17] According to the report, the impact assessment for any such future legal instrument should consider, among other things, the implications of:

> creating a specific legal status for robots in the long run, so that at least the most sophisticated autonomous robots could be established as having the status of electronic persons responsible for making good any damage they may cause, and possibly applying electronic personality to cases where robots make autonomous decisions or otherwise interact with third parties independently.[18]

This notion of robots having a special legal status as 'electronic persons' has been met with scepticism and criticism,[19] and many argue that there is not yet a practical need for such a status.[20] However, given how different legal systems have granted a degree of personhood to various non-human entities (including animals, ships, temples and idols), there is nothing preventing states from granting artificial agents a degree of legal personality.[21]

In addition to electromechanical autonomous systems, the question of the legal status of software agents has also emerged, including whether these entities could or

[15] Ibid, pp. 17–18.

[16] Delvaux (2016).

[17] Ibid, pp. 6–7.

[18] Ibid, p. 18.

[19] See, for example, 'Open Letter to the European Commission Artificial Intelligence and Robotics' (2018) http://www.robotics-openletter.eu. See also Bryson et al. (2017), p. 273.

[20] See, for example, Nevejans (2016), pp. 14–16.

[21] See Chopra and White (2020), p. 160. See also Kurki (2019); Chesterman (2020), p. 819. On the prospect of robot rights, including in the military context, see Singer (2010), 403–407.

should have some form of legal personality.[22] Samir Chopra and Laurence White argue that, while at this stage the law of agency is the most appropriate doctrinal mechanism to deal with the issues relating to artificial agents (both virtual and mechanical),[23] a degree of legal personality is possible in the future.[24] Similarly, others argue that there are practical reasons for why some form of personhood is possible as a way of ensuring there is liability for the actions of these agents, particularly where they make unpredictable decisions.[25] For example, Tomasz Pietrzykowski maintains that the most compelling reason why artificial agents should have some form of personhood (instead of being regarded as mere machines) relates to the benefits of this status for people who could avoid being liable for the effects of the decisions made by these agents. This is the case especially where these agents are capable of learning and adapting their behaviour in dynamic environments and thus where all of the decisions they make are not predictable to the people who programmed or used them.[26] Rafał Michalczak also argues that, even in relation to the current capabilities of 'intelligent software,' the unpredictability of actions taken by the software 'create a gap in the causal link between the actions of the user and the resulting consequences' thus creating conceptual complications for the law.[27]

A similar concern has been highlighted by the United Nations Commission on International Trade Law (UNCITRAL) in relation to the use of electronic agents in contract formation. In an explanatory note to a provision relating to the use of automated systems for contract formation, it is noted that while currently the actions of these agents are attributed to natural or legal persons on the basis that they are only capable of performing within their pre-programmed technical structures, if they begin to act more intelligently and modify their own instructions or develop new instructions, then the law's existing paradigm may no longer be applicable.[28]

Therefore, given the increasing social, political, and economic interactions with these agents, and their growing technical capacity to perform legally significant actions, it has been suggested that a form of legal personality may be possible in the

[22] On how software entities could obtain a degree of legal personality under domestic law within existing legal frameworks and without a legislative act, see Bayern (2016), p. 297. See also Burri (2018).

[23] Chopra and White (n 21), pp. 22–23.

[24] Ibid, pp. 186–188. They argue that, as a relational concept, legal personality of artificial agents will depend on the scope and extent of the social, political and economic interactions with these agents. Further, that the decision to accord or refuse this status will ultimately be based on whether there is a pragmatic need to do so based on the results of this status (opposed to being a decision made based on conceptual claims about this status).

[25] See Pietrzykowski (2017); Michalczak (2017); Hage (2017), p. 255.

[26] Pietrzykowski (2017), p. 64.

[27] Michalczak (2017), p. 98.

[28] See United Nations Commission on International Trade Law, *United Nations Convention on the Use of Electronic Communications in International Contracts* (United Nations 2007), https://www.uncitral.org/pdf/english/texts/electcom/06-57452_Ebook.pdf.

future.[29] While the exact form and the extent of rights and liabilities associated with this status would likely differ across states, it is likely to involve a form of dependent personality where human actors are needed to enforce any rights and obligations held by these entities (similar to a corporation).[30] Some have also proposed personhood for 'highly interdependent cyber systems' which would be structured similar to an international organisation.[31]

As such, there is a possibility that ASAs such as Stuxnet, Mayhem or other systems exercising cyber security functions with a high level of technical autonomy are also given a form of legal personhood. Similar to privatising a state-owned company or creating a company as a separate legal entity, this could be done in an effort to limit or avoid responsibility for the actions of the ASA. The extent of legal personality, including the rights and obligations that these entities have, as well as who has the ability to enforce these rights, can vary among states. Nonetheless, these entities would constitute 'legal persons' within the legal system in which they were granted this status. Where conduct by these agents affects legal rights of other states internationally—such as where they are used in offensive cyber operations or as active cyber defence measures—then their conduct can result in violations of international law and raise questions about state responsibility.

3 International Law on State Responsibility

3.1 Overview of the Law

International law on state responsibility is detailed in the International Law Commission's (ILC) Articles on the Responsibility of States for Internationally Wrongful Acts (ILC Articles).[32] The *Tallinn Manual 2.0 on the International Law Applicable to Cyber Operations* (Tallinn Manual) provides a detailed account about how the rules on state responsibility are considered to apply to state activities in cyberspace specifically.[33] While neither of these are legally binding documents, much of the ILC Articles are widely recognised as an authoritative statement of customary international law,[34] and the Tallinn Manual rules in relation to state responsibility largely align with the ILC articles in terms of the substantive content of the law.

[29] See Chopra and White (n 21), pp. 186–188.

[30] On the distinction between dependent and independent legal personality, see ibid. 159–61. See also Chen and Burgess (2019), pp. 73, 81.

[31] See Kushwaha et al. (2021), pp. 287–288.

[32] International Law Commission, *Responsibility of States for Internationally Wrongful Acts*, UNGA Res 56/83 (12 December 2001) UN Doc A/RES/56/83 ('ILC Articles').

[33] Schmitt (2017).

[34] See *Report of the Secretary-General on responsibility of States for internationally wrongful acts: comments and information received from Governments*, UNGA Res 71/79 (21 April 2016) UN Doc A/71/79; *Report of the Secretary-General on responsibility of States for internationally*

The law on state responsibility consists of secondary rules that determine the circumstances under which a state is responsible for violations of international law. Under this area of law there must be conduct (either an act or omission) that is attributable to a state (the responsible state) which amounts to a violation of a primary rule of international law (the internationally wrongful act), that is, against an international obligation owed to another state (the injured state). Provided that no circumstances precluding wrongfulness exist, such as necessity or self-defence, then the injured state will have the right to a remedy.

In the cyber context, an internationally wrongful act can consist of a cyber operation that is in violation of a primary rule of international law. For example, the use of Stuxnet is generally considered to have constituted a use of force in violation of article 2(4) of the UN Charter because it caused physical damage in Iran.[35] Therefore, provided there were no applicable circumstances precluding wrongfulness (such as self-defence), Stuxnet's use would constitute an internationally wrongful act by the responsible state(s).[36]

For a state to be responsible for an internationally wrongful act, however, the conduct in question must be attributed to it. As abstract legal entities, states can only act through human agents and representatives.[37] The rules on attribution provide the process through which the conduct of a natural person becomes an 'act of state' for which the state is responsible.[38] This is clear where, for example, a state organ such as its armed forces engages in an activity amounting to a violation of international law. However, where the conduct is by other entities, such as private individuals or corporations, the rules of attribution are more complex. As such, the actor in question and its connection to the state will determine whether state responsibility arises in relation to the international wrongful act in question. In the cyber context, attribution can be particularly problematic on a technical level given the frequent use of proxy actors and other technical means to obfuscate the true geographical origin of the operation.[39] However, as long as attribution can be achieved on a technical level, then the rules on state responsibility provide the legal criteria used to determine whether the conduct can be attributed to a state.

A common issue raised in relation to autonomous systems is the question of fault or intention and how—or to what degree—the autonomy of a system impacts on this for the purposes of responsibility. Under the law on state responsibility, the ILC Articles adopt the approach that the intention of the state is only relevant to the extent

wrongful acts: compilation of decisions of international courts, tribunals and other bodies. UNGA Res 71/80 (21 April 2016) UN Doc A/71/80.

[35] See Haataja and Akhtar-Khavari (2018), pp. 99, 109–111.

[36] There is, however, debate around other primary rules of international law and the threshold at which cyber operations amount to violations of international law (especially sovereignty and non-intervention). See Schmitt and Vihul (2017), p. 1639; Corn and Taylor (2017), p. 207.

[37] See Crawford (2013), p. 113.

[38] Ibid.

[39] See Tsagourias and Farrell (2020), p. 941.

that it is an element required to establish a violation of an international legal obligation.[40] In other words, intention is not relevant for the purposes of establishing state responsibility, but it can be relevant for establishing a violation of a primary rule of international law. For example, if a state uses a cyber operation that amounts to a violation of another state's sovereignty, the intention of the responsible state will not be relevant because there is no specific element of intention required for establishing such a violation.[41] In contrast, whether a cyber operation amounts to a violation of the non-intervention principle requires that the responsible state intended to coerce the target state in relation to matters it has the right to decide freely.[42]

3.2 *Attribution of Conduct by Autonomous Software Agents with Legal Personality*

As such, whether conduct by an ASA amounts to an internationally wrongful act will depend on the primary rule of international law in question. However, the conduct in question must also be attributed to the state for it to be responsible.[43] There are various grounds on which this can be done, including where the conduct is by a state organ; where the conduct is by a private entity that has been empowered to exercise inherently governmental functions; and where the conduct is by private persons or groups that are acting under the instructions of, or under the direction or control of a state. While the law on state responsibility is largely indifferent to the legal status (if any) of an entity within a state's domestic legal system, considering a scenario in which ASAs have a degree of legal personality allows analysis and application of the law to the conduct of the ASA (opposed to merely the conduct of the human beings using these capabilities). Accordingly, each of these bases for attribution will be considered in relation to the conduct of ASAs with a separate legal status—that is, agents that are considered legally distinct from the human agents of the state.

[40] According to the ILC, '[i]n the absence of any specific requirement of a mental element in terms of the primary obligation, it is only the act of a State that matters, independently of any intention.' Crawford (2002), p. 84.

[41] Liivoja et al. (n 2), p. 19; Schmitt (2021).

[42] Tsagourias (2020), p. 55.

[43] On the attribution of state responsibility for cyber operations more generally, see, for example, Shackelford and Andres (2011), pp. 971, 986–993; Tsagourias (2012), pp. 229, 236–240; Margulies (2013), pp. 496, 506–516; Banks (2017), p. 29. See also Payne and Finlay (2017), p. 35.

3.2.1 State Organs (Article 4) and Private Actors Empowered to Exercise Governmental Authority (Article 5)

According to article 4 of the ILC Articles, states are responsible for the wrongful conduct of their organs.[44] This is echoed in Rule 15 of the Tallinn Manual which provides that cyber operations conducted by state organs are attributable to the state.[45] The ILC provides that a state's organ includes 'any person or entity which has that status in accordance with the internal law of the State.'[46] Further, pursuant to article 5 of the ILC Articles, the conduct of persons or entities that are not state organs but have been empowered to exercise elements of governmental authority can also be attributed to the state.[47] Similarly, the Rule 15 Tallinn Manual states that, in addition to state organs, persons or entities empowered by domestic law to exercise elements of governmental authority are attributable to the state.[48]

Under article 7 of the ILC articles, the conduct of a state organ is attributable to a state 'even if it exceeds its authority or contravenes instructions' provided that 'the organ, person or entity acts in that capacity'.[49] The same applies to the conduct of entities that have been empowered to exercise elements of governmental authority.[50]

Conceptually, it is not difficult to view ASAs as entities for the purpose of state responsibility analysis. Articles 4 and 5 of the ILC Articles make explicit reference to 'entities' and, while article 8 only refers directly to 'persons and groups', its commentary also makes reference to 'persons or entities'.[51] An entity is generally understood as 'a thing with distinct and independent existence'.[52] In law, the notion of an entity has a more specific meaning, generally referring to either an individual, an association, or other kind of legal or administrative arrangement. However, the ILC Articles use the term 'entity' in a more general sense, meaning that the entity in question (be it an individual or group) does not need to have any distinct legal status under a state's domestic law.[53] As such, the term can be used to refer to various non-human entities both in descriptive terms (as things with a separate existence) and in legal terms (as entities with some form of legal agency, such as a corporation). Similarly, the term 'organ' is used in the ILC articles 'in its most general sense' and

[44] ILC Articles (n 32) Art 4.; Crawford (n 40), p. 94.

[45] Schmitt (n 33), p. 87.

[46] ILC Articles (n 32) Art 4.

[47] Ibid, Art 5.

[48] Schmitt (n 33), p. 87.

[49] ILC Articles (n 32), Art 7.

[50] Ibid. See also Schmitt (n 18), pp. 90–91.

[51] Crawford (n 40), pp. 94, 100, 110.

[52] Stevenson (2010).

[53] The commentary notes that 'person or entity' 'is used in a broad sense to include any natural or legal person, including an individual office holder, a department, commission or other body exercising public authority, etc.' See Crawford (n 40), p. 98. Also, in relation to a draft article on attribution of conduct by private individuals, the term 'individual' was replaced with 'person' so as to cover natural and legal persons. See de Frouville (2010), p. 262.

covers any organ regardless of its legal status, hierarchy or how it is characterised within the state's domestic legal structures.[54] This is echoed in the Tallinn Manual.[55] Accordingly, there would be no conceptual difficulty in considering an ASA as a state organ and an agent of the state under the law of state responsibility.

Even where an entity does not form part of or have the status of a state organ under the state's domestic law, it is possible for it to be equated to one under international law where it acts in 'complete dependence' on the state of which it merely constitutes an instrument.[56] As ASAs need to be programmed by human beings and would likely require some form of registration as legal entities if they have a separate legal status, provided a state is involved in creating this entity and in fact exercises complete control over it, then the entity could be deemed a *de facto* organ of the state.[57] Thus, even where an ASA were not considered an agent of a state organ under a state's domestic law, provided it can be seen to clearly function as one and merely act as an instrument of the state that has a 'great degree of control' over it, then its conduct can be attributed to the state.[58] In this scenario, regardless of its characterisation or legal status as an agent under a state's domestic law, if the ASA is in complete dependence on the state to the extent that it is simply acting as an instrument of it, then it is possible to equate that entity to a state organ for the purposes of attribution.

Conversely, in case an ASA is not considered an agent of a state organ, it is possible to attribute its conduct to the state where it has been empowered to exercise governmental functions pursuant to article 5 of the ILC articles.[59] Here too the ILC takes a broad view of the notion of an entity and notes that it can refer to a range of bodies, including 'public corporations, semi-public entities, public agencies' and even private companies.[60] Importantly, however, this entity has to have been authorised to exercise what are 'quintessential government functions', such as the conduct of foreign affairs, for its conduct to be attributable.[61] Therefore, where an ASA with a degree of legal personality is not acting in complete dependence of a

---

[54] Crawford (n 40), pp. 95–96.

[55] The Tallinn Manual authors adopt a broad construction of the term organ and maintain that it includes all persons or entities with that status in the state's domestic laws. Schmitt (n 33), p. 87.

[56] *Case Concerning the Application of the Convention on the Prevention and Punishment of the Crime of Genocide (Bosnia and Herzegovina v Serbia and Montenegro)* ('*Bosnian Genocide*') (Judgment) [2007] ICJ Rep 43, p. 205, cited in ibid., p. 88.

[57] Crawford (n 37), p. 125. Crawford writes that according to the ICJ in *Nicaragua*, this depends on '(a) whether the nonstate entity was created by the state; (b) whether state involvement exceeded the provision of training and financial assistance; (c) whether complete (as opposed to a degree of or potential for) control was exercised in fact; and (d) whether the state selected, installed or paid the political leaders of the group.'

[58] *Bosnian Genocide* (n 56), p. 205, cited in Schmitt (n 33), p. 88.

[59] Christopher Ford makes a similar point in relation to autonomous weapons systems. See Ford (2017), pp. 413, 476.

[60] Crawford (n 40), p. 100.

[61] Schmitt (n 33), p. 89.

state but has nonetheless been empowered by law to exercise certain elements of government authority—such as defence of government and military networks—it is possible for its actions to be attributed to the state on this basis.

Moreover, when an ASA that is a state organ (either *de jure* or *de facto*) and acts outside the scope of its instructions, the state will be responsible provided the ASA acted with apparent state authority. While it is impossible for an ASA to act contrary to its programming and therefore *ultra vires*, or in a 'private' capacity different from what is has been programmed to do, it is possible for it to act in an unpredictable way resulting in unintended effects. This is particularly the case where complex systems enabled by AI techniques are used which increase the likelihood of unpredictable effects.[62] However, given the approach to attribution under article 7, the state would be responsible for its conduct even where these effects are caused. Hypothetically, if an ASA were capable of acting *ultra vires*, this conduct would likely occur under the apparent authority of the state and also be attributable. For example, if the *ultra vires* conduct occurred while the ASA was in pursuit of its (human determined) goal—for instance, where it had been created and registered to exercise a state's cyber security functions, and it made use of a state's cyber infrastructure—then these factors would likely be sufficient so as to give the appearance of state authority for the ASA's conduct.

3.2.2 Conduct by Persons or Groups Instructed, Directed or Controlled by a State (Article 8)

As such, the conduct of state organs and other entities that have been empowered to exercise governmental authority are attributable to a state. Normally, however, states are not responsible for the conduct of private persons or entities. An exception to this is contained in article 8 of the ILC articles which provides that a person's or group's conduct will be considered an act of the state if they are 'in fact acting on the instructions of, or under the direction or control of, that State in carrying out the conduct.'[63] Consistent with the ILC articles, the Rule 17 of the Tallinn Manual states that '[c]yber operations by a non-State actor are attributable to a State when: (a) engaged in pursuant to its instructions or under its directions or control [...]'.[64] While Article 7 of the ILC articles provides, as discussed above, that the actions of state organs that are *ultra vires* are attributable to the state unless performed in a private capacity, this provision does not apply to conduct attributed under article 8. However, the commentary to article 8 stipulates that where a non-state actor acts in contravention of instructions or directions given by a state, if the 'unlawful or

[62] Scharre (2016), pp. 11–15.

[63] ILC Articles (n 32), Art 8.

[64] Schmitt (n 33), p. 94.

unauthorized conduct was really incidental to the mission' and not 'clearly beyond it', then the state will be responsible.[65]

Under article 8, where an ASA is considered a private entity and not an organ of a state or empowered to exercise elements of governmental authority, its conduct can be attributed to the state provided it is found to be acting under the instructions, directions, or control of a state. Any ASA, regardless of its technical sophistication or legal status, must at some point in time have been designed, developed and used by human beings and given some direction in terms of its goal or purpose, or the parameters of its functioning.[66] This is irrespective of whether it operates according to pre-determined rules or using AI enabled techniques. Further, where an ASA has a degree of legal personhood under a state's domestic law, there would need to be rules and processes around its registration and the enforcement of its rights. While there is some debate about the specificity or generality of instructions required under the law in this context,[67] even if only general instructions are given (for example, its high-level goal) it would suffice because any specific capabilities it decides to execute would be done in pursuit of achieving that goal. For these reasons, where an ASA receives instructions or directions from state actors, even where it has a separate legal status from those actors, its conduct can be attributable under article 8.

The alternative basis for attribution under article 8 is where an ASA is under the 'effective control' of a state.[68] For example, according to the Tallinn Manual, a state is in effective control over the actions of a non-state actor where it 'determines the execution and course of the specific operation', where the state has 'the ability to cause constituent activities of the operation to occur', or where the state is able to order the cessation of those activities that are underway.[69] Given the approach to autonomy adopted in this chapter—that autonomy is a form of control exercised in advance opposed to real-time—an ASA would remain under the control of a state once it has been deployed or activated. Even if an ASA operates for extended periods of time in closed networks without direct or real-time human control, this does not mean the state that created the ASA could claim that it was not under its control in an attempt to avoid responsibility for its conduct. Additionally, the ASA would not be outside the effective control of the state when the low level steps the ASA decides to take to achieve its purpose are unforeseeable, as it will only be capable of operating according to the capabilities it has in pursuit of its overall high level goal.

Therefore, if a state provides an ASA with a degree of legal personality within its domestic legal system, under international law there is little difficulty in conceptualising these as entities or organs within existing rules on state

[65] Crawford (n 40), p. 113.

[66] On the various ways in which human beings are involved in the design, development, testing and use of autonomous weapons systems, see Noorman and Johnson (2014), pp. 51, 58–60.

[67] Crawford (n 37), p. 145.

[68] This is the standard of control adopted by the ICJ and the Tallinn Manual. See Schmitt (n 33), p. 96.

[69] Ibid.

responsibility. This is irrespective of the exact parameters and extent of that agent's legal personality, as the important factor instead is the relationship of that agent with the state and the types of functions it performs.[70] Also, having a degree of legal personhood would likely require some form of registration of those ASAs as legal entities by human beings in the state. Further, even technically sophisticated ASAs with machine learning capabilities are systems created through processes involving human beings at various stages in their development and use.[71] Accordingly, all ASAs will retain a connection to a state's human agents, and the relationship between these agents is crucial in establishing attribution. And even where an ASA acts in an unpredictable way and causes unintended effects, given the way in which the rules of state responsibility are formulated and the approach to fault, the state will be responsible for its conduct.[72]

However, like with cyber operations generally, the ability to attribute the conduct of an ASA on a technical level makes legal attribution difficult. In this respect the legal issues surrounding attribution of the conduct of ASAs to the state—even to those ASAs that have some form of legal personality—are not novel. In fact, compared to cyber operations using, for example, open-source tools and techniques, attributing the conduct of ASAs that have a separate legal status may be less challenging particularly if they have been registered by human actors in a particular state. As such, existing rules on attribution of conduct in the law on state responsibility are compatible with a scenario in which ASAs that perform cyber security functions have a separate legal status under a state's domestic law. Ultimately these agents must be created and programmed by human beings, they are likely to have some form of registration where they exist as separate legal entities, and it is these links to human beings through which their conduct can be attributed. In other words, creating a separate legal status cannot be used as a means of avoiding or obfuscating responsibility for the conduct of ASAs under international law.

[70] As the ILC notes, the state 'is held responsible for the conduct of all of the organs, instrumentalities and officials which form part of its organization and act in that capacity, whether or not they have separate legal personality under its internal law.' Crawford (n 40), p. 93. While under the law on state responsibility the state is responsible and not the agent individually, there are parallels with the 'cog in the machine' doctrine in international criminal law that has been considered in relation to the actions of autonomous weapons systems. See Ohlin (2016), p. 1.

[71] Johnson (2015), pp. 707, 712–713. Even in relation to a futuristic superintelligence, humans will be involved in designing the technology and therefore responsible for it. See Johnson and Verdicchio (2019), pp. 639, 645.

[72] This is provided the primary rule of international law in question does not have intention as a constituent element. See Schmitt (n 41).

4 Conclusion

This chapter considered the rules on attribution of conduct under international law on state responsibility in relation to ASAs used by states in cyber operations. It focused on the conduct of ASAs as entities separate from the human agents of the state using a scenario in which ASAs have been given a degree of legal personality within a state's domestic legal system. It demonstrated that ASAs in this context are conceptually compatible with the rules of state responsibility, and that the rules surrounding attribution of conduct can be extended to artificial non-human agents. Given the approach of the ILC to fault and provisions that provide that states are generally responsible for the conduct of their agents even where it is *ultra vires*, any unpredicted or unintended effects caused by ASAs would also be attributable. Accordingly, even technically sophisticated ASAs in a hypothetical scenario in which they have a separate legal status will have a link to the human beings responsible for their creation or registration, and that link is sufficient to establish attribution under the law on state responsibility.

References

Avgerinos T et al (2018) The mayhem cyber reasoning system. IEEE Secur Priv 16(2):52–60

Banks W (2017) State responsibility and attribution of cyber intrusions after Tallinn 2.0. Tex Law Rev 95(7):1487

Bayern S (2016) The implications of modern business-entity law for the regulation of autonomous systems. Eur J Risk Regul 7(2):297–309

Bryson JJ, Diamantis ME, Grant TD (2017) Of, for, and by the people: the legal lacuna of synthetic persons. Artif Intell Law 25:273–291

Buchanan B, Bansemer J, Cary D et al (2020) Automating cyber attacks: hype and reality. Centre for Security and Emerging Technology. https://cset.georgetown.edu/publication/automating-cyber-attacks

Burri T (2018) Free movement of algorithms: artificially intelligent persons conquer the European Union's internal market. In: Barfield W, Pagallo U (eds) Research handbook on the law of artificial intelligence. Edward Elgar Publishing

Chen J, Burgess P (2019) The boundaries of legal personhood: how spontaneous intelligence can problematise differences between humans, artificial intelligence, companies and animals. Artif Intell Law 27:73–92

Chesterman S (2020) Artificial intelligence and the limits of legal personality. Int Comp Law Q 69(4):819–844

Chopra S, White L (2020) A legal theory for autonomous artificial agents. University of Michigan Press

Corn GP, Taylor R (2017) Sovereignty in the age of cyber. AJIL Unbound 111:207

Crawford J (2002) The International Law Commission's articles on state responsibility: introduction, text and commentaries. Cambridge University Press

Crawford J (2013) State responsibility: the general part. Cambridge University Press

de Frouville O (2010) Attribution of conduct to the state: private individuals. In: Crawford J et al (eds) The law of international responsibility. Oxford University Press

Delvaux M (2016) Report with recommendations to the Commission on Civil Law Rules on Robotics. European Parliament Committee on Legal Affairs Report. https://www.europarl.europa.eu/doceo/document/A-8-2017-0005_EN.html

Falliere N, Murchu L, Chien E (2011) W32.Stuxnet Dossier. Version 1.4. Symantec. https://www.symantec.com/content/en/us/enterprise/media/security_response/whitepapers/w32_stuxnet_dossier.pdf

Ford C (2017) Autonomous weapons and international law. SC Law Rev 69(2):413–478

Franklin S, Graesser A (1997) Is it an agent, or just a program? A taxonomy for autonomous agents. In: Müller JP, Wooldridge MJ, Jennings NR (eds) Intelligent agents III: agent theories, architectures, and languages. Springer

Guarino A (2013) Autonomous intelligent agents in cyber offence. In: Podins K, Stinissen J, Maybaum M (eds) 5th international conference on cyber conflict. NATO CCDCOE Publications

Haataja S, Akhtar-Khavari A (2018) Stuxnet and international law on the use of force: an informational approach. Camb Int Law J 7(1):99–121

Haataja S (2021) Autonomous cyber capabilities and attribution in the law of state responsibility. In: Väljataga A, Liivoja R (eds) Autonomous cyber capabilities under international law. NATO CCDCOE Publications

Hage J (2017) Theoretical foundations for the responsibility of autonomous agents. Artif Intell Law 25:255–271

Halliday J, Borger J (2010) Nuclear plants likely target of foiled cyber sabotage. The Guardian. https://www.theguardian.com/world/2010/sep/25/iran-cyber-hacking-nuclear-plants

Heinl CH (2014) Artificial (intelligent) agents and active cyber defence: policy implications. In: Brangetto P, Maybaum M, Stinissen J (eds) 6th international conference on cyber conflict. NATO CCDCOE Publications

Johnson D (2015) Technology with no human responsibility? J Bus Ethics 127(4):707

Johnson D, Verdicchio M (2019) AI, agency and responsibility: the VW fraud case and beyond. AI Society 34:639–647

Kurki V (2019) A theory of legal personhood. Oxford University Press

Kushwaha N, Giles K, Singer T et al (2021) Cyber personhood. In: Jančárková T, Lindström L, Visky G et al (eds) 13th international conference on cyber conflict: going viral. NATO CCDCOE Publications

Liivoja R, Naagel M, Väljataga A (2019) Autonomous cyber capabilities under international law. NATO Cooperative Cyber Defence Centre of Excellence Working Paper, https://ccdcoe.org/library/publications/autonomous-cyber-capabilities-under-international-law

Lohr S (2016) Stepping up security for an internet-of-things world. The New York Times. https://www.nytimes.com/2016/10/17/technology/security-internet.html

Margulies M (2013) Sovereignty and cyber attacks: technology's challenge to the law of state responsibility. Melb J Int Law 14:496–519

McFarland T (2020) Autonomous weapon systems and the law of armed conflict. Cambridge University Press

McFarland T (2021) The concept of autonomy. In: Väljataga A, Liivoja R (eds) Autonomous cyber capabilities under international law. NATO CCDCOE Publications

Michalczak R (2017) Animals' race against the machines. In: Kurki VAJ, Pietrzykowski T (eds) Legal personhood: animals, artificial intelligence and the unborn. Springer

Nevejans N (2016) European civil law: rules in robotics. Technical report. Directorate-General for Internal Policies, European Parliament. https://www.europarl.europa.eu/RegData/etudes/STUD/2016/571379/IPOL_STU(2016)571379_EN.pdf

Noorman M, Johnson D (2014) Negotiating autonomy and responsibility in military robots. Ethics Inf Technol 16(1):51–62

Ohlin J (2016) The combatant's stance: autonomous weapons on the battlefield. Int Law Stud 92(1)

Open Letter to the European Commission Artificial Intelligence and Robotics (2018). http://www.robotics-openletter.eu

Payne C, Finlay L (2017) Addressing obstacles to cyber-attribution: a model based on state response to cyber-attack. Geo Wash Law Rev 49(3):535–638
Pietrzykowski T (2017) The idea of non-personal subjects of law. In: Kurki VAJ, Pietrzykowski T (eds) Legal personhood: animals, artificial intelligence and the unborn. Springer
Sanger D (2012) Obama order sped up wave of cyberattacks against Iran. The New York Times. http://www.nytimes.com/2012/06/01/world/middleeast/obama-ordered-wave-of-cyberattacks-against-iran.html
Scharre P (2016) Autonomous weapons and operational risk. https://www.cnas.org/publications/reports/autonomous-weapons-and-operational-risk
Schmitt M (ed) (2017) Tallinn manual 2.0 on the international law applicable to cyber operations, 2nd edn. Cambridge University Press
Schmitt M (2021) Autonomous cyber capabilities and the international law of sovereignty and intervention. In: Väljataga A, Liivoja R (eds) Autonomous cyber capabilities under international law. NATO CCDCOE Publications
Schmitt M, Vihul L (2017) Respect for sovereignty in cyberspace. Tex Law Rev 95:1639
Shackelford S, Andres R (2011) State responsibility for cyber attacks: competing standards for a growing problem. Georget J Int Law 42(4):971–1016
Singer P (2010) Wired for war. Penguin Books
Stevenson A (ed) (2010) Oxford dictionary of English, 3rd edn. Oxford University Press
Stuard J, McGhee J (2015) Is Skynet the answer? Rules for autonomous cyber response capabilities. In: Blowers M (ed) Evolution of cyber technologies and operations to 2035. Springer
Tsagourias N (2012) Cyber attacks, self-defence and the problem of attribution. J Confl Secur Law 17(2):229–244
Tsagourias N (2020) Electoral cyber interference, self-determination, and the principle of non-intervention in cyberspace. In: Broeders D, van den Berg B (eds) Governing cyberspace: behaviour, power, diplomacy. Rowman & Littlefield
Tsagourias N, Buchan R (2018) Automatic cyber defence and the laws of war. GYIL 60:203–237
Tsagourias N, Farrell M (2020) Cyber attribution: technical and legal approaches and challenges. Eur J Int Law 31(3):941
Tyugu E (2012) Command and control of cyber weapons. In: Czosseck C, Ottis R, Ziolkowski K (eds) 4th international conference on cyber conflict. NATO CCDCOE Publications
United Nations Institute for Disarmament Research (UNIDIR) (2017) The weaponization of increasingly autonomous technologies: autonomous weapon systems and cyber operations. https://unidir.org/publication/weaponization-increasingly-autonomous-technologies-autonomous-weapon-systems-and-cyber
Väljataga A, Liivoja R (eds) (2021) Autonomous cyber capabilities under international law. NATO CCDCOE Publications
Warrick J (2011) Iran's Natanz nuclear facility recovered quickly from Stuxnet cyberattack. The Washington Post. http://www.washingtonpost.com/wp-dyn/content/article/2011/02/15/AR2011021506501.html

Algorithmic Criminal Justice: Is It Just a Science Fiction Plot Idea?

Athina Sachoulidou

Abstract This chapter examines the use of algorithms in the realm of criminal justice (known as algorithmic criminal justice) and the potential paradigm shift towards pre-emption-driven decision-making. It contributes to debates about the increasing role of enabling technologies in understanding and responding to crime by turning the spotlight on criminal proceedings. It argues that, at first sight, algorithmic decision-making tools may present a strong potential to improve the operational efficiency of criminal justice authorities, but their use remains associated with hard-to-solve challenges, ranging from lack of transparency to questionable compatibility with core principles of substantive and procedural criminal law. Finally, it highlights the need for a balanced dialogue at the crossroads of technological novelty and (criminal) justice.

1 Introduction: Shaping the Background

'Algorithms in the Courtroom', 'Can you make AI fairer than a Judge?', 'All Rise for the Robot Judge' could be titles of science fiction novels dealing with a future dystopia, in which people are judged by machines. Instead of this, these are titles of recently published articles and blog posts[1] discussing an idea called 'algorithmic justice' (often also referred to as 'predictive justice'), i.e., the use of algorithms[2] in judicial settings. Algorithmic justice and predictive policing, which has already

[1] Greengard (2020); Hao and Stray (2019); Obispa (2020).

[2] The term 'algorithm' describes a 'finite sequence of formal rules' that makes it possible 'to obtain a result from the initial input of information': CEPEJ (2018), p. 69. An algorithm 'may be part of an automated execution process and draw on models designed through machine learning': *Idem*.

A. Sachoulidou (✉)
CEDIS, NOVA School of Law, Universidade NOVA de Lisboa, Lisbon, Portugal
e-mail: athina.sachoulidou@novalaw.unl.pt

A. Kornilakis et al. (eds.), *Artificial Intelligence and Normative Challenges*, Law, Governance and Technology Series 59,
https://doi.org/10.1007/978-3-031-41081-9_8

reached continental Europe,[3] are considered part of 'the larger shift towards "algorithmic governance"'.[4]

While predictive policing and the use of artificial intelligence (AI) in the realm of law enforcement in general have attracted a considerable amount of scholarly concern,[5] algorithmic *criminal* justice has recently started attracting attention. For the moment, there is some academic work stemming from the field of computer science that does not exclusively refer to the area of criminal justice[6] and a limited number of legal studies that focus on the *specificities* of criminal law with this regard.[7] The majority of these studies discuss the idea of deploying algorithms to calculate the risk of future misconduct by referring (mostly) to the US legal order. This is not surprising inasmuch as continental European countries may have started using software-based tools in the judicial sector (e.g., Prédicte; Case Law Analytics; JurisData Analytics—all of them deployed in France for analysis and search purposes), but have excluded criminal cases from their scope of application.[8]

The motivation behind employing (predictive) software tools is generally linked to several competing reasons, including, for instance, the need to decrease budgets and increase predictability in the judicial sector.[9] This emerging trend is being monitored by the European Commission for the Efficiency of Justice (CEPEJ), which has published a Feasibility Study on the 'Possible introduction of a mechanism for certifying artificial intelligence tools and services in the sphere of justice and the judiciary', under the umbrella of the Council of Europe.[10] The publication of this study followed the adoption of the 'European Ethical Charter on the use of artificial intelligence in judicial systems and their environments'.[11] These initiatives are part of *a broader debate* taking place at the EU and international levels and addressing the intersection of new technologies and law. Representative examples are the examination of the compatibility of multiple uses of AI with human rights and the rule of law[12] and the ongoing brainstorming on future regulation and policy-

---

[3] See, for instance, Singelnstein (2018); Meuwese (2020).

[4] Završnik (2019), p. 2. For the purposes of this chapter, the term 'algorithmic governance' is understood as 'a form of social ordering that relies on coordination between actors, is based on rules and incorporates particularly complex computer-based epistemic procedures': Katzenbach and Ulbricht (2019), p. 2.

[5] See the overview provided by Fuster (2020); cf. Meijer and Wessels (2019); Strikwerda (2021).

[6] E.g., Aletras et al. (2016).

[7] E.g., Kehl et al. (2017); Robinson (2018); Hannah-Moffat (2019); Wisser (2019); Završnik (2019, 2020); Ofterdinger (2020); Quattrocolo (2020); Oswald (2020); Sachoulidou (2023).

[8] CEPEJ (2018), pp. 14, 17–18.

[9] Završnik (2019), p. 3.

[10] CEPEJ (2020).

[11] CEPEJ (2018).

[12] FRA (2020); CAHAI (2020).

making in this field[13] that led to the release of the EU Commission's Proposal for a Regulation laying down harmonised rules on AI (AI Act) in April 2021.[14]

This chapter interjects in that debate by examining the concept called 'algorithmic justice' with regard to criminal justice settings (Sect. 2). Revisiting the existing scholarly works, it offers a critical analysis of the risks and benefits associated with a shift towards algorithmic decision-making while considering the fundamental principles governing substantive and procedural criminal law (Sect. 3). This chapter's core argument is that the use of new decision-making tools cannot, nor should, be independent of the specificities of the decision-making context and the subject matter of the decision itself – in this specific case: criminal justice and criminal liability as a primarily human-*action*-based, individualised liability leading to an equally individualised sentence. This argument is presented while also examining persistent challenges associated with algorithmic (criminal) justice (Sect. 4). Finally, the spotlight is turned on the broader political and scholarly discourse that takes place at the crossroads of technological novelty and (criminal) justice (Sect. 5).

2 Algorithmic Justice and Criminal Law: Bridging Past Behaviour with Future One?

'In terms of weighing the various factors, I'm ruling out probation because of the seriousness of the crime and because [the defendant's] history, history on supervision, *and the risk assessment tools that have been utilised*, suggest that [he is] extremely high risk to re-offend'.[15]

That excerpt belongs to the *Loomis v. Wisconsin* landmark decision and refers to the COMPAS (Correctional Offender Management Profiling for Alternative Sanctions)[16] risk assessment that classified Loomis as representing 'a high risk of recidivism' in the following categories: pre-trial release risk, general recidivism and violent recidivism.[17] After his probation had been denied, Loomis challenged the use of COMPAS claiming that the algorithm violated his right to be sentenced using accurate information and to have an individualised sentence, as well as arguing

[13] AI HLEG (2019a, b; 2020).

[14] European Commission (EC) (2021) Proposal for a Regulation of the European Parliament and of the Council laying down harmonised rules on Artificial Intelligence (Artificial Intelligence Act) and amending certain Union legislative acts. COM (2021) 206 final. https://eur-lex.europa.eu/legal-content/EN/TXT/?uri=CELEX:52021PC0206. This manuscript was submitted for publication in 2021 and, thus, it does not take into account the European Parliament's negotiating position on the AI Act that was released only in June 2023 and marked the beginning of the trilogue negotiations. See European Parliament (2023).

[15] *Loomis*, 881 N.W.2d, para.755 (emphasis added).

[16] COMPAS is one of the most commonly used risk-assessment algorithms across the US. See Wisser (2019).

[17] *Loomis*, 881 N.W.2d, para.755; Wisser (2019), p. 1814.

that the algorithm impermissibly considered gender when generating the risk assessment.[18] The final judgment was in favour of the State, but limitations were highlighted regarding the use of COMPAS.

More specifically, the court noted: '[Although] we ultimately conclude that a COMPAS risk assessment can be used at sentencing, *we do so by circumscribing its use*. Importantly, we address how it can be used and what limitations and cautions a circuit court must observe in order to avoid potential due process violations'.[19] According to the suggested limitations: (1) risk assessments may not be used as the determinative factor in the sentencing; (2) in addition to the risk assessment, the choice of a specific sentence has to be justified; (3) risk assessments are not to be used to determine whether someone will be incarcerated or not or how severe his/her sentence will be; and (4) written advisement including limitations of and cautions about COMPAS are to be provided to courts deploying it.[20]

Despite the criticism the *Loomis v. Wisconsin* judgment has received,[21] the case itself remains a useful example towards addressing the question of what it actually means to foresee the future when adjudicating a criminal case with the help of algorithms.[2] The formulation of this question already reveals a fundamental contradiction: an attempt to assess the *future* behaviour of the defendant in the context of a procedure designed not only to prevent future crime, but also to reconstruct a *past* behaviour and to ascribe liability to the actor for that *specific* behaviour.[22] What is expected by an algorithm, especially a recidivism algorithm, is to foresee that future behaviour in terms of a risk of (re-)offending by usually scoring the person responsible for a crime committed in the past on the basis of a statistical evaluation of datasets of a *relevant* (compared to the individual actor) population.[23]

The areas of criminal proceedings, where such a prediction may be deployed (or at least deemed useful) predominantly include[24]: pre-trial detention and bail, i.e., coercive measures imposed *before the final assessment of liability*; sentencing, i.e., the organised State response to crime *after a fact-finding-based conviction* consisting of criminal sanctions *stricto sensu* and/or measures of correction and prevention; and the re-evaluation of the sanction *already imposed* in the context of, for instance, parole procedures potentially leading to an early release.[25] While in the first case various risks are considered, such as that of (re-)offending, escaping or tampering with the evidence, in the second and the third case, the focus lies on the risk of behaving wrongfully in the future, and, thus, on the prevention of future

---

[18] *Loomis*, 881 N.W.2d, para.757; Wisser (2019), p. 1814.

[19] *Loomis*, 881 N.W.2d, para.757 (emphasis added).

[20] Summarised by Wisser (2019), p. 1815.

[21] E.g., Wisser (2019); Quattrocolo (2020).

[22] Quattrocolo (2020), p. 131.

[23] *Idem*; cf. Greenstein (2021).

[24] Acknowledging the limits of this book chapter in terms of providing a comprehensive comparative analysis, the focus liese on European jurisdictions that follow the civil law tradition.

[25] Quattrocolo (2020), pp. 132–133.

crime. In this context, it is worthy to underline the difference between firstly retribution-based and secondly prevention-based sanctions, which have to remain proportional to the crime committed and the offender's guilt, and preventive measures seeking to address the individual's dangerousness and to rehabilitate him/her while remaining proportional *lato sensu*—with the approach to the purposes of criminal punishment varying considerably even among European continental jurisdictions.[26] This difference should be taken into account when assessing the completeness of the concept called algorithmic *criminal* justice.

Besides COMPAS, algorithmic risk assessment (for criminal justice purposes) entails, for instance, the use of PSA (Public Safety Assessment) in the US,[27] HART (Hart Assessment Risk Tool)[28] and OASys (Offender Assessment System)[29] in England and Wales.[30] These tools present, however, considerable differences in terms of the input data needed, their design, as well as the goal they seek to achieve. One may distinguish between example-driven and rule-based algorithms. In the first case, the input data consists of various examples (e.g., court decisions on cases presenting similar characteristics), the algorithmic analysis of which results in the creation of various patterns (output data). In the second case, the input data consists of rules and information initially coded by human experts.[31] This is a distinction one may use when examining the use of algorithms not only for risk assessment purposes, but also for further applications, such as the determination of the mental elements of criminal liability, the assessment of the credibility of witness testimonies (aiming to release the court from the so-called halo effect) or the examination of documentary evidence.

The following analysis primarily focuses on algorithmic risk assessment in terms of a project already materialised that is also discussed progressively in European civil-law jurisdictions. However, while attempting to strike the 'right' balance between the benefits and risks associated with algorithmic criminal justice and addressing the transition from science fiction to reality to identify challenges and open questions (Sects. 3 and 4), this chapter also takes into consideration the possibility of deploying an algorithm to decode criminal liability itself, namely to assist a judge in deciding about liability and not "merely" sentencing. The use of algorithms to enhance the predictability of court decisions, including those reached by criminal courts,[32] or to administer justice using open data[33] will not be discussed.

---

[26] *Ibid* (2020), pp. 137–144.

[27] See *ibid* (2020), pp. 151–152.

[28] See Oswald et al. (2018); Palmiotto (2021).

[29] See Lancaster, Lumb (2006).

[30] Kehl et al. (2017); Završnik (2019), p. 3.

[31] Lorenso (2020), p. 19; cf. CEPEJ (2018), pp. 32–33. For the distinction between rule-based systems and machine learning ones see Greenstein (2021).

[32] See Quattrocolo (2020), pp. 181–221.

[33] Cf. CEPEJ (2018), pp. 20–25.

3 Benefits v. Risks: The Focal Points of the Current Scholarly Debate

Based on the existing scholarship on the use of algorithms in courtrooms, it is fair to talk about a *balancing exercise* in the sense of an ongoing attempt to strike a balance between the expected benefits and risks. This exercise is coupled with the need to examine whether algorithmic justice is or may become compatible with fundamental rights, whether enshrined in national constitutions or in supranational charters, and the rule of law.[34] And it becomes considerably complex when shifting the focus onto criminal justice settings, considering the consequences prescribed in criminal law and the impact of the use of algorithmic tools on due process (that, surprisingly or not, is used as both pro- and contra-argument).

Beginning with the expected benefits, the focus lies on two different components of the right to a fair trial: the right to a hearing within a reasonable time and the right to such a hearing by an independent and impartial tribunal (Art. 6 (1) ECHR). Considering the load of (often undermanned) criminal courts, algorithms are expected to accelerate criminal proceedings by enabling risk assessments that are necessary for deciding on matters like pre-trial detention, which would normally require costly and time-consuming processing of a considerable amount of data.[35] This expectation is coupled with the hope that the algorithmic outcome will be issued not only within a reasonable time framework, but will also be free of mistakes compared to the human analysis of the same information – a hope based for the time being on studies showing that algorithms perform better than humans when analysing, for instance, contractual agreements.[36] Nevertheless, this expectation should be pondered carefully, as the acceleration of criminal proceedings—being a component of the fair trial principle—requires not only the efficient organisation of these proceedings timewise, but also the protection of the rights of the vulnerable party, namely the accused person.

Besides saving time, reducing procedural costs and potentially delivering new knowledge, the use of algorithms in the criminal courtroom is expected to safeguard or even enhance independence and impartiality by eliminating arbitrary judgments, including embarrassingly disproportionate ones, that should otherwise be subject to review by a higher court. This goal could be attained by identifying in past case-law, for instance, those parameters that are necessary to independently pinpoint connections between specific clues and the results correlating with those and to develop an (semi-)automated decision-making practice.[37] In this way, there would be no space for developing subjective criteria or sympathies with one or the other side and the decision reached with the help of the algorithmic tools would be free from any other

[34] Cf. Greenstein (2021).

[35] Melzer (2020), p. 148; Ebersbach (2020), p. 32.

[36] Melzer (2020), p. 148.

[37] Dreyer, Schmees (2019), p. 759; Melzer (2020), p. 148.

factors than the predetermined facts.[38] In theory, that could grant the defendants equal opportunities before *all criminal courts*; that is, irrespective of the judge and/or the jury adjudicating their case or the expert witness examining their case and the pre-occupations, whether scientific or not, those persons may have.[39] Besides this, the legitimacy of criminal justice authorities could be enhanced through the increase of the fairness of their decisions. This requires, however, not only access to complete and reliable data (as will be shown below), but also rationalising and translating the different components of judgments into input data for the algorithm—with the measurement of elements such as leniency, human values and social perceptions presenting considerable difficulties. That said, it also remains questionable whether an absolute equality, first, *could* and, second, *should* be achieved in criminal justice settings,[40] in which equal justice does not necessarily mean reaching a decision by matching clues and results in a mathematical way. On the contrary, equal criminal justice is based on *individualised* liability shaped by factors within the control of the accused person and leading to an *individualised* penalty within the penalty framework prescribed in law at a moment prior to the crime commission.[41]

Delving into the question of whether and to what extent these expectations are realistic is a significantly difficult task without access to statistically important empirical data—at least as far as European civil-law jurisdictions are concerned. However, before one takes on such a task, the risks already noted in the scholarship (that remain largely unsolved at technical level) should be systematised and assessed carefully. That is particularly the case when deploying algorithms in a criminal courtroom inasmuch as a considerable number of the decisions reached in this context violates legal interests, such as personal freedom—no matter if this violation corresponds to the organised State reaction to crime.

Since the *Loomis v. Wisconsin* case was adjudicated in 2016, the use of (recidivism) algorithms in criminal matters has raised major legal issues related to potential violations against the equal protection of citizens due to the inclusion of certain variables in the decision-making process, as well as against criminal procedural rights.[42] Before addressing the respective risks, a general problem related to the use of data-driven tools and technologies for decision-making purposes has to be scrutinised, namely that of data accuracy. Accurate data is required in order to offer wide and reliable knowledge, to rationalise human performance and to reach fair decisions on this basis. In other words, the reliability of a data-based decision-making system is inextricably linked to data accuracy.[43] The accuracy of the dataset is not identical to its contextuality that impacts on the meaning ascribed to the data in

[38] Melzer (2020), p. 148.

[39] Cf. Lorenso (2020), pp. 16, 20; Ebersbach (2020), pp. 27, 32–33.

[40] Cf. Holder (2014).

[41] See Papadimitrakis (2019).

[42] Kehl et al. (2017), p. 21; Završnik (2019), p. 4; (2020), pp. 574–579; Sachoulidou (2023).

[43] Cf. CEPEJ (2018), p. 2; Marx (2021), p. 30.

a specific situation,[44] or its completeness. The completeness of the available data is particularly relevant in the case of historical crime data, given the low rates of reporting in certain crime categories, such as white-collar crimes or domestic violence.[45] This phenomenon is associated with a twofold consequence. On the one side, non-reported crime alone constitutes a black box never properly encompassed by the algorithms that seek to predict future, turning it into a future 'calculated from already selected facts about facts'.[46] On the other side, the access to data of more reported crimes, such as those against property, which are often associated with certain demographics and neighbourhoods, inevitably turns the spotlight on individuals presenting certain characteristics or residing in specific neighbourhoods.[47] These individuals are exposed to the stigma associated not only with arrest (when one examines the case of predictive policing), but also to that linked to a criminal conviction covered by the "objectivity veil" of an algorithm or a classification as a potential threat to the society thanks to the recidivism algorithm.[48]

What if one focuses on the ideal scenario? The data may be accurate, complete, collected and processed in the right context and the system processing it may be crafted with the best of intentions, such as the intention to release criminal justice from human bias. That, however, does not necessarily mean that the outcome of data processing will not be biased. This is the point at which equality concerns are raised—with equal protection before the law (cf. Art. 14 ECHR) being a key component of the rule of law and democracy, and a fundamental tenet of criminal justice.[49] In societal contexts, in which discriminatory practices or policies are widespread or inequalities beyond the control of those suffering them simply exist, the data collected will reflect those practices or policies or simply the reality. And the systems deploying that data may end up reproducing and entrenching bias that results in discrimination and inequality, particularly as far as minorities and marginalised or disadvantaged groups are concerned[50]—leading to a transition from human to algorithmic bias.[51] This transition is associated with a further problem related to the way *criminal liability* itself, the ascertainment of which leads to criminal punishment, should be assessed in a judicial system respecting equality as enshrined in national constitutions and supranational charters.

As already mentioned, criminal liability is shaped on the basis of a past behaviour driven by factors *within the individual's control*. Criminal law addresses a freely reached decision to commit a crime, provided that this decision is materialised in the empirical world by harming or endangering a legally protected interest. Such a

---

[44] Greenstein (2021).

[45] FRA (2020), pp. 69–73.

[46] Završnik (2019), p. 7.

[47] FRA (2020), p. 70; cf. Fuster (2020), pp. 40–42.

[48] Cf. Ebersbach (2020), p. 34; Sachoulidou (2023).

[49] Cf. Wisser (2019), p. 1819; Greenstein (2021).

[50] Cf. FRA (2020), p. 69; CEPEJ (2018), p. 55; Sachoulidou (2021).

[51] Mittelstadt et al. (2016), p. 5; Ryan et al. (2019), pp. 31–33.

definition of criminal liability presupposes that variables, such as gender, employment or education, are considered 'inappropriate to bring into [criminal liability assessment] and criminal sentencing',[52] particularly as long as criminal law does not provide *stricto sensu* (in the sense of codifying) any guidelines for that purpose (e.g., when shaping aggravation or mitigation circumstances and with regard to the decision on sentencing). That said, algorithmic risk assessment and sentencing may represent, as Starr empathically points out, 'an explicit embrace of other-wise condemned discrimination, sanitized by scientific language'.[53] Besides this, criminal law and computer science may approach these variables differently. For instance, in the eyes of a programmer, the consideration of gender may promote the accuracy of a prediction without signalling (at a least not automatically) a discrimination risk.[54] The lack of common criteria or a common mindset may allow biases to slip into the design of the algorithm and the interpretation of the calculated results, i.e., the *probabilities* (not certainties),[55] even before those reach the courtroom and get "translated" in the context of criminal proceedings.[56] And this issue arises in a system, within which the determination of liability and sentencing are (or at least should be) originally based on *causation from actual past criminal behaviour* and not on sole correlations with potential future wrongdoing.

Should biases slip into the algorithmic decision-making, how could that outcome (or any other) be validated? Or in a broader sense: How can the use of the algorithm be substantiated? Addressing these questions is a prerequisite for safeguarding transparency in the realm of criminal justice and protecting the right to participate effectively in a criminal trial and to defend oneself being informed in a language[57] that one understands (Art. 6 (3) ECHR). In this context, transparency requires either establishing technical standards that enable *ex ante* reverse engineering or setting review models that offer *ex post* validation of the algorithmic output.[58] That implies a distinction that the court failed to make in the case of *Loomis v. Wisconsin*, namely the distinction between the ability to 'review and rebut the individual pieces of information [. . .] fed into the algorithm' and the ability to 'review how the score itself was calculated'.[59] That presupposes not only a close cooperation between the algorithm designer and the end-user, namely the judge, which cannot be taken for granted, but also the "translation" of the respective information, including the way that information is processed, in a language the affected individual understands.

[52] Kehl et al. (2017), p. 23.

[53] Starr (2014), p. 806.

[54] Wisser (2019), p. 1818.

[55] Mittelstadt et al. (2016), p. 4.

[56] Završnik (2019), p. 10.

[57] The term "language" may have to be interpreted in a broader way in the future, considering the potential inclusion of programming languages into the respective discourse.

[58] Quattrocolo (2020), p. 93.

[59] Kehl et al. (2017), p. 23; cf. Wisser (2019), p. 1822; Završnik (2019), p. 14.

While seeking to achieve that goal, trade secret[60] and technical inability to explain how the algorithm works[61] appear as significant obstacles (or excuses masking the unwillingness to share expertise)[62]—in a field, however, in which there should be no space for 'tensions between life, liberty and property interests'.[63]

To open the black box in terms of accessing effectively all evidence adduced or observations filed and being able to comment on them *with a view to influencing the court's* decision[64] before and after conviction – or, in other words, to address the primary due-process-related concern, the following requirements shall be met[65]: One should (1) be aware of whether, at which stage(s) of the procedure and to what extent an algorithmic tool was deployed; (2) know how and where to request explanations; and (3) have enough information to contest the underlying decision. Even in this case, one cannot exclude possible infringements upon the presumption of innocence (Art. 6 (2) ECHR), should algorithmic tools be deployed to shape judgments not only on sentencing, but also on liability. That risk refers to the consideration of mere probabilities in judicial settings[66] and the future increase of the 'innocence threshold' the affected individual has to overcome,[67] particularly when (s)he is expected to provide more persuasive contra-evidence compared to the algorithmic output that is already surrounded by scientific objectivity and a sense of security[68] – and that within a speedy criminal procedure.[69]

Finally, there is one more risk going beyond equality and due process and referring to a trend of over-focusing on risk management among the *multiple* purposes of sentencing that shall (first) respond to a *past* criminal behaviour.[70] That happens 'without any stable empirical basis, i.e., without any clear indication whether longer imprisonment, for instance, decreases the risk of recidivism'[71] and at a moment when pre-emption-oriented decision-making can also be identified in the field of criminal legislation. That refers to a gradual (but consistent) transition from a post-crime to a pre-crime logic in terms of a change of focus 'from past actions to potential future personal states and circumstances'[72] revealing a transfer of criteria and ideologies shaping other fields of regulation, such as police law, in the area of criminal law. That transition is already reflected in the adoption of the so-called

[60] Cf. CEPEJ (2018), p. 53; FRA (2020), p. 77.

[61] Cf. FRA (2020), p. 58, 77.

[62] Sachoulidou (2021).

[63] Wexler (2018), p. 1343.

[64] See ECtHR (2020), p. 31.

[65] Cf. FRA (2020), p. 76.

[66] Završnik (2019), p. 14; Greenstein (2021).

[67] Galetta (2013); Milaj and Mifsud Bonnici (2014), p. 425.

[68] Cf. Hannah-Moffat (2019).

[69] Sachoulidou (2021, 2023).

[70] Kehl et al. (2017), pp. 26–27.

[71] Završnik (2019), p. 5.

[72] *Ibid*, p.6.

pre-preventive measures, *including criminalisation itself*, as part of various crime prevention policies with the counter-terrorism one offering maybe the most representative example.[73] Against this backdrop, the need to set rule-of-law-based limits that will safeguard proportionality and the protection of fundamental rights—an attempt progressively undertaken, *inter alia*, by the CJEU since the *Digital Rights Ireland* judgment[74]—becomes clearer when facing a step-by-step transition from science fiction to an algorithmic reality, which is future-risk-oriented *by nature*, in judicial settings.

4 From Science Fiction to Pressing Questions

The risks noted above have already led CEPEJ to adopt five principles to govern the use of AI in judicial systems and their environment: (1) the principle of respect for fundamental rights (guaranteed by the ECHR and the CoE Convention on the Protection of Personal Data), including the prioritisation of *ethical-by-design* or *human-rights-by-design* approaches; (2) the principle of non-discrimination, including measures to limit or, if possible, neutralise risks and to raise awareness among the involved stakeholders; (3) the principle of quality and security (regarding the processing of judicial decisions and data), including the need for collaboration among designers of machine learning models, justice system professionals and researchers in the field of legal and social sciences; (4) the principle of transparency, impartiality and fairness, the protection of which requires striking a balance between the intellectual property of certain processing methods and transparency requirements; and (5) the principle 'under user control' that encompasses both the ability of justice system professionals to review the judicial decisions and the data used to produce a certain result, while retaining the right to dissent in the light of particularities of each case, and the protection of the due process rights enshrined in Art. 6 ECHR.[75]

Against this backdrop, the subsequent analysis focuses on issues pertaining to algorithmic justice that can be perceived as persistent challenges or at least as open questions, part of which is associated with the specificities of criminal law and criminal justice.

---

[73] Kaiafa-Gbandi (2019).

[74] *Digital Rights Ireland Ltd v Minister for Communications, Marine and Natural Resources and Others and Kärntner Landesregierung and Others*, Joined Cases C-293/12 and C-594/12, CJEU, 8 April 2014, ECLI: ECLI:EU:C:2014:238. See also *Privacy International v Secretary of State for Foreign and Commonwealth Affairs and Others*, Case C-623/17, CJEU, 6 October 2020, ECLI:EU:C:2020:790; *Quadrature du Net and Others v. Premier ministre and Others*, Joined Cases C-511/18, C-512/18 and C-520/18, CJEU, 6 October 2020, ECLI: ECLI:EU:C:2020:791.

[75] CEPEJ (2018), pp. 8–13.

4.1 *What Does the Algorithm Measure and What Does Really Matter?*[76]

Examining the use of algorithms in criminal justice settings with a focus on algorithmic risk assessment tools, Završnik (2019) identifies, *inter alia*, considerable pitfalls concerning the creation of databases, the design of algorithms and the unpredicted paths the latter may take (in spite of the initial good intentions). In this context, besides the problem of data accuracy and completeness outlined above, he highlights, the (political) *human decisions* inherent in the procedures of collecting, labelling and interpreting data.[77] The end-users, namely the justice system professionals, should be able to "decode" these decisions. This requires *technical literacy*, which varies considerably among the specific end-users, and the *ability to pose the right questions* in order 'to excavate [the] values embedded in calculations'.[78]

Nevertheless, the fact that the judiciary is responsible for asking the right questions does not automatically mean that the engineers building algorithmic models should be the ones shaping the values in the first place, even when, by doing so, they seek to attain a noble goal, such as that of de-biasing the algorithm and supplying it with the "right" data.[79] One should consider not only the gravity of criminal punishment as a violation of fundamental liberties, but also the fact that criminal codes and codes of criminal procedure constitute a "distillation" of the legislative process taken on by democratically elected actors and reflecting (at least in theory) societal interests and values that are translated into legal ones. Until these actors sit together with the engineers, the existing legislative procedure is the one remaining 'relatively open to scrutiny in comparison with a process of de-biasing conducted behind closed doors by computer scientists in a laboratory'.[80]

Additionally, one might also wonder to what extent an algorithm could "perceive" the multiple dimensions and origins of criminality—considering that, first, there is anything but unanimity among criminologists in that regard and, second, human activity is not (necessarily) governed by mathematical formulas.[81] And, even if one decides to let the numbers speak for themselves, data availability cannot be taken for granted inasmuch as it depends on, *inter alia*, the willingness of each individual to reveal information about him–/herself. The next question arising in such a context is how much data would be "too much" when seeking to safeguard

[76] While examining the challenges of prediction in the realm of criminal justice, Robinson (2018, pp. 154–174) identifies three core tensions formulated as follows: 'What Matters Versus What the Data Measure'; 'Current Goals Versus Historical Patterns'; and 'Public Authority Versus Private Expertise'.

[77] Završnik (2019), pp. 8–9; cf. Melzer (2020), pp. 148–149.

[78] Završnik (2019), p. 9.

[79] *Ibid*, p.11.

[80] *Idem.*

[81] See Hildebrandt (2018).

proportionality and compliance with the fundamental right to informational self-determination and the core principles of data protection, such as purpose limitation and data minimization, which remain applicable in the realm of law enforcement and criminal justice (Art. 4 (1) Directive 2016/80/EU).[82]

Shifting the focus from risk to liability assessment via algorithms, the structural challenge that arises is associated with the perception of crime as a normative phenomenon that not only reflects certain human values changing over time and place,[83] but is also structured in a specific way (varying depending on the concerned legal order). No matter what the algorithm measures, what matters is to what extent those measurements reflect the normative decisions reached in this specific field of regulation. In the case of European civil-law jurisdictions, the algorithmic output should match concrete material and mental elements and address the codified or otherwise recognised grounds upon which the wrongfulness of an act can be excluded or the liability itself can be excluded, aggravated or mitigated[84]—in order to facilitate the decision-making procedure in compliance with the defendant's right to an *individualised* judgment that is not solely based on a mass of data and algorithmically indicated links.[85]

The technical challenges associated with this task arise from: (1) the multitude and the complexity[86] of the variables shaping criminal liability and the risk of oversimplifying the outcome of the democratically organised criminal justice; (2) the lack of a universal approach to crime and criminal liability in a universal technological environment; and (3) the need to preserve the unique character of national criminal law. In addition, one should also consider that legal regulation may usually lag behind technological development, but the latter does not necessarily "capture" the complex and often difficult-to-predict human life.[87] That presupposes having enough time to train the algorithm accordingly, as well as identifying possible understanding gaps, bridging different mindsets and mitigating the risks arising from the fact that future data may always disrupt the predictive accuracy of the initial hypothesis.[88] These goals cannot be achieved without bringing legal, social, and computer scientists together—in *both* the amphitheatre and the laboratory. Otherwise, it is already too late, when the warnings or the instructions reach the courtroom[89] without the specificities of the decision-making procedure and its subject matter having been taken into account when designing the algorithm and supplying it with data.

---

[82] Cf. CEPEJ (2018), pp. 56–57; Ebersbach (2020), pp. 32, 35.

[83] Završnik (2019), p. 7.

[84] See Quattrocolo (2020), pp. 214–215.

[85] Cf. Wisser (2019), p. 1823; Ebersbach (2020), p. 34.

[86] Cf. CEPEJ (2018), p. 36.

[87] See *ibid* (2018), p. 61; Završnik (2019), p. 12.

[88] See Hildebrandt (2019).

[89] As suggested in the *Loomis v. Wisconsin* case; cf. Wisser (2019), p. 1816.

4.2 *First Things First: Independence, Accountability and Trust*

Should those two different "worlds", crime and criminal liability on the one side and algorithmic decision-making on the other, be bridged, it still seems over-optimistic to proceed with employing algorithms in criminal justice settings (or in the judicial field in general). Before that (and even if the use of algorithms is limited to small-scale projects), independence of the judiciary has to be safeguarded, accountability questions have to be addressed carefully, remedies have to be designed accordingly, and trust in the new decision-making system has to be ensured.

Independence presupposes knowledge and the ability to assess critically the data presented to oneself. It is not only the defendant as a layperson that needs to comprehend the explanation provided to him/her (or more accurately: the code translated into an explanation),[90] but also the judge. The latter has to be educated accordingly and trained regularly throughout his/her career following all possible system updates the same way that (s)he is expected to keep pace with legislative amendments.[91] Otherwise, it is highly unlikely to reach an informed (non-arbitrary) decision about, first, how much to rely on the algorithmic output, and, second, liability and sentencing—the same way that the judge is expected to assess critically the expert opinions presented to him/her. Without knowledge, it is highly unlikely that a judge will leave the algorithmic "comfort zone" and reach the courageous decision to distance him/herself from the algorithmic output.[92]

Defining accountability for the final decision and designing effective legal remedies remain a sine-qua-non, even when the algorithmic output is not a binding one—considering that there is actually no guarantee that the courts will not use, for instance, risk assessments available to them 'to determine whether or not someone will be incarcerated or to determine the severity of a sentence',[93] unless an explicit prohibition or limitation is incorporated into the set of rules governing the criminal procedure. In the absence of such rules, the responsibility of the person training the algorithm, "feeding" it with data or shaping the rules, according to which it reaches a conclusion, should be clearly defined to the extent that the algorithm "usurps" part of the judicial decision-making power.[94] Besides the ethical standards required, similar to the judge's (legal) obligation to explain his/her decision publicly and in a thorough and understandable way, the algorithm designers/trainers should also be responsible for explaining the algorithmic output 'in written, protracted, published opinions'.[95] In other words, '[they] should not be allowed to hide behind the actions

[90] See Wisser (2019), p. 1829.

[91] Cf. *ibid*, pp.1827–1828; Ebersbach (2020), p. 36.

[92] Cf. CEPEJ (2018), p. 56; Greenstein (2021).

[93] *Loomis*, 881 N.W.2d, para.760.

[94] Wisser (2019), p. 1831.

[95] *Idem.*

of the tools they have designed, sold and deployed'.[96] This is generally required, and particularly in a field of decision-making with a direct impact on the individuals' personal freedom,[97] within which there should be no place for proprietary interests and black boxes.

Trust in algorithmic decision-making in general and algorithmic criminal justice in particular requires social consensus—the same way that the function of a legal order as a whole presupposes adequate social consensus obtained through elections in democratic societies. Consensus shall cover the values governing algorithmic decision-making and the outcome of the "merger" of justice and technology to the widest possible extent.[98] This presupposes that citizens understand the added value (if any) of employing such a model in the field of criminal justice, in order to be able to judge individually whether it is a privilege (or exactly the opposite) to have their cases adjudicated by a judge assisted by an algorithm or even solved by an algorithm instead of a judge.

5 Outlook: Revisiting the Intersection of (Criminal) Justice and Technology

As stated by the European Commission in the Communication titled 'Building Trust in Human-Centric Artificial Intelligence', 'AI is not an end in itself, but a tool that has to serve people *with the ultimate aim of increasing human well-being*'.[99] To attain that goal in the case of algorithmic criminal justice, 'trustworthiness shall be ensured'.[100] This presupposes acknowledging not only the tremendous opportunities, but also potential drawbacks when employing new technologies, as well as realizing that those should not be deployed without the necessary precautions and distinctions.[101] There can be no algorithmic criminal justice—or more accurately: no justice—without transparency, due process, independence, and accountability, and without filling the understanding gap. Otherwise, the impact upon society and human rights will be simply too high.[102] To make that happen, interdisciplinarity should reach a much deeper level than achieved so far, something that requires time and courageous investments at multiple levels, including (but not limited to) the educational sector.

Before moving on with such a project, the priorities should also be revisited. What if, for instance, we first invest resources to decode and prevent crime in terms

[96] *Idem.*

[97] CEPEJ (2018), p. 54; CEPEJ (2020), p. 3.

[98] Cf. Završnik (2019), p. 8.

[99] EC (2019), p. 1 (emphasis added).

[100] *Ibid*, p. 2.

[101] CEPEJ (2018), p. 54.

[102] Cf. Završnik (2019), p. 16.

of understanding its social, structural and psychological drivers before seeking to predict or punish it by means of algorithms?[103] And once the priorities are (re-)set, it should be examined whether the 'code executes correctly' *and* whether it promotes social well-being.[104] In other words, it is not enough to incentivize innovative technologies. It is of equally central importance to preserve "sustainability" by carefully considering the specificities of each field of application, and to detect and attest empirically the added value.

References

Aletras N et al (2016) Predicting judicial decisions of the European court of human rights: a natural language processing perspective. PeerJ Comput Sci 2(2):1–19. https://doi.org/10.7717/peerj-cs.93
Barabas C et al (2018) Interventions over Predictions: Reframing the Ethical Debate for Actuarial Risk Assessment. Available via Cornell University. https://arxiv.org/abs/1712.08238
Council of Europe Ad Hoc Committee on Artificial Intelligence (CAHAI) (2020) Feasibility Study on AI Legal Standards. https://rm.coe.int/cahai-2020-23-final-eng-feasibility-study-/1680a0c6da
Council of Europe European Commission for the Efficiency of Justice (CEPEJ) (2018) European Ethical Charter on the use of artificial intelligence in judicial systems and their environment. https://www.coe.int/en/web/cepej/cepej-european-ethical-charter-on-the-use-of-artificial-intelligence-ai-in-judicial-systems-and-their-environment
Council of Europe European Commission for the Efficiency of Justice (CEPEJ) (2020) Possible introduction of a mechanism for certifying artificial intelligence tools and services in the sphere of justice and the judiciary: Feasibility Study. https://rm.coe.int/feasability-study-en-cepej-2020-15/1680a0adf4
Dreyer S, Schmees J (2019) Künstliche Intelligenz als Richter? Wo keine Trainingsdaten, da kein Richter – Hindernisse, Risiken und Chancen der Automatisierung gerichtlicher Entscheidungen. Computer und Recht 35(11):758–764. https://doi.org/10.9785/cr-2019-351120
Ebersbach M (2020) Big Data, Algorithmen und Bewährungsentscheidungen. In: Momsen C, Schwarze M (eds) Strafrecht im Zeitalter von Digitalisierung und Datafizierung. pp 26–37. https://kripoz.de/wp-content/uploads/2020/06/Ebersbach-Big-Data-Algorithmen-und-Bew%C3%A4hrungsentscheidungen.pdf
European Commission (EC) (2019) *Building Trust in Human-Centric Artificial Intelligence*. COM (2019) 168 final. EUR-Lex - 52019DC0168 - EL - EUR-Lex (europa.eu)
European Court of Human Rights (ECtHR) (2020) Guide on Article 6 of the European Convention on Human Rights. Right to a fair trial [criminal limb]. https://www.echr.coe.int/documents/GuideArt6criminalENG.pdf
European Parliament (2023) Amendments adopted by the European Parliament on 14 June 2023 on the proposal for a regulation of the European Parliament and of the Council on laying down harmonised rules on artificial intelligence (Artificial Intelligence Act) and amending certain Union legislative acts. COM (2021)0206 –C9-0146/2021– 2021/0106(COD), 14 June, https://www.europarl.europa.eu/doceo/document/TA-9-2023-0236_EN.html

[103] Barabas et al. (2018); Završnik (2019), p. 8.

[104] Hulette (2017); Završnik (2019), p. 9.

European Union Agency for Fundamental Rights (FRA) (2020) Getting the future right. Artificial intelligence and fundamental rights. https://fra.europa.eu/en/publication/2020/artificial-intelligence-and-fundamental-rights

Fuster GG (2020) Artificial Intelligence and Law Enforcement. Impact on Fundamental Rights. Study requested by the LIBE Committee. https://www.europarl.europa.eu/thinktank/en/document.html?reference=IPOL_STU(2020)656295

Galetta A (2013) The changing nature of the presumption of innocence in today's surveillance societies: rewrite human rights or regulate the use of surveillance technologies? EJLT 4(2) https://ejlt.org/index.php/ejlt/article/view/221/377

Greengard S (2020) Algorithms in the Courtroom. Available via Communications of the ACM. https://cacm.acm.org/news/244263-algorithms-in-the-courtroom/fulltext

Greenstein S (2021) Preserving the rule of law in the era of artificial intelligence (AI). Artif Intell Law. https://doi.org/10.1007/s10506-021-09294-4

Hannah-Moffat K (2019) Algorithmic risk governance: big data analytics, race and information activism in criminal justice debates. Theor Criminol 23(4):453–470. https://doi.org/10.1177/1362480618763582

Hao K, Stray J (2019) Can you make AI fairer than a judge? Play our courtroom algorithm game. Available via MIT Technology Review. https://www.technologyreview.com/2019/10/17/75285/ai-fairer-than-judge-criminal-risk-assessment-algorithm/

High-Level Expert Group on Artificial Intelligence (AI HLEG) (2019a) Ethics Guidelines for Trustworthy AI. https://ec.europa.eu/futurium/en/ai-alliance-consultation/guidelines#Top

High-Level Expert Group on Artificial Intelligence (AI HLEG) (2019b) Policy and Investment Recommendations for Trustworthy AI. https://ec.europa.eu/digital-single-market/en/news/policy-and-investment-recommendations-trustworthy-artificial-intelligence

High-Level Expert Group on Artificial Intelligence (AI HLEG) (2020) The Assessment List for Trustworthy Artificial Intelligence (ALTAI) for self-assessment. https://ec.europa.eu/digital-single-market/en/news/assessment-list-trustworthy-artificial-intelligence-altai-self-assessment

Hildebrandt M (2018) Preregistration of machine learning research design. In: Bayamlioglu E et al (eds) Being profiled: Cogitas ergo sum. Amsterdam University Press, Amsterdam, pp 102–105

Hildebrandt M (2019) 'Privacy as protection of the incomputable self': from agnostic to agonistic machine learning. Theor Inq Law 19(1):83–121

Holder E (2014) Attorney General Eric Holder Speaks at the National Association of Criminal Defense Lawyers 57th Annual Meeting and 13th State Criminal Justice Network Conference. Available via the United States Department of Justice Official Website. https://www.justice.gov/opa/speech/attorney-general-eric-holder-speaks-national-association-criminal-defense-lawyers-57th

Hulette D (2017) Patrolling the intersection of computers and people. Available via Princeton University. https://www.cs.princeton.edu/news/patrolling-intersection-computers-and-people

Kaiafa-Gbandi M (2019) Information exchange for the purpose of crime control: the EU paradigm for controlling terrorism – challenges of an 'open' system for collecting and exchanging personal data. Eur Crim Law Rev 2:141–174. https://doi.org/10.5771/2193-5505-2019-2-141

Katzenbach C, Ulbricht L (2019) Algorithmic governance. Internet. Pol Rev 8(4):1–18. https://doi.org/10.14763/2019.4.1424

Kehl D, Guo P, Kessler S (2017) Algorithms in the criminal justice system: assessing the use of risk assessments in sentencing. Responsive Communities Initiative, Berkman Klein Center for Internet & Society, Harvard Law School. Available via Harvard Library. https://dash.harvard.edu/handle/1/33746041

Lancaster E, Lumb J (2006) The assessment of risk in the National Probation Service of England and Wales. J Soc Work 6(3):275–291. https://doi.org/10.1177/1468017306071176

Lorenso T (2020) Nutzung von Big Data und Algorithmus-basierter Datenanalyse in der Beweisführung zum Nachweis des Vorsatzes. In: Momsen C, Schwarze M (eds) Strafrecht im Zeitalter von Digitalisierung und Datafizierung. pp 15–25. https://kripoz.de/wp-content/

uploads/2020/06/Lorenso-Nutzung-von-Biig-Data-und-Algorithmus-basierter-Datenanalyse-in-der-Beweisf%C3%BChrung-zum-Nachweis-des-Vorsatzes.pdf
Marx G (2021) Introduction: the ayes have it – should they? Police body-worn cameras. In: Newell BC (ed) Surveillance, privacy, and accountability. Routledge, London, pp 24–51
Meijer A, Wessels M (2019) Predictive policing: review of benefits and drawbacks. Int J Public Adm 42(12):1031–1039. https://doi.org/10.1080/01900692.2019.1575664
Melzer J (2020) Auswirkungen von künstlicher Intelligenz auf Völkerrecht, insbesondere die Gewährleistung der Garantien des Art. 6 EMRK. Zeitschrift zum Innovations- und Technikrecht 3:145–150
Meuwese A (2020) Regulating algorithmic decision-making one case at the time: a note on the Dutch 'SyRI' judgment. Eur Rev Digital Adm Law 1(1–2):209–211
Milaj J, Mifsud Bonnici JP (2014) Unwitting subjects of surveillance and the presumption of innocence. Comput Law Secur Rev 30(4):419–428. https://doi.org/10.1016/j.clsr.2014.05.009
Mittelstadt BD et al (2016) The ethics of algorithms: mapping the debate. Big Data Soc 3(2):1–21. https://doi.org/10.1177/2053951716679679
Obispa G (2020) All Rise For The Robot Judge. Available via Profound. https://profoundprojects.com/insight/all-rise-for-the-robot-judge/
Ofterdinger H (2020) Strafzumessung durch Algorithmen? Zeitschrift für Internationale Strafrechtsdogmatik 9:404–410
Oswald M (2020) Technologies in the twilight zone: early lie detectors, machine learning and reformist legal realism. Int Rev Law Comput Technol 34(2):214–231. https://doi.org/10.1080/13600869.2020.1733758
Oswald M, Grace J, Urwin S, Barnes GC (2018) Algorithmic risk assessment policing models: lessons from the Durham HART model and 'experimental' proportionality. Inform Commun Technol Law 27(2):223–250. https://doi.org/10.1080/13600834.2018.1458455
Palmiotto F (2021) The black box on trial: the impact of algorithmic opacity on fair trial rights in criminal proceedings. In: Ebers M, Cantero Gamito M (eds) Algorithmic governance and governance of algorithms. Legal and ethical challenges. Springer, Cham, pp 49–70
Papadimitrakis G (2019) Big data and algorithmic risk studies. New challenges in the area of penology. [in Greek]. Poiniki Dikaiosyni 10:1045–1054
Quattrocolo S (2020) Artificial intelligence, computational modelling and criminal proceedings. A framework for a European legal discussion. Springer, Cham
Robinson D (2018) The challenges of prediction: lessons from criminal justice. J Law Policy Inf Soc 14(2):151–186. https://core.ac.uk/download/pdf/185249983.pdf
Ryan M et al (2019) Report on Ethical Tensions and Social Impacts. WP 1. D1.4 SHERPA. https://doi.org/10.21253/DMU.8397134
Sachoulidou A (2021) OK Google: is (s)he guilty? J Contemp Eur Stud. https://doi.org/10.1080/14782804.2021.1987863
Sachoulidou A (2023) Going beyond the "common suspects": to be presumed innocent in the era of algorithms, big data and artificial intelligence. Artif Intell Law. https://doi.org/10.1007/s10506-023-09347-w
Singelnstein T (2018) Predictive Policing: Algorithmenbasierte Straftatprognosen zur vorausschauenden Kriminalintervention. Neue Zeitschrift für Strafrecht 37(1):1–9
Starr S (2014) Evidence-based sentencing and the scientific rationalization of discrimination. Stanford Law Rev 66(4):803–872
Strikwerda L (2021) Predictive policing: the risks associated with risk assessment. Police J Theor Pract Principl 94(3):422–436. https://doi.org/10.1177/0032258X20947749
Wexler R (2018) Life, liberty, and trade secrets: intellectual property in the criminal justice system. Stanford Law Rev 70:1343–1429

Wisser L (2019) Pandora's algorithmic black box: the challenges of using algorithmic risk assessments in sentencing. Am Crim Law Rev 56:1811–1832

Završnik A (2019) Algorithmic justice: algorithms and big data in criminal justice settings. Eur J Criminol 18(5):1–20. https://doi.org/10.1177/1477370819876762

Završnik A (2020) Criminal justice, artificial intelligence systems, and human rights. ERA Forum 20:567–583. https://link.springer.com/article/10.1007/s12027-020-00602-0

Part IV
Intellectual Property Protection and Patentability of AI

The Patentability of AI-Related Subject Matter According to the EPC as Implemented by the EPO

Eleni Tzoulia

Abstract This chapter comments upon the necessity and the feasibility of patenting AI-related subject matter, considering AI's distinguishing features, i.e., its technical complexity, autonomy, and self-evolving capacities. These issues are examined in light of the European legal order. The investigation endeavours to identify grounds advocating for a change of tack on the handling of AI patent applications within the European Patent System.

1 Introduction

This chapter firstly defines the concept of Artificial Intelligence (AI) and identifies its relation to software, algorithms, and big data. Subsequently, it investigates the linkages between AI, intellectual property, and patent law. Patents are indicated as a suitable legal instrument to protect one's intellectual property on AI technologies. In view of that, the chapter outlines the patent granting procedure as arranged in the so-called European Patent System in particular. And then, it reviews the implementation of the European Patent Convention (EPC) by the European Patent Office (EPO) in the context of patent applications directed to AI.

This research is co-financed by Greece and the European Union (European Social Fund- ESF) through the Operational Programme "Human Resources Development, Education and Lifelong Learning" in the context of the project "Reinforcement of Postdoctoral Researchers - 2nd Cycle" (MIS-5033021), implemented by the State Scholarships Foundation (IKY). The paper was partly written within the framework of an Austrian Standards Fellowship at the Faculty of Law of the University of Graz.

E. Tzoulia (✉)
Department for Economic and Commercial Law, Law School, Aristotle University of Thessaloniki, Thessaloniki, Greece

School of Science and Technology, Hellenic Open University, Patras, Greece
e-mail: elenitzoulia@law.auth.gr

A. Kornilakis et al. (eds.), *Artificial Intelligence and Normative Challenges*, Law, Governance and Technology Series 59,
https://doi.org/10.1007/978-3-031-41081-9_9

Within this frame of reference, the study endeavors to identify those features determining the technical or non-technical character of AI inventions. Subsequently, it investigates the patentability of technical AI inventions, according to the criteria set by the EPC in its Arts. 52 and 53. In this respect, it is contemplated whether ethical controversies may impede AI patenting, as well as how novelty and not obviousness shall be examined taking into consideration AI's self-evolving capacities. Moreover, the chapter reflects on adversities posed by the involvement of AI in the inventive process, relating to the designation of the inventor and the disclosure of the invention.

The above analysis seeks firstly to substantiate whether the doctrines currently applied to implement EPC rules can safeguard a coherent and consistent legal treatment of AI patent applications. A stance is also envisaged to be taken as regards the appropriate responses of patent law in view of the increasing software automation. The long-debated espousal of AI inventorship will be weighed against any interests put at stake and antinomies induced by such a prospect.

2 AI Concept and Peculiarities

Any set of procedures and routines associated with the operation of a computer belongs to its software. This is the opposite of hardware, which comprises the physical components of electronic devices. Software in the above sense is a catalyst for automation, i.e., machine operation with minimal human intervention. It namely enables electronic devices to autonomously control and coordinate their internal functions, respond to external stimuli, and accomplish human orders. Such capacities derive from the simulation of human intelligence made possible through "programming".

Programming refers to the procedure by which humans communicate to computers instructions for performing specific tasks and producing requested outcomes. It first entails outlining the steps to be followed in a logical and finite sequence, i.e., formulating the problem-solving "algorithm". The description of this algorithm in plain language is known as the program's "pseudocode". This initial outline is then encoded in a programming language, thus formulating the program's "source code". The latter will be finally compiled in binary language, the so-called "machine" or "object" code, which is intelligible and executable by the computer's hardware.

The above state of art signifies an elementary form of artificial intelligence (AI), which is called "symbolic". Because symbolic AI relies on previous programming, i.e., encoded human knowledge, it is inherently narrow. It namely endows hardware with the capacity to act autonomously to the extent that it is accordingly instructed. When the solution to specific problems is too complex to be manually modelled, symbolic AI reaches its limits.

Over the last decades, however, computer autonomy has improved dramatically, thanks to software deploying self-learning techniques rather than programming to fulfill its assignments. In this case, the software is taught to develop on its own the suitable algorithm to achieve a set goal, instead of following predetermined steps dictated by human experts. This procedure, known as Machine Learning (ML), in broad terms entails that the system gets trained on data, thus gradually identifying patterns, and deducting rules towards a desired outcome.

ML technologies currently revolutionizing AI are the so-called Artificial Neural Networks (ANNs). Each ANN is a collection of layered processing units, which simulates the neurons in a biological brain. The network responds to given tasks on the basis of probability-weighted associations made possible through the processing of input data. In the context of the relevant data training, the network recognizes errors in its behavior by comparing each output produced with a target output. This way it develops learning rules, according to which it configures its structure and comes up with updated responses, until it gradually achieves the pursued outcome. The use of massively multilayered ANNs, which are capable to develop more abstract conceptualizations of problems and to deliver more nuanced responses, comes under the generic term "deep learning".[1]

Once combined with other revolutionary technologies, like the Internet of Things (IoT), AI can automate any household and business practice, manufacturing, primary production, health, transportation, etc.[2] Moreover, contemporary AI confers software with the capacity to generate products that resemble figments of human intellect, like works of art.[3] However, the evolutionary machine learning techniques employed nowadays arguably make software operation untraceable and therefore inexplicable for the average specialist in the relevant technical field. This lack of transparency, often referred to as "algorithm blackbox",[4] is considered as a major issue of concern with respect to AI booming.

In more detail, machine learning as described above serves the objective of enabling computer programs to respond to unspecified situations by developing their own judgement rules. In this context, the inferences on which algorithmic reasoning is based in each given case, may become opaque, even for AI experts. This possibility increases in proportion to the complexity of the machine learning process. The chance that this process is unsupervised, i.e., relies on unlabeled training datasets, may also lead to lack of transparency in AI operation. Algorithm blackbox is supposed to complicate the attribution of liability for AI-facilitated law infringements, as well as the designation of ownership for creations involving AI contributions.

---

[1] European Parliament Briefing, *How Artificial Intelligence works*, March 2019, PE 634.420. European Parliament (2019a).

[2] European Parliament Briefing, *State of art and future of artificial intelligence*, February 2019, PE 631.051. European Parliament (2019b).

[3] See, for instance, Guadamuz (2017), pp. 169–186; Bonadio and McDonagh (2020), pp. 112 et seq.

[4] The European Consumer Organization (BEUC) (2018), p. 5 et seq.

3 Protecting AI as Intellectual Property

Large investments associated with AI development justify the interest of AI stakeholders in protecting their products from unauthorized use. Relevant claims may be based on civil or unfair competition law in each jurisdiction. In principle, however, the several components of AI applications, like computer programs, underlying algorithms, machine learning models, and databases, are subject to intellectual property rights (IPRs). This term refers to exclusive rights that are established either automatically or following an administrative procedure on creations of the human intellect.

International treaties classify IPRs in two main categories, i.e., copyright, and industrial property. According to the Berne Convention of 1886 (Art. 2), in particular, copyright shall protect original productions of any kind within the literary, scientific, or artistic domain. On the other hand, the Paris Convention of 1883 (Art. 1 para. 2), and the TRIPS Agreement that followed it (Art. 29), classify under an entity's industrial property its trademarks, patents, industrial designs, designations of origin and geographical indications, as well as its trade secrets. This systematization is currently adhered to on a global level and also instructs EU legislation.

3.1 AI and Copyright

According to Art. 10 paras 1 and 2 of the TRIPS Agreement, computer programs and data compilations shall be subject to copyright protection as literary works within the meaning of the Berne Convention. These provisions have influenced IP law on a worldwide level, being embraced in particular by the EU legislator. Indeed, on the basis of Directives 2009/24/EC[5] and 96/9/EC,[6] software and dataset protection is traditionally entrusted to copyright law in the EU. Copyright applies automatically as soon as the work is documented in material form and lasts for up to 70 years after the death of the author, i.e., the programmer and the data scientist respectively in the given case.

As apparent from the preceding analysis, the term AI refers to software which emulates natural cognitive abilities either as a result of prior programming by human experts or due to self-programming mechanisms based on training data. This interpretation is espoused by the EU legislator, as evident from the "Artificial Intelligence

[5] *Directive 2009/24/EC of the European Parliament and of the Council of 23 April 2009 on the legal protection of computer programs*, OJ L 111, 5.5.2009, pp. 16–22.

[6] *Directive 96/9/EC of the European Parliament and of the Council of 11 March 1996 on the legal protection of databases*, OJ L 77, 27.3.1996, pp. 20–28, last amended by *Directive (EU) 2019/790 of the European Parliament and of the Council of 17 April 2019 on copyright and related rights in the Digital Single Market and amending Directives 96/9/EC and 2001/29/EC*, OJ L 130, 17.5.2019, pp. 92–125.

Act",[7] i.e., a Regulation Proposal introducing a risk-based approach to regulating AI applications in the common market. Since it basically comprises software and data compilations, AI falls in principle under the scope of copyright law.

It is to be noted, however, that copyright protection only covers the source or object code of a computer program.[8] Namely, it does not extend to any effects produced by the execution of that code on electronic devices.[9] Besides, ideas and principles substantiating the elements of a computer program, e.g., the algorithm it encapsulates, are excluded from copyright protection.[10] As far as training datasets are moreover concerned, copyright is conditional upon them constituting original creations by virtue of their content's selection and arrangement.[11]

3.2 Protecting AI Training Data with the Sui Generis IP Right on "Databases"

To circumvent the originality requirement prescribed by copyright law, training data collections may also claim the 15-year-long protection provided by Directive 96/9/EC, Art. 7 et seq., for "databases". In order for a training data collection to be regarded as a database, pursuant to Art. 1 para. 2 Directive 96/9/EC, it is expected to comprise systematically arranged pieces of information, each of which demonstrates individual significance and can be separately accessed. In this sense, only labeled data intended for supervised machine learning may be considered for the *sui generis* protection in question. However, for the pertinent rights to be ultimately established the database maker is expected to have invested considerable human, technical and/or financial resources, i.e., time, effort, energy, money, and/or infrastructure, to obtain, verify, and/or present the database contents.[12] The fulfilment of these requirements can only be assessed on a case-by-case basis.

---

[7] See Art. 3(1) of the *Proposal for a Regulation of the European Parliament and of the Council laying down harmonized rules on artificial intelligence (Artificial Intelligence Act) and amending certain Union legislative acts*, COM/2021/206 final; Spindler (2021), pp. 362 et seq.

[8] See Art. 10 para 1 TRIPS; C-393/09 of 22.12.2010, *Bezpečnostní softwarová asociace*, ECLI:EU:C:2010:816, rec.37–42.

[9] C-406/10 of 02.05.2012, SAS Institute Inc., ECLI:EU:C:2012:259, rec.39–41.

[10] See Art. 1 par. 2 Directive 2009/24.

[11] See also the reflections of Jakl (2019), p. 714, on further limitations set to the copyright protection of AI training data by Art. 5 para. 3(d) *Directive 2001/29/EC of the European Parliament and of the Council of 22 May 2001 on the harmonization of certain aspects of copyright and related rights in the information society*, OJ L 167, 22.6.2001, pp. 10–19, in accordance with C-476/17 of 29.07.2019, Pelham, ECLI:EU:C:2019:624, rec.74.

[12] See Art. 7 and recitals 7 and 40 of the Preamble of Directive 96/9/EC.

3.3 Trade Secret Protection for Smart Software

The term "trade secret" refers to information which is treated as confidential by its holder through reasonable protective measures, and which gains commercial value by its very secrecy. This definition adheres to internationally binding standards,[13] having been also adopted in all EU Member States through Directive (EU) 2016/943.[14] Any kind of knowledge which is or may prove valuable for an undertaking, like know-how, business, and technological information, may be treated as a trade secret.[15] The pertinent regulatory framework is postulated as the suitable legal basis for algorithm protection, which is explicitly excluded from copyright and patent law.[16] It is arguably also appropriate for protecting collections of training data serving machine learning purposes, since it does not set any requirements for originality or substantial investments.[17]

The legal protection of trade secrets prohibits their unauthorized acquisition, use or disclosure by third parties. However, it does not entail the establishment of an absolute right on the information concerned. Therefore, the independent acquisition or development of identical knowledge through, e.g., research and analysis, or even reverse engineering, remains permitted.[18]

From another perspective, unpublished innovations do not qualify as "prior art". Thus, trade secret holders are exposed to the risk that third parties of good faith may obtain priority IP rights on the same subject matter. It should be also considered that the confidentiality required for trade secret protection may impede the commercialization of technical information.[19]

3.4 Justifying the Growing Global Interest in AI Patents

In view of the drawbacks identified in the above fields of IP law, stakeholders involved in AI industry have consistently sought for alternative or complementary means of protection for their intellectual property. This has incited in recent years remarkable interest in patenting AI worldwide.[20] Patents are legal titles establishing IP rights on "inventions". For a patent to be granted, an application must be filed

---

[13] Art. 39 para. 2 TRIPS.

[14] See Art. 2 para. 1 *Directive (EU) 2016/943 of the European Parliament and of the Council of 8 June 2016 on the protection of undisclosed know-how and business information (trade secrets) against their unlawful acquisition, use and disclosure*, OJ L 157, 15.6.2016, pp. 1–18.

[15] See rec. 14 Directive (EU) 2016/943.

[16] See Scheja (2018), pp. 485–492; Söbbing (2019), pp. 192–194.

[17] BGH, *Decision of 28 January 2014*, VI ZR 156/13, BGHZ 200, para.38–51.

[18] See rec. 16 Directive (EU) 2016/943.

[19] See EPO (2018), p. 3; Papadopoulou (2021), p. 416.

[20] See EPO (2017).

before the competent authorities. A patent holder is entitled to exclusive use of his/her protected invention for a period of 20 years from the filing date.

In comparison to copyright, patent law promises the establishment of exclusive rights on whole AI applications, i.e., the AI-driven products intended for the market. It, therefore, extends the IP protection provided beyond the program's source code, to the tangible results of its execution. Thus, it ultimately prevents the achievement of competing results by means of different program code. Furthermore, patent granting presupposes the disclosure of all details about how to make and use the claimed invention. Therefore, it is supposed to contribute to future innovation, while circumventing the competitive risks associated with information confidentiality.[21] The following sections examine the prerequisites for patenting AI in the European legal order.

4 Abstract Patentability of AI Technologies in the European Patent System

The exclusive rights deriving from a patent are territorial, i.e., only applicable within the country where the patent has been granted. Therefore, to protect an invention in multiple jurisdictions, one has to file a patent application before each national competent authority separately. To circumvent the adversities associated with the principle of territoriality, international treaties have established unified procedures for patent granting. The European Patent Convention (EPC) is such a treaty establishing the legal framework for the granting of "European patents", in particular, as well as special bodies for the implementation of its provisions.

4.1 The European Patent System in a Nutshell

European patents may be granted through a single application and investigation process before the European Patent Office (EPO). Subsequently, they can be validated in all EPC contracting states, i.e., most EU Member States and several third countries. European patents can be also revoked both at a centralized and at the national levels.

In particular, first-instance decisions by the EPO can be appealed before the EPO boards of appeal. The boards' decisions form the case-law of the EPO, which serves as non-binding guidance for the national courts. More generally, its position and role enable EPO to exert significant influence on patent policy in the EPC contracting states, and, thus, in the EU as a whole.

[21] European Commission (2016), pp. 3 et seq.

According to Art. 52 para. 1 of the EPC, as it currently stands, *"European patents shall be granted for any inventions, in all fields of technology, provided that they are new, involve an inventive step and are susceptible of industrial application"*. This provision is meant to prescribe three patentability requirements for any claimed subject matter, i.e., its novelty, non-obviousness, and industrial applicability. The implementation of the pertinent examination presupposes, however, that the subject matter concerned is patent-eligible.

4.2 *The Rules Determining Software Patent-Eligibility According to the EPC*

The invention concept is not defined in the EPC. However, Art. 52 para. 2 provides a non-exhaustive list of negative examples in that regard. Accordingly, as non-inventions are declared any scientific theories and mathematical methods, aesthetic creations, schemes, and rules to make business, as well as presentations of information and computer programs. Consequently, software is explicitly declared as patent-ineligible. However, paragraph 3 of the same Article associates patent-ineligibility with filing a patent application for the excluded subject-matter "as such". This reservation is considered to be making the admissibility of software patent applications conditional upon them "serving a technical purpose" according to their claims.

4.2.1 The EPO's Two-Hurdle Approach

The EPO outlined a "two-hurdle approach" to identify whether the claimed subject matter is technical or not in any given case.[22] In this context, the technical character is examined in two successive stages. Firstly, it is assessed whether the claimed subject matter refers to an activity excluded from patent protection "as such", thus falling foul of the invention concept according to Art. 52 paras 2 and 3 EPC. If this hurdle is overcome, it is subsequently examined whether the claimed invention provides a technical contribution to the prior art. It will be deemed patentable if it solves a technical problem by technical means in a novel and non-obvious manner.

4.2.2 The "any Hardware" Approach

In the first stage of the above investigation, the EPO determines whether the patent application should be dismissed for referring to purely conceptual subject matter. In the context of this assessment, the EPO applies the so called "any hardware"

[22] T 0641/00 (*Two identities/COMVIK*) of 26.9.2002.

approach,[23] which prescribes that any claim involving technical means shall be deemed patent eligible. This approach renders automatically patent eligible any claim involving a physical device, e.g., an apparatus. Similarly, claims related to software may avoid exclusion under Articles 52(2) and (3) EPC by merely explicitly mentioning the use of a computer[24] or a computer-readable storage medium or a computer peripheral for presenting information, like its monitor.[25]

4.2.3 The "Technical Effect" Criterium

It appears that the formula applied for software patent applications overcoming the eligibility hurdle is based on a formality. It merely requires formulating a claim as a computer implemented method or as a computer program product, i.e., mentioning the word "computer". This ascertainment does not render, however, meaningless the exclusions listed in Article 52(2) EPC. The technical character of a patent-eligible software invention will be re-assessed when evaluating its concrete patentability.

As mentioned above, to be deemed patentable an invention must satisfy the requirements of novelty, inventive step, and industrial applicability. Novelty and inventiveness can be based only on technical features, which must be clearly defined in the claim. It is expected, in particular, that the claim contains a technical feature, which produces a hitherto not known and non-obvious "technical effect".[26]

The technical effect criterion is fulfilled in any case where the claimed subject matter solves a technical problem using technical means. Accordingly, a technical effect is produced by computer software managing, e.g., an industrial process or the operation of a piece of machinery. Software may produce a technical effect also by influencing the internal functioning of a computer. However, the common physical effects of the program execution on an electronic device, e.g., any electrical currents produced, do not suffice to consolidate a patentable technical effect. In such cases, the technical character of the invention is associated with the "further effects" deriving from the software execution on the hardware.[27]

[23] First outlined in the decision T 0931/95 (*Controlling pension benefits system*) of 8.9.2000 and established by T 0258/03 (*Auction method/HITACHI*) of 21.4.2004. See also T 0424/03 (*Clipboard formats I/MICROSOFT*) of 23.2.2006.

[24] G 0003/08 (*Programs for computers*) of 12.5.2010, rec.10.1 et seq.

[25] See also T 0154/04, *Estimating sales activity/DUNS LICENSING ASSOCIATES*, of 15 November 2006, rec.21: Data stored as electric signals fulfil the requirements of the critical approach. However, the term "database" does not imply technicality per se, since it encompasses data collections which may be performed without using any technical means at all.

[26] T 0154/04, ibid., rec.16.

[27] T 1173/97, *Computer program product/IBM*, of 01.07.1998, rec.6 et seq.

4.2.4 The Concept of a "Further" Technical Effect

According to the EPO's case-law, no further technical effect is produced by software that merely automates conceptual tasks and business methods.[28] Inventions tackling managerial issues by means of technology, have no technical character.[29] The enhanced speed achieved through the computerized execution of the task, and any related energy and time saving effects, are no technical solutions. Besides, modelling information in a way that a viewer may regard as appealing, lucid, or logical, e.g., presenting data as vector diagram charts on a computer display, does not represent a solution to any technical problem.[30] Similarly, modifications to a programming language that enable experts to develop computer programs with greater ease, speed, and accuracy, do not confer a technical contribution to the art.[31]

By contrast, a patentable computer program is expected to involve technical teaching, addressed to the person skilled in the art, as to how to solve a particular technical problem using technical means. This requirement may be fulfilled in any case where a computer program affects the physical functioning or the operating parameters of an electronic device. For instance, it may fix a malfunction, like delays in the propagation of information, or add a new functionality that does not merely address a human mental process, like splitting the touchscreen on a smart device.[32] Also, modifying the technical parameters of an electronic application to circumvent a technical problem which hampers its operation, represents a technical subject matter.[33] On the contrary, modifying the operation rules of an electronic application so that any technical problems, e.g., data transmission delays, become irrelevant, has been deemed not technical.[34]

As far as the presentation of information is concerned, it might exceptionally contribute to the technical character of an invention. To this end, the presentation of information is expected to assist the user in performing a technical task by means of a continued and guided human-machine interaction process.[35] In a similar vein,

[28] T 1865/17 (*Generating two-dimensional visual objects/GMC SOFTWARE*) of 4.12.2020, rec.10.3.

[29] This is the case, for example, when it comes to systems computerizing order placing, T 0172/03 of 27.11.2003, (*Order management/RICOH*), the management of supply needs, BGH X ZB 23/74 of 22.06.1976, (*Dispositionsprogramm*), the classification of data records for billing or rating purposes, T 1784/06, *(Classification method/ COMPTEL)*, of 21.09.2012, etc.

[30] See T 49/99 of 5.3.2002; T 244/00 of 15.11.2001; T 0125/04 of 10.05.2005.

[31] T 1630/11 (*Modelling a multiprocessor system/THE MATHWORKS*) of 13.1.2017, rec.9.2.

[32] See T 0172/03 (*Order management/RICOH*) of 27.11.2003; BGH X ZB 23/74 (*Dispositionsprogramm*) of 22.06.1976; T 1784/06 (*Classification method/COMPTEL*) of 21.09.2012.

[33] See T 1422/19 (*Content item visibility/GOOGLE*) of 19.5.2021.

[34] See T 0258/03 (*Auction method/HITACHI*) of 21.4.2004.

[35] T 1741/08 (*GUI layout/SAP*) of 2.8.2012, rec. 3.3; T 0336/14 (*Presentation of operating instructions/GAMBRO*) of 2.9.2015; T 1802/13 (*Brain stimulation/CLEVELAND*) of 10.11.2016; T 2084/18 (*Suspicious behaviour/AIC*) of 18.6.2021, rec. 3.2.

technical character has been attributed to a method of arranging images on the display of electronic devices in a side-by-side manner at a low resolution, so that users would not have to go through the images one by one at a high resolution to select a specific image for output.[36]

4.3 The Technical Character of AI Inventions

To sum up, software patentability entails that the critical technology is presented as a computer implemented innovation intended to produce a technical effect capable to solve a technical problem. This is not the case for software designed to automate cognitive tasks in order to accelerate their performance, to save energy, to achieve greater accuracy, etc. Neither fulfills the "technical character" criterion any information modelling or user interface improvement, which only serve aesthetic purposes or convenience needs.

The EPO also applies the above rules to patent applications referring to "smart" software, i.e., software administered by machine-learning technologies.[37] In order to be deemed patent-eligible the claimed subject matter must be presented as a computer implemented method, or must, more generally, mention an inherent technical feature. As long as this requirement is fulfilled, the claimed invention is then examined with regard to its novelty, inventiveness, and practical utility. In this context, only those features of the invention are taken into consideration, which demonstrate technical character. The use of machine learning per se renders the claimed features neither technical nor inventive.[38]

It has been repeatedly ruled, for instance, that classification methods based on machine learning algorithms are not technical. Automated text classification, including email filtering, simulates a mental task regardless of the machine learning model governing the performance of the underlying algorithm. More specifically, it is irrelevant whether the latter relies on linguistic analysis,[39] predetermined features,[40] previous classification paradigms,[41] or user preferences. In particular, the intervention of user preferences in the algorithm training is considered to be rendering the whole classification process conditional upon human cognitive functions, thus

[36] T 0643/00 (*Searching image data/CANON*) of 16.10.2003.

[37] See EPO (2021a) Guidelines for examination, Part G, Chapter II, para.3.3.1.

[38] T 1510/10 (*Ranking of live web applications/ERICSSON*) of 4.12.2013, rec. 8.

[39] See T 0022/12 (*Spam classification/MICROSOFT*) of 16.11.2015.

[40] Ibid, e.g., particular words, sender addresses and domains (".com", ".net", etc.), message delivery attributes (time of delivery, at night, after hours, etc.).

[41] T 1358/09 (*Classification/BDGB ENTERPRISE SOFTWARE*) of 21.11.2014.

waiving its technical character.[42] This approach is based on the theory dictated by the EPO's jurisprudence which is known as "broken technical chain fallacy".[43]

However, automated decision-making systems based on machine-learning models are not excluded per se from patentability either. For instance, methods related to detecting malware on the basis of decision tree learning algorithms[44] have been deemed technical, on the grounds that (a) a computer virus has a direct impact on the computer hardware, and (b) antivirus software does not depend on the preferences of a user.[45] A technical character has been also attributed to a reputation-based system for identifying messages as undesired. The claimed invention was meant to achieve a "more fine-grain assessment" of whether or not a received message qualifies as spam based on metrics delivered by a "reputation engine". The latter refers in principle to a data analysis algorithm attributing scores to each message based on certain identifiers, like its IP address. According to the EPO, the application concerned deals with telecommunication messages, like SIP and emails, thus referring to a technical issue. Moreover, the features composing the invention are "part of the functional computer", thus being technical.[46]

In view of the above, it can be argued that the technicality of machine learning algorithms and smart software is conditional upon the following cumulative requirements. *First*, the software must deal with a technical problem. Any issue related to the operation of a computer's hardware is regarded as in principle technical. Therefore, the design of a patentable piece of software must have been motivated by technical considerations of the computer's internal functioning. *Second*, the software must attempt to resolve the pertinent technical problem through technical means. Therefore, automated decision-making and machine learning may be considered technical as long as they take account of only technical parameters. In this respect, user preferences constitute a non-technical criterion, while, e.g., an email's size is a technical one.

[42] Accordingly, a spam filter algorithm cannot have a purely technical purpose if the classification depends on the personal preferences of a user. T 2363/16 (*URL based email filtering/MICROSOFT TECHNOLOGY LICENSING*) of 6.12.2019.

[43] See T 2147/16 of 7.9.2021, rec. 5.3.18; T 1741/08 (*GUI layout/SAP*) of 2.8.2012, rec.2.1.6; T 1670/07 (*Shopping with mobile device/NOKIA*) of 11.7.2013, rec.11.

[44] Such algorithms gradually filter the available input data through successive classification queries which test different parameters. Thus, ultimately a classification decision is reached. See T 0340/14 (*Detection of previously unknown malware/KASPERSKY*) of 5.11.2019.

[45] T 2147/16, ibid., rec.5.3.19.

[46] T 1028/14 (*Non-technical features*) of 22.8.2017, rec.1.1.2 to 1.1.4.

5 AI Normative Challenges to the European Patent Law

Undoubtedly, the exact features determining the technical or non-technical character of AI inventions according to the EPO's two-hurdle approach have not been identified and systematized consistently yet. However, the interplay between AI and patent law raises several issues of concern which extend far beyond the technicality of AI inventions. The following section highlights normative challenges posed to patent law by AI and critically presents the corresponding responses of the EPO to date.

5.1 Issues of Concern Related to the Concrete Patentability of Inventions Directed to AI Technologies

For the sake of clarity, the pertinent analysis is allocated in two sub-sections. This one relates to AI technologies constituting the subject matter of European patent applications. The second one following further below deals with the issue of patenting innovations generated by AI.

5.1.1 Ethically Controversial AI

With reference to patenting AI technologies, the ban contained in Art. 53 (a) EPC in relation to ethically controversial inventions should be firstly taken into account. Autonomous decision-making facilitated by AI has been linked to serious restrictions on the individual's freedoms and with negative effects on one's interests, e.g., unjustified discrimination and market segmentation. Therefore, the scope of application of the above provision and its relevance for AI inventions should be investigated and defined.

5.1.1.1 The Concept of "Ordre Public" and Morality

Art. 53 EPC, in line with Art. 27 para. 2 TRIPS, prohibits patent granting for inventions the commercial exploitation of which is contrary to "ordre public" or morality. The prohibition is specified by the Biotechnology Directive 98/44,[47] with reference to its scope of application, through a non-exhaustive list of inventions which are considered not patentable on the ground of the ethical controversy they raise. Accordingly, excluded from patentability shall be (a) inventions for cloning human beings, (b) inventions for modifying the germ line genetic identity of human

[47] *Directive 98/44/EC of the European Parliament and of the Council of 6 July 1998 on the legal protection of biotechnological inventions*, OJ L 213, 30.7.1998, pp. 13–21.

beings, (c) inventions involving the use of human embryos for industrial or commercial purposes, (d) inventions for modifying the genetic identity of animals that is likely to cause them suffering without any substantial medical benefit to human beings or animals, or an invention that is an animal resulting from such a process.[48]

In EU law the terms "ordre public" and morality are used interchangeably, thus ultimately being regarded as synonyms.[49] According to the ECJ, in addition to the perturbation of the social order involved in any infringement of the law, restrictions in the name of "ordre public" and morality presuppose the existence of a genuine and sufficiently serious threat to the requirements of public policy affecting one of the fundamental interests of society.[50] Such interests certainly comprise human, animal and plant life and health, as well as environmental conservation.[51] In broader terms, any subject matter grossly obscene or likely to incite criminality, riot, or discriminatory propaganda may be deemed contrary to "ordre public" and morality.[52]

5.1.1.2 Ethical Considerations on AI's Distinguishing Features

AI is a revolutionary technology, which has raised ethical concerns since its very infancy. The increasing autonomy of modern software and its skills to improve by learning and to take initiatives in decision-making and problem-solving procedures are regarded as the major controversial features in this respect. It has been speculated that AI may in future surpass human intellect and become an uncontrollable risk factor.[53] Part of the scholarly debate places this scenario in the realm of science fiction.[54] However, it is commonly accepted that even contemporary AI applications may jeopardize fundamental legal goods, freedoms, and interests of individuals.[55]

Indeed, today, the individual as a citizen and consumer is subject to continuous monitoring and profiling, which is used for automated decision-making that serves scoring and targeted advertising purposes. Such automated decisions are goal-oriented, detached from any ethical considerations and likely to blindly reproduce social prejudices. Under these circumstances, the individual may lose his/her freedom of choice and self-determination and be exposed to unjustified discrimination.[56]

[48] See Article 6, in conjunction with recitals 36, 38, and 39 of the Directive's preamble.

[49] See *Opinion of Advocate General on the ECJ case C-377/98 of 14.06.2001, Netherlands v Parliament and Council*, ECLI:EU:C:2001:329, rec.99.

[50] C-30/77 of 27.10.1977, *Régina v Pierre Bouchereau*, ECLI:EU:C:1977:172, rec.35.

[51] See Art. 27 para.2 TRIPS and rec.36 of the Directive's 98/44 Preamble.

[52] See EPO (2021a) Guidelines for examination, Part 1, Chapter III, para.8.1.

[53] European Parliament (2017), pp. 6 et seq.

[54] See for instance Kim (2020), pp. 443–456.

[55] See Tzoulia (2021), pp. 451 et seq.

[56] See especially on the "filter bubble" or "echo chamber" phenomenon, European Parliament Briefing, *Artificial Intelligence: Challenges for EU Citizens and Consumers*, 2019, PE 631.043, pp. 4 et seq.

From another perspective, the increased machine autonomy may put users of, e.g., self-driving vehicles and other autonomous devices at serious risks concerning their life and health, while disrupting the causal link between fault, damage, and human liability.[57]

These AI aspects have been acknowledged by legal orders around the world, thus prompting the drafting of non-binding guidelines and recommendations with a view to enforcing specific ethical principles and safety standards for the manufacture and use of AI technologies.[58] Only recently have the first legislative initiatives implementing AI ethics as prescribed at a global level been enacted. Such an initiative constitutes the proposed EU Regulation prescribing certain obligations for the operators of "high-risk" AI ("AI Act")[59]. The institutionalization of AI ethics in the EU has been first attempted in the context of the GDPR.[60]

To date, AI patent applications handled by the EPO have not raised ethical concerns. It should be considered, however, whether Art. 53 EPC could give rise to well-founded objections to smart software patent granting. Could that provision preclude patent protection, e.g., for the long-heralded artificial "general" and "super" intelligence?[61] Is the EPO entitled to grant a patent for, e.g., a fully automated driving system not allowing any human driver intervention? Would the same approach apply in the case of a "face recognition" mobile app?

5.1.1.3 AI Inventions under the Scrutiny of Art. 53 EPC

Art. 53 EPC and 6 of the Biotechnology Directive are condemned for both legislative inefficacy and lego-political inexpediency. The reason is that they entrust the EPO and the respective national authorities with *ex ante* ethical assessments about the possible future consequences of an invention's commercial exploitation. On the one hand, it is argued that the social impact of an invention's commercial exploitation is unrelated to the issue of its IP protection and monopolization. On the other hand, the precepts of public order and morality are allegedly variable and fluid, something which impedes their reliable assessment in advance.[62]

---

[57] See Spindler (2015), pp. 766–776; Grützmacher (2016), pp. 695–698.

[58] See, for example, *European Parliament resolution of 20 October 2020 with recommendations to the Commission on a framework of ethical aspects of artificial intelligence, robotics, and related technologies*, 2020/2012(INL), rec.27 et seq; Executive Office of the President of the United States (2019), pp. 19 et seq.

[59] Supra, note 7.

[60] *Regulation (EU) 2016/679 of the European Parliament and of the Council of 27 April 2016 on the protection of natural persons with regard to the processing of personal data and on the free movement of such data and repealing Directive 95/46/EC (General Data Protection Regulation)*, OJ L 119, 4.5.2016, pp. 1–88. See on that supra note 55, pp. 462 et seq.

[61] These terms refer to software countervailing and surpassing human intelligence respectively.

[62] Enerson (2004), pp. 696 et seq.

In any case, the application of the critical provisions by the EPO is rare and limited to problematic cases of biotechnological inventions, related, e.g., to genetic chimerism.[63] This case-law suffices, however, to consolidate a number of principles which may also guide the handling of cases involving AI inventions with dubious ethical implications. *First*, an AI invention cannot be excluded from the protection of patent law merely because it infringes legal provisions, e.g., the GDPR or the forthcoming Artificial Intelligence EU Act. *Second*, the EPO cannot reject an AI patent application on the grounds provided by Art. 53 EPC, based merely on speculations. There must be scientific evidence of the harm invoked. *Lastly*, Art. 53 EPC prescribes a balancing test to be applied, in the context of which any potential hazards of the claimed invention are weighed against its usefulness to mankind.[64]

5.1.2 Substantiating the Novelty and Non-obviousness of AI Inventions

In view of the above, it appears that ethical concerns are currently very unlikely to hinder AI patent granting. In the discourse of the pertinent examination, however, further concerns may arise with reference to the concrete patentability of the filed AI invention. A relevant issue currently challenging European patent law refers to the appropriate benchmark for assessing the novelty and non-obviousness of AI inventions.

In this respect, Art. 56 EPC prescribes that *"an invention shall be considered as involving an inventive step if, having regard to the state of the art, it is not obvious to a person skilled in the art"*. The state of the art comprises *"everything made available to the public by means of a written or oral description, by use, or in any other way, before the date of filing the patent application"*.[65] Moreover, something is "obvious" if it does not involve the exercise of any skill or ability beyond that to be expected of the person skilled in the art. This notional person represents the skilled practitioner in the pertinent field of technology who is possessed of average knowledge and ability.[66]

AI challenges these principles. As implied above, each advanced AI product is the result of collective research and joint contributions from various disciplines, such as computer science, data analysis, logic, cognitive modelling, etc. It is therefore difficult to determine the technical field (the "art"), to which AI inventions pertain in each given case. Moreover, the self-improvement capacities of modern algorithmic codes blur the lines between prior and novel art. In other words, whether the claimed

---

[63] See, for instance, Application No EP 0 322 240 A2 of 28.06.89, *Chimeric immunocompromised mammals and their use ("the Stanford patent").*

[64] Supra note 61.

[65] T 0939/92 (*Triazoles*) of 12.9.1995, rec.2.3.

[66] T 0004/98 (*Liposome Compositions/SEQUUS*) of 9.8.2001. See also T 0172/03 (*Order management/RICOH*) of 27.11.2003.

features are known and not obvious is rather opaque, given that the full cognitive potential of already known AI products remains inevitably unexplored. Under these circumstances, it is questionable whether human experts remain competent to evaluate the novelty and non-obviousness of AI inventions. It is also debatable, whether the premise of inventive step remains relevant for assessing the patentability of AI inventions or needs to be abandoned, as postulated occasionally in the literature.[67]

Concerning the above issues, the EPO Guidelines for Examination note that the skilled person might also be a team of human experts.[68] The knowledge available to the competent person or team may derive from any, even undocumented source in the relevant field of technology.[69] Consequently, the expert or team of experts skilled in the art of smart software is supposedly aware of those AI technologies which are openly used in industrial practice, as well as of information contained in previous AI patent specifications and related scientific publications.[70] The examiner must give fair weight to arguments or evidence submitted by the applicant concerning the background of the AI invention.

To date, all EPO decisions related to AI applications have effortlessly identified the state of prior art in the pertinent field of technology. In the domain of distributed gaming systems, for instance, prior art equates to the knowledge possessed by the average gaming/betting program expert on the date of patent filing.[71] A novel way to generate input data (colored images) for training a machine learning algorithm (semantic classifier) has been found to contribute to the prior art in the relevant field in a non-obvious way.[72] Also, a well-known AI technology for identifying audio content may be patented, if used to tackle a different technical problem.[73]

Nevertheless, European patent applications having been examined so far have not given EPO the opportunity to comment upon the implications of increased software autonomy for the consolidation of inventive step. This arguably justifies the assumption that, despite any contrary speculations, software automation is currently subject to certain limitations and lies under human control. It may also signify, however, that the occasional confrontation of the EPO with AI inventions hinders it from outlining a realistic and up-to-date European AI patenting policy.

5.1.3 Disclosing AI Inventions Sufficiently

Art. 83 EPC states that the patent application shall disclose the invention in a manner sufficiently clear and complete for it to be carried out by a person skilled in the art.

---

[67] See relevant reflections in Blok (2017), pp. 70 et seq.

[68] T 0164/92 (*Electronic computer components*) of 29.4.1993.

[69] T 0766/91 (*Decorative laminates/BOEING*) of 29.9.1993, rec.8.2.

[70] See Nägerl et al. (2019), pp. 338 et seq.

[71] T 0683/17 of 3.12.2020, rec.3.8.

[72] T 1286/09 (*Image classifier/INTELLECTUAL VENTURES*) of 11.6.2015.

[73] T 2123/16 (*Audio-content identification/ROVI GUIDES*) of 5.2.2019.

The question what exactly needs to be disclosed is particularly relevant for inventions that concern AI products and machine or deep learning models. The EPO has recently dealt with a relevant case, rejecting the patent application on the ground of insufficient disclosure of the claimed subject-matter.

Indeed, case T 0161/18 dealt with the patentability of a heart monitoring apparatus comprising a sensor for receiving electrocardiograph signal from the patients and a neural network for identifying arrhythmia. The EPO board of appeal noted that with reference to the training of the ANN, the application merely stated that the input data should cover a broad spectrum of patients of different age, gender, constitutional type, health condition, etc., to avoid specifying the network. However, the application did not disclose which input data would be suitable for training the ANN of the invention, or at least a data record suitable for solving the underlying technical problem.[74]

The EPO had already made clear in the discourse of an earlier case that, where a software patent application invokes machine learning features, it must define the particular machine learning method used and describe it thoroughly.[75] Through the above decision, the EPO has further declared that, in this context, the learning process itself must be outlined and substantiated. This requirement serves the objective of enabling examiners to verify that by means of the identified learning process the claimed software reaches the desired outcomes, i.e., solves the crucial technical problem.

Consequently, for sufficient disclosure to be achieved, it is not enough for the applicant to just mention the categories of data used in the training process. However, it is neither necessary to reveal one's whole training database. On the contrary, a minimum exemplary dataset adequate and suitable for testing the learning process of the invention would suffice. The applicant is expected, in particular, to provide the examiners with those training data determining the weighting factors of the machine learning model.

With respect to unsupervised machine learning, which demonstrates dynamic character and stimulates increased self-reliance in software operation, endeavours for sufficient disclosure may prove challenging. The said features may potentially render AI functioning unpredictable and any related technical effect untraceable and unjustifiable. Therefore, revealing the operation of unsupervised machine learning models in a verifiable and reproducible manner may, apart from providing any training data used, also entail a comprehensible description of the model's internal structure, and/or the disclosure of the training algorithm administering its performance.[76]

It is speculated that the requirement to precisely disclose the input data and algorithms used to train a machine learning model may expose the applicant's trade secrets to competitors.[77] Similar contemplations have been prompted by data

[74] T 0161/18 (*Äquivalenter Aortendruck/ARC SEIBERSDORF*) of 12.5.2020, rec.2.2.

[75] T 1510/10, ibid.

[76] Meniere, Pihlajamaa (2019), p. 335.

[77] See ad hoc BGH, Decision of 28 January 2014, VI ZR 156/13, BGHZ 200, 38–51.

protection legislation. For instance, the GDPR endows data subjects with the right to not only be aware of, but also to understand any automated decision-making affecting them.[78] Such obligations may conflict with the interest of undertakings to handle confidentially any competitively sensitive information they possess, such as the algorithms and training datasets administering AI applications employed in their business practice. In such cases, trade secret holders are arguably expected to reconcile themselves the conflicting interests by finding the less intrusive way to disclose the operation of their automated decision-making systems to the data subjects concerned.[79]

When it comes to patent disclosure, however, reconciliation does not seem to be an option for such conflicting interests. Directive 2016/943 provides, in rec. 39 of its Preamble, that the protection of trade secrets shall not affect the application of any intellectual property rights. Moreover, Art. 5 of that Directive legitimizes any trade secret disclosure which serves the purpose of protecting a legitimate interest recognized by law. Accordingly, in the context of patent filing the applicant's interest to establish a right for exclusive use on the claimed invention precludes the protection of any underlying trade secrets.

5.2 Issues of Concern Related to "AI-Generated Inventions"

The ability of modern software to interpret external stimuli and learn enables it to deliver products that would have appertained to intellectual property, had they been created by humans. Indeed, in recent years, machines have been featured in the media for having created artistic works, written literary or scientific scripts, and composed music. Legal theory has been notably preoccupied with the question of who can claim the paternity of those creations, if not the software involved itself.[80]

The same contemplations arise in the case of AI-generated inventions.[81] This term refers to technical innovations having been developed exclusively or partly through contributions made by smart software. Examples of such inventions having been known so far comprise dental care devices, innovations from the pharmaceutical industry, etc.[82]

The involvement of AI in the inventive process challenges fundamental principles of intellectual property law. This legal branch recognizes only natural persons and, under certain conditions, legal entities as the beneficiaries of the related rights. Therefore, inventorship is regarded as a human-centered notion. This may not be

[78] See Art. 13(2)(f), 14(2) (g) and 22(3) of the GDPR, as well as the recital 71 of its Preamble.

[79] Supra note 55, pp. 462 et seq.

[80] See for instance De Wachter (2020), pp. 12–20; Lauber-Rönsberg (2019), pp. 244–253; Hristov (2017), pp. 431–454.

[81] See Hetmank and Lauber-Rönsberg (2018), pp. 575 et seq.

[82] Supra note 66, pp. 69 et seq; Bonadio et al. (2021), p. 50.

explicitly acknowledged in the EPC, it is derived however implicitly from its Art. 81, as well as from the Guidelines for Examination released by the EPO, in particular from rule No 19(1). There, it is mentioned that a patent application shall designate the inventor by stating that "person's" family and given name, as well as place of residence, while also bearing his/her signature. It is evident that the European Patent System takes the human nature of an inventor for granted.[83] This approach is embraced worldwide.[84]

Nevertheless, patent offices around the world have recently dealt with patent applications naming AI systems as the inventor.[85] In two renowned cases dealt by EPO,[86] the Office has taken a stance on the issue of AI inventorship by declaring that only human beings may qualify as inventors. Third parties may acquire rights on non-proprietary inventions by virtue of law or contractual agreements. However, smart software lacking any kind of personhood can neither own nor transfer IP rights.[87]

The above premise has been condemned as outdated and erroneous by several scholars.[88] Accordingly, the EPC should be interpreted broadly or even be amended to embrace non-human inventorship. The lack of legal capacity currently impeding the ownership of IP rights by machines has been suggested to be tackled either by acknowledging a sort of electronic personality for advanced AI applications,[89] or by establishing a *sui generis* IP right intended to protect specifically AI-devised products.[90] Despite the ongoing debate in legal theory, however, the EPO perceives the legal regime in force as adequate to successfully handle any inventive capacities of contemporary smart software.

For the sake of brevity, the analysis at hand shall not delve into each one of the above positions. It shall align itself with the view that in the current stage of technological advancement AI remains a tool for human experts irrespective of any self-evolving capacities it may demonstrate. Therefore, the inventorship of innovations devised through the engagement of AI technologies can be traced back at all times to a person bearing legal capacity pursuant to the legislation in force. The one to be designated as inventor, among all those persons involved in AI industry, often in the capacity of an employer or an employee (e.g., software developers, machine learning supervisors, data controllers and processors, investors,

---

[83] Supra note 75.

[84] World Economic Forum (2018), p. 9.

[85] See US patent applications of the kind in supra note 69, footnote 36; Bonadio et al. (2021), supra note 81, pp.56 et seq.

[86] Cases J 8/20 and J 9/20 corresponding to the applications No EP3564144 - *FOOD CONTAINER*; EP3563896 - *DEVICES AND METHODS FOR ATTRACTING ENHANCED ATTENTION*.

[87] Recently the EPO's Legal Board of Appeal (2021b) announced its decision to also dismiss the appeal in cases J 8/20 and J 9/20.

[88] See for instance Stierle (2021), pp. 115–133; Stierle (2020), pp. 918–924.

[89] See European Parliament (2017) *Report with recommendations to the Commission on Civil Law Rules on Robotics*, p. 18.

[90] Stierle (2021), supra note 87, pp. 131 et seq.

etc.), shall be identified in accordance with the general principles of patent law. This approach also evades any inconsistencies and the legal uncertainty associated with the recognition of a new IP right and/or a new subject of law.

The above considerations do not suggest, however, that AI ingenuity is devoid of any legal consequences. While being used and exploited by a licensee, smart software may deliver by-products which fall independently under the concept of intellectual property. It is, therefore, to be contemplated who shall be the beneficiary of IP rights on "secondary" inventions being delivered by means of patented AI during its licensing period. It has been argued that any conflicting interests of the patent owner and the licensee may be contractually reconciled in such cases by means of "experimental-use-exemption" clauses, "reach-through" and "grant-back" agreements.[91] Such arrangements and their enforcement shall be scrutinized in light of their IP and competition law implications.

6 Concluding Remarks and Further Research Recommendations

This chapter evaluated the suitability and effectiveness of patents as a means for AI protection in comparison to other intellectual property rights, such as copyright and trade secrets. It identified the doctrines determining patentability for inventions from the IT sector, as prescribed by the EPO, and examined their implementation in the case of smart software in particular. It appeared that, when it comes to AI, the commonly problematic relationship between software and patent law reaches new dimensions. Not only the patentability and inventorship requirements need to be reconsidered in light of any AI peculiarities, but also the contractual relationships developed in the context of the economic exploitation of patented AI need to be explored and the consequences of AI patenting on the functioning of market competition need to be contemplated. In this respect, EPO case-law issued on the occasion of AI patent filings can offer only limited contribution. To realistically assess the need for a change of paradigm in the European patent system at the jurisprudential or/and legislative level, one would need feedback derived from the AI industry and market practice. Obviously, a promising field of interdisciplinary research is emerging in this area.

References

Blok PH (2017) The inventor's new tool: artificial intelligence – how does it fit in the European patent system? Eur Intell Prop Rev 39(2):69–73

[91] See Goddar (2021), p. 197.

Bonadio E, McDonagh L (2020) Artificial intelligence as producer and consumer of copyright works: evaluating the consequences of algorithmic creativity. Intell Prop Q 2:112–137
Bonadio E, McDonagh L, Dinev P (2021) Artificial intelligence as inventor: exploring the consequences for patent law. Intell Prop Q 1:48–66
De Wachter J (2020) Software written by software – is copyright still the appropriate tool to protect it? CRi 11(1):2–20
Enerson BD (2004) Protecting society from patently offensive inventions: the risk of reviving the moral utility doctrine. Cornell Law Rev. 89:685–720
European Commission (2016) Report on the trends and current practices in the area of patentability of computer implemented inventions within the EU and the U.S.
European Parliament (2017) Report with recommendations to the Commission on Civil Law Rules on Robotics. A8-0005/2017. https://www.europarl.europa.eu/doceo/document/A-8-2017-0005_EN.html.%20Accessed%2031%20October%202021
European Parliament Briefing (2019a) How Artificial Intelligence works. PE 634.420
European Parliament Briefing (2019b) State of art and future of artificial intelligence. PE 631.051
European Patent Office (EPO) (2017) Patents and the fourth industrial revolution. The inventions behind digital transformation. ISBN 978-3-89605-200-1. http://documents.epo.org/projects/babylon/eponet.nsf/0/17FDB5538E87B4B9C12581EF0045762F/$File/fourth_industrial_revolution_2017__en.pdf
European Patent Office (EPO) (2018) Patenting Artificial Intelligence. Conference Summary, 30 May 2018, Munich. https://e-courses.epo.org/pluginfile.php/23523/mod_resource/content/2/Summary%20Artificial%20Intelligence%20Conference.pdf
European Patent Office (EPO) (2021a) Guidelines for Examination in the European Patent Office. https://www.epo.org/law-practice/legal-texts/guidelines.html
European Patent Office (EPO) (2021b) Press Communiqué on decisions J 8/20 and J 9/20 of the Legal Board of Appeal. https://www.epo.org/lawpractice/case-law-appeals/communications/2021/20211221.html
Executive Office of the President of the United States (2019) US National AI R&D Strategic Plan: 2019 Update. https://www.nitrd.gov/pubs/National-AI-RD-Strategy-2019.pdf
Goddar H (2021) Patent system solutions for AI and IoT inventions. GRUR 123:196–199
Grützmacher M (2016) Die deliktische Haftung für autonome Systeme – Industrie 4.0 als Herausforderung für das bestehende Recht? Ein Plädoyer für die Nutzung von Beweislastregeln und wider den vorschnellen Ruf nach der Einführung einer Gefährdungshaftung. CR 32(10): 695–698
Guadamuz A (2017) Do Androids dream of electronic copyright? Comparative analysis of originality in artificial intelligence generated works. IPQ 2:169–186
Hetmank S, Lauber-Rönsberg A (2018) Künstliche Intelligenz – Herausforderungen für das Immaterialgüterrecht. GRUR 120(6):574–582
Hristov K (2017) Artificial intelligence and the copyright dilemma. IDEA 36:431–454
Jakl B (2019) Das Recht der Künstlichen Intelligenz. Möglichkeiten und Grenzen zivilrechtlichen Regulierung. MMR 22(11):711–715
Kim D (2020) 'AI-Generated Inventions': time to get the record straight? GRUR Int 69(5):443–456
Lauber-Rönsberg A (2019) Autonome "Schöpfung" – Urheberschaft und Schutzfähigkeit. Gewerblicher Rechtschutz und Urheberrecht (GRUR) 121(3):244–253
Meniere Y, Pihlajamaa H (2019) Künstliche Intelligenz in der Praxis des EPA. GRUR 4:332–336
Nägerl J, Neuburger B, Steinbach F (2019) Künstliche Intelligenz: Paradigmenwechsel im Patentsystem. GRUR 121(4):336–341
Papadopoulou (2021) Creativity in crisis: are the creations of artificial intelligence worth protecting? JIPITEC 12(3):408–418
Scheja K (2018) Schutz von Algorithmen in Big Data Anwendungen – Wie Unternehmen aufgrund der Umsetzung der Geschäftsgeheimnis-Richtlinie ihre Algorithmen wie auch Datenbestände besser schützen könne. CR 34(8):485–492

Söbbing T (2019) Schutz von Algorithmen. Rechtliche Anforderungen und vertragliche Gestaltung. ITRB 8:192–194

Spindler G (2015) Roboter, Automation, künstliche Intelligenz, selbst-steuernde Kfz – Braucht das Recht neue Haftungskategorien? Eine kritische Analyse möglicher Haftungsgrundlagen für autonome Steuerungen. CR 31:766–776

Spindler G (2021) Der Vorschlag der EU-Kommission für eine Verordnung zur Regulierung der Künstlichen Intelligenz (KI-VO-E). CR 37(6):361–374

Stierle M (2020) Artificial Intelligence designated as inventor – An analysis of the recent EPO case law. GRUR Int 69(9):918–924

Stierle M (2021) A de lege ferenda perspective on artificial intelligence systems designated as inventors in the European Patent System. GRUR Int 70(2):115–133

The European Consumer Organization (BEUC) (2018) Automated decision making and artificial intelligence – A consumer perspective. BEUCX-2018-058. https://www.beuc.eu/publications/beuc-x-2018-058_automated_decision_making_and_artificial_intelligence.pdf

Tzoulia E (2021) Targeted advertising in the digital era: modern challenges to consumer privacy and economic freedom: the responses of the EU legal order. In: Synodinou TE et al (eds) EU internet law in the digital single market. Springer Nature, Switzerland, pp 447–477

World Economic Forum (2018) World Economic Forum White Paper, Artificial Intelligence Collides with Patent Law. REF 160418 - case 00048540. https://www3.weforum.org/docs/WEF_48540_WP_End_of_Innovation_Protecting_Patent_Law.pdf

International Perspectives on Regulatory Frameworks: AI Through the Lens of Patent Law

David Tilt

Abstract This chapter considers the approach to regulating artificial intelligence (AI) from a patent law perspective, exploring how existing forms of regulation can help inform our stance vis-à-vis AI. The focus is on contextualising the developments in software and pharmaceutical regulation through patent law, and then applying these lessons to AI. The EU, US and Japan all represent different approaches to the regulation of AI, and this diversity already impacts the existing relationship between AI and the patent system. The chapter concludes by recommending that self-regulation for AI inventions (but supported by robust systems of data protection) will be important in encouraging the commercial growth of AI. The patent system represents an important normative filter for AI, but the experience of software and pharmaceuticals in patent law highlights how it is more successful at excluding the most extreme iterations of a technology.

1 Introduction

Artificial intelligence (AI) is perhaps the most legally disruptive innovation of recent history because it not only pushes the boundaries on our understanding of technology, but also reframes our societal relationships. The human aspect of this disruption is particularly significant because it has *already* started—the lives of ordinary citizens in areas like finance, crime, and privacy are being shaped by complex applications of AI that have varying degrees of transparency.[1]

Establishing a regulatory regime that can deal with the definitional issues in AI and the societal risks at such a global scale is challenging because of the complex balancing of values—as explored in this chapter, Japan, the US, and the EU all attempt to balance the commercialisation of AI technologies with their normative

[1] Kovač (2020), p. 30.

D. Tilt (✉)
International Business Law at Central European University (CEU), Vienna, Austria
e-mail: tilt_david@phd.ceu.edu

A. Kornilakis et al. (eds.), *Artificial Intelligence and Normative Challenges*, Law, Governance and Technology Series 59,
https://doi.org/10.1007/978-3-031-41081-9_10

risks but from different perspectives. Intellectual property, as well as, specifically, the patent system, is central in this process of commercialisation because it represents a robust tool for businesses in protecting their AI products.[2] The patent system itself has a normative dimension because it deals with issues such as transparency, disclosure and whether the application of the technology is truly novel.

But beyond this relationship in terms of normative values and technology, the reality is that patent law is already being used to protect AI inventions. Even without a regulatory framework that specifically deals with applications of AI,[3] the patent system (as one of many relevant systems) is key for exploring the normative regulation of AI, because it reflects a type of policymaking that takes place *within* institutions and outside the normal legislative process.

Normative developments in this context are then made not only by bodies with specific institutional arrangements or processes, but also from a specific perspective. In the case of patent law, the patent offices are an important actor in this type of regulation, but with a perhaps more restricted perspective than when AI regulation is considered in a legislative context. [4] The focus here is on a comparative analysis between the US, Japan, and the EU that brings together a more conventional doctrinal analysis with a greater institutional emphasis that considers the role of specialised agencies and patent offices.

Considering the normative dimensions of AI through the patent system also reveals the interconnected nature of technological development. While the scale of AI and its societal impact is new, the challenges that it presents are not—software in the 1980s, pharmaceuticals (perhaps more recently), and data protection all have a societal dimension that was mirrored in the more technical challenge that they pose to the patent system. The process of managing the normative dimensions of technology (and of regulating them) is then one that necessarily involves the patent system but cannot be achieved solely through it.

This chapter contextualises the development of pharmaceuticals and software through the patent system from a comparative perspective, considering whether the patent system's response to their respective normative challenges could be applied to AI. These two technologies represent two fundamentally different aspects of regulation: one that represents an internal approach that relies on patent eligibility principles to minimise normative challenges and another in which an external framework is used to supplement the internal approach.

It is clear from this that AI and its impact on human welfare must be addressed while the industry is still in its relative infancy and strong welfare considerations form the basis of legal treatment in this area. This chapter suggests that the baseline normative elements of the patent system will be important as harmonised, international regulation of AI remains a difficult proposition.

---

[2]Bereuter et al. (2020), p. 156.

[3]Of which the EU AI Draft Regulation is a notable example.

[4]The role of the patent office – and its legitimacy – represents its own complex dynamic: Thambisetty (2017), p. 221.

2 Internal Perspectives

2.1 The Challenging Development of Software in Patent Law

2.1.1 Connecting the Development of Software and AI

A robust understanding of how software has shaped (and has been shaped by) the development of patent law is key to the development of a regulatory response to AI inventions because, in many practical applications,[5] inventions utilising AI can be seen as an evolution of the software or 'computer-implemented inventions' (CIIs) of the last four decades.[6] AI is perhaps a more complex subject matter from a technological point of view because, while sharing with software a similarly broad scope of application, the innovation is not always software-focused and has led to projects aimed at establishing an accurate taxonomy for AI and its applications.[7]

These taxonomies for AI operate essentially along two interconnected axes. The first focus in AI research is an exploration and categorisation of whether the AI is 'strong' or 'weak', with a second area of focus on how the AI is integrated, in order to distinguish (almost functionally) between applications of AI as they pertain to areas like robotics, algorithmic decision-making, and smart devices.[8] The Japanese approach has a considerable focus on the physical implementations of AI and the potential for AI-enabled robots to revolutionise society.[9]

These two directions are more properly understood as a spectrum in which applications of AI can be both weaker or stronger and cross disciplinary boundaries. Understood from an intellectual property perspective and evidenced across the history of software protection in the US, EU, and Japan,[10] this complexity in the framing of a technology makes it difficult to construct a response to its normative challenges because a developer of AI has several options in protecting its invention.

An applicant could file a patent that is focused on the software perspective of AI as a technical application of software to solve a technical problem and therefore cast

---

[5] Many applications of AI are fundamentally related to the development of software, with capability drastically improved, with increased computational power and data availability: Fenwick et al. (2018), p. 87.

[6] With an equally long heritage of AI and its precursors: from McCarthy in 1955 to the even earlier efforts of Turing: Girasa (2020), p. 6.

[7] Categorising exactly what 'AI' is is difficult from a functional and a technical perspective, with many types of AI levels of function and actual subsets of discipline: ibid., p. 13.

[8] AI inventions can be found in the development of deep learning, robotics, and computational vision, though, importantly, not all of these have a normative dimension. Girasa refers to the development of AI used to recolour black and white images which lacks the normative threat of other applications such as autonomous vehicles or personalized medicine: ibid., p. 14.

[9] Garcia (2019), p. 7.

[10] Even in the early framing of the European doctrine in VICOM, the emphasis is not necessarily on whether the software itself is innovative (a patent for software) but whether the inventive quality is found in the solving of a technical problem (a computer-implemented invention): Murray (2019), p. 246.

in the same way as CIIs,[11] or the applicant could otherwise patent the AI element indirectly by filing for patent protection over an innovation that addresses the technical problem as an integrated whole.[12]

2.1.2 The Early Regulation of Software in the Patent System

This flexibility is one of the drivers of heterogeneity between the major patent jurisdictions and, specifically for applications of AI that are more clearly framed as software, comes at least in part from the fractured history of software patent protection.[13] Japan exhibits a broader theoretical dissonance (rather than a practical one) in that patent law explicitly exists to further technological development and economic growth,[14] minimising the types of 'form' discussions that dominated the early stages of the software industry in the US and the EU.[15] The European and US approach to the patenting of both AI and software, on its part, is a process of navigating established patent law and crafting exceptions or complex doctrine to legitimize the patenting of technologically disruptive innovations in a way that is not present in the Japanese context.[16]

The early period of any industry is a legally disruptive time that involves finding the appropriate method of regulation. Yet for AI, the risks to society are so profound that it is difficult to endorse the same type of regulatory experimentation that occurred with software. Understanding regulation in this context as a balance between commercial interests and normative tensions highlights the difficulty in pursuing a strict regulatory paradigm—the early software industry benefited from a

[11] The emphasis on overall invention and the technical contribution of the invention beyond the mere automation of 'mental steps', means that AI can be patented not as the invention itself but as a component that contributes to the overall technical means of addressing a technical problem: Hashiguchi (2017), p. 23.

[12] Japan's approach to software patents, and therefore AI, combines parts of the US approach and the EU approach, in a way that emphasises not on the technical character of the invention, but on how it supports or assists humans: ibid., p. 26.

[13] The protection of software is not harmonised internationally and suffers significantly from crucial complexities even at the EU level, with overlapping copyright and patent protection but complicated by the lack of effective harmonisation (for example, through the Unitary Patent) and the prominent role of the national patent offices: Ghidini and Arezzo (2008), p. 372.

[14] Japan is unique in that 'invention' is defined in legislation and that software, as an application of laws of nature, is explicitly patentable: Article 2(1), Japan Patent Act 1959; whereas the EU frames software as unpatentable: Hellstadius (2010), p. 362.

[15] In Europe, there were many cases that developed the patentability of software, through the 'technical character principle' to the 'technical effect' doctrine, to gradual arrive at a situation in which software is understood as patentable (only excluding software 'as such' from patentability): Booton (2007), pp. 92, 115.

[16] The industrial objective of Japanese patent law is theoretically clearer by defining in Article 2, paragraph 1 of Japan's Patent Act 1959 an invention as the "*highly* advanced creation of technical ideas utilizing the laws of nature.". Europe and the US lack this positive definition and define invention from a negative perspective: Kageyama (2019), pp. 542, 548.

lack of specific regulation that promoted commercialisation and questions have been raised about how rapidly software would have developed if it were subject to the current standards of regulation.[17]

2.2 *Patent Law and its Internal Normative Framework*

2.2.1 The Fundamentals of the Patent System

Patent law perhaps does not stand out immediately as incorporating a strong normative dimension, particularly in contrast to the history and development of trademark and copyright law.[18] Yet its very structure means that, when an applicant attempts to patent her AI-related invention, this is implicitly filtered through a set of criteria that can be considered the internal or baseline normative response to technology. Two of these criteria and their potential to mitigate or otherwise address the welfare dimension of AI inventions will be considered here.

2.2.2 Subject Matter Eligibility

Subject matter eligibility is the first criterion that fulfils an overtly technological role in barring inventions in certain areas while performing a more muted normative function. The impact of subject matter eligibility in both contexts is necessarily narrow because it is a low standard that prevents the patenting of only the most extreme cases of technological or normative threat.

Subject matter eligibility is usually elaborated through a combination of legislative underpinning and practice of a patent office to investigate whether a technology falls within the accepted boundaries for a patent application—excluding mere discoveries, rules and laws of nature, and abstract ideas.[19] These criteria have a clear technological justification in the promotion of industrial growth by rewarding, in combination with the legal concepts of novelty and inventiveness, inventors who

[17]Riley (2007), p. 593.

[18]In copyright, the right of the author is a clear normative mechanism by which the author can prevent distortion, modification, or mutilation that would impact their reputation or character: Paterson, Karjala (2003), p. 642; while trademark functions as a safeguard for a business's investment in its image and reputation, it has a strong function of protecting the consumer from being misled: Abbott et al. (2019), p. 446.

[19]In Europe, subject matter eligibility comes from Article 52(2) of the European Patent Convention in framing ineligible subject matter; Japan, Article 2(1) (though novelty and the destruction of novelty are dealt with in 29(1)) of the Patent Act 1959; and in the US, 35 USC § 101.

innovate (as opposed to those who seek to obtain property rights over a universal truth).[20]

But it is the more muted normative dimension of subject matter eligibility that speaks to the potential of managing the disruptive societal aspects of innovations in AI. Across the US, Japan, and the EU, there are several exceptions that reflect this and prevent the patenting of innovations in areas such as atomic weapons and innovations produced solely for the killing of humans.[21] There is also the broader *ordre public* threshold, though the scale (and severity) of this exception would only appear to apply exceptionally to AI inventions.[22]

Together, subject matter eligibility and other thresholds that prevent patentability based on the subject of the invention are important in preventing these extreme examples of technological development that could threaten society. But it is because of this broad approach that it is unlikely that subject matter exclusions or *l'ordre public* would apply to AI. Software already has developed methods for overcoming subject matter exclusions (which are jurisdiction-specific anyway), and it is unlikely that an application of AI would be judged to be so contrary to public morality that it would be barred from the patent system.[23]

2.2.3 Disclosure in the Patent System

The second fundamental element of the patent system that has both a technological and normative function is disclosure, forming a part of the justification of the patent system itself.[24] Disclosure is essential to the patent system because it provides the basis for the exchange with the inventor—in that the inventor provides information about how the invention works, and in return, a period of exclusivity is granted for its exploitation.[25]

[20] The EPC outlines the requirement of novelty in Article 52(1), while the US deals with it in the same section as subject matter eligibility (§ 101).

[21] Japan provides a clear example in Article 32 of the Patent Act 1959, preventing the patenting of any invention 'liable to injure public order, morality, or public health'.

[22] Though reflected in the national legislation, Article 8 of the TRIPS Agreement outlines the functioning of a *l'ordre public* exceptions in permitting denial of patentability on the basis that it would violate public morality or national security; though on the broader construction of 'public interest' as used in TRIPS: Weckström Lindroos (2020), p. 210.

[23] As an example, social credit systems are prohibited under Title II in the EU Draft AI Regulation. It is not that *l'ordre public* would not apply, it is that it would be prohibited at a more general level before it emerges as an issue within the patent system. The technology would have to be so egregious to come under *l'ordre public* that it would interact with more general areas of law first.

[24] The patent, as a powerful economic instrument, is often constructed as an incentive for the inventor to disclose the functioning of the invention which otherwise may have remained private and is, therefore, one of the fundamental justifications of the patent system: Perera and Sugden (2017), p. 335.

[25] While the disclosure of the functioning of the invention is a core aspect of the patent system, the duty to disclose relevant prior art varies across the US, Japan, and EU, with the US representing

This requirement of disclosure is embodied in the patent document itself as a record of how the invention functions, though there are some difficulties when the patent regime does not distinguish substantively between technologies because the effectiveness (or accuracy) of this disclosure varies between disciplines.[26] The disclosure element of a patent is intended to provide others skilled in the field with the technical know-how of the invention and to, at least in principle, enable them to replicate it. Thus, it can be particularly problematic for inventions in AI.[27]

This relates back to the flexibility that an implementation of AI has as it enters the patent system, where it can be framed as *part* of a broader invention. The disclosure requirement in the patent system is, therefore, only a limited response to the issues of transparency that AI presents—though this is also a jurisdiction-specific issue. The EU framework is particular in that this technology-focused approach of the patent system is complemented with a risk-based approach in the General Data Protection Regulation (GDPR) and the proposed AI Regulation ensures that there is some transparency in the outcome.[28]

Japan has a similar to the EU approach to data protection and implements high standards around data privacy (with a similar extraterritorial reach),[29] though this also means that it has some of the same limitations in terms of AI. The US, in contrast, currently lacks this complementary relationship between disclosure as constructed by the patent system and institutional framework provided for by data protection.[30]

The data protection framework is significant for the normative challenges in AI because so much of the transformative potential in AI relies on processing data at a scale that would be impossible for humans.[31] The three jurisdictions here, then, represent a spectrum of the relationship between patent disclosure, data protection, and AI regulation: the EU has both a strong regulatory approach to AI and data protection, Japan has high standards of data protection and is yet unenthusiastic about AI-specific regulation,[32] and the US lacks a harmonised data protection

perhaps the strictest approach in the duty of candour and the EPO technically with no prior art disclosure requirement: Erstling (2011), pp. 329, 332.

[26]While in principle a technologically unitary system, patent law in practice is very much technology-specific: Burk and Lemley (2002), p. 1156.

[27]One of the major concerns that are also present with the patenting of software is that much of the technical know-how is not in published works, something particularly notable in the US context: Jaffe and Lerner (2006), pp. 27, 57.

[28]Article 22, GDPR.

[29]And the reform of Japan's data protection framework was a key element in the EU-Japan trade relationship and an 'adequacy decision' under the GDPR: Greenleaf (2018), p. 8.

[30]Though there are initiatives that propose a federal agency for privacy through a data protection act: Taylor Hatmaker (2021).

[31]Lodder and Loui (2018), p. 375.

[32]With some amendments made in 2020 to the data privacy framework: Amended Act on the Protection of Personal Information 2020 (tentative translation available at: https://www.ppc.go.jp/files/pdf/APPI_english.pdf.

framework but its agencies have emphasised the importance of the values in AI regulation.[33]

While it is complemented by the broader framing, the disclosure in the patent system is important because it involves the disclosure of the working of the invention. The GDPR, by contrast, can require that an explanation be provided as to an automated decision, [34] but this does not necessarily mean that an in-depth, technical (and, for the patent system, reproducible) explanation will be provided. The decision through the GDPR, for an individual seeking to understand how their information was processed by AI, is only a narrow disclosure, not just because it focuses on output (rather than a technical working), but also because it is not communicated to society at large. The patent system, however, is premised on a societal disclosure, rather than a limited one to a specific individual.

3 External Regulatory Regimes

3.1 Pharmaceutical Patents as a Model for Normative Regulation

3.1.1 The Emergence of Pharmaceutical Patents

Pharmaceuticals, in terms of interactions with the patent system,[35] have a longer history of intellectual property protection when compared to software, yet it is perhaps only in the last three decades that the normative dimension of pharmaceutical patent protection has become a prominent international issue. The visibility of normative issues became more prominent with the creation of the World Trade Organisation (WTO) and the conclusion of the Agreement on the Trade-Related Aspects of Intellectual Property (TRIPS),[36] which brought pharmaceutical products *and* processes under the ambit of patent protection.[37] Prior to this, there had been significant global variation as to the patent eligibility of pharmaceuticals and this variation could be identified in both developing and developed countries alike.[38]

[33] US FTC (2021).

[34] Article 22, GDPR.

[35] The patenting of pharmaceuticals has a long history in both the US and Europe, though one prominent early example is the ‘bilious pills’ that were patented in late eighteenth century Connecticut: Gabriel (2014), p. 10.

[36] On the ‘birth defect’ of TRIPS as the split between the Global North and South: Guan (2018), p. 91.

[37] On the historical lack of protection for pharmaceutical process patents: Shu-Acquaye (2016), p. 375.

[38] France and its lack of pharmaceutical product patents is one prominent example: La Croix and Liu (2017), p. 438.

While the intellectual property treatment of pharmaceuticals appears, at first, to be separate from both the experience of software and the burgeoning regulation towards AI inventions, pharmaceuticals are an indicator as to how complex issues of accessibility can emerge. Reconciling the accessibility dimension is key in situating the patent system as a complementary framework to more specific forms of AI regulation, and is particularly important as AI continues to be applied in more explicitly medical contexts.

Pharmaceuticals have a clear accessibility dimension when a patient's ability to receive adequate treatment is predicated on the ability to pay the high cost of the medication—of which a patent, as an economic device, directly contributes to.[39] Once considered an issue predominantly in lower-income countries, the concerns over medicine scarcity—because of the price impact of patents—have reached the US, Japan, and the EU in varying intensities.[40] In the last year, the interaction of patents and medicine availability has become of direct importance because of the COVID-19 pandemic.[41] Even countries that are not typically considered vulnerable to medicine shortages experienced vocal discussions about the difficulties in securing enough doses of the vaccine that are very much tied to issues of patent law.[42]

Applications of AI at the intersection of medicine and intellectual property highlight the distinct concern in the process by which AI technology is integrated into the patented innovation. Considering first the integration of AI in patented products, it is important to remember that the patent system is inherently a normative framework and, as such, one of the general exclusions to patent eligibility is therapeutic techniques.[43]

3.1.2 Accessibility, AI, and Commercialisation

There is ample scope for the introduction of AI elements into this process that would negatively impact the resulting accessibility to the innovation, the clearest of which would be the use of a trained AI to establish the most efficient or effective dose of a new compound across a variety of patients (based on gender, weight, or other material factors) in the general trend of personalised medicine that has huge potential for improved medical outcomes.[44]

---

[39] High medicine cost as a direct result of patent protection was less immediately obvious until the end of the twentieth century because strict intellectual property laws were generally confined to economically healthier states: Pogge (2010), p. 138.

[40] While medicine scarcity was once a concern for only lower-income countries, recent years have seen increased attention to the risks of scarcity in developed countries: Jenzer et al. (2019), p. 2.

[41] Kianzad and Wested (2021), pp. 71, 72.

[42] Guarascio (2020).

[43] On the general restriction of patenting therapeutic methods or medical treatment procedures: Devarapalli (2018), pp. 54, 55.

[44] Blasiak et al. (2019), p. 95.

In this hypothetical example, the AI itself is a fundamental component in the novelty of the innovation, but most crucially, it is not the sole subject of the patent. Jurisdictions around the world are struggling to deal with, in particular, the patenting of AI applications that involve training with a dataset, because the disclosure in the patent document does not constitute an accurate description of the product's functioning of the product in practice.[45]

The EU Draft Regulation on AI approaches this issue of training of the datasets again from a risk perspective like in the GDPR,[46] by requiring that high-risk implementations of AI be subject to mandatory regulation.[47] One of these provisions specifically highlights that the quality and accuracy of the dataset used to train an algorithm must be of sufficient quality and be monitored.[48] Generally, the Japanese approach to AI, on its part, does not support mandatory regulation and instead seeks to rely on design principles that would promote the creation of trustworthy applications of AI.[49] Both approaches highlight the importance of the data used to train algorithms being accurate, though, currently, Japan is seemingly opposed to mandatory regulation because of the impact on commercialisation.[50]

The US approach reflects a similar concern as to the importance of commercialisation, but with more vocal support for regulating AI sooner rather than later.[51] Applying this commercial focus to a medical context—that necessarily implicates the patent system—without a broader framework of AI regulation provides a potentially chilling scenario for accessibility. AI could be patented as part of a medical innovation (such as an advance in imaging,[52] for example) that could introduce accessibility concerns for not just physical products but medical devices more generally *without* any broader mechanisms to provide even baseline levels of transparency.

3.2 External Frameworks of Pharmaceuticals

3.2.1 Multifaceted Regimes of Regulation

From a regulatory perspective, the treatment of pharmaceuticals in the context of intellectual property is particularly useful for understanding the challenge of

[45] The European response in terms of machine learning appears to have been to consider computational models and algorithms as prima facie abstract mathematical constructs whether or not they can be trained: EPO Guidelines for Examination, 3.3.1.

[46] EU Draft Regulation, 1.

[47] Ibid, Title III.

[48] EU Draft Regulation 29.

[49] Cabinet Office (undated).

[50] METI/Expert Group on Architecture for AI Principles to be Practiced (2021).

[51] Burt (2021).

[52] Pesapane et al. (2018), p. 1.

moderating the normative impact of AI inventions because it more accurately presents the regulatory landscape. Pharmaceuticals are actually subject to a constellation of regulatory regimes, of which intellectual property is a small part, that contributes towards the overall normative aspect of pharmaceuticals as private property and medicine.

This multifaceted approach towards regulation presents an integration of internal and external frameworks that work together to limit the normative damage of pharmaceuticals. Given the already accepted use of patents in the protection of AI,[53] it is important to understand how these regulatory regimes interact to ensure that applications of AI have a robust normative foundation.

By contextualising these complementary frameworks, the role of the patent—and, by extension, why external regulation is somewhat preferable to the internal, snapshot approach discussed with software earlier—is understood as fundamentally limited in scope. While the patent system inherently has a normative dimension, the patent itself is a negative right and, therefore, it only prevents third parties from using the patented technology.[54]

The patent itself is not a licence to sell or distribute the product and neither is it inherently a tool of market dominance[55]—which, for AI, suggests that there is a space for external or non-intellectual property systems of regulation that are complementary to the objectives of the patent system. Like with pharmaceuticals, these systems of regulation would nevertheless be centred on the patent and the patented product. This use of supplementary systems is somewhat reflected in the legislative initiatives in the US and the EU, though it also raises the possibility of applying specific regimes to patented AI inventions that go beyond the generalised framework.

3.2.2 Patent Rights as Normative Screening

It would then appear that there is at least an argument for the regulation of AI that starts with an intellectual property right as an initial normative screening, subsequently supported by one or more external regulatory regimes. The introduction of standards for efficacy and safety certainly finds some analogy in the current development of AI, and pharmaceuticals show that, in contrast to some academic opinion

[53] The patent boom of AI applications is already, and has been, happening: WIPO (2019), pp. 38–39.

[54] Patent rights, though of intellectual property more generally, are negative rights that exclude others but do not necessarily permit the owner additional freedoms: Guan (2016), p. 421.

[55] Patent rights are more correctly understood as a 'temporary form of monopoly': Weyand and Haase (2005), p. 655; and may certainly contribute to a strong market position it does not guarantee market success.

regarding the early software industry,[56] an industry can thrive even within a substantive regulatory context *if* these additional standards are transparently communicated and established with clear normative objectives.

This is in stark contrast to the functioning of the *implicit* systems of normative regulation that have dominated the discussions of pharmaceuticals in the late twentieth century, where arguments based on the right to health or the right to food have been advanced.[57] Human rights, as one form of external implicit regulation for law, form a network of generalised principles that provide a vocabulary with which the negative impact of a phenomenon can be constructed and deconstructed, ensuring that victims can articulate their grievances.[58]

While this flexibility is essential to deal with the complexities of human rights violations, the evolving nature of these rights has a much less positive impact in an industrial context, because it introduces a lack of clarity as to the expectations of products, innovation, and the industry more generally. This type of flexible framework suggests that AI may need the type of specific regulation that is being currently developed in the EU.

While the Draft Regulation mentions commercialisation and unlocking the potential of Digital Europe,[59] the dominant focus of the document is the human rights of European citizens and minimising the negative potential of AI. Japan, and, to an extent, the US, both construct AI as having a negative potential, but the perspective in the documents produced by METI and the Expert Group is one that appears to prioritise commercial interests.[60]

For Japan, commercialisation is key to realising the societal benefits of AI and this requires an approach that places minimum burden on businesses (particularly as Japan promotes voluntary guidelines and design principles, though only briefly considering the governmental use of AI).[61] In the absence of an effective AI-specific regulation like in Japan, the use of human rights (or other normative frameworks) essentially becomes an attempt to resolve these incidents *after* they have occurred.

Given the profound technological and societal impact of AI (and recognising that this ex-post approach is still a valuable part of an effective system), regulating it through dispute settlement means that the AI would have already entered the market and whatever damage would have already occurred. There is also the issue that this type of approach requires an elaborate and comprehensive human rights protection regime, like the one adopted in Europe. For instance, a potential weakness in the

[56] Another example of rapidly developing industries benefiting from an absence of singular control from a strong firm is modern telephony, specifically the loss of control by AT&T and subsequent boom in products: Barton (1997), pp. 449, 455.

[57] Cullet (2003), pp. 139, 140.

[58] On the role of human rights as a 'vocabulary' in different contexts: Gross (2016), p. 51.

[59] EU Draft Regulation 6.

[60] METI/Expert Group on Architecture for AI Principles to be Practiced (2021).

[61] Ibid, p. 29.

Japanese context is that there are some gaps in the legal protection against discrimination.[62] The potential for discrimination through AI is a central concern for regulators, and would be even more challenging without clear legislative standards.

4 Reorienting the Normative Dimensions of Industry

4.1 Existing Initiatives on Normative Control in AI

4.1.1 Legislative Initiatives

In a departure from the emergence of software in the early 1970s and 1980s,[63] industry and governments have been quick to recognise the value and huge technological impact of AI inventions, while several initiatives aimed at regulating AI have emerged. As explored below, these existing approaches can be broadly divided into systems of regulation that emerged as a public response and those that represent initiatives by private industry.

The development and implementation of the General Data Protection Regulation (GDPR) in the EU has an important regulatory impact on the normative footprint of AI inventions, not only in terms of its substantive requirements that directly affect the applications of AI, but also in terms of the reach and significance of a harmonised approach to the issue (as well as of the normative identity of the actor implementing the harmonisation). The publication of the Draft Regulation in the EU (which followed its leak earlier in the year) builds upon many of the design principles of the GDPR.[64]

The Draft Regulation differentiates between AI based on the risk that it poses to society, rather than the underlying technology or its specific technical characteristics. On that basis, it involves an outright prohibition of social credit systems,[65] mandatory regulation for high-risk technologies such as biometric processing and access to essential public or private services,[66] and minimal transparency requirements for specific low-risk implementations of AI.[67] This is coupled with an extraterritorial reach that takes the same approach as the GDPR, meaning the provisions apply whether or not the AI processing took place within the EU, or the AI product was present in the EU market.[68]

[62] In particular, gender identity and sexual orientation: Amnesty International (2021).

[63] As essentially a by-product of managing hardware: Ruiz Durán (2007), p. 314.

[64] Heikkilä (2021).

[65] Title II, EU Draft Regulation, p. 13.

[66] Ibid.

[67] Ibid, Title IV.

[68] Ibid, p. 20.

The strong external framework of regulation that the GDPR and the Draft Regulation represent constitutes an important normative control on the impact of AI because it fundamentally restricts the freedom with which data can be gathered and transmitted.[69] Many forms of AI either directly rely on data gathering as preparation for a dataset in a trained algorithm or act upon the data in a more direct fashion that involves their processing.[70] In this, both cases would be covered by the provisions of the GDPR.[71]

This data protection framework also means that the baseline provisions of the patent system as to disclosure and transparency are being gradually supplemented through a broader, harmonised approach to AI technologies. The development of AI regulation in both Japan and the US is somewhat less developed than in the EU, though this seems to stem from legislative difficulties at the federal level in the US while Japan considers strong regulation to be unnecessary.[72]

4.1.2 Private Industry Initiatives

Private industry has also responded to the normative threat (and potential commercial opportunity) posed by unregulated AI development. The most significant private proposal is the idea of a form of AI auditing, in which a digital auditor reviews a company's use of algorithms and assesses its performance against a set of benchmark criteria that consider values such as transparency and accountability.[73] While constituting an important development, the auditing approach in a commercial private industry context has several limitations.

The first limitation is that, in a similar way to the patent eligibility criteria, this auditing represents a snapshot of an algorithm's performance. Given the multitude of applications of AI and its capacity to refine or otherwise iterate its functional output in a semi-autonomous manner,[74] a snapshot understanding of an algorithm's impact is fundamentally incomplete.

The timing of this auditing would also be significant because an algorithm that is audited in terms of its functioning as represented in a patent application as a part of a complete innovation would not necessarily correspond exactly with the functioning

---

[69] Alkemada and Toet (2021), p. 177.

[70] Zhuang et al. (2017), p. 4.

[71] The processing of data is one of the significant focuses of the GDPR provisions, and therefore includes processing by AI creations: Wrigley (2018), p. 184.

[72] Broadbent, Arrieta-Kenna (2021).

[73] Several initiatives have entered the auditing space, such as the Smith Institute for Industrial Mathematics and System Engineering: https://www.smithinst.co.uk/what-we-do/algorithm-auditing/; and Deloitte forecasting that algorithmic auditing will be a major role by 2025: https://www2.deloitte.com/content/dam/insights/us/articles/4767_FoW-in-govt/DI_Algorithm-auditor.pdf.

[74] AI systems are dynamic by nature, involving 'repeated or continuous learning rather than being static': Girasa (2020), p. 242.

of that invention in 6 months.[75] The auditing approach in this manifestation is also limited across jurisdictions and industries because, in the absence of a central authority or harmonised framework, there is no inherent degree of comparability between one company's digital auditing standards over that of another in a different jurisdiction.

4.2 The Contextual Role of Commercial Actors

4.2.1 The Potential in Self-Regulation

It is, therefore, clear that AI requires some form of response to the challenge it presents—both in terms of ensuring that the industry of AI applications has the requisite flexibility *and* the freedom to develop rapidly while addressing the immediate normative threat that we can already observe.[76] As increasingly specialised instruments of AI regulation will inevitably emerge, this chapter suggests that the importance of self-regulation—of implementing provisions beyond the mandatory minimum—will increase as AI becomes more integrated into everyday life.

Rather than the strict gatekeeping of the pharmaceutical approach and multiple external agencies, using the baseline provisions of the patent system and the framework of a more specialised instrument provides space for commercial actors to develop their own approaches that fit with their business style. The internal dimension of intellectual property—of simply excluding specific technologies or implementations of AI on the basis of subject matter—is not a sustainable method of ensuring damaging AI can be dynamically minimised, though an explicit external institution—in the style of a medicine authority—requires a degree of time and cooperation that (given the immediate impact of AI inventions) would not be appropriate.[77]

Self-regulation as a supplement to mandatory regulation could be increasingly incorporated by businesses as AI matures, in much the same way that businesses are already recognising the commercial value in their approach to privacy. Like with an overarching AI regulatory instrument, in data protection, these voluntary undertakings allow companies to market their technology based on how it respects data privacy or data sovereignty. As could be the case for AI, this type of commercial perspective and adoption of standards is happening in a global context in which there

[75] With the FDA requiring periodic updates to monitor what changes were implemented in the approved pre-specifications: FDA (2021).

[76] Predictive policing is one such example, in which an algorithmic data processing becomes self-reinforcing and does not adequately reflect the human relationship between law enforcement and the community (particularly in the context of poor communities of colour): Ferguson (2017), p. 3.

[77] The GDPR took 4 years to negotiate, which while not an immensely long time, 4 years in the context of a rapidly developing industry would be significant: GDPR Timeline https://edps.europa.eu/data-protection/data-protection/legislation/history-general-data-protection-regulation_en.

is a much more developed understanding and awareness of binding data protection instruments (like the EU GDPR or the Japanese Act on the Protection of Personal Information 2003).[78]

4.2.2 Contextualising the Role of Guidelines and Self-Regulation

While this initially seems as a particularly weak way of encouraging higher standards above a legally mandated minimum, there are successful examples across various industries. In particular, the recent example of privacy standards and the Apple App Store demonstrates both the normative strength and the actual impact of decisive action by private companies.[79]

For Apple, this commitment to privacy and new safeguards for consumer welfare clearly functions in a commercial dimension as a marketable reflection of its corporate values, though the impact on the consumer is undeniable, since consumers using the software hosted on the App Store now have greater information as to how the applications they use impact their privacy.[80]

Self-auditing principles or guidelines designed at an international governmental level—even if they simply promote understanding between different jurisdictions as to the values that should drive commercial implementations of AI—would carry some normative weight, not only in terms of globally inspiring similar standards on AI inventions, but also in terms of consumer understandings and expectations around the impact of AI inventions.

It is important to remember that, while the EU has produced a draft text of an AI regulation, it remains a draft and one of the only examples of AI-specific regulation. While self-auditing or self-regulation may not be suitable for the EU if the regulation is successful, there exists a variety of political and legal contexts in which this approach could be a meaningful development. The approach to self-regulation is no guarantee against the negative impact of AI, but if promoted correctly, it does provide consumers with more information about a highly relevant technology.

The self-auditing could take on various forms, functioning either as a blanket declaration that the AI in a particular product or service has been tested and presents no significant human welfare risk, or as a more granular approach that identifies specific dimensions of transparency or recommends periodic review (reflecting the weaknesses of snapshot approaches in AI inventions).[81] A blanket statement-style declaration of welfare impact for AI inventions could be incorporated into the patent system with little modification—as an easy complement to the disclosure process already required—to establish at least a baseline of normative protection for welfare.

---

[78] Japanese Act on the Protection of Personal Information (Act No. 57 of 2003), subsequently amended most recently in 2020.

[79] Hay Newman (2020).

[80] Perez (2021).

[81] FDA (2021).

5 Conclusion

Given that the patent system across many jurisdictions allows for the granting of patents for inventions that incorporate AI, it is important to investigate the normative underpinnings of the system. The challenges that AI presents—issues of transparency, accountability, and accessibility—may appear to be new because of the disruptive potential and the sheer scope of implementation. However, the broader technological context reveals that these issues can more correctly be understood as embodying existing tensions within the patent system. These tensions can be identified clearly through the treatment of software and pharmaceuticals in the patent system.

The patent system presents an important complement to more explicit forms of regulating the normative impact of AI because it necessarily touches upon some of the current policy design choices that are being made around the world, specifically about whether to pursue binding regulation or to centre the interests of industry. Two ways that the patent system manages normative disruption that are considered in this chapter—subject matter eligibility and disclosure—must be recognised as complements to specific AI regulation because they are limited in application to successfully registered inventions.

The EU is most prominent in the development of AI-specific regulation that builds on the success of the GDPR, though Japan—with a comparably developed data protection framework—represents a firm shift *away* from binding horizontal regulation in favour of commercial flexibility. Self-regulation based on principles of AI may be of only minimal importance to the EU, but it represents a way of balancing commercial interests with consumer safety in other jurisdictions. This is particularly the case in jurisdictions that lack the same type of human rights enforcement present in the EU.

It is clear that the shifts that AI is propelling—normative, societal, and technological—have only just begun. It is also apparent that robust data protection provisions are a core aspect of regulating AI, suggesting that the current discussions over whether or not to regulate AI at the outset or as it matures (as was the case with software) are misguided. AI is already, in a meaningful way, regulated by data protection principles across Japan, the EU, and the US to varying degrees.

References

Abbott FM, Cottier T, Gurry F (2019) International intellectual property in an integrated world economy. Wolters Kluwer, Alphen aan den Rijn

Alkemada G, Toet J (2021) Data protection regulation in the Netherlands. In: Kiesow Cortez E (ed) Data protection around the world: privacy laws in action. Springer, Berlin, pp 165–188

Amnesty International (2021) Japan: Government Must Deliver an LGBTI Bill that Ensures Zero Tolerance of Discrimination. https://www.amnesty.org/en/latest/news/2021/06/japan-government-must-deliver-an-lgbti-bill-that-ensures-zero-tolerance-of-discrimination/

Barton JH (1997) Patents and antitrust: a rethinking in light of patent breadth and sequential innovation. Antitrust Law J 65(2):449–466

Bereuter T, Ménière Y, Rudyk I (2020) Market success and challenges facing European SMEs: results from EPO's patent commercialization scoreboard. Les Nouvelles LV(2):156–164

Blasiak A, Khong J, Kee T (2019) CURATE.AI: optimizing personalized medicine with artificial intelligence. SLAS Technol 25(2):95–105

Booton D (2007) The patentability of computer-implemented inventions in Europe. IPQ 92(1): 92–116

Broadbent M, Arrieta-Kenna S (2021) AI Regulation: Europe's Latest Proposal is a Wake-Up Call for the United States. Available via CSIS. https://www.csis.org/analysis/ai-regulation-europes-latest-proposal-wake-call-united-states

Burk DL, Lemley MA (2002) Is patent law technology-specific? Berkeley Technol Law J 17(4): 1155–1206

Burt A (2021) New AI regulations are coming: is your organization ready? Available via Harvard Business Review. https://hbr.org/2021/04/new-ai-regulations-are-coming-is-your-organization-ready

Cabinet Office (undated) Realizing Society 5.0. https://www.japan.go.jp/abenomics/_userdata/abenomics/pdf/society_5.0.pdf

Cullet P (2003) Patents and medicines: the relationship between TRIPS and the human right to health. Int Aff 79(1):139–160

Devarapalli P (2018) Patenting therapeutic methods: statutes and strategies. J Commer Biotechnol 24(2):54–58

Erstling J (2011) Patent law and the duty of candor: rethinking the limits of disclosure. Creighton Law Rev 44:329–366

FDA (2021) Artificial Intelligence and Machine Learning in Software as a Medical Device. https://www.fda.gov/medical-devices/software-medical-device-samd/artificial-intelligence-and-machine-learning-software-medical-device

Fenwick M, Vermeulen EPM, Corrales M (2018) Business and regulatory responses to artificial intelligence: dynamic regulation, innovation ecosystem and the strategic management of disruptive technology. In: Corrales M, Fenwick M, Forgó M (eds) Robotics, AI, and the future of law. Springer, Singapore, pp 81–104

Ferguson AG (2017) The rise of big data policing: surveillance, race, and the future of law enforcement. NYU Press, New York

Francesco Guarascio, EU Warns not Enough COVID Vaccines for All in Europe until 2022 (Reuters, 27 October 2020) <https://www.reuters.com/article/health-coronavirus-eu-vaccines-idUSKBN27C2DQ>

Gabriel JM (2014) Medical monopoly: intellectual property rights and the origins of the modern pharmaceutical industry. University of Chicago Press, Chicago

Garcia G (2019) Artificial intelligence in Japan: industrial cooperation and business opportunities for European companies. EU-Japan Centre for Industrial Cooperation. https://www.eu-japan.eu/publications/artificial-intelligence-japan-and-opportunities-european-companies

Ghidini G, Arezzo A (2008) One, none, or a hundred thousand: how many layers of protection for software innovations?'. In: Drexl J (ed) Research handbook on intellectual property and competition law. Edward Elgar Publishing, Cheltenham, pp 346–372

Girasa R (2020) Artificial intelligence as a disruptive technology: economic transformation and government regulation. Palgrave Macmillan, London

Greenleaf G (2018) Japan: EU Adequacy Discounted. Privacy Laws & Business International Report 8-10 UNSW Law Research Paper No. 19-5

Gross A (2016) The righting of the law of occupation. In: Bhuta N (ed) The frontiers of human rights: extraterritoriality and its challenges. Oxford University Publishing, Oxford, pp 21–54

Guan W (2016) IPRs, public health, and international trade: an international law perspective on the TRIPS amendment. LJIL 29(2):411–440

Guan W (2018) Diversified FRAND enforcement and TRIPS integrity. WTR 17(1):91–120

Hashiguchi M (2017) The global artificial intelligence revolution challenges patent eligibility laws. J Bus Technol Law 13(1):1–35
Hay Newman L (2020) Apple's app "Privacy Labels" are here – and they're a big step forward. Available via Wired. https://www.wired.com/story/apple-app-privacy-labels/
Heikkilä M (2021) Europe eyes strict rules for artificial intelligence. Available via Politico. https://www.politico.eu/article/europe-strict-rules-artificial-intelligence/
Hellstadius A (2010) Software patents. In: Wahlgren P (ed) Information & communication technology: legal issues. Stockholm Institute for Scandinavian Law, Stockholm, pp 362–396
Jaffe AB, Lerner J (2006) Innovation and its discontents. Innovation policy and the economy. The MIT Press
Jenzer H et al (2019) The European medicines shortages research network and its mission to strategically debug disrupted pharmaceutical supply chains. In: Barbosa-Povoa AP, Jenzer H, Luis de Miranda J (eds) Pharmaceutical supply chains—medicines shortages. Springer, Switzerland, pp 1–22
Kageyama K (2019) Invention and comparison of patenting and the examination guidelines about inventive step in Japan, the USA, and the EU: based on the opinion focusing on principles and their uses. Beijing Law Rev 10(3):539–578
Kianzad B, Wested J (2021) "No-One is Safe Until Everyone is Safe" – Patent Waiver, Compulsory Licensing and COVID-19. EPLR 5(2):71–91
Kovač M (2020) Judgment-proof robots and artificial intelligence: a comparative law and economics approach. Palgrave Macmillan, London
La Croix S, Liu M (2017) Patents and access to essential medicines. Volume 2. In: Maskus KE (ed) Intellectual property, growth and trade. Elsevier Group Publishing Limited, Amsterdam, pp 423–464
Lodder AR, Loui RP (2018) Data algorithms and privacy in surveillance: on stages, numbers and the human factor. In: Barfield W, Pagallo U (eds) Research handbook on the law of artificial intelligence. Edward Elgar Publishing, Cheltenham, pp 375–384
METI/Expert Group on Architecture for AI Principles to be Practiced (2021) AI Governance in Japan Ver. 1.0. https://www.meti.go.jp/press/2020/01/20210115003/20210115003-3.pdf
Murray A (2019) Information technology law, 4th edn. Oxford University Press, Oxford
Paterson RK, Karjala DS (2003) Looking beyond intellectual property rights in resolving protection of the intangible cultural heritage of indigenous peoples. Cardozo J Int Comp Law 11(2): 633–667
Perera A, Sugden P (2017) Myriad Genetics Inc.: patenting of isolated human DNA – a missed policy opportunity or judicial interpretation supporting a judicial minimalist status quo (Part I). EIPR 39(6):334–343
Perez S (2021) Following Apple's Launch of Privacy Labels, Google to Add a "Safety" Section in Google Play. Available via TechCrunch. https://techcrunch.com/2021/05/06/following-apples-launch-of-privacy-labels-google-to-add-a-safety-section-in-google-play/
Pesapane F, Codari M, Sardanelli F (2018) Artificial intelligence in medical imaging: threat or opportunity? Radiologists again at the forefront of innovation in medicine. Eur Radiol Exp. 2(35). https://doi.org/10.1186/s41747-018-0061-6
Pogge T (2010) The health impact fund: better pharmaceutical innovations at much lower prices. In: Pogge T, Rimmer M, Rubenstein K (eds) Incentives for global public health: patent law and access to essential medicines. Cambridge University Press, Cambridge, pp 135–154
Riley C (2007) The need for software innovation policy. JTHTL 5(589):589–630
Ruiz Durán C (2007) Mexico: the management revolution and the emergence of the software industry. In: Giovannetti E, Kagami M (eds) Tsuji M. Edward Elgar Publishing, Industrial agglomeration and new technologies: a global perspective, pp 312–352
Shu-Acquaye F (2016) The decline of HIV/AIDS: a new paradigm in Sub-Saharan Africa? AJICL 24(3):362–388

Taylor Hatmaker T (2021) A Senate Proposal for a New US Agency to Protect Americans' Data is Back. Available via TechCrunch. https://techcrunch.com/2021/06/17/data-protection-agency-bill-antitrust-gillibrand/
Thambisetty S (2017) The construction of legitimacy in European Patent Law. IPQ 3:221–244
US FTC (2021) Aiming for truth, fairness, and equity in your company's use of AI. Available via FTC. https://www.ftc.gov/news-events/blogs/business-blog/2021/04/aiming-truth-fairness-equity-your-companys-use-ai
Weckström Lindroos K (2020) Fairness and Ordre public in certified global food chains. In: Gervais DJ (ed) Fairness, morality, and Ordre public in intellectual property. Edward Elgar Publishing, Cheltenham, pp 195–214
Weyand J, Haase H (2005) Patenting computer programs: new challenges. IIC 36(6):647–663.
WIPO (2019) WIPO Technology Trends 2019 – Artificial Intelligence. https://www.wipo.int/publications/en/details.jsp?id=4386
Wrigley S (2018) Taming artificial intelligence: "Bots", the GDPR and regulatory approaches. In: Corrales M, Fenwick M, Forgó N (eds) Robotics, AI, and the future of law. Springer, Singapore, pp 183–208
Zhuang YT et al (2017) Challenges and opportunities: from big data to knowledge in AI 2.0. Front Inf Technol Electr Eng 18(1):3–14

Part V
AI and Human Rights

What Role for Social Rights During the Leap to Post or "Enhanced" Humanism?

Themistoklis Tzimas

Abstract The chapter examines the relationship between posthumanism and social rights. It identifies the potential impact of the path towards posthumanism on social cohesion. On such grounds, the role of social rights, as guarantors of maximum social equality is addressed. More specifically, the rights to science and health are analyzed in relation to posthumanism. Social rights are approached as binding norms, within the framework of the human rights legal regime. The case for a cooperative and centralized model of governance is made and, in this context, the significance of international law is presented.

1 Introduction

We are in 2050: fully autonomous, general, artificial intelligence (AGI) or super artificial intelligence (ASI) still seem distant. We can be relieved; no "Terminator" or "Matrix" scenario seems even remotely close. The international community decided soon enough that investing on AGI or ASI constitutes a far too dangerous concept.

Instead of these, the choice has been to develop highly intelligent AI but still at a -relatively at least- narrow level. More specifically, a choice was made to develop narrow AI (ANI)[1] that can help us, humans, enhance our capacities even ontologically, up to the extent of reaching the threshold of trans- or post-humanism. The extent of human enhancement has already reached ontological levels. People "internalize" AI so that they can live longer, healthier lives, providing themselves with a variety of choices, from altering their own bodies and minds to engineering or "hacking" their own DNAs.

[1] AI that supersedes our intellectual capacities, albeit in a specific area, and not in all aspects of intelligence.

T. Tzimas (✉)
School of Economics and Political Sciences, Aristotle University of Thessaloniki, Thessaloniki, Greece
e-mail: thtzimas@polsci.auth.gr

A. Kornilakis et al. (eds.), *Artificial Intelligence and Normative Challenges*, Law, Governance and Technology Series 59,
https://doi.org/10.1007/978-3-031-41081-9_11

There is however one, among others, problem: these technologies are not for all. Only few have the economic capacity to enjoy such scientific developments. The rest have to cope with traditional medicine, bodies and minds. Inequalities were obviously already nothing new. Still, it was quite different to have better access to health services compared to someone else—which constituted an already significant type of inequality—from being or becoming better ontologically, with some free of disease and aging, victorious over death, whereas the majority of the population has to cope with the unavoidability of biological limits.

Social and political systems actually begin to crumble: it is obvious that next to *homo sapiens*, an engineered form of humanity is emerging, on the basis of advanced technology and of the economic capacity to harvest the "miracles" of science and of AI. This new type of humanity feels that it is held back by the inferior masses, while, conversely, the latter face the unique situation of having to cope with a biologically superior species-in-the-making. It is difficult to imagine how the humanity of the previous decades did not see it coming: societies need at least some extent of equality, in order to enjoy—again at least—some form of cohesion and therefore viability. The impact of this new type of inequality derails political and social models and the consequences are being felt globally.

Back to the present: we are already well aware of the impact of AI on human lives and on our societies. Literally, almost no aspect of human life evades its impact. It is also evident that AI has an actual effect and will most likely have an even bigger one in the future on what we consider life, living and human ontology.[2] The merging of artificial with human intelligence is one of the "next big things" in science. As machines surpass human intelligence in narrow areas—and could do so at a general level as well—and as we incorporate their intelligence into ours, we need to wonder where will we go from there? Are we becoming the architects and the creators of new forms of life-enhancement or are we approaching the moment of opening a "Pandora's box"? Are we at the verge of liberating our lives from the hardship of social and economic models based on exploitation of humans by humans or are we about to enter an era of socio-economic catastrophe because of inequality and the suffocation of productive forces?[3]

The advance of AI and its merging with human intelligence raises a variety of moral and legal issues. Here the focus is on the role of international law, in light of the potential leap to posthumanism and from the perspective of the need to secure the maximum possible, social cohesion. It is in this framework that social rights are addressed.[4] The chapter first addresses the themes of AI, posthumanism or enhanced- humanism. It then moves onto social rights, under international law. Last but not least, it examines how social rights can contribute into the governance of AI evolution towards posthumanism.

[2] Kang (2011), p. 84.

[3] Good (1966), pp. 32–33; Muggleton (2006); McGinnis (2010), p. 371; Soskis (2005), p. 38.

[4] Mumford (2010), pp. 9–51.

2 AI and Posthumanism

2.1 AI: its Multifaceted Impact

AI as a concept, dates back to the '50s constituting not only the outcome of computing technology but also a vision of some of the brightest minds raising the prospect of an alternative form of intelligent beings.[5] As Professor McCarthy would state, the goal of AI is "to proceed on the basis of the conjecture that every aspect of learning or any other feature of intelligence can in principle be so precisely described that a machine can be made to simulate it."[6]

From the ambition of a simulation of the human mind, scientific progress has made us envisage an emulation of the human intelligence or of aspects of it.[7] Not simply a repetition or "copy", but an autonomous, self-developing mind and consciousness, of non-biological origin. The levels of intellectual autonomy—may or will—vary, ranging from existing, limited autonomy[8] to intelligence equal or superior to human.[9]

The fundamental element of AI is its autonomy, which differentiates it from mere automation.[10] While the need for an initial human design exists in both of them, autonomy provides to AI the capacity to move beyond its initial design. The prospect is that at some point AI may self-replicate or even re-write its own code.[11] Autonomy thus, provides to AI its adaptability to new environments, beyond the need for direct or even remote human control, though it equally raises the danger of unpredictability, since AI is expected to be "taught" how to act, through machine-learning, instead of mere programming.[12] After all, machine-learning, exactly enhances the capacities of AI as it provides to it the ability to act thanks to what it has "learned", instead of solely pre-determined instructions.[13]

---

[5] Gerdes (2018), p. 678.

[6] Dartmouth (1956); Gerdes (2018), p. 678.

[7] Kurzweil (2005); p. 33.

[8] The so-called, weak or narrow AI (ANI), where "[t]he computer is merely an instrument for investigating cognitive processes".

[9] The so-called strong AI (AGI or ASI), where "[t]he processes in the computer are intellectual, self-learning processes"; see Wisskirchen et al. (2017), p. 10; Urban (2015).

[10] "The mechanization of well-defined processes, in which routine tasks are translated into some formalized structure that allows human operators to delegate some level of control to an automated system"; Sheridan and Verplank (1978), pp. 6–12; Noorman and Johnson (2014), p. 52; Singer (2009), p. 5.

[11] Martinez (2019), p. 1027.

[12] Kowert (2017), p. 183; Tanz (2016); Scherer (2016), p. 365; Cuellar (2017), p. 33; Schuller (2017), p. 396.

[13] Bostrom and Ćirkovic (2008), p. 25.

In various sectors (i.e. military, finance,[14] health, education, environment, governance) AI, in the form of ANI, is already present,[15] building expectations and creating risks. Its consequences are roughly distinguished between two main categories: the ones referring to ontological issues and those to social and economic. The ontological ones are in principle related to the emergence of non-biological entities with equal or superior, intelligence than humans. The social and economic ones are mainly pre-occupied with the role of AI in the working environment and in the economic circuits.

While they seem distinct, these categories are in fact interlinked: as more autonomous and more intelligent AI entities emerge, the capacity to produce wealth with less—or even no—human interference will maximize,[16] which on the basis of the present socio-economic model could be exploited by ruling elites among us.[17] In case such a condition is not—to say the least—balanced through a social rights-oriented access to the benefits of science, instead of a market-oriented one, we will easily end up with a situation of an intensifying and widening vicious circle of inequality, which may reach even ontological levels.

Such a condition of ontologically established inequality will be historically unique in case it is materialized. It could merge social and biological inequality in ways resembling to racist pseudo-science perspectives. In order to address this issue, we need to give a brief look onto posthumanism or transhumanism as it is often mentioned, as well as to potential developments which could occur while moving towards this direction.

2.2 Trans or Post-Humanism

Posthumanism or transhumanism refer to a variety of different situations. The polarization between "bioconservatives" and "technoprogressives"—or transhumanists and "dethists"—is indicative of the hopes or threats that science breeds.[18] Posthumanism is essentially a path leading to a situation within which humans and humanity, in general or at least in the way we currently comprehend both, will not constitute the dominant being and form of existence; they will seem too obsolete, bound by existing, biological limitations.[19]

[14] Karppi and Crawford (2016), pp. 74 and 77.

[15] Renn and Klinke (2004), p. S41; van Asselt and Renn (2011), pp. 436–438; Spier (2011); Frey and Osborne (2017), p. 261; Acemoglu and Restrepo (2017), pp. 7–10; Xiang (2018).

[16] Xu et al. (2018), p. 91; Schwab (2015); Lucas (2004); Banerjee and Duflo (2005); Mathiason et al. (2016) paras. 1.2 and 2; Jee (2017), pp. 255–256.

[17] Acemoglu and Restrepo (2017), pp. 7–10; Xiang (2018).

[18] Fukuyama (2004), pp. 42–43.

[19] Pollock (2011), p. 238; Bostrom (2003).

A post-human reality may take several forms: it can be a future of generally enhanced human intelligence; a reality comprised of super-humans with all human beings enjoying unprecedented capacities, based on the collaboration of machines and humans, describing the ideal of augmentation[20]; it can be a post-human reality where only a few among us will have reached the level of super-humans or even a future with humanity extinct.[21] As technology advances, it becomes an issue of social and political choice, as well as of legal regulation, which way will prevail.

In terms of terminology, both transhumanism and posthumanism have been put in use, quite often interchangeably. Here the term "posthumanism" is chosen as it depicts the shift towards a non-human-centered world, whereas transhumanism mainly depicts a situation of merging of the two intelligences, namely, the human and the artificial. In such a sense, the latter constitutes only one potential means towards the former. However, the focus of both is on human enhancement, with the help of AI. The idea is omnipresent: we, humans, enhance ourselves, from wooden legs to glasses and from antibiotics to modern medicine. The effort has always been to improve our bodies and minds.

What is different now, is the ambition to overcome fundamental biological limitations with the help of AI. As AI capacities expand, in terms of microchips, nanorobots, implants which can augment our senses and enrich our cognitive capacities, provide us with cybernetic abilities,[22] connect us to memory chips, read our minds so that our mental orders will be remotely executed overcoming distance,[23] and reverse the aging of our brains and of the rest of our bodies, they "promise" to deliver our enhanced versions. They promise even a victory over death through potentially silicon or cyber, alternative embodiments of our minds or even through collective consciousness forms.[24] Hence, such capacities can lead to the de-humanization of our world or to an improved version of humanity. Ultimately, by merging man and machine, science is expected to create humans who have vastly increased cognitive and emotional intelligence, strength and lifespans, surpassing

---

[20] Hooker and Kim (2019), p. 63.

[21] The evolution of human mind towards post-humanism under the impact of AI will raise a variety of existential and ontological issues, on top of "simpler" ones- which in fact will not be simple at all-related to liability cases. For example, what will be the role of human emulations? Once, human and artificial intelligence begin to merge, what will be the threshold distinguishing artificial from human intelligence? When do we stop being humans? Are we ethically allowed to experiment with human consciousness, possibly destroying it? In spite of their significance, they cannot be addressed here, where the emphasis is placed on the theme of social rights.

[22] McKie (2018).

[23] RT (2022).

[24] Braidotti (2013), pp. 13–55.

what we comprehend as our widest capacities;[25] a near embodiment of gods. The growth of human capacities will outpace our wildest imagination.[26]

Within this debate however, what is already under way, together with the existing technology—and in fact is rapidly intensifying as technology grows—is inequality too; one that could reach a level of ontologically established or internalized inequality, that is, a level where actual biological or post-biological superiority and inferiority are established.[27] We must not forget that post-humanism already bears significant similarities or even coincides with a "new-eugeneticist discourse of human improvement", which seems relatively innocent at first glance.[28] In this sense, if the existing trends of widening inequality due to the model of encompassment of AI-driven technologies into production seem significant—and indeed they are[29]—the repercussions from potential ontological inequality will be disastrous.[30]

This is why social rights become crucial: a universal accessibility to such technologies will co-shape the future of humanity.[31] In this framework, the rights to science and to health, in particular, become absolutely critical and even more their incorporation into AI governance, especially in light of posthumanism.[32]

3 Social Rights

3.1 A Teleological Approach to Social Rights

Posthumanism is a phenomenon that cannot escape the ambit of human rights, and particularly of social rights, since it impacts so crucially on our social evolution. Given such an approach, in order to further develop the relationship between posthumanism and social rights, our suggestion is that we should comprehend the latter as a whole, on accounts of their general scope and therefore interpret them

[25] Bostrom (2008), p. 112.

[26] Miah (2008), pp. 51–71 (concerning the philosophical and legal questions about whether such a procedure should be allowed in the first place); Susen (2022) (here the focus is solely on the potential social consequences).

[27] Bostrom (2005), p. 4.

[28] Leach (2018); Vint (2007), pp. 79–101.

[29] Manyika et al. (2017), p. 14; The Economist (2017); Manyika (2017);Executive Office of the USA President (2016), p. 2; The Crypto Oracle (n.d.).

[30] Floridi et al. (2018), pp. 692–694.

[31] The best-known effort in the business world is probably the one of Neuralink; see Clifford (2020); Cellan-Jones (2020).

[32] Marshall and Bottomore (1992), pp.??; Rawls (1971), pp. 294–346; Taylor (2007), pp. 667–668; International Covenant on Cultural, Economic and Social Rights (adopted 16 December 1966 entered into force 3 January 1976) 993 UNTS 3, Preamble; Wiessner and Willard (1999), p. 318.

teleologically.[33] By "nature" after all, social rights are keen to teleological interpretation so that they can adjust to social and economic developments, which are obviously dynamic.

Yet, since social rights mainly function within an—in principle—hostile economic model, we often come across the proposal for a "static" comprehension of social rights. This approach envisages social rights as encompassing a bare minimum of social protection invoking lack of resources, or, argues at the normative level for a supposedly less binding status compared to the rest of human rights.[34] The idea in this approach is that social rights are already too many and too ambitious and that therefore we should limit them to a core of rights, which further can be fulfilled only up to the extent that political decision-makers decide, without any normative "upward" restraints, other maybe than the avoidance of such a level of deprivation or de-finance that breaches their most fundamental elements.[35]

As a result, if this approach prevails in the course towards posthumanism, human enhancement inventions and interventions will remain outside the provisions of health systems as unnecessary luxuries. They will be considered as too costly to be offered freely and universally, as part of national health systems or as elements of freely accessible science.

Still, and although an analysis of the economics of welfare states globally must be avoided, we can identify whether the argument of too costly social rights, stands.[36] As data from the World Bank show, the global GDP has grown from 1.369 trillion $, in 1960, to 84.68 trillion $, in current US dollars.[37] On the contrary and while global GDP has more than doubled, during the last 20 years, with the highly industrialized states being the pioneers in this explosion of wealth, the gross public social spending within the same states during these last decades has stagnated, reduced or very narrowly expanded.[38] Further, the "conventional wisdom" that social spending and the welfare state—comprising of the material implementation of social rights—harm economic growth has been systematically negated.[39]

Thus, while obviously each state constitutes a different case, in principle and per average, there is no material reason justifying a static approach to social rights, limiting them to minimum protection.[40] On the contrary, the scope of social rights is

---

[33] For example, the UN Human Rights Committee, endorses in the protection of life the positive measures for the elimination of malnutrition and epidemics. Such diastolic approach prerequisites a teleological interpretation. See, for instance, International Human Rights Instruments (2003), p. 128.

[34] Portugal Gouvêa (2013), pp. 460–461.

[35] Young (2008), p. 113.

[36] After all, in particular, these arguments have normative implications as well.

[37] World Bank (n.d.).

[38] Lindert (2021).

[39] Sen (1983), p. 12.

[40] In such a framework, one must look at the UN Committee on Economic and Social Rights (CESCR); CESCR (2000), para 47; CESCR (1999b), para 57; CESCR (1999a), para 8; Lehmann (2006), p. 163.

to redistribute wealth among the most and least privileged ones within our societies—through state activism practically—in order not to solely guarantee some minimum protection to the latter ones, but to achieve as egalitarian as possible conditions, in furtherance of cohesive and viable societies.[41]

Social rights, therefore, are addressed in this chapter as the legal framework which attempts to achieve the greatest possible equality. When new developments such as AI and posthumanism create new potentials but only for few, intensifying the risk of social fragmentation, social rights must cover the inequality gap through the establishment of universal access to these developments. Under these circumstances, the most important is not the cost of financing the implementation of social rights but their significance for sustaining social cohesion. It is the former that must be valued in furtherance of the latter and not vice versa.

Therefore, once the potential for a general improvement of human well-being emerges, through scientific progress, the question should not be how costly is in the short-term the universal enjoyment of such progress, but how significant it is for the general well-being and how destructive it would be for social cohesion to let this progress be regulated in accordance with market-oriented policies. This must be the attitude towards developments and achievements in the course towards posthumanism, in light with a teleological interpretation of social rights.

3.2 *The Bindingness of Social Rights*

The additional question of course is whether social rights are actually binding internationally and therefore whether despite what is politically right or not, it is also obligatory to take them into account as compulsory, for posthumanism's regulation. It is not rare for legal scholars to consider social rights as somehow less binding in comparison to traditional, individual rights- which refer only to the abstention of the state from the private sphere- or as external to the human rights' legal regime.[42]

Nevertheless, such an approach to social rights does not align with their legal foundations neither in international law, nor in most national constitutions. In terms of international law, social rights constitute part of the human rights' framework,[43] as the International Covenant on Economic, Social and Cultural Rights (ICESCR) and the Universal Declaration of Human Rights (UDHR) attest. Social rights are, thus, an indivisible and interdependent part of human rights. Given the high number

[41] Eide (2000), p. 115; Yeshanew (2013) p. 280. Contrary to what is often considered, the baseline approach to the implementation of social rights, does not mean to weaken them but to impose the minimum from which, the realization of social rights must begin; not the point where social rights may "end" if the relevant government wishes to do so; CESCR (1990), paras 2 and 9.

[42] Alston (1987); Pollis (1996), p. 318; Muzaffar (1999), p. 29; Wright (1979), p. 19.

[43] World Conference on Human Rights (1993); Whelan and Donnelly (2007), p. 922.

of contracting parties in the relevant international treaties, there is no legal reason to treat them as external to human rights or as less binding than the rest of human rights.

After all it is ICESCR article 2, para. 1, which, with a sense of urgency, requires that all parties take measures towards the full enjoyment by everyone of all the rights, "immediately", implying legislative, political, economic, administrative and judicial means that may be necessary, use the available resources so that any limitations to them by states must conform with the nature of these rights and not endanger the promotion of the general welfare.[44] In addition, the Universal Declaration of Human Rights in two articles makes mention to social rights and more specifically, on the one side, to social security and economic, social and cultural rights,[45] and, on the other side, to standard of living that is adequate for health, well-being, medical care, housing, social services, "...and the right to security in the event of unemployment, sickness, disability, widowhood, old age or other lack of livelihood in circumstances beyond his control."[46] In the UN Charter too, social rights are endorsed in article 55 both in principle and in terms of more specific obligations, as it sets forth that "the United Nations shall promote: higher standards of living, full employment, and conditions of economic and social progress and development; solutions of international economic, social, health, and related problems."[47]

The fact that social rights are new in comparison to civil or political rights does not mean that they are less binding but that on the contrary they constitute the "state-of-the-art" of human rights.[48] In fact, they both enrich critically our normative perception about what human rights are, how far their regulatory impact is extended, and impose upon states the requirement to act positively, towards materially sustaining the whole structure of human rights.[49]

Parenthetically and complementarily to international law, we must also keep in mind that most states in their constitutions include provisions on social rights. In this sense, a status of general principle of law could be inferred for them.[50]

---

[44] Ibid., p. 6; Andreassen (1992), p. 333; Samnøy (1999), p. 11.

[45] Universal Declaration of Human Rights (UDHR), Article 22.

[46] UDHR, Article 25(1).

[47] Charter of the United Nations (adopted 26 June 1945 entered into force 24 October 1945) 1 UNTS XVI (UN Charter), Article 55. There is a significant extent of debate regarding the normative bindingness of this provision, ranging from the recognition of complete bindingness to the identification only of a general requirement of cooperation with no normative content. One particularly interesting approach argues that the "...UN Charter, the Universal Declaration, the various international conventions, resolutions of UN organs and other multilateral bodies, and the practices of states have combined to create customary, or a blend of customary and conventional legal obligations binding upon all states to respect at least some human rights norms"; see Henkin (1990), pp. 55–56.

[48] Marshall (1950), pp. 10–82.

[49] Atria (2015), p. 598; Garty and Mantouvalou (2011), pp. 88, 116 and 170.

[50] Ssenyonjo (2009), p. 201; Fordham (2013), pp. 382–383. Höffe (2007), p. 47.

Summing up, both the significance of social rights for the furtherance of maximum social cohesion and of the aversion of ontological inequality and fragmentation, as well as their bindingness in legal terms, explain why they must be crucial in terms of access to posthuman technologies and in the scientific progress towards them. The focus in particular is in relation to the rights to science and health, as the most relevant.[51]

3.3 *The Right to Science*

The right to science remains one of the most neglected social rights. We tend to approach it as somehow too general to raise concrete results, whereas in reality not only can it produce concrete and binding results but it is also critical, taking into account the extent of scientific progress and its social impact.

According to article 15 of ICESCR, "*[t]he States Parties to the present Covenant recognize the right of everyone: (b) To enjoy the benefits of scientific progress and its applications; (c) To benefit from the protection of the moral and material interests resulting from any scientific, literary or artistic production of which he is the author. 2. The steps to be taken by the States Parties to the present Covenant to achieve the full realization of this right shall include those necessary for the conservation, the development and the diffusion of science and culture*."[52] A similar provision can be found in article 27 of the UDHR.[53]

The right to science is not *static* per definition as it must keep track both of scientific developments and the economic interests gathering around the use of scientific progress.[54] In this sense, it is important to determine whether the use of science will remain primarily market-oriented or on the contrary—as the Venice Statement characteristically advocates—will be directed towards the benefit of all humanity, even at the expense of profit and intellectual property.[55]

[51] As ECOSOC/Commission on Human Rights (2003), para. 12, held, "[t]ransnational corporations and other business enterprises shall respect economic, social and cultural rights as well as civil and political rights and contribute to their realization, in particular the rights to development, adequate food and drinking water, the highest attainable standard of physical and mental health, adequate housing ... and shall refrain from actions which obstruct or impede the realization of those rights."

[52] ICESCR, Article 15.

[53] Between the two documents, a number of significant documents on this issue emerged, mainly at the initiative of the UN General Assembly (GA) such as the 1974 Charter of Economic Rights and Duties of States; the 1975 Declaration on the Use of Scientific and Technological Progress in the Interests of Peace and for the Benefit of Mankind; the 1997 Universal Declaration on the Human Genome and Human Rights, adopted by UNESCO's General Conference and endorsed by the UN General Assembly in 1998; and the 2003 International Declaration on Human Genetic Data, adopted by the General Conference of UNESCO. See Donders (2011), p. 372.

[54] UNESCO (2009), para. 3.

[55] Ibid, paras. 6 and 10.

The prevalence of the second approach, as well the extent of it, can be inferred among other sources and means of interpretation from CESCR's GC n. 25, which stipulates that "*[a]pplications [of science] refer to the particular implementation of science to the specific concerns and needs of the population. Applied science also includes the technology deriving from scientific knowledge, such as the medical applications, the industrial or agricultural applications, or information and communications technology*".[56] The term "benefits" of science describes the material results of science, namely, the information, the knowledge, which is produced by science, as well as the latter's social impact.[57]

From the above, it becomes evident that the right to science is not *abstract* either. It does not include only access to scientific progress in general but also its applications. Obviously, the rights of intellectual property raise barriers; still the general and in principle superior direction is to put first the social right to science, while trying to combine it with existing norms of ownership and intellectual property, without undermining it.[58] More specifically, the full-scale privatization of scientific research and progress—even further of scientific research with huge social and existential implications—must be seen with extreme cautiousness, due to the fact that the right to science—as we can schematically call it—involves a precautionary principle too, which is intended to control potential and future harm.[59]

It is the impact of the specific scientific development, on potential inequality in case these benefits are not shared by all of humans. Among other things, it is that which will determine the role of social rights' provisions in light of intellectual property and vice versa.[60] Still, the openness of science must be the rule. The quest for balance between competing interests and norms does not mean that they are all equally prioritized; social rights come first.

---

[56] CESCR (2020), para. 7.

[57] Ibid, para. 8.

[58] Ibid, para. 12.

[59] Participation, also, includes the right to information and participation in controlling the risks involved in specific scientific processes and its applications. In this context, the precautionary principle plays an important role. This principle demands that, in the absence of full scientific certainty, when an action or policy may lead to unacceptable harm to the public or the environment, actions will be taken to avoid or diminish that harm. Unacceptable harm includes harm to humans or to the environment that is: (a) threatening to human life or health; (b) serious and effectively irreversible; (c) inequitable to present or future generations; or (d) imposed without adequate consideration of the human rights of those affected. Technological and human rights impact assessments are tools that help to identify potential risks early in the process and the use of scientific applications; CESCR (2020).

[60] Müller (2010), pp. 765 and784.

3.4 The Right to Health

Equally important in this discussion is the right to health, especially in light of the holistic definition of health, as provided in the constitution of the World Health Organization, according to which "[h]ealth is a state of complete physical, mental and social well-being and not merely the absence of disease or infirmity".[61] A series of observations should be formulated regarding the right to health. First, it is already apparent that the pioneer force behind the gradual formation of posthumanism and of the road towards it will be the preservation and improvement of human health. As of now, all of the scientific progress that is related to posthumanism is built on the grounds of health issues. As Nick Bostrom eloquently expounds, at the heart of "transhumanism" one can find the "radical extension of human health-span, eradication of disease, elimination of unnecessary suffering, and augmentation of human intellectual, physical, and emotional capacities".[62] It is therefore expected to constitute the most (or one of the most) significant developments regarding human enhancement.[63]

Within such a context, the right to health becomes central. Again, the question is how we are going to interpret it. Is a twofold interpretation in terms of the universality of public health systems and in relation to whether health systems must include posthuman technologies and interventions too, feasible? In order to tackle these questions, it must be kept in mind that the right to health establishes the provision of "the highest attainable standard of health".[64] This, in correlation to the description of the right to health in the WHO Constitution leads to the dynamic interpretation of the core of the right. In other words, this right should require the provision of the essentials for health not only as they were comprehended a few decades ago or even today, but in line with the new developments on the wider area of health and well-being. Hence, posthumanism, as long as it enhances our health, must be included as well.

Most importantly, the right to health is an inclusive one referring to a variety of sub-rights or entitlements, among which the most relevant one is "the right to a system of health protection providing equality of opportunity for everyone to enjoy the highest attainable level of health."[65] On this basis, we are led to think of the right to health as inherently incompatible with inequality. As the Declaration of Alma-Ata held, "[t]he existing gross inequality in the health status of the people particularly between developed and developing countries as well as within countries is

[61] Constitution of the World Health Organization (adopted 22 July 1946 entered into force 7 April 1948) 14 UNTS 185.

[62] Bostrom (2003/2005), p. 1.

[63] Verdoux (2009), pp. 62–69.

[64] Office of the United Nations High Commissioner for Human Rights/WHO (2008), p. 1.

[65] Ibid., p. 3.

politically, socially and economically unacceptable and is, therefore, of common concern to all countries."[66]

In this framework, the right to health establishes the three obligations of the states: to respect, to protect, to fulfil. Among them, the obligation to protect stands out, since it imposes on States the obligation, among other ones, to "ensure that private actors conform with human rights standards when providing health care".[67] This (sub-) obligation must be executed in conformity with the general direction of the right to health, meaning in furtherance of equal access to health too.

From all the above, it becomes evident that the right to health is inextricably linked to social justice and politics, transferred into the domain of law.[68] This does not mean that social rights belong to the domain of politics but that the domain of politics is up to some extent assessed regarding its legitimacy and regulated through the prism of social rights and in particular of the specific right to health.

This perception of social rights and more specifically of the right to health means that on the one hand every state can regulate the role of the private sector (i.e. pharmaceuticals, industry etc.) in accordance with its own laws and intellectual property requirements. On the other hand, and at the same time however, under international law—and in most cases under national constitutional law too—states bear the obligation to safeguard "the highest attainable standard of health". This is the primary goal of the right to health and is expected to determine both the policies in this area as well as the implementation of other rights -such as to intellectual property- when they contradict the right to health.[69]

What does this mean if we look at it more thoroughly? Not that states can guarantee complete health for everyone.[70] It means that states must mobilize their resources to attain the best possible fulfilment of the right to health. In such a framework, universal access to posthumanism technologies can be advocated.

4 Means of the Incorporation of Social Rights During the Road to Posthumanism

One last critical question is how should social rights could be incorporated into the regulation of the course to posthumanism. There are multiple ways to achieve this. Most of them however necessitate a model for the governance of the technologies which are crucial in the road to posthumanism, with AI being the most prominent among them. For instance, machine-learning, which is the foundation of AI autonomy could be mandatorily conducted in conformity with social rights, imposing

[66] International Conference on Primary Health Care (1978), para. II.

[67] Office of the United Nations High Commissioner for Human Rights/WHO (2008), p. 26.

[68] Yamin (2005), p. 1159; Toebes (1999).

[69] Mzikenge Chirwa (2003), pp. 542–543.

[70] den Exter et al. (2001), pp. 10–11.

relevant regulations on AI creators and programmers.[71] That could produce AI that preserves the role of social rights, as guarantees of a "*ius commune*" of human dignity.[72] Further, the provisions of the Council of Europe about a system of Human Rights Impact Assessment (HRIA) for AI could explicitly include a similar criterion dedicated to social rights and be further adopted as an international model.[73]

Such proposals and policies imposing internationally uniform standards for AI presuppose a governance model, which can be *cooperative* regarding state and private actors, *centralized* and with a *dominant public aspect*. Such a model must bear the capacity to coordinate, monitor and regulate, to implement standards, codes of conducts and good practices and therefore to fine-tune technical and technological progress.[74] Therefore, international law must lie at its heart.[75]

The imposition of a governance model is not an easy task, given both the established lack of transparency regarding AI developments,[76] and the evolving, de-centralized, often low-cost, diffused nature of them.[77] A further complication emerges from the expanding area of AI applications as well as from the economic interests in relation to AI.[78] However, exactly because of the above unique characteristics of AI and because of the threats that could be raised on the basis of them, it becomes even more imperative to move on with a co-operative, centralized model of governance, with social rights- and human rights in general- at its "heart".

The procedure towards such a model of governance, as the above-mentioned, will necessitate both an extensive public debate and eventually some type of international treaty as well. The international community must face issues such as the impact of AI on human rights and on human- centrism of both our societies and our legal systems. We will need to keep in mind that once we comprehend human rights in general and holistically, as guarantors of human centrism, human rights' legal regime could "tolerate" a path towards posthumanism, only up to the extent that human-centrism remains prevalent.[79]

In addition, and in the same context, social rights, as part of the human rights' legal regime, align to posthumanism as long as the latter does not lead to a complete social fragmentation and to the widening of inequalities up to ontological, existential, biological levels.[80]

---

[71] Saslow and Lorenz (2019), p. 18.

[72] Carozza (2008), p. 932.

[73] Council Of Europe (2019), pp. 7–8; Edri (2018).

[74] Palmerini et al. (2015), p. 11.

[75] Mokhtarian (2018), p. 149.

[76] McGinnis (2010), p. 375.

[77] Fenwick et al. (2017), pp. 563–568.

[78] Butenko and Larouche (2015) p. 66; Brownsword (2008), p. 162; Collingridge (1980), p. 19; Bennett Moses (2011), pp. 768–769; Shah et al. (2015); Black (2008), p. 14; Mandel (2013), p. 62; Marchant and Wallach (2013), p. 136; Schuck (1984), p. 197.

[79] Tzimas (2021), pp. 131–147.

[80] Ibid.; Tzimas (2020), pp. 1–25.

Such perceptions of the role of human rights, and within them of social rights, make it necessary to reach a level of consensus about an international treaty for posthumanism, which requires a philosophical, biological, medical, political, social, psychological, economic and ultimately an extensive legal debate too. The existing system of international law and the organs of the international community, in the system of the UN, will have to adjust as well. It is very much likely that new institutions and norms will be needed.[81] In the end, it is not going to be a risk-free or easy attempt. Still, as the stakes become higher, the need for this endeavor grows.[82]

5 Conclusions

The scope of this chapter is to present an overview of the role of social rights in relation to posthumanism. The discussion has entered the level of science from that of science fiction. Not only is it fascinating and inherently interdisciplinary; it is also critical for the future of humanity, AI and for the viability of our societies.

Posthumanism can be addressed as a blessing or as a curse; there are two inherent aspects in this issue: the one is whether our human-centric legal systems—but most importantly our societies—can existentially accept a posthuman future, especially in case such future will be perceived as non-human. The promise however is that essentially it will not be a non-human future but a future of enhanced humanity, that is, of a humanity enjoying unprecedented well-being, longevity and intellectual capacities. The essential argument of this chapter is that such promises must be shared by all in order not to turn this evolution into a catastrophic scenario of growing inequality, with ontological and existential impact. It is mainly a matter of political and social determination how our quest for posthumanism will evolve. Within this general framework, however, social rights constitute the specific norms that can and must guarantee maximum possible equality, universal accessibility to scientific progress and therefore, social viability.

Further, the risks which are presented by AI and posthumanism make it necessary to have a centralized and cooperative model of governance, aiming at and capable of standardization, metrology, monitoring and enforcement at the international level too. That is easier said than done. For legal norms it is always difficult to maintain a regulatory role in uncertain domains the evolution of which is far from being finalized. Despite all these obstacles, the argument is that it is absolutely necessary

[81] IEEE (2019), p. 20. Characteristically, in the AI4People- An Ethical Framework document, an extended list of 20 action points is proposed, which involve aspects of assessment of AI technology, of development of the necessary ethical, legal and framework, of incentivization in financial terms, of support to self- regulatory codes, corporate bonds and educational activities. Floridi et al. (2018), pp.701–705; Tito (2017), pp. 44–48

[82] Floridi et al. (2018), p. 691; Tito (2017), pp. 44–48; U Pagallo et al. (2019); Crosnier (2018), pp. 1–12; Sinclair (1997), p. 544; Rubinstein (2016); Michael (1996), pp. 541–544; Cowls and Floridi (2018).

to move on with the debate and the actions which are required in order to shape the future of AI as well as our future with AI. From this aspect too, legal norms such as social rights can play a significant role in the sense of providing concrete ground—as concrete as law can be—regarding the regulation of the evolution of AI and the determination of its "friendliness" or not, towards us.

Consequently, the role of social rights is perceived here as the main guarantor of coherent societies via equality—as much as possible—within the capitalist model. Their role is already under strain and facing polemic. In relation to sectors where colossal economic interests and power games are at stake, their role is further endangered. The initiative, the pioneer force for such a development can be primarily only social movements for social justice in the way that AI—and, in general, modern technologies—evolve and are used.

The technological breakthrough is getting more closely to what was once considered to be science fiction. AI is already capable of improving itself,[83] design machine-learning chips,[84] create fake faces in order to generate the data with which they are going to be trained[85] and surprise us with the "beauty" of the moves they make on games like Go.[86] It "promises" to us victory over disease and death. The temptation is almost an impossible one to resist.

References

Acemoglu D, Restrepo P (2017) Robots and jobs: evidence from US labor markets. MIT Department of Economics Working Paper No. 17-04. https://papers.ssrn.com/sol3/papers.cfm?abstract_id=2940245

Alston P (1987) Out of the abyss: the challenges confronting the new U.N. Committee on economic, social and cultural rights. Hum Rights Q 9:332–381

Andreassen B-A (1992) Article 22. In: Eide A et al (eds) The universal declaration of human rights: a commentary. Scandinavian University Press, Oxford, pp 319–356

Atria F (2015) Social rights, social contract, socialism. Soc Leg Stud 24:598–613

Banerjee A, Duflo E (2005) Growth theory through the lens of development economics. In: Aghion P, Durlauf S (eds) Handbook of economic growth. Elsevier, Amsterdam, pp 473–552

Bennett Moses L (2011) Agents of change: how the law 'Copes' with techno logical change. Griffith Law Rev 20:763–794

Black J (2008) Forms and paradoxes of principles based regulation. LSE L, Society & Econ Working Papers 13/2008

Bostrom N (2003) The Transhumanist FAQ: A General Introduction, Version 2.1. Available via the World Transhumanist Association. https://www.nickbostrom.com/views/transhumanist.pdf

Bostrom N (2005) Transhumanist values. J Philos Res 30(Supplement):3–14

Bostrom N (2008) Why I want to be a Posthuman when I grow up. In: Gordijn B, Chadwick R (eds) Medical enhancement and posthumanity. Springer, The Netherlands, pp 107–137

[83]Heaven (2021).

[84]Vincent (2021).

[85]Hao (2021).

[86]Wood (2016).

Bostrom N, Ćirkovic M (2008) Introduction. In: Bostrom N, Ćirkovic M, Rees M (eds) Global catastrophic risks. Oxford University Press, Oxford, pp 1–30
Braidotti R (2013) The posthuman. Polity Press, Cambridge
Brownsword R (2008) Rights, regulation, and the technological revolution. Oxford University Press, Oxford
Butenko A, Larouche P (2015) Regulation for innovativeness or regulation of innovation? Law Innov Technol 7:52–85
Carozza PG (2008) Human dignity and judicial interpretation of human rights: a reply. Eur J Int Law 19:931–944
Cellan-Jones R (2020) Is Elon Musk Over-Hyping His Brain-Hacking Neuralink Tech? Available via BBC. https://www.bbc.com/news/technology-53987919
CESCR (1990) General Comment No. 3: The Nature of States Parties' Obligations (Art. 2, Para. 1, of the Covenant). UN Doc E/1991/23(SUPP)
CESCR (1999a) General Comment No. 12 The Right to Adequate Food (Art. 11). UN Doc E/C.12/1999/5
CESCR (1999b) General Comment No. 13: The Right to Education (Art. 13). UN Doc E/C.12/1999/10
CESCR (2000) General Comment No. 14: The Right to the Highest Attainable Standard of Health (Art. 12). UN Doc E/C.12/2000/4
CESCR (2020) General Comment No. 25 on Science and Economic, Social and Cultural Rights (Article 15 (1) (B), (2), (3) And (4) of the International Covenant on Economic, Social and Cultural Rights). E/C.12/GC/25
Clifford C (2020) Elon Musk's Brain-Computer Interface Company Neuralink Has Money and Buzz, But Hurdles Too. Available via CNBC. https://www.cnbc.com/2020/12/05/elon-musks-neuralink-bold-ideas-hurdles.html
Collingridge D (1980) The social control of technology. St. Martin's Press, New York
Council Of Europe (2019) Commissioner for Human Rights: Unboxing Artificial Intelligence: 10 Steps to Protect Human Rights. https://www.coe.int/en/web/commissioner/-/unboxing-artificial-intelligence-10-steps-to-protect-human-rights
Cowls J, Floridi L (2018) Prolegomena to a White Paper on an Ethical Framework for a Good AI Society. Available via SSRN Electronic Journal. https://doi.org/10.2139/Ssrn.3198732
Crosnier HL (2018) Communs numériques et communs de la connaissance Tic & Société 12:1–12
Cuellar MF (2017) A simpler world? On pruning risks and harvesting fruits in an orchard of whispering algorithms. UC Davis Law Rev 51:27–49
Dartmouth (1956) Artificial Intelligence (AI) Coined at Dartmouth. https://250.dartmouth.edu/highlights/artificial-intelligence-ai-coined-dartmouth
den Exter A et al (2001) Right to health. In: van Krieken PJ (ed) Health, migration and return: a handbook for a multidisciplinary approach. T.M.C. Asser Press, The Netherlands, pp 9–30
Donders Y (2011) The right to enjoy the benefits of scientific progress: in search of state obligations in relation to health. Med Health Care Philos 14:371–381
ECOSOC/Commission on Human Rights (2003) in its resolution about 'Economic, Social and Cultural Rights: Norms On The Responsibilities Of Transnational Corporations And Other Business Enterprises With Regard To Human Rights, E/CN.4/Sub.2/2003/12/Rev.2, 26 August 2003, para. 12
Edri (2018) UN Special Rapporteur Analyses AI's Impact on Human Rights. https://edri.org/our-work/un-special-rapporteur-report-artificial-intelligence-impact-human-rights/
Eide A (2000) Economic and social rights. In: Symonides J (ed) Human rights: concept and standards. Routledge, London, pp 109–174. https://www.corteidh.or.cr/Tablas/R28245.Pdf
Executive Office of the USA President (2016) Artificial Intelligence, Automation, And The Economy. https://obamawhitehouse.archives.gov/sites/whitehouse.gov/files/documents/Artificial-Intelligence-Automation-Economy.PDF
Fenwick M, Kaal WA, Vermeulen EPM (2017) Regulation tomorrow: what happens when technology is faster than the law? Am Univ Bus Law Rev 6:561–594

Floridi L et al (2018) AI4People—an ethical framework for a good AI society: opportunities, risks, principles, and recommendations. Minds Mach 28:689–707
Fordham M (2013) Social rights. Judicial Rev 18:379–387
Frey CB, Osborne MA (2017) The future of employment: how susceptible are jobs to computerisation? Technol Forecast Soc Chang 114:254–280
Fukuyama F (2004) Transhumanism. Foreign Policy 144:42–43
Garty C, Mantouvalou V (2011) Debating social rights (debating law). Hart Publishing, Oxford
Gerdes A (2018) An inclusive ethical design perspective for a flourishing future with artificial intelligent systems. Eur J Risk Regul 9:677–689
Good IJ (1966) Speculations concerning the first Ultraintelligent machine. Adv Comput 6:31–88
Hao K (2021) These Creepy Fake Humans Herald a New Age in AI. Available via MIT Technology Review. https://www.technologyreview.com/2021/06/11/1026135/ai-synthetic-data/
Heaven WD (2021) AI Is Learning How to Create Itself. Available via MIT Technology Review. https://www.technologyreview.com/2021/05/27/1025453/artificial-intelligence-learning-create-itself-agi/
Henkin L (1990) The age of rights. Cambridge University Press, Cambridge
Höffe O (2007) Democracy in an age of globalization. Springer, Dordrecht
Hooker J, Kim TW (2019) Ethical implications of the fourth industrial revolution. In: Wasieleski DM, Weber J (eds) Business ethics business and society 360, vol 3. Emerald Publishing Limited, Bingley, pp 35–63
IEEE (2019) Ethically Aligned Design, 1st edn. https://standards.ieee.org/content/dam/ieee-standards/standards/web/documents/other/ead1e.pdf?utm_medium=undefined&utm_source=undefined&utm_campaign=undefined&utm_content=undefined&utm_term=undefined
International Conference on Primary Health Care (1978) Declaration of Alma-Ata, 6-12 September 1978. https://cdn.who.int/media/docs/default-source/documents/almaata-declaration-en.pdf?sfvrsn=7b3c2167_2
International Human Rights Instruments (2003) Compilation of General Comments and General Recommendations Adopted by Human Rights Treaty. UN Doc. HRI/GEN/1/Rev.6
Jee YS (2017) Exercise rehabilitation in the fourth industrial revolution. J Exercise Rehabil 13:255–256
Kang M (2011) Sublime dreams of living machines, the automation in the European imagination. Harvard University Press, Harvard
Karppi T, Crawford K (2016) Social media, financial algorithms and the hack crash. Theory Cult Soc 33:73–92
Kowert W (2017) The foreseeability of human-artificial intelligence interactions. Texas Law Rev 96:181–204
Kurzweil R (2005) The singularity is near: when humans transcend biology. Viking, New York
Leach A (2018) Iain M. Banks – Human, Posthuman and Beyond Human. ELOPE 15:69–81. doi: https://doi.org/10.4312/elope.15.1.69-81
Lehmann K (2006) In defense of the constitutional court: litigating economic and social rights and the myth of the minimum core. Am J Int Law 22:163–197
Lindert P (2021) Social Spending and the Welfare State. In: OECD, How Was Life? Volume II: New Perspectives on Well-being and Global Inequality since 1820. OECD Publishing, Paris. https://doi.org/10.1787/3d96efc5-en
Lucas RE (2004) The industrial revolution: past and future. Annual Report of The Federal Reserve Bank of Minneapolis 18:5–20
Mandel GN et al (2013) Emerging technology governance. In: Marchant GE, Abbott KW, Allenby B (eds) Innovative governance models for emerging technologies. Elgar, Cheltenham, pp 44–62
Manyika J (2017) Technology, jobs, and the future of work. Available via McKinsey Global Institute. https://www.mckinsey.com/Featured-Insights/Employment-And-Growth/Technology-Jobs-And-The-Future-Of-Work
Manyika J et al (2017) A Future that Works: Automation, Employment and Productivity. Available via McKinsey Global Institute. https://www.mckinsey.com/~/media/mckinsey/featured%20

insights/Digital%20Disruption/Harnessing%20automation%20for%20a%20future%20that%20works/MGI-A-future-that-works-Executive-summary.ashx
Marchant GE, Wallach W (2013) Governing the governance of emerging technologies. In: Marchant GE, Abbott KW, Allenby B (eds) Innovative governance models for emerging technologies. Elgar, Cheltenham
Marshall T, Bottomore TB (1992) Citizenship and social class. Pluto Press, London
Marshall TH (1950) Citizenship and social class. Cambridge University Press, Cambridge
Martinez R (2019) Artificial intelligence: distinguishing between types & definitions. Nevada Law J 19:1015–1041
Mathiason G et al (2016) The Transformation of the Workplace Through Robotic Artificial Intelligence, and Automation. Available via Litter https://www.littler.com/publication-press/publication/transformation-workplace-through-robotics-artificial-intelligence-and.
McGinnis JO (2010) Accelerating AI. Northwest Univ Law R Colloquy 104:366–381
McKie R (2018) No death and an enhanced life: is the future Transhuman?. Available via The Guardian. https://www.theguardian.com/technology/2018/may/06/no-death-and-an-enhanced-life-is-the-future-transhuman
Miah A (2008) A critical history of posthumanism. In: Gordijn B, Chadwick R (eds) Medical enhancement and Posthumanity. Springer, The Netherlands, pp 71–94
Michael DC (1996) Cooperative implementation of federal regulations. Yale J Regul 13:535–601
Mokhtarian E (2018) The bot legal code: developing a legally compliant artificial intelligence. Vanderbilt J Entertain Technol Law 21:145–207
Muggleton SH (2006) Exceeding human limits. Nature 440:409–410
Müller A (2010) Remarks on the Venice Statement on the Right to Enjoy the Benefits of Scientific Progress and its Applications (Article 15(1)(B) ICESCR). Human Rights Law Rev 10:765–784
Mumford L (2010) Technics & civilization. The University of Chicago Press, Chicago
Muzaffar C (1999) From human rights to human dignity. In: van Ness P (ed) Debating human rights: critical essays from the United States and Asia. Routledge, New York, pp 25–31
Mzikenge Chirwa D (2003) The right to health in international law: its implications for the obligations of state and non-state actors in ensuring access to essential medicine. South Afr J Human Rights 19:541–566
Noorman M, Johnson DG (2014) Negotiating autonomy and responsibility in military robots. Ethics Info Technol 16:51–62
Office of the United Nations High Commissioner for Human Rights/WHO (2008) The Right to Health, Fact Sheet No. 31. https://www.ohchr.org/documents/publications/factsheet31.pdf
Pagallo U et al (2019) On Good AI Governance. 14 Priority Actions, A S.M.A.R.T. Model of Governance, and a Regulatory Toolbox. https://www.eismd.eu/wp-content/uploads/2019/11/AI4Peoples-Report-on-Good-AI-Governance_compressed.pdf
Palmerini E et al (2015) Robolaw, regulating emerging robotic technologies in Europe: Robotics Facing Law and Ethics. https://cordis.europa.eu/project/id/289092/reporting
Pollis A (1996) Cultural relativism revisited: through a state prism. Hum Rights Q 18:316–334
Pollock G (2011) What is Posthumanism? By Cary Wolfe (2009). J Crit Animal Stud IX:235–241
Portugal Gouvêa C (2013) Social rights against the poor. Vienna J Int Const Law 7:454–475
Rawls J (1971) A theory of justice. Harvard University Press, Harvard
Renn O, Klinke A (2004) Systemic risks: a new challenge for risk management. EMBO Rep 5:S41–S46
RT (2022) Mind-reading Robot Tested on Humans – Reports. https://www.rt.com/news/545324-mind-reading-robot-china/
Rubinstein IS (2016) The future of self-regulation is co-regulation. In: Selinger E, Polonetsky J, Tene O (eds) The Cambridge handbook of consumer privacy. Cambridge University Press, Cambridge
Samnøy A (1999) The origins of the universal declaration of human rights. In: Alfredsson G, Eide A (eds) The universal declaration of human rights: a common standard of achievement. Martinus Nijhoff, The Hague, pp 3–22

Saslow K, Lorenz P (2019) Artificial Intelligence Needs Human Rights. Available via Stiftung Neue Verantwortung. https://www.stiftung-nv.de/sites/default/files/ai_needs_human_rights.pdf
Scherer MU (2016) Regulating artificial intelligence systems: risks, challenges, competencies, and strategies. Harv J Law Technol 29:353–400
Schuck PH (1984) When the exception becomes the rule: regulatory equity and the formulation of energy policy through an exceptions process. Duke Law J 1984:163–300
Schuller AL (2017) At the crossroads of control: the intersection of artificial intelligence in autonomous weapon systems with international humanitarian law. Harv Natl Secur J 8:379–425
Schwab K (2015) The Fourth Industrial Revolution: What It Means and How to Respond. Available via Foreign Affairs. https://www.foreignaffairs.com/articles/2015-12-12/fourth-industrial-revolution
Sen A (1983) Poverty and famines: an essay on entitlement and deprivation. Oxford University Press, Oxford
Shah S et al (2015) The Regulator of Tomorrow. Rulemaking and Enforcement in an Era of Exponential Change. Available via Deloitte. https://www2.deloitte.com/content/dam/Deloitte/tr/Documents/public-sector/Regulator-of-tomorrow_vFINAL.pdf
Sheridan TB, Verplank WL (1978) Human and Computer Control of Undersea Teleoperators. https://apps.dtic.mil/sti/pdfs/ADA057655.pdf
Sinclair D (1997) Self-regulation versus command and control? Beyond false dichotomies. Law Policy 19:529–559
Singer PW (2009) Wired for war: the robotics revolution and conflict in the 21st century. Penguin Books, New York
Soskis B (2005) Man and the machines. It's time to start thinking about how we might grant legal rights to computers. Available via Legal Affairs. https://www.legalaffairs.org/issues/January-February 2005/feature_sokis_janfeb05.msp
Spier J (2011) Uncertainties and the state of the art: a legal nightmare. J Risk Res 14:501–510
Ssenyonjo M (2009) Economic and social rights in international law. Hart Publishing, Oxford
Susen S (2022) Reflections on the (post-)human condition: towards new forms of engagement with the world? Soc Epistemol 36:63–94
Tanz J (2016) Soon We Won't Program Computers. We'll Train Them Like Dogs. Available via WIRED. https://www.wired.com/2016/05/the-end-of-code/.
Taylor C (2007) A secular age. Harvard University Press, Harvard
The Crypto Oracle (n.d.) The Fourth Industrial Revolution: The Rise of the Autonomous Economy. https://medium.com/the-capital/the-fourth-industrial-revolution-the-rise-of-the-autonomous-economy-cfe0886ad8b3
The Economist (2017) Automatic for the People: How Germany's Otto Uses Artificial Intelligence. https://www.economist.com/business/2017/04/12/how-germanys-otto-uses-artificial-intelligence
Tito J (2017) Destination unknown: exploring the impact of artificial intelligence on government. Available via Centre for Public Impact. https://www.centreforpublicimpact.org/assets/documents/Destination-Unknown-AI-and-government.pdf
Toebes BCA (1999) The right to health as a right in international law. Intersertia, Antwerpen
Tzimas T (2020) Artificial intelligence and human rights: their role in the evolution of AI. ZaöRV 80:1–25
Tzimas T (2021) Legal and ethical challenges of artificial intelligence from an international law perspective. Springer, Switzerland
UNESCO (2009) The Right to Enjoy the Benefits of Scientific Progress and Its Applications. https://unesdoc.unesco.org/ark:/48223/pf0000185558
Urban T (2015) The AI revolution: the road to superintelligence. Available via WAIT BUT WHY. https://waitbutwhy.com/2015/01/artificial-intelligence-revolution-1.html
van Asselt MBA, Renn O (2011) Risk governance. J Risk Res 14:431–449
Verdoux P (2009) Transhumanism, progress and the future. J Evol Technol 20:49–69

Vincent J (2021) Google is Using AI to Design its Next Generation of AI Chips More Quickly Than Humans Can. Available via The Verge. https://www.theverge.com/2021/6/10/22527476/google-machine-learning-chip-design-tpu-floorplanning

Vint S (2007) Bodies of tomorrow. Technology, subjectivity, science fiction. University of Toronto Press, Toronto. https://doi.org/10.3138/9781442684072

Whelan DJ, Donnelly J (2007) The west, economic and social rights, and the global human rights regime: setting the record straight. Hum Rights Q 29:908–949

Wiessner S, Willard AR (1999) Policy-oriented jurisprudence and human rights abuses in internal conflict: toward a world public order of human dignity. Am J Int Law 93:316–334

Wisskirchen G et al (2017) Artificial intelligence and robotics and their impact on the workplace. IBA Global Employment Institute

Wood G (2016) The Sadness and Beauty of Watching Google's AI Play Go. Available via WIRED. https://www.wired.com/2016/03/sadness-beauty-watching-googles-ai-play-go/

World Bank (n.d.) GDP. https://data.worldbank.org/indicator/NY.GDP.MKTP.CD

World Conference on Human Rights (1993) Vienna Declaration and Programme of Action. UN Doc A/CONF.157/23

Wright JT (1979) Human rights in the west: political liberties and the rule of law. In: Pollis A, Schwab P (eds) Human rights: cultural and ideological perspective. Praeger, New York

Xiang F (2018) AI Will Spell the End of Capitalism. Available via The Washington Post. https://www.washingtonpost.com/news/theworldpost/wp/2018/05/03/end-of-capitalism/

Xu M, David JM, Kim SH (2018) The fourth industrial revolution: opportunities and challenges. Int J Financ Res 9:90–95

Yamin AE (2005) The right to health under international law and its relevance to the United States. Am J Public Health 95:1156–1161

Yeshanew SA (2013) The justiciability of economic, social and cultural rights in the African regional human rights system: theory, practice and prospect. Intersentia, Cambridge

Young KG (2008) The minimum Core of economic and social rights: a concept in search of content. Yale J Int Law 33:113–175

Artificial Intelligence vs Data Protection: How the GDPR Can Help to Develop a Precautionary Regulatory Approach to AI?

Joanna Mazur

Abstract In the chapter I analyse how experience drawn from the implementation of data protection impact assessment (DPIA) to the General Data Protection Regulation (GDPR) can be helpful when developing a precautionary regulatory approach to artificial intelligence (AI) in the European Union's (EU) law. I begin with the examination of the shortcomings of the regulatory framework concerning DPIA. Next, I move on to the analysis of the regulatory proposal concerning AI, presented by the Commission in April 2021. The proposal strengthens the precautionary approach to the regulation of new technologies in EU law by e.g., implementation of the category of an unacceptable risk. However, to guarantee effective precautionary approach to the regulation of AI in the *AI Act*, it is necessary to learn the lesson from the shortcomings which became evident in the case of the GDPR's provisions concerning DPIA.

Funding: This research was funded by the National Science Centre (Poland) under grant "Automated decision-making versus prohibition of discrimination in the European law" (project number 2018/29/N/HS5/00105). Joanna Mazur is supported by the Foundation for Polish Science (FNP).
Acknowledgments: I would like to thank the organizers and the participants of the Colloquium on "Artificial Intelligence and Normative Challenges: International and Comparative Legal Perspectives" for the opportunity to present my work during the Colloquium and the participants of DELab Seminar "Digitalization under the closer look of science" during which my paper was discussed, for their insightful comments.

J. Mazur (✉)
University of Warsaw, Warsaw, Poland
e-mail: j.mazur@delab.uw.edu.pl

A. Kornilakis et al. (eds.), *Artificial Intelligence and Normative Challenges*, Law, Governance and Technology Series 59,
https://doi.org/10.1007/978-3-031-41081-9_12

1 Introduction

Neither the term 'artificial intelligence' (AI) nor other terms strictly connected to AI, such as 'machine learning' or 'edge computing', appear in the General Data Protection Regulation (GDPR).[1] Despite the lengthy motives included in the regulation's text, the European Union (EU) did not decide to directly refer to these particular new technologies in this legal act, which might be perceived as a sign of the GPDR's technological neutrality.[2] This does not mean that the GDPR fails to provide regulatory measures which should be perceived as having a direct influence on the regulation of AI.

As I show in Sect. 2, one of such measures is the data protection impact assessment (DPIA), introduced in the GDPR. DPIA, as an instrument whose purpose is to ensure systemic accountability of data processing, is focused on the analysis of the systems used for data processing. In the chapter, I analyse situations in which it may be obligatory to perform a DPIA when AI-based solutions are used for the processing of personal data. In Sect. 3, I analyse the conditions under which a DPIA is obligatory in the light of the GDPR's provisions. In Sect. 4, I examine if the necessity to perform a DPIA in case of use of AI may be strengthened on the national level, since the member states are granted a certain degree of liberty in terms of e.g., drawing up the list of the types of processing which should be subjected to a DPIA (Table 1). The chapter presents results of the analysis of the blacklists of operations subjected to DPIAs adopted by the national supervisory authorities in the member states of the EU and in the countries of the European Economic Area (EEA). The purpose of the analysis is to examine the manners in which the national blacklists may indicate the necessity to perform DPIAs when using AI based tools for personal data processing. In Sect. 5, I show what kind of lessons do the experiences with DPIAs' regulation teach us in the context of the future regulatory framework for AI in the EU, namely, the proposal of the *AI Act.*[3]

These lessons concern both the procedural aspects of the precautionary measures adopted in relation to new technologies, and the issue of relation between the level on which a given aspect of these precautionary measures is regulated (national or EU law). The analysis concerning DPIA refers to the AI algorithms and systems, which are developed using personal data or whose use involves personal data. This limitation results from the scope of the GDPR and, therefore, the extent of the situations in which the regulatory measures foreseen in the GDPR may be used.

[1] *Regulation (EU) 2016/679 of the European Parliament and of the Council of 27 April 2016 on the protection of natural persons with regard to the processing of personal data and on the free movement of such data, and repealing Directive 95/46/EC (General Data Protection Regulation)* [2016] OJ L119/1.

[2] Which can be identified in Art 2(1) GDPR and is explicitly mentioned in its Recital 15.

[3] Commission, *Proposal for a Regulation of the European Parliament and of the Council Laying Down Harmonised Rules on Artificial Intelligence (Artificial Intelligence Act) and Amending Certain Union Legislative Acts*, COM/2021/206 final.

Table 1 Links to the national blacklists

State	Short link	State	Short link
Austria	https://bit.ly/3ivkZss	Luxembourg	https://bit.ly/392MoyI
Belgium	https://bit.ly/3iwR8Qi	Malta	https://bit.ly/3c0n9io
Bulgaria	https://bit.ly/3YjQzNl	Netherlands	https://bit.ly/2Nhz4hu
Croatia	https://bit.ly/3o5NwpI	Poland	https://bit.ly/39NyeAK
Cyprus	https://bit.ly/2LKor6J	Portugal	https://bit.ly/3RtWUnb
Czech Republic	https://bit.ly/3odw9n3	Romania	https://bit.ly/3c1aE6u
Denmark	https://bit.ly/3p9yQau	Slovakia	https://bit.ly/3c0Oxg7
Estonia	https://bit.ly/2Y0dsZ5	Slovenia	https://bit.ly/2Y0uuGB
Finland	https://bit.ly/35YZhYG	Spain	https://bit.ly/3c7xZ6a
France	https://bit.ly/2Y7pbFb	Sweden	https://bit.ly/40tB2wk
Germany	https://bit.ly/3jOufL0		
Greece	https://bit.ly/392mQ4H	Iceland	https://bit.ly/2NlVmPb
Hungary	https://bit.ly/3c1fWPc	Liechtenstein	https://bit.ly/3p9xYm3
Ireland	https://bit.ly/3614m2K	Norway	https://bit.ly/363kKzJ
Italy	https://bit.ly/2NrsbKL		
Latvia	https://bit.ly/3sKhL99	United Kingdom	https://bit.ly/39Tij3L
Lithuania	https://bit.ly/3qFdQZl		

However, it does not mean that the conclusions drawn from the analysis of the GDPR's provisions on DPIA may not inspire providing better regulatory solutions in the legal acts whose scope differs from the GDPR's. For example, the evident drawbacks of DPIA in terms of its accessibility for the broader public can, as I show in the text, indicate the necessity to provide certain safeguards in the legal acts which specifically address the challenges related to AI, as for example the proposal of *AI Act*.

2 GDPR's and DPIA's Significance for AI Regulation

The significance of the GDPR for AI regulation results from the fact that a number of AI-based solutions developed nowadays use personal data processing for training of the algorithms.[4] Therefore, the rights of the data subject and obligations of the data controller set out in the GDPR have an influence on the requirements which need to be fulfilled when implementing AI-driven tools based on personal data processing.[5]

[4]The need of compliance of AI applications with the data protection regulatory framework is stressed in: Commission, *White Paper: On Artificial Intelligence - A European approach to excellence and trust*, COM/2020/65 final, pp. 11, 20–22; Commission, *AI Act*, section 1.2.

[5]For a comprehensive overview of the GDPR's impact on AI's regulation, see Centre for Information Policy Leadership (CIPL) (2020).

The impact of the data protection regulatory framework on the AI's applications is twofold. Firstly, there is a perspective which focuses on the rights of the data subject. For example, in order to guarantee the compliance with the provisions, which provide the data subject with a right to receive 'meaningful information about the logic involved, as well as the significance and the envisaged consequences of such processing for the data subject' (Art 13(2)f, Art 14(2)g and Art 15(1)h) in case of automated decision making, it is necessary to support the development of the explainable AI solutions. One could argue that this right should actually prevent the use of AI systems which do not allow the provision of such 'meaningful information'. However, the controversies concerning the meaning of the term 'meaningful', as well as the lack of relevant case law, hamper the possibility of such an interpretation.[6] Thus, a lack of clarity concerning the actual meaning and scope of certain data subjects' rights limits the influence of these provisions on the implementation of AI-based systems using personal data.

Secondly, there is a perspective which stresses the necessity to adopt a precautionary, risk-based approach to the processing operations themselves. For example, principles relating to processing of personal data enumerated in Art 5, as well as more specific requirements such as data protection by default and by design (Art 25), or the requirement to conduct a DPIA in cases of processing, which are likely to result in a high risk to the rights and freedoms of natural persons, constitute the elements of the regulatory framework which have to be respected independently of the type of technology used for personal data processing and, thus, are of importance for the use of AI-based tools. Some of these provisions are equally imprecise as those which constitute the data subjects' rights (e.g., data protection by design and by default). Others, as, for instance, the provisions concerning DPIAs (Arts 35–36), consist of more specific obligations. Therefore, it is worth examining the extent to which such an influence can take place and what are the consequences of the necessity to comply with the GDPR's provisions when implementing AI-based tools which are based on personal data processing.

Additionally, the decision to focus on the DPIA and its impact on the regulation of AI results from its similarity to the tools which are proposed in discussions concerning AI's regulation in the EU. In the *White Paper: On Artificial Intelligence* (*White Paper*) and the *AI Act*—discussed in detail in Sect. 5 of this chapter—the Commission proposes to create a category of high-risk uses of AI which would be subject to requirements regarding, for example, the representativeness of data used for training the algorithms, or documentation of the programming. As I show below, this concept resembles the DPIA, as both of these solutions are based on the assumption that high-risk use of new technologies should be subject to certain precautionary measures which would allow to assess the risks linked to this new solution and develop measures to address them.

[6] For the relevant literature on this, so called, right to explanation, see Wachter et al. (2017), pp. 76–92; Selbst and Powles (2017), pp. 233–242; Malgieri and Comandé (2017), pp. 243–265; Brkan (2019), pp. 91–121; Kaminski (2019), pp. 189–218.

3 The DPIA and AI in the GDPR

The DPIA, a novelty in the European data protection law,[7] was introduced in Art 35 of the GDPR.[8] It is referred to as an 'accountability'[9] measure or an 'auditing'[10] instrument, as its purpose is to ensure *ex ante* control of processing operations which are likely to result in a high risk to the rights and freedoms of individuals. The DPIA is a regulatory measure focused on guaranteeing systemic accountability: what is scrutinised is not the situation of a particular individual and the processing of his or her personal data, but the way of conducting the processing operation.

Conducting a DPIA has an obligatory character when a type of processing falls under the criteria described in the GDPR. Thus, failure to carry out a DPIA when it is required, conducting a DPIA in an incorrect manner, as well as the lack of the obligatory consultations with the competent supervisory authority, can lead to an administrative fine.[11] Therefore, it seems vital to provide precise indications determining the necessity to conduct a DPIA.

The general criteria determining when it is compulsory to carry out a DPIA are enumerated in Art 35(1): processing which is likely to result in a high risk to the rights and freedoms of natural persons should be subjected to a DPIA. The factors which should be taken into account include the nature, scope, context, and purposes of the processing, and whether the processing is conducted using new technologies. Thus, it seems necessary—in any case of processing—to conduct a preliminary analysis in order to assess if it is likely to result in a high risk to the rights and freedoms of natural persons[12] and, therefore, whether it should be subjected to a DPIA. Such an analysis is especially significant in terms of processing which takes place using new technologies, as Art 35(1) explicitly mentions their use as a

[7] However, the DPIA is already present in other data protection laws, e.g., in New Zealand, Australia and Canada, see Kloza et al. (2017), p. 1.

[8] For an elaborate commentary on Art 35 and, additionally Art 36, which refers to prior consultation which should, in certain cases, take place before conducting a DPIA, see Kosta (2020), pp. 665–687.

[9] Kosta (2020), op.cit., p. 668; Kaminski and Malgieri (2021), p. 1; Article 29 Data Protection Working Party, *Guidelines on Data Protection Impact Assessment (DPIA) and determining whether processing is "likely to result in a high risk" for the purposes of Regulation 2016/679*, Adopted on 4 April 2017. As last Revised and Adopted on 4 October 2017, 17/EN WP 248 rev.01, p. 4.

[10] Goodman (2016), p. 4.

[11] 'Failure to carry out a DPIA when the processing is subject to a DPIA (Article 35(1) and (3)–(4)), carrying out a DPIA in an incorrect way (Article 35(2) and (7) to (9)), or failing to consult the competent supervisory authority where required (Article 36(3)(e)), can result in an administrative fine of up to 10 M€, or in the case of an undertaking, up to 2% of the total worldwide annual turnover of the preceding financial year, whichever is higher.' – Article 29 Data Protection Working Party (2017), op. cit., p. 4.

[12] As confirms e.g., the graph in Article 29 Data Protection Working Party (2017), op.cit., p. 7. Casey, Farhangi and Vogl note: 'demonstrating that a DPIA is not necessary will, in many instances, itself require a DPIA.' – Casey et al. (2019), pp. 143–188, 175.

condition which may indicate the existence of a high risk ('a type of processing in particular using new technologies').

Moreover, Art 35(3) enumerates three specific types of processing when a DPIA should be required. This is so, firstly, in cases of automated processing which constitutes the basis for decisions that produce legal effects concerning the natural person or similarly significantly affect the natural person. Such processing, if it involves 'a systematic and extensive evaluation of personal aspects relating to natural persons' (Art 35(3)a), and is automated, should be subjected to a DPIA. Secondly, DPIA is required when processing on a large scale of special categories of data, and processing of personal data which relate to criminal convictions and offences. Thirdly, the same applies to a systematic monitoring of a publicly accessible area on a large scale. The list is non-exhaustive and seems to serve as an 'illustration'[13] of what should be understood under the term 'is likely to result in a high risk'.[14]

GPDR's provisions also enumerate four obligatory elements of the DPIA (Art 35(7)).[15] More specifically, it should include: (a) the description of the envisaged processing and its purposes; (b) an assessment of the necessity and proportionality of the processing in the light of its purposes; (c) an assessment of the risks to the rights and freedoms of individuals; and (d) the description of the measures which would be adopted in order to cope with the identified risks. What is important to mention is the lack of obligation to publish the DPIA's results.[16] Even in cases when the DPIA indicates the existence of 'a high risk in the absence of measures taken by the controller to mitigate the risk' (Art 36(1)) and the controller is obliged to consult the supervisory authority (Art 36), still, it is not compulsory to make neither the DPIA nor its parts (e.g., summary) publicly available. Thus, the scale on which conducting DPIAs currently takes place remains unknown.

The question which should be raised, in the context of the use of products and services which use AI, is how the provisions of the GDPR concerning DPIAs may influence the regulatory requirements referring to the products and services which are developed using AI. Firstly, the expression 'in particular using new technologies', which describes the types of processing that should be carefully scrutinised as possibly creating a high risk for the rights and freedoms of natural persons, stresses the need to consider the necessity of performing DPIAs when using tools based on technologies referred to as AI. Secondly, in case of using AI-based tools for one of the types of processing included in the catalogue in Art 35(3), automatically the need to perform a DPIA appears. Thirdly, the Article 29 Data Protection Working Party (Art 29 WP) *Guidelines on Data Protection Impact Assessment (DPIA) and determining whether processing is "likely to result in a high risk" for the purposes of*

[13] See Article 29 Data Protection Working Party (2017), op.cit., pp. 8–9.

[14] On the term 'high risk' and its lack of clarity, see Demetzou (2019).

[15] On the complex literature review concerning the methods of conducting DPIA described in the literature, ss Georgiadis and Poels (2022).

[16] Confirmed by the Guidelines, see ibid., p. 18.

Regulation 2016/679 (Guidelines), despite their non-binding character, provide additional information on how to assess the existence of a high risk. Art 29 WP enumerates nine factors which should be considered when assessing the need to carry out a DPIA,[17] one of them being 'innovative use or applying new technological or organisational solutions.' According to the Guidelines, meeting two and more criteria should be considered as an indication of the need to conduct a DPIA. Thus, processing which uses AI-based solutions may be considered as quite likely to fall into the category of operations which require a DPIA.

4 DPIA and AI: Analysis of National Blacklists

Additionally, the GDPR foresees one more solution which should 'provide a more concrete set of processing operations that require a DPIA due to their inherent high risk',[18] namely the lists adopted at the national level.[19] According to Art 35(4): 'The supervisory authority shall establish and make public a list of the kind of processing operations which are subject to the requirement for a data protection impact assessment.' The lists, called blacklists, were adopted by the supervisory authorities of all of the member states and of the countries of the EEA (see Appendix). Additionally, the supervisory authorities may, but are not obliged to, adopt whitelists which include the types of processing which do not require performance of a DPIA. Considering that the national blacklists often mention the criteria proposed in the Guidelines, they are an interesting source of information on how the general criteria proposed by the Art 29 WP[20] may be translated into more specific categories of types of processing which require carrying out a DPIA.

The results of the analysis presented below describe the types of processing identified in the national blacklists which may lead to an unequivocal inclusion of the processing performed using AI among the types of processing which require an obligatory DPIA. For the purposes of the analysis,: (1) I collected the available language versions of national blacklists of the types of processing which should be subjected to a DPIA; (2) if available, I used the English version;[21] if no English version was available, I used automated translation of the list (when possible, revised by myself); (3) additionally, I checked the translated lists against the opinions of the EDPB in order to verify that the translation achieved in the above-described manner is correct.

[17] See Article 29 Data Protection Working Party (2017), op.cit., pp. 9–11.

[18] Ibid., p. 9

[19] For the analysis of national blacklists, see also Demetzou (2020).

[20] Currently the European Data Protection Board (EDPB). The Guidelines were prepared by this body under its previous name.

[21] Preferably provided by the national supervisory authority, however, when available, I also used other sources. When quoting or referring to the list I indicate the source of the text.

On the basis of their content, I attempted to identify how the national blacklists indicate the inclusion of processing with use of AI-based tools among the types of processing subjected to DPIAs. Three manners in which solutions which use AI for data processing may be influenced by the national blacklists include: (1) technologically sensitive approach, which results from explicit enumeration of AI or new technologies in the blacklists; (2) technologically neutral approach, which is characterised by indirect impact on AI-based solutions due to the purpose of the processing performed or the type of data used in it; and (3) mentioning the size of the processed dataset. Below I describe these manners in detail.

4.1 Technologically Sensitive Approach: AI and New Technology

The term ‘new technology’, used in Art 35(1) of GDPR, is explained in its Recital 91 as in ‘accordance with the achieved state of technological knowledge’. However, such an approach does not seem to clarify which technologies should be treated with special attention. While the majority of the national blacklists include the reference to ‘new technologies’, ‘new technology’ or ‘new technological’,[22] only a few of the national blacklists include what seems to be an attempt at explaining what this term actually means.

‘Artificial Intelligence’ is explicitly mentioned in blacklists adopted by the supervisory authorities of Austria,[23] Czech Republic,[24] Germany,[25] Greece,[26] Italy,[27] and United Kingdom, as can be seen in Table 2.[28] On the German list, the use of AI constitutes a separate point describing a type of processing requiring a DPIA, while for Austrian, Greek, Italian, and British lists AI is mentioned as an

---

[22] From my calculation: 16 of the blacklists include one of these expressions.

[23] Verordnung der Datenschutzbehörde über Verarbeitungsvorgänge, für die eine Datenschutz-Folgenabschätzung durchzuführen ist (DSFA-V). Access: https://www.ris.bka.gv.at/eli/bgbl/II/2018/278/20181109.

[24] List of processing operations subject to data protection impact assessment. Access: https://iapp.org/media/pdf/resource_center/czech_blacklist.pdf.

[25] Liste der Verarbeitungstätigkeiten, für die eine DSFA durchzuführen ist. Access: https://www.lda.bayern.de/media/dsfa_muss_liste_dsk_de.pdf.

[26] List of the kind of processing operations which are subject to the requirement for a data protection impact assessment according to article 35 par. 4 of GDPR. Access: https://iapp.org/media/pdf/resource_center/hellenic_blacklist.pdf.

[27] Elenco delle tipologie di trattamenti, soggetti al meccanismo di coerenza, da sottoporre a valutazione d’impatto. Access: https://www.garanteprivacy.it/home/docweb/-/docweb-display/docweb/9058979.

[28] Type of processing operation(s) requiring a DPIA. Access: https://ico.org.uk/for-organisations/guide-to-data-protection/guide-to-the-general-data-protection-regulation-gdpr/data-protection-impact-assessments-dpias/examples-of-processing-likely-to-result-in-high-risk/.

Table 2 The elements of the national blacklists explicitly mentioning the phrase 'artificial intelligence' or 'AI'

Country	The relevant point on the blacklist
Austria	4. Processing of data using or using new or novel technologies or organizational solutions that make it difficult to estimate the effects on the data subjects and the social consequences, in particular through the use of **artificial intelligence** and the processing of biometric data, provided that the processing not just the real-time reproduction of face images.
Czech Republic	Processing of personal data in technically complex or advanced infrastructures or platforms (partially criteria 6, 5, and 1 of the guidelines): [the highest level of the risk:] Automated expert systems including **artificial intelligence**.
Germany	11. Use of **artificial intelligence** to process personal data for controlling the interaction with those affected or for assessment of personal aspects of the data subject.
Greece	3.1 Innovative use or application of new technological or organizational solutions, which can involve novel forms of data collection and usage, possibly with a high risk to individuals' rights and freedoms, like the combined use of fingerprint and face recognition for improved physical access control, or mHealth applications, or other "smart" applications from which user profiles are generated (e.g. daily habits), or **artificial intelligence** applications as well as publicly accessible blockchains that include personal data.
Italy	7. Treatments carried out through the use of innovative technologies, also with particular organizational measures (e.g., IoT; **artificial intelligence** systems; use of online voice assistants through voice and textual scanning; monitoring performed by wearable devices; tracking proximity such as e.g., wi-fi tracking) whenever at least one of the criteria identified in WP 248, rev. 01.
United Kingdom	1. Innovative technology—Processing involving the use of new technologies, or the novel application of existing technologies (including **AI**). A DPIA is required for any intended processing operation(s) involving innovative use of technologies (or applying new technological and/or organisational solutions) when combined with any other criterion from WP248rev01.

example of 'new' or 'innovative' technology or 'technically complex or advanced infrastructures'.

Such a direct mention of AI included in a blacklist may facilitate the assessment of the need to perform a DPIA. Despite the difficulties concerning, for instance, what should be understood by the term AI, providing examples of technologies which should be treated as 'new' seems to be an input of the national blacklists to the general criteria included in the GDPR's provisions. Moreover, the inclusion of the 'innovative use' criterion in the reference to AI in three of the national blacklists which explicitly mention AI potentially addresses the question 'when the technology is not new anymore?'. Even if technologies based on AI were to become quite widespread and standard in the future, there would still be a need to conduct DPIA in a situation of its innovative use.

4.2 *Technologically Neutral Approach: Purpose of the Processing and Types of Data Used in the Processing*

The second manner in which the blacklists may stress the need to perform DPIAs when using AI is mentioning particular purposes of the processing or the types of data used in the processing. This scenario focuses on non-technological aspects of the processing and is independent of the use of AI-based solutions. However, the uses of AI for the purposes included in the blacklists or for the processing of the types of data explicitly mentioned in the blacklists would result with the need to conduct a DPIA.

The criterion of the purpose of the processing requires that a data controller, who intends to use AI-based solutions for the purposes mentioned in the blacklists, considers whether the solution which he or she develops falls into one of the categories included in the blacklist. An example from the Belgian blacklist is:

> 14. Large-scale processing of data generated by devices with sensors that sent data over the Internet or any another means (i.e., Internet of Things applications such as smart TV, smart household appliances, connected toys, smart cities, smart energy systems) for the purpose of analysing or predicting individuals' economic situation, health, preferences or personal interests, reliability or behaviour, localization or movements.[29]

It seems that even if such a processing is conducted solely for the purpose of analysis of data subjects' situation or preferences, in the cases enumerated in the blacklist, a DPIA should be conducted. This approach widens the scope of the obligatory DPIA when compared to Art 35. Thus, inclusion of the purpose of analysis may be perceived as a manner of broadening of the scope of situations when the obligation to perform a DPIA arises.

An example of the situation when the use of a particular type of data may result in the obligation to perform a DPIA is the inclusion in the blacklists of the reference to 'biometric' data'. While Art 35(3) mentions 'processing on a large scale of special categories of data'—biometric data included—all of the blacklists somehow refer to biometric data. In certain cases, they do not refer to the requirement of the 'large scale' processing; for instance, the Finnish blacklist foresees a number of various situations in which the use of biometric data should be subjected to a DPIA, 'large scale' processing being only one out of eight types of processing included in the

[29] Vlaamse Toezichtcommissie voor de verwerking van persoonsgegevens: Beslissing VTC nr. O/2020/01 van 14 januari 2020 betreffende Aanname van de lijst met verwerkingen waarvoor een Gegevensbeschermingseffectbeoordeling dient te worden uitgevoerd conform artikel 35.4 van de Algemene Verordening Gegevensbescherming door Vlaamse bestuursinstanties. Access: https://overheid.vlaanderen.be/sites/default/files/media/VTC/VTC_O_2020_01_DPIA_lijsten_v1_voor_web.pdf.

list.[30] It seems that any AI-based technology which uses the types of data mentioned in the national blacklists in cases enumerated in them[31] should result in the need to carry out a DPIA.

4.3 Size of the Processed Dataset: Large-Scale Processing

The third manner in which, indirectly, the national blacklists may influence the scope of the situations in which it is obligatory to perform a DPIA when using AI, are the references to 'large-scale processing'. It seems that, usually, it is necessary for the development of AI-based solutions to process large amounts of data. Thus, in cases in which the blacklists refer to 'large scale' processing, the need to perform a DPIA—when using AI—would often appear.

It is noteworthy, that the blacklist may refer to large scale processing without specifying any other additional criteria. An example is the Polish blacklists which simply include a category of data processing on a large scale, with the explanations that 'the notion of large scale' means: the number of people whose data are processed, the scope of processing, the data storage period and the geographical scope of processing.[32] Thus, any AI-based solution which requires processing of personal data on a large scale may be considered as requiring a DPIA.

4.4 The National Blacklist's Characteristics and DPIA of the Processing Performed Using AI

It must be stressed that the blacklists are not to be treated as exhaustive.[33] Thus, it is the criterion of the existence of a 'high risk' which ultimately determines the need to perform a DPIA. However, the national blacklists can play an important role for entrepreneurs and other organisations in the process of deciding whether it is necessary to perform a DPIA. Therefore, despite their non-exhaustive character, it seems crucial to provide clear description of the examples that illustrate the types of processing in which the obligation to carry out a DPIA arises.

[30] List compiled by the Office of the Data Protection Ombudsman of processing operations which require data protection impact assessment (DPIA). Access: https://tietosuoja.fi/en/list-of-processing-operations-which-require-dpia.

[31] The most commonly appearing on the blacklists being 'for the purpose of uniquely identifying a natural person'.

[32] As explained in the Guidelines and repeated on the Polish blacklist. Komunikat Prezesa Urzędu Ochrony Danych Osobowych z dnia 17 czerwca 2019 r. w sprawie wykazu rodzajów operacji przetwarzania danych osobowych wymagających oceny skutków przetwarzania dla ich ochrony. Access: https://monitorpolski.gov.pl/M2019000066601.pdf.

[33] Which is often mentioned in the EDPB opinions on the national lists.

The example of mentioning AI in the blacklists illustrates that the margin of freedom granted to the states in some of the GDPR's provisions leads to diversification of the national blacklists. Subsequently, this may result in the diversification of the standards of data protection due to the variety of catalogues of processing types which should be subjected to a DPIA. Such a situation seems to go against the concept of unifying the regulatory framework for data protection. However, as there is no obligation to publish DPIA results, we lack the tools for assessing to what an extent DPIAs are actually conducted and, as a result, to estimate to what an extent such a diversification takes place.

5 DPIA and the Proposal of the AI Act

The influence of the regulatory framework created by the GDPR on the solutions which use AI can provide certain insights into the question of how to proceed with the regulation of AI technologies. To provide such an analysis, this section presents an overview of the solutions proposed in the *AI Act.* Despite—or maybe because of—the preliminary character of this document, it is worth considering how the regulatory strategy presented by the Commission could benefit from the lessons learned from the regulation of new technologies in data protection law. Such a comparison is performed in the second part of this section.

The regulation of AI has been declared as one of the priorities by Ursula von der Leyen in the *Political Guidelines for the Next European Commission*.[34] The promise to 'put forward legislation for a coordinated European approach on the human and ethical implications of Artificial Intelligence'[35] in her first 100 days in office, seemed to have been an overly optimistic statement. In February 2020, the *White Paper* was presented, as one of three documents prepared in order to set out the conceptual framework of the EU's approach to the regulation of new technologies.[36] None of these documents constituted a legislative proposal and all of them were of a rather general character, describing the approach to the issues discussed both in terms of the regulatory strategy and in terms of the planned actions concerning e.g., funding. Finally, in April 2021, the legislative proposal of *AI Act* has been published. Although it is strongly based on the ideas presented in the *White Paper*, it also

[34] Ursula von der Leyen (2019).

[35] Ibid., p. 13.

[36] The other two being Commission, *Communication from the Commission to the European Parliament, the Council, the European Economic and Social Committee and the Committee of the Regions: A European strategy for data*, COM/2020/66 final, and Commission, *Communication from the Commission to the European Parliament, the Council, the European Economic and Social Committee and the Committee of the Regions: Shaping Europe's Digital Future*, COM/2020/67 final.

contains certain novelties (e.g., the category of unacceptable risk).[37] As this proposal constitutes a basis for further discussion on the regulation of AI in the EU, it is the main subject of the analysis in this section.

The *AI Act* includes the proposal of the legal definition of AI systems, which is based on an enumeration of techniques and approaches, e.g., machine learning or logic- and knowledge-based approaches[38] used in software for the purpose of generating outputs such as content, predictions, recommendations, or decisions influencing the environments they interact with (Art 3(1)). Compared to the definition proposed by the Commission in a document from 2018, where AI referred to 'systems that display intelligent behaviour by analysing their environment and taking actions—with some degree of autonomy—to achieve specific goals',[39] the new proposal provides more specific guidelines on what is bound to be regulated by the *AI Act*. It is also more detailed (even though, therefore, more limited) than the category used in the GDPR in the provision on DPIA ('new technologies'). Although the catalogue of techniques and approaches may raise controversies and will probably be subjected to significant revisions during the legislative process, the concept of definition based on the references to specific methods seems to be a path for guaranteeing a higher level of legal certainty in terms of what does the term AI mean in EU law.

In terms of how AI systems are to be regulated, the *AI Act* follows the risk-based approach.[40] The Commission puts forward the proposal of introducing three levels of the risk which AI systems create: prohibited AI practices, high-risk systems, and other AI systems.[41] The division into unacceptable, high and low risk uses of AI leads to the differentiation of the obligations arising from the implementation of such systems. In the case of low-risk AI use the Commission proposes the mechanisms of voluntary certification (Art 69, *AI Act*). The idea resembles, for example, the certification foreseen in the GDPR's provisions (Art 42, GDPR). While encouraging the development of certification mechanisms, there would be no obligation to enter such schemes and their role for the development of risk-based approach to AI would probably be marginal.

---

[37] Both the White Paper and the AI Act are to a certain extent based on the work of Independent High-Level Expert Group on Artificial Intelligence set up by the European Commission, which strongly encouraged risk-based approach to AI, see Independent High-Level Expert Group on Artificial Intelligence set up by the European Commission (2019).

[38] The list is included in Annex I to the AI Act which, accordingly to Art 4, could be updated by the delegated act of the Commission.

[39] Commission, *Communication from the Commission to the European Parliament, the European Council, the Council, the European Economic and Social Committee and the Committee of the Regions on Artificial Intelligence for Europe*, COM/2018/237 final.

[40] For an insightful analysis of this issue, see Mökander et al. (2022).

[41] Additionally, Title IV refers to the category of 'AI systems intended to interact with natural persons', which I understand as a category which may include AI systems belonging to any of the risk groups.

The other two categories would be potentially more significant for the development of a risk-based approach to AI. The category of unacceptable risk, which results in the proposal of four types of AI systems which should be prohibited (Art 5, *AI Act*), was not present in the *White Paper*. The idea of establishing a catalogue of AI uses which should be prohibited, by itself, strengthens the risk-based approach. However, the specific catalogue proposed by the Commission leads to several critiques. Especially the prohibition of 'real-time' remote biometric identification systems in publicly accessible spaces for the purpose of law enforcement (Art 5(1)d) is problematic, as the exceptions allowed by the proposal (Art 5(2)-(4)) undermine the unequivocal character of the ban.[42] Additionally, the terminology applied in other positions of the proposed catalogue is problematic. For instance, a reference made to 'AI system that deploys subliminal techniques beyond a person's consciousness in order to materially distort a person's behaviour in a manner that causes or is likely to cause that person or another person physical or psychological harm' (Art 5(1)), is quite ambiguous. If interpreted strictly, one could claim that any recommendation system operates beyond a consumer's consciousness in purpose of changing his or her behaviour something which is likely to result in psychological harm (e.g., addiction). Thus, a heated debate on how to phrase the catalogue of prohibited uses of AI systems is to be expected.

The category of high-risk use of AI was proposed already in the *White Paper*. The *AI Act* includes two main categories of AI uses which should be considered as high risk (Art 6). The first category concerns AI systems, which constitute a safety component of a product or are themselves a product, covered by the Union harmonisation legislation enumerated in Annex II to the proposal, e.g., aviation, cars, or toys. Secondly, Annex II includes a number of specific areas and uses of AI systems which should be considered as high risk, such as in the area of the judiciary AI systems intended to assist a judicial authority in researching and interpreting facts and the law and in applying the law to a concrete set of facts (Annex II, 8a) or AI systems intended to be used for recruitment or selection of natural persons, notably for advertising vacancies, screening or filtering applications, evaluating candidates in the course of interviews or tests in the area of employment, workers management and access to self-employment (Annex II, 4a). Such an approach limits the precautionary approach adopted in the proposal when compared to the *White Paper*, by closing the catalogue of the AI's uses which should be considered as high risk. However, it also provides more clarity on the EU level than the way that the category of data processing which should be subjected to DPIA is defined in the GDPR.

The solution foreseen for the uses of AI defined as high risk includes the proposal of the requirements which such systems would have to fulfil (Arts 8–15) and the list of the obligations of the providers of such systems (Arts 16–29). The requirements proposed by the Commission refer to various steps and aspects of high-risk AI systems, e.g., training, validation and testing data, technical documentation, and

---

[42]The proposed solution was criticised by the European Data Protection Supervisor, see European Data Protection Supervisor (2021).

record keeping. Proposed solutions also include certain requirements which refer to the users of AI systems, understood as 'any natural or legal person, public authority, agency or other body using an AI system under its authority, except where the AI system is used in the course of a personal non-professional activity' (Art 3(4)). The requirements concerning human oversight demand that an AI system must be subjected to effective oversight 'by natural persons during the period in which the AI system is in use' (Art 14(1)). The measures which should allow for such an oversight, include, e.g., ensuring that a user is capable to 'fully understand the capacities and limitations of the high-risk AI system and be able to duly monitor its operation, so that signs of anomalies, dysfunctions and unexpected performance can be detected and addressed as soon as possible' (Art 14(4)a) or 'be able to correctly interpret the high-risk AI system's output, taking into account in particular the characteristics of the system and the interpretation tools and methods available' (Art 14(4)c). This may be interpreted as the obligation to guarantee that in case, for example, of a system which supports judges in making decisions, the system and its outputs should be understandable for judges as users of this AI system.

These examples show that the requirements proposed in the *AI Act* are different from the ones enumerated in the provisions concerning DPIAs as they refer, for instance, to technical aspects of the developed AI-based solutions. Moreover, many of them—e.g., human oversight mechanisms—concern the users of AI systems, not the individuals subjected to decisions taken on the basis of AI's recommendation or by AI.[43] Simultaneously, the risk-based approach adopted in the *AI Act* is similar to the reasoning behind the introduction of the DPIA.[44] Both the DPIA and the requirements in the *AI Act* stress the necessity to consider risks linked to the processing operation (DPIA) or application of AI (requirements in the *AI Act*) and to develop measures which would allow countering them. Due to this similarity, it is worth considering what kinds of lessons can be drawn from the DPIA to support the effectiveness of the regulatory strategy which is to be adopted towards a high-risk AI application.

Firstly, the above-described discrepancies between the national blacklists concerning types of processing which should be subjected to DPIA suggest that the potential problems with the assessment of a particular use and its high-risk character should be solved on the EU level. Thus, the concept of a common list of potentially high-risk uses of AI should be welcomed, although its limited scope shall

---

[43] As it is the case in the GDPR (e.g., data subjects rights concerning automated decision-making). For the comparison of various approaches to explanation of technology in EU law, see Hacker and Passoth (2022).

[44] In terms of the relation between the obligation to carry on DPIA and the obligation to assess risks linked to the development of high-risk AI system, Art. 29 of the AI Act states that the users of high-risk AI system shall use information provided by the providers of AI System on the basis of Art 13 of the AI Act to carry out a DPIA. This solution may raise certain doubts, as it seems to divide the responsibility for conducting DPIA not accordingly to the criteria foreseen in the GDPR (in which this obligation is placed on the data controller) but on the user of AI system, which must not necessarily be data controller.

be perceived as a drawback of the Commission's proposal. Secondly, the experience with DPIAs shows a strong need to provide more specific requirements regarding the publication of the information produced when complying with such requirements. The example of the DPIA shows that despite its character of being a preventive, precautionary measure, it is quite impossible to assess whether it is used as such. Due to a lack of any obligations regarding the publications of DPIAs' results, the only control which can take place is the one which may be conducted *ex post* by the supervisory authority.

The obligation to share information about the manners in which the legal requirements referring to the AI-based systems would be fulfilled is a necessary element of the regulatory framework which aims to build the 'ecosystem of trust' for AI systems. The proposal of *AI Act*, to a certain extent, goes in this direction, as shows the concept of registration of high-risk AI uses in a publicly accessible database (Art 60). However, the limited scope of information which will be available to the individuals, which, for instance, does not include information on risk management systems,[45] hampers the capability of exercising *ex ante* control of AI systems and, therefore, seems to perpetuate DPIA's shortcomings.

6 Conclusions

The analysis shows that the data protection regulatory framework in EU law covers certain applications of AI. An example of this situation is the obligation to carry out a DPIA introduced in the GDPR. On the basis of the GDPR's provisions, AI-based solutions which use the processing of personal data and are 'likely to result in a high risk to the rights and freedoms of natural persons' should be subjected to a DPIA. Additionally, the national blacklists specify types of processing in relation to which DPIA should be conducted.

There are at least three manners in which data processing with the use of AI-technologies can be covered by the obligation to perform a DPIA on the basis of the national blacklists. Firstly, certain states decided to explicitly mention AI in their blacklists as a criterion which makes it obligatory to conduct a DPIA. Secondly, some of the states include references to use of 'new technologies / new technology / new technological...' as a reason to obligatorily conduct a DPIA. Thirdly, it can be assumed that some of the solutions using AI may come under scrutiny when a blacklist includes criteria referring to the term 'large scale [e.g., processing]', as developing such algorithms is linked to large scale data processing. These three categories of processing present in the national blacklists, which may result with an obligation to perform a DPIA in cases of use of AI, must be interpreted in the context of the GDPR's provisions which define the necessity to conduct a DPIA if 'the processing which is likely to result in a high risk to the rights and freedoms of natural

[45] See Veale and Zuiderveen Borgesius (2021), p. 12.

persons'. Thus, even if a particular type of processing does not fit in any of the categories enumerated on the national blacklist, the obligation to carry out a DPIA may still appear. Such an approach to the DPIA may cause a number of difficulties, e.g., companies may find the national blacklists misleading due to their non-exhaustive character.

Simultaneously, the shortcomings of the GDPR's provisions referring to the DPIA seem to limit the practical significance of this tool as a precautionary measure. On the one hand, the DPIA should serve as a tool which leads to the identification and management of risks posed by data processing, including that which takes place using AI-based tools. On the other hand, lack of obligations concerning e.g., the publication of its results, does not allow to assess the effectiveness of this tool. Due to the internal character of the DPIA, there are hardly any possibilities for the broader public to get information on identified risks and measures adopted in order to manage them. The control concerning carrying out a DPIA may be performed by the supervisory authorities and may lead to financial sanctions. However, such an *ex post* control limits the significance of the DPIA as a regulatory measure which could support a preventive approach to the threats caused by e.g., large-scale data processing.

These concerns illustrate that the analysis of the DPIA's impact on AI regulation provides grounds to consider the weaknesses of the regulatory strategy adopted in the GDPR as a source of inspiration for the development of the normative framework for AI. The analysis of the differences between the national blacklists indicates the importance of establishing one, common list on the EU level. Additionally, the experience with DPIAs exhibits the importance of mechanisms which increase the transparency of automated tools. Therefore, it is important to ensure that the final shape of the *AI Act* will include provisions obliging the providers of AI systems to share information on the results of the conducted risk assessments with the public. The experiences drawn from data protection law show that without the introduction of such safeguards, which would ensure the possibilities to execute broad *ex ante* control over implemented solutions, the precautionary character of such measures is undermined.

References

Brkan M (2019) Do algorithms rule the world? Algorithmic decision-making and data protection in the framework of the GDPR and beyond. Int J Law Info Technol 27(2):91–121

Casey B, Farhangi A, Vogl R (2019) Rethinking explainable machines: the GDPR's 'Right to Explanation' debate and the rise of algorithmic audits in enterprise. Berkeley Technol Law J 34: 143–188

Centre for Information Policy Leadership (CIPL) (2020) Artificial Intelligence and Data Protection How the GDPR Regulates AI. Available via Hunton Privacy Blog. https://www.huntonprivacyblog.com/wp-content/uploads/sites/28/2020/03/cipl-hunton_andrews_kurth_legal_note_-_how_gdpr_regulates_ai__12_march_2020_-1.pdf

Datenschutzkonferenz (DSK) (2018) Liste der Verarbeitungstätigkeiten, für die eine DSFA durchzuführen ist. https://www.lda.bayern.de/media/dsfa_muss_liste_dsk_de.pdf

Demetzou K (2019) Data Protection Impact Assessment: a tool for accountability and the unclarified concept of 'high risk' in the General Data Protection Regulation. Comp Law Sec Rev 35(6):105342. https://doi.org/10.1016/j.clsr.2019.105342

Demetzou K (2020) Processing operations 'Likely to Result in a High Risk to the Rights and Freedoms of Natural Persons'. In: Antunes L, Naldi M, Italiano G, Rannenberg K, Drogkaris P (eds) Privacy Technologies and Policy. 8th Annual Privacy Forum, APF 2020, Lisbon, Purtugal, October 22–23, 2020, Proceedings (Lecture Notes in Computer Science, vol. 12121), Springer, Cham, pp 25–42

European Data Protection Supervisor (2021) Artificial Intelligence Act: a welcomed initiative, but ban on remote biometric identification in public space is necessary. https://edps.europa.eu/press-publications/press-news/press-releases/2021/artificial-intelligence-act-welcomed-initiative_en

Garante per la Protezione dei Dati Personali (2018) Elenco delle tipologie di trattamenti, soggetti al meccanismo di coerenza, da sottoporre a valutazione d'impatto. https://www.garanteprivacy.it/documents/10160/0/ALLEGATO+1+Elenco+delle+tipologie+di+trattamenti+soggetti+al+meccanismo+di+coerenza+da+sottoporre+a+valutazione+di+impatto

Georgiadis G, Poels G (2022) Towards a privacy impact assessment methodology to support the requirements of the general data protection regulation in a big data analytics context: a systematic literature review. Comp Law Sec Rev 44:105640. https://doi.org/10.1016/j.clsr.2021.105640

Goodman BW (2016) A step towards accountable algorithms? Algorithmic discrimination and the European Union general data protection. Paper presented at the 29th Conference on Neural Information Processing Systems (NIPS 2016), NIPS Foundation, Barcelona, 5–10 December 2016. http://www.mlandthelaw.org/papers/goodman1.pdf

Hacker P, Passoth JH (2022) Varieties of AI explanations under the law. From the GDPR to the AIA, and beyond. In: Holzinger A, Goebel R, Fong R, Moon T, Müller KR, Samek W (eds) xxAI - Beyond Explainable AI. xxAI 2020 (Lecture Notes in Computer Science, vol. 13200). Springer, Cham, pp 343–373

Hellenic Data Protection Authority (2018) List of the kind of processing operations which are subject to the requirement for a data protection impact assessment according to article 35 par. 4 of GDPR. https://iapp.org/media/pdf/resource_center/hellenic_blacklist.pdf

Independent High-Level Expert Group on Artificial Intelligence set up by the European Commission (2019) Ethics Guidelines for Trustworthy AI. https://ec.europa.eu/digital-single-market/en/news/ethics-guidelines-trustworthy-ai

Kaminski ME (2019) The right to explanation, explained. Berkeley Technol Law J 34:189–218

Kaminski ME, Malgieri G (2021) Algorithmic impact assessments under the GDPR: producing multi-layered explanations. Int Data Priv Law 11(2):125–144. https://doi.org/10.1093/idpl/ipaa020

Kloza D, van Dijk N, Gellert R, et al (2017) Data protection impact assessments in the European Union: complementing the new legal framework towards a more robust protection of individuals. d.pia.lab Policy Brief No. 1/2017. https://cris.vub.be/ws/portalfiles/portal/32009890/dpialab_pb2017_1_final.pdf

Kosta E (2020) Section 3 Data protection impact assessment and prior consultation. In: Kuner C, Bygrave LA, Docksey C (eds) The EU general data protection regulation (GPDR). A commentary. Oxford University Press, Oxford, pp 665–687

Malgieri G, Comandé G (2017) Why a right to legibility of automated decision-making exists in the general data protection regulation. Int Data Priv Law 7(4):243–265

Mökander J, Axente M, Casolari F, Floridi L (2022) Conformity assessments and post-market monitoring: a guide to the role of auditing in the proposed European AI regulation. Minds Mach 32:241–268. https://doi.org/10.1007/s11023-021-09577-4

Monitor Polski (2019) Komunikat Prezesa Urzędu Ochrony Danych Osobowych z dnia 17 czerwca 2019 r. w sprawie wykazu rodzajów operacji przetwarzania danych osobowych wymagających

oceny skutków przetwarzania dla ich ochrony. https://monitorpolski.gov.pl/M2019000066601.pdf
Office for Personal Data Protection of the Czech Republic (undated) List of processing operations subject to data protection impact assessment. https://iapp.org/media/pdf/resource_center/czech_blacklist.pdf
Rechtsinformationssystem des Bundes (2018) Verordnung der Datenschutzbehörde über Verarbeitungsvorgänge, für die eine Datenschutz-Folgenabschätzung durchzuführen ist (DSFA-V). https://www.ris.bka.gv.at/eli/bgbl/II/2018/278/20181109
Selbst AD, Powles J (2017) Meaningful information and the right to explanation. Int Data Priv Law 7(4):233–242
Veale M, Zuiderveen Borgesius F (2021) Demystifying the Draft EU Artificial Intelligence Act — analysing the good, the bad, and the unclear elements of the proposed approach. Comp Law Rev Int 22(4):97–112. https://doi.org/10.9785/cri-2021-220402
Vlaamse Overheid (2020) Vlaamse Toezichtcommissie voor de verwerking van persoonsgegevens: Beslissing VTC nr. O/2020/01 van 14 januari 2020 betreffende Aanname van de lijst met verwerkingen waarvoor een Gegevensbeschermingseffectbeoordeling dient te worden uitgevoerd conform artikel 35.4 van de Algemene Verordening Gegevensbescherming door Vlaamse bestuursinstanties. https://overheid.vlaanderen.be/sites/default/files/media/VTC/VTC_O_2020_01_DPIA_lijsten_v1_voor_web.pdf
von der Leyen U (2019) A Union that strives for more: My agenda for Europe. https://op.europa.eu/en/publication-detail/-/publication/43a17056-ebf1-11e9-9c4e-01aa75ed71a1
Wachter S, Mittelstadt B, Floridi L (2017) Why a right to explanation of automated decision-making does not exist in the general data protection regulation. Int Data Priv Law 7(2):76–92

Part VI
AI and Jus ad Bellum-Jus in Bello Questions

The Use of AI Weapons in Outer Space: Regulatory Challenges

Anthi Koskina

Abstract The new era in space exploitation is characterized by the rise of artificial intelligence (AI) multiplying the capabilities of space systems, and the growing awareness of (space) environmental constraints. It is already apparent that the inevitable consequence of these developments will be the growth of economic and political tensions. The need to ensure the continuity of benefits derived on Earth from space systems—and to protect space assets—seems to be more or less related to the growing debate on the militarisation and weaponization of space. In this context, AI and Autonomous Weapon Systems (AWS) will most probably be harnessed and the laws possibly applying to potential conflicts in space will have to be discussed, taking into account the characteristics of these new technologies. As the UN Charter rules on the use of force apply *expressis verbis* in space, pursuant to Art. III of the Outer Space Treaty (OST), this chapter will primarily examine under what conditions States could use AWS in space, i.e., where it is considered that a threat to the peace (Art. 39 of the UN Charter) and/or an armed attack to a UN member State (Art. 51 of the UN Charter) are effectively occurring in this particular environment (*jus ad bellum*). Following this analysis, the specific operating mode of AWS potentially used in the context of a space war will be addressed, to clarify whether such activity could be in line with the rule established in Art IV of the OST, as well as with international humanitarian law (*jus in bello*).

1 Introduction

The *Treaty on Principles Governing the Activities of States in the Exploration and Use of Outer Space, including the Moon and Other Celestial Bodies* or *Outer Space Treaty* (OST, Treaty) signed in 1967, is the *lex specialis* regulating space activities in

A. Koskina (✉)
IdEF College-Sorbonne Paris North University, Athens, Greece

AthensPIL, National and Kapodistrian University of Athens, Athens, Greece
e-mail: akoskina@law.uoa.gr

A. Kornilakis et al. (eds.), *Artificial Intelligence and Normative Challenges*, Law, Governance and Technology Series 59,
https://doi.org/10.1007/978-3-031-41081-9_13

this environment.[1] The freedom of exploration and use of outer space for all States (established in Art. I of the OST), the non-appropriation of space, including the Moon and other Celestial bodies (Art. II of the OST) and the conduct of space activities in accordance with International Law, including the Charter of the United Nations, in the interest of maintaining international peace and security[2] (Art. III of the OST) are among its guiding principles.

The key provisions of the OST (such as Arts. I, II and III) are regarded as being legally binding on all States, because of both the Treaty's high level of recognition, and its customary character.[3] Hence, any use of Autonomous Weapon Systems (AWS) in outer space must conform to the OST[4] in conjunction with general international law,[5] as developed below.

First, the OST prohibits particular uses—such as to place in orbit around the Earth; install them on celestial bodies, or station them in outer space, in any manner—of a specific category of weapons, namely "nuclear weapons or any kind of weapons of mass destruction (WMD)", pursuant to its Art. IV para 1.[6] Scholars argue that the OST does not place an absolute ban on the use of military force in outer space,[7] but rather establishes a principle of non-aggression, on the basis of Art. III of the OST. It lays down "an affirmative duty on States not to station weapons of an aggressive nature in outer space. It does not prohibit States from placing weapons of a defensive nature in space (. . .) or from placing weapons required by order of the Security Council in order to maintain international peace and security".[8]

Second, according to international law and the UN Charter—applying in outer space pursuant to Art. III of the OST–, the use of force is legitimate if developed in accordance with Chapter VII of the UN Charter (i.e., to maintain or restore international peace and security, following a UN Security Council decision)[9] or for

[1]Adopting the Outer Space Treaty (OST) was deemed necessary, given that "(n)ot all rules are directly translatable into the space environment (. . .), see Blount (2009).

[2]Art. III of the OST ["(. . .) shall carry on activities in the exploration and use of outer space (. . .) in accordance with international law, including the Charter of the United Nations, in the interest of maintaining international peace and security (. . .)"] is reiterating Art. 1 para 1 of the UN Charter ["The purposes of the United Nations are: (1) to maintain international peace and security, and to that end: to take effective collective measures for the prevention and removal of threats to the peace (. . .)"].

[3]*Inter alia,* Hofmann and Bergamasco (2020).

[4]When not in contradiction with the UN Charter (see Art. 103), due to its nature as *lex specialis*.

[5]"The space law regime inherits the concept of international peace and security from the Charter of the United Nations (. . .)", see Blount (2018), p. 2.

[6]OST, Art. IV para 1: "(. . .) undertake not to place in orbit around the Earth any objects carrying nuclear weapons or any kind of weapons of mass destruction, install such weapons on celestial bodies, or station such weapons in outer space in any manner".

[7]In fact, the OST provides that States may use military personnel for scientific research or any other peaceful purposes, see OST, Art. IV para 2.

[8]Blount (2009), p. 4.

[9]Pursuant to Art. 2 para 4 of the UN Charter, States "(. . .) shall refrain from the threat or use of force against the territorial integrity or political independence of any state, or in any other manner (. . .)".

individual or collective self-defense, pursuant to Art. 51 of the UN Charter[10] (*jus ad bellum*). Once the armed conflict has started, military operations should be in accordance with the principles of international humanitarian law (*jus in bello*). However, in practice, specific features of space, such as its vastness—justifying, at the same time, the non-appropriation principle—call into question the applicability of *jus in bello* and *jus ad bellum* as such, in this complex environment.

On a technological level, the rise of Artificial Intelligence (AI)[11] led to considerable changes in robotics, due to its ability to act autonomously—without being bounded by the cognitive limitations of the human brain—and adopt "*solutions that humans may not have considered*, much less attempted to implement".[12] On this basis, new types of weapons were developed, driven by AI in their critical functions, with on-board sensors and algorithms able to identify and damage targets without human intervention,[13] like AI Weapon Systems (AWS) mostly consisting in 'killer robots'. However, AWS may also be used as, *inter alia*, a new capability for disrupting and destroying (space) objects without causing material damage, such as in the form of radio-frequency jamming. AI[14] and AWS are a valuable instrument *per se*, but their use in outer space is expected to raise a number of challenges for law enforcement in this environment.[15]

As the UN Charter rules on the use of force apply *expressis verbis* in space,[16] this chapter will primarily examine under what conditions States could use AWS in space, i.e., how *jus ad bellum* key concepts should be interpreted in this context (Sect. 2). Following this analysis, the specific operating mode of AWS will be addressed; the purpose is to debate whether they can be used in accordance with the principles of *jus in bello* (Sect. 3) given their potential and weaknesses, in the theoretical context of a conflict in space. In the final Sect. (4), some conclusions will be drawn.

However, Chapter VII of the UN Charter lays down that in case the Security Council determines the existence of a threat to the peace, breach of the peace or act of aggression, it may make recommendations or decide –in a mandatory and binding upon the Member States manner– measures to "maintain or restore international peace and security" (Art. 39 of the UN Charter). Art. 42 of the UN Charter provides that in the case of inadequate measures, "it may take such action by air, sea or land forces as may be necessary to maintain or restore international peace and security".

[10] Martinez and Bouvier (2006), pp. 109–112.

[11] For the purposes of this chapter, AI can be regarded as a "a goal-oriented, problem-solving thinking process, with at least some human-level (or better) capabilities", "*embodied by machine learning based on data*" [emphasis added], see Abney (2020), p. 63.

[12] Scherer (2016).

[13] Other applications of AI in space include extensive mapping of the solar system and beyond, new telescopes, new human-rated space launchers etc.; see OECD (2019), Chapter 4. Experts refer to a "fourth industrial revolution" and to "new space" or "space 4.0", see Bohinger (2017), p. 25.

[14] E.g., a first ESA satellite was launched with AI onboard, strongly improving the efficiency of sending remote sensing data back to Earth, Daws (2020).

[15] Gal et al. (2020).

[16] This chapter does not examine the case of aggressions or threats to the peace etc. occurring on Earth, following the use of space assets.

2 Threats & Attacks in Space, as a Condition to Use AWS (*Jus Ad Bellum*)

The principles of *jus ad bellum*, enshrined in the UN Charter and applying in space pursuant to Art. III of the OST, establish the right to use force to maintain or restore international peace and security (as decided by the UN Security Council) and/or for individual or collective self-defense. Hence, the triggering event for the use of AWS in space would be the "existence of any *threat to the peace, breach of the peace, or act of aggression* (Art. 39 of the UN Charter)" or the "occurrence of an armed *attack against a member* of the UN (Art. 51 of the UN Charter)".

However, the fundamental characteristic of space is that it is not subject to national appropriation; States may not claim sovereignty over any of its part(s) or element(s), following Art. II of the OST. Therefore, no threat to territorial integrity *stricto sensu* could materialize in space, in the traditional meaning of the UN Charter; as a matter of fact, "(s)everal decades after humankind's conquest of space, there has not yet been a case of force being actively used in outer space by one nation against another".[17] At the same time, attacks to space-based assets may well occur, equally posing threats to international peace or States security;[18] in this respect, the rules for invoking concepts established in Art. 39 or Art. 51 of the UN Charter should be kept flexible, to ensure that the UN Charter principles are applied in space, as well.

Thus, the question arises as to what should be considered as a threat to the peace or an attack against a UN Member State in space, and how the UN Charter conditions should be applied. On the one hand, concepts such as territorial integrity and political independence,—or other ones[19] recognized as threats to the peace and protected *via* the rules of *jus ad bellum*—do not apply as such (Art. II of the OST). On the other hand, Art. III of the OST requires that space activities are carried out in the interest of maintaining international peace and security. It is, therefore, a legitimate objective to seek to ensure that space activities are carried out in a manner which takes account of the interests of all States (as stipulated in Art. I of the OST),[20] and that *jus ad bellum* is interpreted to allow the effective implementation of both the OST (Art. I) and UN Charter (Art. 1 para 1).

---

[17] Maogoto and Freeland (2007), p. 1091.

[18] "(. . .) new means, and methods of using force will also give rise to new means of making threats, including those from space (Major Ramey)", see Maogoto and Freeland (2007), p. 1111.

[19] Such as, 'deliberate targeting of civilian populations in armed conflict'; 'drug trafficking and organized crime'; 'terrorism' etc., see UN-LEGAL (2016).

[20] OST, Art. I: "The exploration and use of outer space (. . .) shall be carried out for the benefit and in the interests of all countries (. . .)".

2.1 Threats to the Peace, Breach of Peace & Acts of Aggression, in Space (Art. 39)

To decide measures involving the use of force in space,[21] a threat to the *peace*, a breach of the *peace* or an act of *aggression* is required (Art. 39 of the UN Charter, in conjunction with Art. I and Art. III of the OST). However, the meaning of "maintaining international peace and security" in space, mentioned in Art. III of the OST, is not defined in the Treaty; neither is the right of States to conduct space activity for peaceful purposes, established in Art. IV and IX of the OST. In fact, "(w)hile the principle of the use of outer space for peaceful purposes has most likely entered customary international law, the content of that term is somewhat nebulous, because different nations apply it in different ways".[22]

In practice, space operators and law experts focused on a more application-oriented approach, and the right to peacefully use space was interpreted as the right to ensure (mainly) assets security. The concept of *space security* was first negotiated in the 1950s and defined according to political criteria—as the right to freely access and use space with respect to its military use and to the military security of States[23]—but was gradually broadened. Today, it refers to the safe use of space in the context of military operations (or to activities in relation to those), as well as to the objective of ensuring a sustainable environment *per se,* based on a "network of international and domestic laws" governing *a wide variety* of space activities.[24]

As a corollary, the concept of a *threat to the peace* in space—related, first, to the use of (space) weapons, within the broad framework of hostilities—crystallized around the idea of a threat to assets, and its consequences on the Earth and Space environment.[25] In truth, any deliberate damage to space infrastructures (e.g., a purposeful destruction of satellites) would have widespread repercussions for States on earth (i.e., impossibility to use satellites signal for national security purposes etc.) but also for operators in space, as more space debris would be created, posing additional risks to the safe operation of objects.[26] At the same time, such an attack

[21] Following Art. 42 of the UN Charter, *lato sensu*, see Lee (2002).

[22] And "the specific content of military endeavors consistent with the peaceful uses of outer space is not made explicit in the treaty", Blount (2009), p. 2.

[23] It was first defined "in bipolar terms as part of the strategic balance between the United States and the Soviet Union, and it was focused on military and environmental aspects of accessing and using space", see Hays (2015).

[24] Blount (2018).

[25] "While the armed forces of another country might represent a clear security threat for the people of specific countries, this situation might be different in many other countries, where issues like food and water shortages or endemic diseases would be perceived as real security threats to the survival of populations (…). As a result, while military security was retained as a crucial security sector, new ones such as economic, societal, and environmental securities were added to the concept", see Sheehan (2015).

[26] In this regard, the concept of space sustainability was developed, to raise awareness on the necessity to ensure a space environment that would be safe for both operators and assets, and

could be detrimental to the survival of large parts of the population, given the growing reliance of Earth on space infrastructure, in everyday life as well as exceptional circumstances and natural disasters.[27]

Following this reasoning, if such an event were to occur, it could possibly be regarded as a threat to the peace or act of aggression, materializing in space. In this scenario, it would be legitimate to allow the use of AWS in space, provided such use is in line with the principles of *Jus in bello*.

2.2 The Occurrence of an Armed Attack against a UN Member, in Space (Art. 51)

From a different angle, Art. 51 of the UN Charter would require the occurrence of an armed attack against a UN Member State in space. The provision may not be used to protect a State's national territory in space, since this concept does not apply *as such* on the basis of Art. II of the OST. However, despite the exclusion of sovereignty in space, Art. VIII of the OST provides for the exercise of certain sovereign rights, by establishing that "A State Party (. . .) on whose registry an object launched into outer space is carried *shall retain jurisdiction and control over such object*, and over any personnel thereof, while in outer space or on a celestial body". Hence, States do exercise a quasi-territorial jurisdiction over their space objects and the personnel thereof.[28]

On this basis, the question arises whether States would be entitled to protect their space assets and/or the continuity of benefits derived on Earth from their activities, on the sole basis of Art. VIII of the OST in conjunction with Art. 51 of the UN Charter. In theory, such an attack could be aimed at a State's military asset, but also at satellites programmed to gather and process (military and/or non-military) data, other types of space objects such as launchers etc. As the matter remains to be resolved, the U.S. hastened to declare that any "*purposeful interference*" with their space systems "*will be viewed as an infringement on (their) sovereign rights*", and

---

defined as "*the ability of the space environment to continue to be a place where space activities can be successfully conducted (. . .) it draws attention to the crucial issue of the long-term management and use of space, and it links the military, scientific and economic dimensions of space security*", Sheehan (2015), p. 15. This approach is in line with Art. 44.2 of the ITU Constitution: "In using frequency bands for radio services, Member States shall bear in mind that radio frequencies and any associated orbits (. . .) are limited natural resources and that they must be used rationally, efficiently and economically (. . .)".

[27] E.g., numerous satellites were used to coordinate disaster relief operations after the Haiti earthquake in 2010 and the Fukushima nuclear accident in 2011, Sheehan (2015), p. 18.

[28] *Inter alia*, Zhang (2019), p. 148.

any attack on their spacecraft considered as an attack on the sovereignty of the U.S. and possibly on its territorial integrity.[29]

In truth, causing damage in space—such as *via* an attack using kinetic, incendiary, or explosive energy against a space asset—would immediately raise the question of the international responsibility of the attacking State, on the ground of Art. VI[30] and Art. VII of the OST, laying down that: "Each State Party (. . .) that launches or procures the launching of an object into outer space (. . .) is *internationally liable for damage* to another State Party (. . .) or to its natural or juridical persons by such object or its component parts" (and as established further in the 1972 Liability Convention). The attacking State would also probably engage its responsibility pursuant to Art. IX of the OST,[31] on the protection of the space environment, due to the numerous space debris resulting from this attack. However, should we consider that all peaceful means of resolution were exhausted, it is reasonable to consider that Art. 51 of the UN Charter could then apply; in this case, the response should be again in accordance with the principles of *Jus in bello*.

Having determined under which circumstances States could resort to AWS in outer space (i.e., how the conditions of *Jus ad bellum* could be interpreted, to take into account the specific features of this environment), the issue arises as to whether the use of AWS in response to such an attack could be consistent with the rules of *Jus in bello*.

3 Use of AWS in Line with the OST and the Principles of IHL (*Jus in Bello*)

In the event of an armed conflict in space, States could use AWS in accordance with both the OST and the principles of *Jus in bello*, as developed hereafter.

According, first, to the OST, there is no absolute ban on the use of military force in outer space. The Treaty does not impose its complete demilitarization,[32] but rather prohibits the use of specific categories of weapons, namely *nuclear weapons,* and *any kind of weapons of mass destruction* (Art. IV para 1 of the OST). On the

---

[29]Blount (2018), p. 3. In the same direction: "(g)iven the growing dependence on satellite communication and information (. . .), these factors need to be included in proportionality analysis. Consequently, attacks against satellites prompt the requirements for the application of International Humanitarian law. It may therefore be that the balance of proportionality will generally be against attacks on satellites", Mosteshar (2019). Also, Hostbeck (2015), p. 956.

[30]OST, Art. VI: "States (. . .) shall bear international responsibility for national activities in outer space (. . .)".

[31]In conjunction with Art. IX stipulating that: "In the exploration and use of outer space (. . .) States (. . .) shall conduct all their activities in outer space (. . .) with due regard to the corresponding interests of all other States (. . .)".

[32]For the difference between militarization and weaponization of space, see *inter alia* Zahoor (2017), p. 113.

contrary, the regime applying to the Moon and other celestial bodies is stricter, as they are to be used "exclusively for peaceful purposes" (Art. IV para 2 of the OST).[33] The OST aims at ensuring the peaceful use of space by establishing effective safeguards against the proliferation of *well-known types* of weapons which is reiterated in other instruments, such as the Nuclear Test Ban Treaty[34] prohibiting the conduct of nuclear explosions in outer space.

At the same time, the principles applying to the use of force in international relations between states as established by the ICJ,[35] are of relevance. In particular, the Court clarified that "*civilians must not be the object of attacks, so States 'must consequently never use weapons that are incapable of distinguishing between civilian and military targets'. The second principle is that 'it is prohibited to cause unnecessary suffering to combatants*'"[36] and use weapons having an indiscriminate wide-area effect. These principles emerge from several international treaties and instruments aiming at limiting the use of weapons (such as Additional Protocol I[37] placing limits on attacks on civilians and civilian objects,[38] and protecting the environment against "widespread, long-term and severe damage")[39] and constitute the corpus of International Humanitarian Law (IHL). All these limitations—referred to as *Jus in bello*—apply to space operations likewise, on the basis of customary international law[40] (despite the fact that general international law does not refer to space weapons, *expressis verbis*).

Due to the particular features of AWS, it is necessary to examine first, whether their use in space is consistent with the specific rule established in Art. IV of the OST, and second (i.e., in case their use would be considered legitimate), whether they may effectively be used in accordance with the rules of IHL.

---

[33] The rule is reiterated in Art. 3 of the Moon Agreement: "The Moon shall be used by all states parties exclusively for peaceful purposes".

[34] Treaty banning nuclear weapon tests in the atmosphere, in outer space and under water (Partial Test Ban Treaty) (adopted 5 August 1963 entered into force 10 October 1963) 480 UNTS 43, Art. I.

[35] *Legality of the Threat or Use of Nuclear Weapons (Advisory Opinion)* [1996] ICJ Rep. 266.

[36] Blount (2009), p. 5.

[37] Protocol Additional to the Geneva Conventions of 12 August 1949 and Relating to the Protection of Victims of International Armed Conflicts (adopted 8 June 1977 entered into force 7 December 1978) 1125 UNTS 3 (Additional Protocol I).

[38] According to Additional Protocol I, Art. 51.4, indiscriminate attacks are prohibited.

[39] Additional Protocol I, Art. 55.

[40] "(...) international humanitarian and the *jus in bello* and *jus ad bellum* applicable to warfare apply equally in space (ref. to Boothby (2017), p. 179)", Mosteshar (2019); Blount (2009), p. 5.

3.1 Do AWS Used in Space Meet the Requirements Set Out in Art IV of the OST?

Given on the one hand the ban on nuclear weapons and *any kind of weapons of mass destruction* in space (Art. IV para 1 of the OST) and on the other hand, the multifaceted nature of AWS, the first task is to define the precise category to which AWS belong.

In general, weapons are categorized according to their type and/or their use and purpose,[41] the *summa divisio* being that between conventional arms (causing material damage by using kinetic, incendiary, or explosive energy, such as small arms, bombs, rockets, missiles, missile launchers)[42] and non-conventional ones. The second category refers to nuclear, chemical, and biological weapons; the term is used as a synonym for weapons of mass destruction (WMD)[43] and includes "*any weapons developed in the future which might have characteristics comparable in destructive effect to those of (...) other weapons mentioned above*".[44] Space weapons are defined as weapons designed to be used in space, under specific conditions of gravity and velocity. They may cause a wide range of damage[45] due to the vastness of space; hence, a detailed examination of their operating mode is required, before including them in a category of weapon.

3.1.1 Traditional Space Weapons Vs AWS (Space) Technology

Conventional space weapons[46] are already being used. Lars Hostbeck distinguishes three categories, based on their trajectory: (i) *Earth-to-Space weapons*, namely missiles or directed energy weapons launched from the Earth; their target is in space, and usually consists in a satellite or anti-ballistic missile system/ABM. (ii) *Space-to-Space weapons* (i.e. missiles or directed energy weapons) placed and launched from Space, either prior to the time they are being used, or after the target has been identified; their launching platform is a satellite—or another space object—and their target is either a satellite or an Intercontinental Ballistic Missile (ICBM).[47] Finally, (iii) *Space-to-Earth weapons* (SEW), with a launching platform in space and

[41] Mosteshar (2019).

[42] "Conventional arms are weapons other than weapons of mass destruction", see UNODA(a). Missiles are the most frequently used in the context of space.

[43] The UN mentions "nuclear, chemical and biological weapons", see UNODA(b).

[44] UNGA, 'Prohibition of the development and manufacture of new types of weapons of mass destruction and new systems of such weapons', GA Res 32/84[B], 12 December 1977.

[45] Such as when used for counterspace actions, Hitchens (2017).

[46] For additional approaches to space weapons, Sheehan (2015), p. 12.

[47] "The launch of Sputnik in 1957 (...) demonstrated intercontinental ballistic missile (ICBM) technology for the first time. This demonstration globalized the threat of nuclear war by diminishing the time and ability of a state to defend against such an attack", Blount (2018).

a target in any place on Earth.[48] From a different perspective, Lyall & Larsen propose a distinction between: (a) weapons in orbit used to strike the surface of the Earth or targets in air-space, (b) weapons in orbit used to strike other space objects and (c) weapons in space used to target ballistic missiles being boosted from the surface of the Earth (ASAT), eventually used to paralyze radio frequencies and energy sources.[49]

Their key feature is that reference is still made to guns, bombs, and missiles, which are, however, carried by—or aimed at—weapon platforms such as satellites, spaceships, and space planes.[50] They allow reaching targets that cannot be reached differently (they are inaccessible to other types of weapons) and may cover a large distance within a very short period of time,[51] which makes them less vulnerable to attacks.[52] Nonetheless, they remain observable and their trajectory predicable—despite being in orbit–, and may create a significant amount of debris, if destroyed.

AI offers clear advantages when used onboard space objects and allows significant improvements in terms of (i) decision-making, by processing infinite amounts of data (Space Big Data) at a very high speed; (ii) identifying situations and objects from a long distance; and (iii) processing data to make estimates without being dependent on communications to Earth, in environments that are inaccessible—or forbidden—to humans. Using this technology, AWS in space will not only be able to adapt an object's course, by improving their trajectory so as to avoid collisions with other objects, but more than that, act—during an armed conflict—in an "intelligent"[53] way.

3.1.2 Nature & Extent of the Injury Potentially Resulting from the Use of AWS in Space

The general concepts of *injury*, *attack*, or *harm* allow to evaluate when and in which manner it is appropriate to use force—to maintain peace or in self-defense (UN Charter), and/or according to IHL during a war–, but also to categorize weapons. As concepts, they are mainly defined by reference to material damage being caused by using kinetic, incendiary, or explosive energy. Nonetheless, reference is increasingly made to damage being caused by measures involving a use of

[48] Hostbeck (2015), p. 956.

[49] Lyall and Larsen (2018), p. 448.

[50] *Idem*.

[51] They could offer response times from several minutes to several hours, Preston et al. (2002), p. XX.

[52] However, their launching is expensive, and many would be required to be put into orbit to ensure that one of them would be in the right place when needed: "dozens of weapons in orbit for each needed to engage targets at a particular time and place. (. . .) constellations could be as small as three to six weapons for each needed to engage a target at a particular time and place", Preston et al. (2002), p. XXI.

[53] This viewpoint is developed in the conclusions.

force without, however, constituting an armed attack[54] *stricto sensu* (e.g., in the case of cyber-attacks). Hence, the use of digital or cyber technology—as a weapon of war—must comply with *Jus ad bellum* and *Jus in bello*,[55] since despite substantive differences between cyber and kinetic measures, "the latter could theoretically prove monumentally destructive, in many cases more so than kinetic ones".[56]

Following this reasoning, weapons using non-kinetic, non-incendiary and non-explosive energy (like digital technology, AI etc.) should be assessed in light of their overall effects, to determine if they should be assimilated to conventional weapons or WMD. In other words, it is appropriate to examine the full extent of damage possibly caused by AWS in space, and whether such potential allows to really include AWS in the category of conventional weapons, contingently authorized in space by an argument *a contrario* based on Art. IV of the OST.

In reality, the key feature of AI is to automatically collect and process data (usually on the basis of a machine learning technology), having eventually reached remote and inaccessible areas and/or changed or adapted its targeting parameters over time; thus, it will not necessarily differentiate between data related to Space or conflict *stricto sensu* (i.e., with a direct impact on the conduct of operations, or related to weapons trajectory etc.) and those providing information of an economic, political, and strategic nature.[57] It will also allow conducting attacks of a different character—such as radio-frequency jamming—resulting in the complete destruction of targets, as these would "no longer be able to perform (their) proper function".[58] Overall, AI could also lead to unintended and unpredictable consequences[59]; the period for decision-making will be substantially reduced, eventually paving the way for an escalation of hostilities, as there will be no time to mull over decisions[60] or reverse the course of war.[61]

---

[54] In the Nicaragua Judgement, the ICJ clarified that there are 'measures which do not constitute an armed attack but may nevertheless involve a use of force' and distinguished 'most grave forms of the use of force from other less grave forms.', Schmitt (2012), p. 286.

[55] "The International Court of Justice had opined in its Nuclear Weapons advisory opinion that the type of weapon used is immaterial to the application of Articles 2(4) and 51", Schmitt (2012), pp. 286–287.

[56] *Idem.*

[57] *Inter alia*, the National Defense Operations Center of the Russian Federation is designed to "collect, summarize, and analyze information on the military and political situation in the world (...) its software and hardware system monitors and analyzes information from open sources, simulates forecasts of key world events, and prepares recommendations in an automated mode", Kozyulin (2019), pp. 25–28.

[58] Sheehan (2015), p. 13.

[59] Their use will be favorable to developed countries; such changes to military organization could at the same time bring stability, an overall decrease in war or the strong leadership of the economically developed world; see Spindel (2019), p. 7.

[60] Humans using AWS lack alternative information allowing them to contest data outpout, Bode and Huelss (2021).

[61] Spindel (2019).

However, *until now*, such technology is not directly used, *via* outer space, for the purpose of causing injury or death to human beings. It is therefore reasonable to consider that AWS in space should not be regarded as (a priori) WMD and could possibly be considered to be lawful, as conventional weapons. As a reference point—since it also precludes the creation of material debris–, cyber technology used for military purposes is likewise regarded as failing to qualify as WMD.[62]

3.2 May AWS Be Used in Space, in Accordance with IHL?

In case AWS were regarded as being possibly usable in space, their use should comply with the *jus ad bellum* principles of necessity (i.e., force may only be employed defensively, and to the extent that non-forceful measures are unlikely to suffice) and proportionality, allowing only that degree of force required for an effective defense.[63]

3.2.1 Applying the Principle of Necessity: Dual Use Systems and Programming Errors

Article 48 of Additional Protocol I requires parties to always "distinguish between the civilian population and combatants and between civilian objects and military objectives.".[64] Therefore, the use of AWS in space would be legitimate only if it aimed at military targets, thereby offering a definite military advantage, or at an object normally dedicated to civilian purposes which is, however, "used to make *an effective contribution* to military action".[65] In this context, it appears that targets (in space) of a dual use character—e.g., dual use satellites—will pose specific problems.

Differentiating between well-known military and civilian targets is easy to do (AI is already used on Earth, to avoid putting human lives at risk and reduce human and other losses).[66] However, the task is more complex when the targets constitute high technology devices—such as space objects–, that are mainly of a dual use nature, for reasons of affordability. In fact, satellites are programmed to conduct operations like communication, navigation, observation etc., and often used either

[62] Carr (2013).

[63] Schmitt (2012), p. 286.

[64] Additional Protocol I, Art. 48.

[65] Additional Protocol I, Art. 52 para 3; Schmitt (2010), p. 795.

[66] Sisson (2019).

for civil or for military application.[67] They may easily switch from one to another, without that being a case of malfunction.[68] Thus, defining the nature of space objects as military or civilian targets, only on the basis of an automated processing (i.e., by AWS), is inherently risky.

In practice, a correct differentiation (i.e., between military and non-military targets and/or activity) could only result from the appropriate training and programming of AWS, based—first of all—on a sufficient amount of training data. This, in reality, requires that *clear examples of military tasks conducted by dual-use space objects are really detectable* (to be pre-labelled as positive and negative values) and, following that, provided to the algorithm to help it recognize them and act accordingly. It is, however, doubtful whether such differentiation will be possible in the event of simple data collecting processes or signal transfers, whatever their intended use.

Second, AWS should be trained to *recognize (and distinguish) an attack or military threat, from a programming error or bias*. This task is likewise difficult to accomplish in practice; questions will arise as to whether an AWS operation was, in reality, "accidental or caused deliberately by outside parties using techniques like hacking or data poisoning".[69] In addition to that, the specific scenario of a military threat or attack occurring in space will most probably consist in situations that are not yet defined and/or categorized (and, therefore, that cannot be used as training data); for example, should an "interference with the optimum efficiency of a frequency, or damage to an inanimate piece of metal"[70] be regarded as such?

The correct recognition of a military threat coming from a (dual use) space object will determine the right to use force in accordance with the principle of necessity, and *vice versa*, exclude a State's international responsibility for damage caused by its space object.[71] Arguably, the approach on cyber infrastructure and data stocks—i.e., that the determination that a civilian computer is (. . .) used to make an effective contribution to military action may *only be made after a careful assessment*. Should substantive doubts remain (. . .) it shall be presumed not to be so used[72]—could similarly be applied to space targets aimed by AWS. A question remains as to whether such careful assessment could be efficiently conducted by AWS, which

[67] "The Navstar GPS positioning satellite system, designed as military satellite, has been made available to civilian users and has become an indispensable tool for an astonishing variety of purposes (. . .)", Sheehan (2015), pp. 13–14.

[68] Technologies useful for verifying a space arms control agreement may be at the same time, potential ASATs themselves (e.g., satellites which can maneuver to inspect other satellites or lasers that can track satellites). Hence, there was a massive reliance on civilian satellite systems to accomplish military goals, e.g. during the 1991 and 2003 Gulf Wars; see Sheehan (2015), pp. 10 and 14.

[69] Mélanie Sisson (2019).

[70] Sheehan (2015), p. 18.

[71] On the grounds of Art. VI and VII of the OST, see *supra*, Sect. 2.2.

[72] NATO (2021).

are by definition trained to enable a better (but at the same time much faster) decision-making process at all levels.

3.2.2 Practical Difficulty to Comply with the Proportionality Principle

The second key principle of IHL to be respected when using AWS in space is the principle of proportionality (i.e., the prohibition to cause damage that would be excessive in relation to the concrete and direct military advantage anticipated). In this regard, AWS will respond by using data processing and autonomy in communication-denied environments, or when action happens at speeds beyond human cognition.[73]

Due to this feature, AI is expected to change the whole character of war,[74] by having an unprecedented impact on military organization and combat philosophy.[75] It is not regarded as a type of weapon but rather as a qualitative improvement of existing military systems, which gives them "new capacities (...) and reliable communication *that ultimately allow the hardware to adapt to the environment*".[76]

However, to be able to respond in an adapted and proportionate manner, AWS must be provided (again) with data, prelabelled as positive and negative examples.[77] Once more, the lack of *real wartime space data* able to train the algorithm will be the main inconvenience (e.g., "there are not many pictures of mobile missile launchers available publicly, which raises concerns about the risk of false negative");[78] the problem is amplified in the case of nuclear weapons. In fact, contrary to AI designed to be used in everyday life[79]—such as autonomous vehicles–, space AWS cannot be tested under *real* operational conditions until wartime.[80] Hence, even if AWS were developed in a well-adapted training environment, this could "*never fully recreate the chaos and violence of war*",[81] especially given the complex conditions of space temperature, pressure, and velocity.[82] How will an attack be perceived in space, without proper AI training, in a context of possible sensitivity errors, confusion etc.?

[73] Sisson (2019), p. 4.

[74] Spindel (2019), p. 6.

[75] "France reportedly plans to equip Syracuse telecommunication satellites with cameras and self-defense devices, such as blinding lasers or machine guns for breaking solar panels of an approaching satellite", Kozyulin (2019), p. 28.

[76] *Idem.*

[77] This is difficult *per se*, both for technological (due to the space gravity etc.) and financial reasons (a large investment is needed to keep pace with space robotics developments, and AI technology).

[78] Spindel (2019), p. 7.

[79] Scharre (2019), p. 12.

[80] Spindel (2019).

[81] Scharre (2019), p. 14.

[82] "There is a seemingly infinite number of possible interactions between the system's programming and its environments", *idem.*

Any error of analysis could result in a problematic (i.e., disproportionate) response, and unintended escalation of tension.

It is an open question whether AWS used in space will allow to make accurate estimates and a refined understanding of the war situation, to correctly perceive a (real) (space) threat and to respond in accordance with IHL. As the lack of training data could hamper the safe and controlled use of AI in a proportionate manner—which is, however, required by IHL–, major decisions should always be taken by human decision-makers.

4 Conclusions

The picture emerging from this analysis is that AWS, in the theoretical context of a space war (which will hopefully never occur), could be used in an "intelligent" manner, that will take into account the fundamental need to protect both humanity and the space environment to the benefit of all. Regarded as an "*all-round and all-weather combat capability (with) a robust survivability on the battlefield, as well as lower cost*",[83] they will allow using new types of threat—e.g., radio-frequency jamming, lasers used to disrupt or degrade space-based systems—and avoid creating either losses of human lives or space debris which pose tangible dangers to all space activities.

On the one hand, a broad interpretation of the OST prohibition to use force in space would probably put at risk a wide range of legitimate space activities and deter potential investors, particularly when AI dual-use technology is involved. The use of AWS could for this reason be considered-though under very strict conditions-as lawful (e.g., if they are not used in an offensive and destructive manner).

On the other hand, the growing interest in space resources exploitation—for both commercial and military purposes—and the use of AI[84] in space robotics, in conjunction with the awareness of (space) environmental constraints, will increase political tensions.[85] It is expected that in this context, new technologies will be harnessed; AWS could be possibly used to deter the enemy—without creating a visible accident or collision damages–, but should be regulated in line with international law.

In proposing solutions, scholars already suggest dissociating destructive from non-destructive effects of (space) weapons and concentrate efforts on controlling "*the destructive approaches because they produce long-lasting environmental side*

[83] China Arms Control and Disarmament Association (2019).

[84] Space policies are getting reframed [e.g. Regulation (EU) 2021/696 of the European Parliament and of the Council of 28 April 2021 establishing the Union Space Programme and the European Union Agency for the Space Programme and repealing Regulations (EU) No 912/2010, (EU) No 1285/2013 and (EU) No 377/2014 and Decision No 541/2014/EU, OJ 2021 L 170/69]; Also, efforts are made to regulate the use of AI [e.g., European Commission (2020)].

[85] AJIL-Contemporary Practice of the United States (2020).

effects, whereas nondestructive techniques do not".[86] From a different perspective, "*the rising number of 'dual-use' satellites further complicates matters and asserts that there is a growing need to reach consensus on additional legal regulation*".[87] It is therefore clear that any laws applying to potential conflicts in space will have to be debated, taking into account the characteristics of new technologies, such as AWS, while continuing to use space for peaceful purposes.

Until then, to ensure that international law is duly applied, AWS should only be used for defensive purposes and all the ultimate decisions taken by decision-makers.[88] If this is not possible (e.g. AWS without access to communication with Earth), decision-makers and their States should be held responsible for *any* damage caused by their AWS in space,[89] in line with the OST provisions, as a means to encourage them to remain vigilant and avoid any kind of escalation.

Acknowledgement The author would like to thank Professor Vassilis Pergantis and Dr. Themistoklis Tzimas for providing timely and insightful comments on an earlier version of the manuscript.

References

Abney KA (2020) Space war and AI. In: Masakowski YR (ed) Artificial intelligence and global security. Emerald Publishing Limited, Bingley, pp 63–79

AJIL-Contemporary Practice of the United States (2020) United States creates the U.S. space command and the U.S. space force to strengthen military capabilities in space. Am J Int Law 114:323–326. https://doi.org/10.1017/ajil.2020.13

Blount PJ (2009) Limits on space weapons: incorporating the law of war into the *Corpus Juris Spatialis*. In: Proceedings of the 51st Colloquium on the Law of Outer Space. Available via SSRN. https://ssrn.com/abstract=1393321

Blount PJ (2018) Space security law. In: Read P (ed) Oxford Research Encyclopedia of Planetary Sciences. https://doi.org/10.1093/acrefore/9780190647926.013.73

Bode I, Huelss H (2021) Artificial Intelligence, Weapons Systems and Human Control. Available via E – International Relations. https://www.e-ir.info/2021/02/16/artificial-intelligence-weapons-systems-and-human-control/

Bohinger S (2017) New space and the transitional phase of the space sector. In: Nardon L (ed) European space programs and the digital challenge. Available via IFRI. https://www.ifri.org/en/publications/etudes-de-lifri/european-space-programs-and-digital-challenge

Boothby B (2017) Space weapons and the law. International law studies 93:180-Carr J (2013) the misunderstood acronym: why cyber weapons aren't WMD. Bull At Sci 69:32–37

---

[86] Sheehan (2015), p. 13.

[87] Hays (2015), p. 4.

[88] The presence of humans on the battlefield will strongly decrease, thereby allowing human analysts to focus directly on data points, critical images and/or decisions, Spindel (2019), p. 7. See, also, China Arms Control and Disarmament Association (2019), p. 20: "When hypersonic weapons and cluster operations arise, war will enter the era of flash wars during which the autonomous fighting between intelligent systems might be the only way out".

[89] Such as for other AI uses in space, see *inter alia,* Kyriakopoulos et al. (2021).

Carr J (2013) The misunderstood acronym: Why cyber weapons aren't WMD. Bulletin of the Atomic Scientists 69(5)

China Arms Control and Disarmament Association (2019) Artificial intelligence and its military applications. In: Stanley Center for Peace and Security (eds) The militarization of artificial intelligence. United Nations, New York, pp 19–24

Daws R (2020) Intel, Ubotica, and the ESA launch the first AI satellite. Available via AINews. https://artificialintelligence-news.com/2020/10/20/intel-ubotica-esa-launch-first-ai-satellite/

European Commission (2020) White Paper on Artificial Intelligence – A European approach to excellence and trust. Available at EUR-lex. https://eur-lex.europa.eu/legal-content/EN/TXT/?uri=CELEX%3A52020DC0065

Gal GA, Santos C, Rapp L, Markovich R, van der Torre L (2020) Artificial Intelligence in Apace. arXiv:2006.12362

Hays PL (2015) International space security setting: an introduction. In: Schrogl KU, Hays PL, Robinson J, Moura D, Giannopapa C (eds) Handbook of space security: policies, applications and programs. Springer, New York, pp 3–6

Hitchens T (2017) Space Weapons Technology and Policy. AIP Conference Proceedings 1898: 030006. https://doi.org/10.1063/1.5009221

Hofmann M, Bergamasco F (2020) Space resources activities from the perspective of sustainability: legal aspects. Glob Sustain 3:e4. https://doi.org/10.1017/sus.2019.27

Hostbeck L (2015) Space weapons' concepts and their international security implications. In: Schrogl KU, Hays PL, Robinson J, Moura D, Giannopapa C (eds) Handbook of space security: policies, applications and programs. Springer, New York, pp 955–998

Kozyulin V (2019) Militarization of AI. In: Stanley Center for Peace and Security (eds) The militarization of artificial intelligence. United Nations, New York, pp 25–32

Kyriakopoulos G, Pazartzis F, Koskina A, Bourcha C (2021) Artificial Intelligence and Space Situational Awareness: Data Processing and Sharing in Debris-Crowded Areas. In: Proceedings of the 8th European Conference on Space Debris ESA/ESOC. https://conference.sdo.esoc.esa.int/proceedings/list

Lee RJ (2002) The Jus ad bellum in outer space: The interrelation between Article 103 of the Charter of the UN and Article IV of the Outer Space Treaty. Proceedings of the 45th Colloquium on the Law of Outer Space 45:139–148

Lyall F, Larsen PB (2018) Space law: a treatise, 2nd edn. Routledge, London

Maogoto JN, Freeland S (2007) Space weaponization and the United Nations charter regime on force: a thick legal fog or a receding mist? Int Lawyer 41:1091–1119

Martinez J, Bouvier A (2006) Assessing the relationship between jus in Bello and jus ad bellum: an "orthodox" view. Proc Ann Meet Am Soc Int Law 100:109–112

Mosteshar S (2019) Space law and weapons in space. In: Read P (ed) Oxford Research Encyclopedia of Planetary Sciences. https://doi.org/10.1093/acrefore/9780190647926.013.74

NATO – CCDCOE (2021) Military objectives: National Positions- Germany. https://cyberlaw.ccdcoe.org/wiki/Military_objectives

OECD (2019) The space economy in figures: how space contributes to the global economy. OECD Publishing, Paris

Preston B, Johnson DJ, Edwards S, Miller M, Shipbaugh C (2002) Space weapons earth wars. RAND Corporation, Santa Monica

Scharre P (2019) Military applications of artificial intelligence: potential risks to international peace and security. In: Stanley Center for Peace and Security (eds) The militarization of artificial intelligence. United Nations, New York, pp. 11–18

Scherer MU (2016) Regulating artificial intelligence systems: risks, challenges, competencies, and strategies. Harv J Law Technol 29:354–400

Schmitt MN (2010) Military necessity and humanity in international humanitarian law: reserving the delicate balance. Virginia J Int Law 50:795–839

Schmitt MN (2012) "Attack" as a term of art in international law: the cyber operations context. In: Czosseck C, Ottis R, Ziolkowski K (eds) 4th international conference on cyber conflict. NATO CCD COE Publications, Tallinn, pp 283–293

Sheehan M (2015) Defining space security. In: Schrogl KU, Hays PL, Robinson J, Moura D, Giannopapa C (eds) Handbook of space security: policies, applications and programs. Springer, New York, pp 7–22

Sisson M (2019) Multitaskholder perspectives on the potential benefits, risks and governance options for military applications of artificial intelligence. In: Stanley Center for Peace and Security (eds) The militarization of artificial intelligence. United Nations, New York, pp 3–5

Spindel J (2019) Artificial intelligence, nuclear weapons, and strategic stability. In: Stanley Center for Peace and Security (eds) The militarization of artificial intelligence. United Nations, New York, pp. 6–9

UN-LEGAL, Repertory of Practice of United Nations Organs (2016) Chapter VII- Action with respect to Threats to the Peace, Breaches of the Peace, and Acts of Aggression: Article 39, Supplement No. 10 (2000–2009). https://legal.un.org/repertory/art39.shtml

UNODA(a) Conventional Arms. https://www.un.org/disarmament/conventional-arms/

UNODA(b) Weapons of mass destruction. https://www.un.org/disarmament/wmd/

Zahoor S (2017) Maintaining international peace and security by regulating military use of outer space. Policy Persp 14:113–135

Zhang W (2019) Extraterritorial jurisdiction on celestial bodies. Space Policy 47:148–157

Performance or Explainability? A Law of Armed Conflict Perspective

Jonathan Kwik and Tom van Engers

Abstract Machine learning techniques lie at the centre of many recent advancements in artificial intelligence (AI), including in weapon systems. While powerful, these techniques utilise opaque models whose internal workings are generally quite difficult to explain, which necessitated the development of explainable AI (XAI). In the military domain, both performance and explainability are important and legally required by international humanitarian law (IHL). In practice, however, these two desiderata are in conflict, as improving explainability may involve paying an opportunity cost in performance and vice versa. It is unclear how IHL requires States to address this dilemma. In this article, we attempt to operationalise normative IHL requirements in terms of P (performance) and X (explainability) to derive qualitative guidelines for decision-makers on this issue. We first explain the explainability-performance trade-off, what causes it, and what its consequences are. Then, we explore relevant IHL principles that include P and X as requirements, and develop four tenets derived from these principles. We demonstrate how IHL prescribes minimum values for both P and X, but that once these values are achieved, P should be prioritised over X. We conclude by formulating a general guideline and provide an example of how this would impact model choice.

1 Introduction

The adoption of artificial intelligence (AI) is ubiquitous in both private and public domains, including that of the defence sector. The empowerment of weapon systems with more AI has been a dominant strategy in recent years and has been identified as

J. Kwik (✉)
T.M.C. Asser Institute, The Hague, The Netherlands
e-mail: j.kwik@asser.nl; h.c.j.kwik@uva.nl

T. van Engers
Leibniz Institute, TNO/University of Amsterdam, Amsterdam, The Netherlands
e-mail: T.M.vanEngers@uva.nl

A. Kornilakis et al. (eds.), *Artificial Intelligence and Normative Challenges*, Law, Governance and Technology Series 59,
https://doi.org/10.1007/978-3-031-41081-9_14

a key strategic goal of many militaries.[1] These high expectations can largely be attributed to the increased performance of modern AI, which over the recent years has shifted from knowledge-driven to data-driven machine learning (ML) techniques. These techniques boast excellent general performance and the ability to operate in complex or difficult-to-model situations.[2] Nevertheless, they also come with inherent weaknesses, such as data reliance,[3] overfitting, underfitting and data-shift problems,[4] and, particularly relevant to the topic addressed in this chapter, opacity.[5]

The opaque nature of many modern algorithms has been a significant stumbling block: Samek & Müller note that "the lack of transparency and explainability, which reduces the trust in and the verifiability of the decisions made by an AI system" actively slows or hinders their integration into many sectors.[6] The military domain is no different.[7] Growing concerns about the opaque nature of modern models have led to the development of XAI (eXplainable AI), i.e. techniques aimed at rendering them more interpretable. Nevertheless, implementing XAI often comes with a downside in the form of a reduction in performance.[8] This 'performance/XAI trade-off' introduces an important dilemma for decision-makers wanting to implement modern AI: should performance be prioritised at the expense of explainability, or performance be sacrificed for more explainability?

For military entities, this decision must also be made in light of applicable rules of international humanitarian law (IHL), the legal framework regulating the conduct of hostilities during armed conflict.[9] However, because AI is a relatively new development, there is no specific rule which directly provides an answer to this trade-off problem. A further complication is that both performance and explainability are relevant and possibly obligatory elements for determining the legality of weapon systems: low-performance systems would jeopardise the weapon's reliability and possibly introduce an element of uncontrollability or indiscriminateness to the system, while a lack of explainability would prevent decision-makers from properly foreseeing the consequences of the use of the weapon and, if violations do occur, frustrate ex-post evaluations.

In this article we discuss this performance/XAI dilemma for AI-enabled weapon systems (AIWS) in light of the normative requirements set by IHL. We attempt to answer the following question: *Ceteris paribus, given a choice between more performance or more explainability for the same (envisaged) AIWS, would IHL*

[1] Knight (2019).

[2] Nguyen et al. (2014), p. 1; Lipton (2016), p. 2.

[3] Samek and Müller (2019), p. 6; Russell and Norvig (2010), p. 27.

[4] Cummings (2018), p. 12; Gillespie (2014).

[5] Deng (2015), p. 25; Hofman (2020).

[6] Samek and Müller (2019), p. 6 (emphasis removed).

[7] ICRC (2019b), p. 10.

[8] Molnar (2019), p. 15.

[9] Fleck (2013), para 102.1.

mandate more accuracy at the cost of explainability or to sacrifice performance for more XAI? This question is relevant both when a weapon is being adopted and during operations. In the former case, it is important for States to know whether the performance/XAI ratio of prospective AIWS would permit the weapon to pass for legal use. In the latter, commanders may have to choose between several weapons with different performance/XAI ratios and determine which one allows them to best fulfil their IHL obligations.

This article is structured as follows. First, we briefly outline why opaque models are being used in a military context, what opacity exactly entails and what causes it, and why XAI is needed to combat this opacity. Then, we discuss the performance/XAI trade-off by examining different XAI techniques to show that generally, performance is an opportunity cost of more transparent or explainable models. In this section, we also make a distinction between 'inherent' and 'post-hoc' XAI techniques. Subsequently, we review the relevant IHL framework and identify which (sub-)principles are affected by a weapon's performance (P) and explainability (X) factors. By formalising these relevant principles, we demonstrate in comparative terms that there are baseline minimums which an AIWS must fulfil in terms of both P and X, but that after this minimum value is reached, P generates a greater comparative utility than X, indicating that P should be prioritised.

The scope of this article primarily concerns AIWS, i.e., physical capabilities which interact with the real world and have AI embedded in them to serve a certain operational function (such as target classification or selection), as different rules in IHL apply to domains such as data analysis or decision support. We do not consider artificial general intelligence systems which are expected to make advanced decisions usually reserved for humans, such as those related to military advantage. We also only consider norms flowing from IHL; in practice, many additional factors may influence the performance/XAI trade-off decision, such as policy, politics, ethics, and cost. By eliminating all other factors, we hope instead to present an uncompromised answer to the dilemma from a normative perspective, which decision-makers can subsequently weigh against other factors.

Finally, this analysis is based on the premise that 'performance is a cost'. However, it has been argued that in some scenarios, the opportunity cost may shift. Barredo Arrieta et al. for instance argued that with enough time, investment and effort, inherent solutions can achieve the same P as less-explainable alternatives.[10] That explainable algorithms in some cases come quite close to their opaque alternatives was also confirmed by Schwartzenberg & Van Engers in their study on surrogate models.[11] In that case, the trade-off changes from 'performance is a cost' to 'time/effort is a cost'. This scenario, however, requires a separate analysis and falls outside the scope of this chapter.

[10] Barredo Arrieta et al. (2020), pp. 83–100.

[11] Schwartzenberg et al. (2020).

2 Opaque Models in Weapon Capabilities

2.1 The Need for XAI

In a military context, the ability to delegate decisions to AI offers distinct advantages. Many different reasons for incorporating more autonomy have been cited in literature, such as shortening the decision-making cycle,[12] allowing operations in communications-disrupted environments,[13] avoiding human biases and weaknesses,[14] improving information processing capacity and speed, and even improving respect vis-à-vis IHL.[15] Envisaged functions to be delegated to AI include target detection, identification, tracking, prioritization, and engagement,[16] and may also require the AIWS to possess mobility functions to properly navigate its surrounding terrain efficiently.[17] While previously too difficult to model manually,[18] ML techniques allowed systems to develop their own model of the world using patterns discerned from large amounts of data, and are now the dominant solutions for many AI applications.[19]

One major disadvantage of ML techniques, particularly complex models such as deep neural networks, is their opacity. Also referred to as black boxes, these models obscure the way data is computed behind a level of complexity and high dimensionality that is often impossible for humans to understand.[20] Chakraborty et al. describe such models as offering "little to no explanation/visibility into why specific features are selected over others during training, or how the correlations in the training data are represented in the choice of the features, or why a specific pathway in the network ... is selected over others".[21] Such models are often contrasted with rule-based and linear regression models, whose decision-making logic is relatively simple for humans to grasp.[22]

Explainability has been identified as important for several reasons. Many authors cite user trust as an important goal that can only be achieved by improving one's understanding of an AI's workings.[23] For our purposes, explainability offers even more indispensable benefits. Firstly, explainability allows the provision of proof *ex ante* of a model's qualities. For any decision-maker to agree to the use of a system, it

12 Wilson (2020), p. 126.
13 SIPRI (2017), p. 133.
14 Singer (2009), p. 63.
15 Rosenberg and Markoff (2016); Sassoli (2014), p. 310.
16 Abaimov and Martellini (2020), p. 151.
17 Theunissen and Suarez (2015), p. 171.
18 Boulanin (2016), p. 23.
19 Engstrom et al. (2019), p. 1.
20 Bathaee (2018), p. 901.
21 Chakraborty (2017), p. 1.
22 Mueller et al. (2019), p. 5.
23 Biran and Cotton (2017), para 1; Tolk (2015), p. 300.

must be sufficiently explainable so they can be convinced that its decision-making process will be reasonable.[24] Explainability is also important for error mitigation: debugging, testing for biases, and elucidating the limits of the system all require knowledge beyond merely input and output mappings.[25] Finally, explainability is important in case something goes wrong: when a system does not operate as intended, the problem must be fixed and someone may have to be held accountable. Without explainability, legally holding someone accountable would be challenging because the outcome would have been unforeseeable and causality tests might fail.[26]

There is no consensus on the definitions of terms such as 'explainability', 'transparency' and 'interpretability'.[27] For the purposes of this article, we make no distinction between these terms and will use 'explainability' as a general term to refer to the condition where a human designer, user or auditor can understand the workings of an algorithm and thereby make predictions or deductions as to how it will behave or why it did behave in a certain way. We also use the concept as a spectrum instead of a dichotomy, meaning that some solutions can provide comparatively less understanding than others.

The increasing deployment of opaque systems for consequential decisions such as recidivism prediction, loan risk prediction and weapon systems has generated a push to address this issue in the form of eXplainable AI (XAI).[28] XAI is a rapidly evolving field of study and it is beyond the scope of this article to explore all solutions proposed in literature in detail,[29] but it is relevant to briefly discuss two major strains of XAI solutions. At the broadest level, XAI can be divided into *inherent* and *post-hoc* solutions.[30] The main difference lies in whether the explainability of the model derives from the nature of the base model itself, or from an outside source (applied to a base black box): "[E]ither the model is interpretable itself or some other technique is applied on the black box model to extract interpretations."[31]

In literature, inherent solutions are also referred to as 'transparent' or 'interpretable' models.[32] These models often derive their explainability from resort to an architecture that is inherently understandable to humans,[33] such as a decision tree or rule list. In essence, this solution consists of "providing a model which is locally or

[24] Hoffman et al. (2018), p. 1.

[25] Molnar (2019), pp. 17–19.

[26] Bathaee (2018). Specifically for IHL, see Kwik and Van Engers (2021), pp. 56–58.

[27] Adadi and Berrada (2018), p. 52154.

[28] Kuang (2017).

[29] For a full and detailed taxonomy of XAI approaches, see Barredo Arrieta et al. (2020).

[30] It should be added that hybrid solutions also exist; see for example Barredo Arrieta et al. (2020), p. 98.

[31] Karim et al. (2018), p. 1.

[32] Lipton (2016); Barredo Arrieta et al. (2020), p. 87.

[33] Biran and Cotton (2017), para 3.

globally interpretable on its own".[34] In the taxonomy list provided by Barredo Arrieta et al., they list regression models, decision trees, k-nearest, rule-based, general additive and Bayesian models as inherently explainable.[35]

Post-hoc approaches, in contrast, do not incorporate explainability considerations when designing the base model itself and focus mainly on performance. Instead, separate models are used afterward which target the base model so as to *explain* how the latter (seems to) function.[36] Put another way by Biran & Cotton, post-hoc solutions interpret instead of being transparent.[37] The fact that post-hoc solutions, by design, provide less comprehensive explanatory power than inherent XAI is emphasised in literature.[38] *Fidelity*, for example, is a measure of a XAI accuracy vis-à-vis the original model, indicating that the explanation is merely an approximation. Rudin asserts that 100% fidelity can only exist with inherently explainable models.[39] Thus, while post-hoc solutions have the advantage of requiring fewer compromises when constructing the base model, they provide lower explanatory power in general.

2.2 When Explainability Comes at a Cost

Explainability in AI is often seen as something inherently positive. Weller, however, warns that there may be "settings where, perhaps surprisingly, transparency may lead to a worse outcome. Transparency is often beneficial but it is not a universal good."[40] One of these situations is when the implementation of XAI leads to reduced performance of the model. There is a significant consensus in literature that achieving the 'best of both worlds' is unlikely; rather, there is usually a trade-off between performance (*P*) and explainability (*X*).[41] Put simply, "accuracy and simplicity (interpretability) are in conflict".[42] Very complex models boast high predictive power, but with this complexity, the model drifts away from inherent explainability, requiring post-hoc solutions which result in lower *X*. On the other hand, inherently explainable models pay for their simplicity with performance.[43] To illustrate, one cited benefit of post-hoc models is that "we can interpret opaque models after-the-fact, without sacrificing predictive performance".[44]

[34] Guidotti et al. (2018), p. 11.
[35] Barredo Arrieta et al. (2020), p. 93.
[36] Rudin (2018), p. 1.
[37] Biran and Cotton (2017), para 3.
[38] Doshi-Velez et al. (2017), p. 16; Lipton (2016), p. 2.
[39] Rudin (2018), p. 3.
[40] Weller (2017), p. 23.
[41] Molnar (2019), p. 15; House of Lords (2018), p. 37.
[42] Hansen and Rieger (2019), p. 42.
[43] Bastani et al. (2017), p. 1.
[44] Lipton (2016), p. 5.

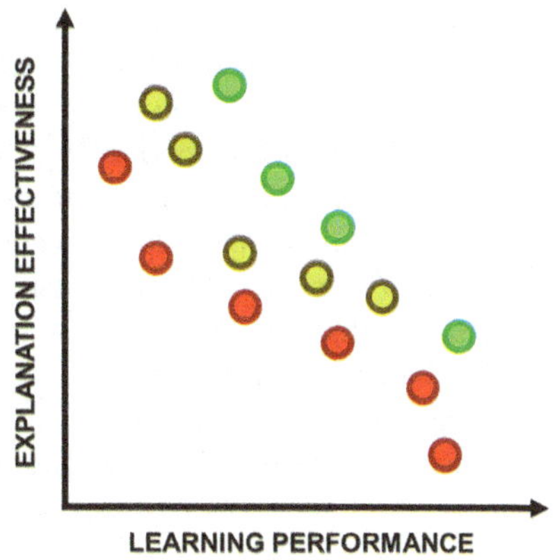

Fig. 1 Opportunity cost illustration (Authors' own interpretation of data from DARPA (2016), p. 14.)

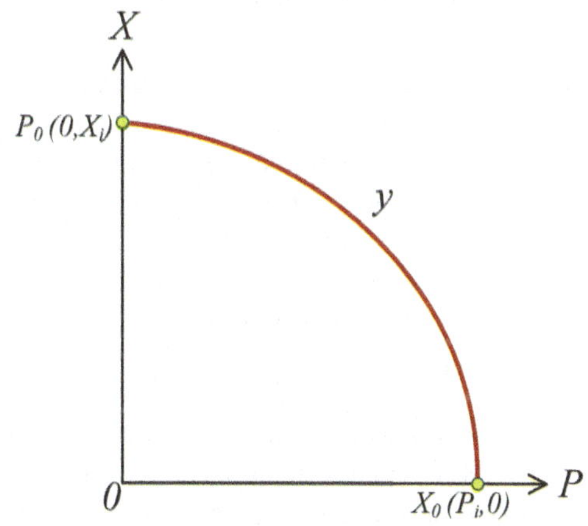

Fig. 2 Simple P vs X trade-off

The dilemma is represented in a 2016 DARPA report as a trade-off where a choice must be made between 'performance' and 'explanation effectiveness', representing a *P*-versus-*X* trade space (Fig. 1).[45] In other words, when designing AI with XAI in mind, a conscious decision should be made as to how much accuracy we are willing to give up for more explainability. The graph is useful as it represents *P* versus *X* as a general function, in accordance with our non-dichotomic use of 'explainability'.[46] Note that the graph has been criticised for appearing empirically-based, when in fact it does not represent any quantitative data.[47] As such, we propose the simplified graph in Fig. 2, where each point on the function *y* represents a possible *P* versus *X* trade-off ('P/X Ratio').

While this relation between *P* and *X* has always existed, AI design philosophy has traditionally neglected the value of *X* in determining the viability of the overall

[45] DARPA (2016), p. 7.

[46] See Sect. 2.1.

[47] Rudin (2018), p. 2.

system. Before the realisation that fully opaque models could cause societal problems, programming had focused purely on maximising P.[48] However, as indicated by the y function, "[i]f you focus only on performance, you will automatically get more and more opaque models."[49] The inverse is also true. Experts argued that "if we restricted ourselves only to techniques which we could fully understand, we would also limit what could be accomplished with AI".[50] Below, we demonstrate that X_0 or P_0 are not desirable states and can be ruled out.[51] Consequently, it is necessary to discern which point on y (i.e., which P/X Ratio) is most ideal, which we attempt based on normative guidelines present in IHL. We also consider if there are minimum values which must be attained in both the P and X axes and whether IHL contains a predilection for either more performance or explainability.

3 Applicable Rules of IHL

IHL is a special branch of international law that regulates conduct during armed conflict. IHL attempts a precarious balance between the necessities of war and maintaining minimum standards of humanity by regulating the methods and means with which parties wage their wars.[52] Any weapon, including AIWS, is subject to these limitations. Failure to respect these rules renders the weapon illegal and any misuse subject to disciplinary or criminal repercussions.[53] IHL is largely a principled rather than a prescriptive legal framework, which offers benefits and disadvantages: its relative flexibility has allowed most of its rules to remain relevant even in light of technological developments,[54] but it provides no direct answers to novel dilemmas such as the P-versus-X problem. Guidance on this matter, then, must be derived by analysing applicable principles.

In IHL, a weapon's legality is tested twice: once as a "general assessment" and later "in light of various circumstances".[55] For the former, it is relevant to look at the rules applicable for legal reviews, an important step in the adoption process where States consider whether the prospective weapon is legal according to its international obligations. For the latter, IHL requires decision-makers to take into consideration principles such as precautions and distinction for the attack to be legal, and should anything go wrong, further steps must be taken to prevent repetition and hold responsible parties accountable. In this light, we perform the analysis on a single

[48] Freitas (2014), p. 1.

[49] Molnar (2019), p. 15.

[50] House of Lords (2018), p. 37.

[51] Section 4.1.

[52] Sandoz et al. (1987), para 1389.

[53] Switzerland (2016), para 8; Department of Defense (2015), para 6.5.9.2.

[54] Kellenberger (2010), p. 800.

[55] Doswald-Beck (1997), p. 45.

function *y*, focusing purely on a linear *P*-versus-*X* comparison, simulating one of the following situations:

(1) *Adoption*: A State is commissioning or purchasing an AIWS and must choose between more performance or more explainability.
(2) *Operation*: A commander tasked with a certain operation has several AIWS available with different P/X Ratios, and must choose the most appropriate one.

Note that in practice, other factors will also be relevant, such as details of the operation, the weapon's ammunition, ethics, internal policy, and interoperability and compatibility. The purpose of isolating the P/X factors is to provide a motivated answer concerning this specific dilemma, which can then be weighed against other relevant factors by the appropriate decision-makers.

Section 3 only provides an overview of the relevant principles to consider. In Sect. 4 we formalise these principles to fit within the diagram introduced in Fig. 2.

3.1 Adoption Phase

When procuring a new AIWS, States can either contract companies to develop new arms for them, or obtain existing weapons domestically or from foreign producers.[56] With the former method, States have a more direct involvement in the design of the weapon, while with the latter, the choice lies more in determining which weapon to buy from which producer. Irrespective of the method, new weapons usually go through a review process to ensure that the weapon's characteristics are consistent with IHL.[57] For Parties of the First Additional Protocol to the Geneva Conventions ('API'), the legal obligation to review is made explicit in Article 36.[58] Even for non-Parties, however, it is evidently inefficient to procure weapons which cannot be used because they are incompatible with IHL.[59] As such, even if the review is non-formal, there is a vested interest for States to know whether to prioritise performance or explainability in their adoption process.

The matter of which elements of IHL to take into consideration during such reviews is more complicated. Many principles in IHL, such as proportionality and precautions, are practically-oriented and meant primarily for consideration at the 'field-level'.[60] API only asks to consider provisions in "this Protocol or by any other rule of international law applicable to the High Contracting Party",[61] and non-Parties are obviously free to apply their own list of legal criteria during reviews. A full

[56] Pamp and Thurner (2017), p. 458.
[57] Parks (2005), p. 114.
[58] Additional Protocol I (1977), Art. 36.
[59] Lawand (2006), p. 925.
[60] Ibid., p. 928.
[61] Additional Protocol I (1977), Art. 36.

comparative study of literature and practice goes beyond the scope of this article, but three factors are generally present in any framework: treaty obligations of the State, indiscriminateness, and superfluous harm.[62]

The first factor pertains to specialised restrictions or prohibitions in treaties such as the Conventional Weapons Convention, although evidently, a treaty on the P/X Ratio does not exist yet this time. *Indiscriminateness* refers to determining whether the weapon in question will be "capable of being used in compliance with the discrimination rule",[63] which is the basic rule in IHL that distinction must be made at all times between military and civilian persons and objects.[64] Specifically, it prohibits a "method or means of combat which cannot be directed at a specific military objective".[65] *Superfluous harm*[66] requires the State to determine if the weapon is of "a nature to cause superfluous injury or unnecessary suffering".[67] The application of these principles is inextricably linked to circumstantial (operational) factors, but it is still possible to apply them during acquisition by taking a more *in abstracto* perspective.

3.2 Operational Phase

During operations, the fundamental concepts of distinction and necessity once again become relevant but with improved context. As decision-makers have more concrete information available on the prospective operation, weapon selection based on IHL principles is carried out while taking into account specific intelligence available on the target, the surrounding environment, mission goals and other relevant factors. Therefore, even if a weapon has been cleared during its 'general assessment', it is still possible to use the weapon illegally under the specific operational circumstances.

In this light, *distinction* prohibits indiscriminate attacks, which take the form of attacks not directed at a specific military target, using weapons which cannot be directed in this way or using weapons which have indiscriminate effects,[68] the second of which is most relevant for our discussion.[69] In literature, there is some disagreement as to whether a weapon which 'inherently' cannot be directed at a

[62] Department of Defense (2015), para 6.2.2; Boothby (2016), para 19.5.3; Parks (2005), p. 129.

[63] Boothby (2016), para 19.5.3.

[64] Additional Protocol I (1977), Art. 48.

[65] Additional Protocol I (1977), Art. 51(4)(b).

[66] We use this term as a more direct translation of the French term *maux superflus*, which has the unwieldy English translation 'superfluous injury and unnecessary suffering'.

[67] Boohtby (2016), para 19.5.3

[68] Additional Protocol I (1977), Art. 51(4).

[69] The first and third pertain more to how an attack is conducted and 'effects' such as poison or biological contaminants respectively; see Doswald-Beck (1997), n. 16.

specific target even exists, with opponents arguing that any weapon can be 'discriminate' or 'indiscriminate' depending on how it is used.[70] Schmitt provides a more nuanced perspective, arguing that a weapon's 'indiscriminateness' is inherently linked to the intended operational environment.[71] For example, an AIWS that does not have an AI installed to distinguish between combatants and civilians would be 'indiscriminate' if the operation takes place in an urban centre, but would be perfectly legal if this particular classification needs not to be made (e.g., underwater). Thus, as long as the AIWS can be confirmed to exhibit sufficient performance to make the necessary distinctions for the envisaged operation, it would not be indiscriminate.

Given the weapon is not indiscriminate, decision-makers still need to take various *precautions* to ensure no unnecessary harm is inflicted. Most importantly in the context of our analysis, this involves *verification*, *proportionality* (the prohibition of excessive collateral damage not justified by the military advantage gained) and *minimising harm* (formulated as taking "all feasible precautions in the choice of means and methods of attack with a view to avoiding, and in any event to minimizing, incidental loss of civilian life, injury to civilians and damage to civilian objects").[72] Finally, IHL also establishes the obligation to *respect and ensure respect*, which includes the duty to address any breaches that may occur during operations.[73] This provision refers to a wide range of measures: armed forces should "take measures to stop violations", "not ignore breaches", and "cooperate to report and where possible investigate".[74] In other words, if a breach does occur involving an AIWS, the incident must be investigated, its causes determined and fixed to prevent repetition, and disciplinary action may be taken. If the violation was particularly serious, responsible parties may have to be referred to a criminal procedure.[75]

4 How IHL Affects the P/X Decision

Having outlined the most important principles to be considered during both Adoption and Operational Phases, we now consider how these principles factor into *P* and *X*. In this Section, we attempt a qualitative formalisation of the legal principles in terms of their effect on *P* and *X*, in order to draw an informed conclusion on how to proceed given the choice to opt for a higher or lower P/X Ratio. We will not make an

[70] See Boothby (2016), para 6.4.1; Department of Defense (2015), para 6.7.1

[71] Schmitt (2013), p. 11.

[72] Additional Protocol I (1977), Arts. 57(2)(a)(i), 57(2)(a)(iii) and 57(2)(a)(ii) respectively. See in general Art. 57.

[73] Additional Protocol I (1977), Arts. 80(1) and 86(1).

[74] Gill and Fleck (2010), para 24.02(5).

[75] Additional Protocol I (1977), Art. 85(1).

attempt to quantify the proposed benchmarks or guidelines. The reason for this is twofold: the legal principles which function as baselines for our analysis are inherently qualitative, and there is not yet an agreed quantifiable scale of 'explainability' in literature.[76] Instead, the purpose is to provide decision-makers with a general indication of important factors to consider when making this particular choice.

4.1 *P_0 and X_0*

Before moving to the more substantive analysis, we briefly address our prior statement[77] that P_0 and X_0 are never legal outcomes. A model at P_0 (zero accuracy, maximum explainability) is difficult to even envisage: it would have to be completely ineffectual as a tool, perhaps generating random outputs (its explainability being derived from its predictable randomness). Given that the indiscriminateness rule requires a relatively solid standard of performance before a weapon can be deployed legally, we can ignore P_0 as a consideration. In contrast, X_0 models do exist, being the default before more attention was brought to the importance of XAI.[78] There are comprehensive reasons listed in literature why deploying fully opaque systems would be undesirable or illegal,[79] but specifically for IHL, we extensively argued elsewhere that the pervasiveness of the notions of prediction and foreseeability in IHL renders X_0 models illegal per se.[80] This applies during both Phases. During Adoption, reviewers are required to determine the working of the proposed weapon in the intended working environment *in abstracto*, which requires a global understanding of the system's behaviour. The same assessment applies during operations:

> In order to comply with IHL, those who plan or decide on an attack using an autonomous weapon system must understand its capabilities and limitations in the given circumstances, in order to determine whether it will perform lawfully in the given circumstances.[81]

Finally, addressing failures requires *ex post* local explainability to trace the cause of the issue, repair it, and determine responsible parties. Thus:

$$P_0 \text{ and } X_0 \text{ are always illegal} \quad (1)$$

[76] Most sources visually depicting the P/X trade-off similarly use qualitative graphs with no empiric data behind them; see e.g. DARPA (2016), p. 7; Barredo Arrieta et al. (2020), p. 100.

[77] See Sect. 2.2.

[78] Freitas (2014), p. 1.

[79] See Hoffman et al. (2018), p. 4.

[80] Kwik and Van Engers (2021).

[81] ICRC (2019a), p. 3.

4.2 Adoption Phase

In this analysis we will ignore the step of testing the weapon against weapons treaty rules to which the State is Party. If a treaty obligation hypothetically requires a certain P/X Ratio to be applied, or perhaps even to abstain from using AIWS altogether, the State only needs to apply these provisions irrespective of their substantive merit. However, in all other cases, States must refer to indiscriminateness and superfluous harm for guidance to determine the appropriate P/X Ratio.

Similarly to the discussion of the principle during the Operational Phase,[82] there is disagreement whether an 'inherently indiscriminate weapon' exists.[83] Arguably, the determination is even harder to make during the Adoption Phase, because there is no concrete operational reference to base the evaluation on. To resolve this issue, when testing both indiscriminateness and superfluous harm as a general assessment, it is relatively settled doctrine that the test needs only be conducted with respect to foreseeable circumstances of use.[84] According to an authoritative commentary, "[t]he determination is to be made on the basis of normal use of the weapon as anticipated at the time of evaluation."[85] A weapon needs not be a swiss army knife: as long as it can be proven to function legally and effectively within the boundaries of the intended task and environmental conditions, it can pass the review process.

This detail is relevant with respect to AI as even the most powerful classifiers function poorly outside of environments for which they were designed. Fortunately, review processes allow specific instructions to be annexed to reviews which prevents operational use in situations outside of the referential circumstance(s) upon which the evaluation is based.[86] Through these 'conditional positives', reviews can safely make general pronouncements about the legality of weapons as long as they are used within specific boundaries (which normally also reflect the original intent of the weapon's designers).[87] The corollary of this is that reviewers must be able to determine the following: (a) What are the 'intended circumstances of use', and (b) How will the algorithm behave in these 'intended circumstances of use'?

Crucially, reviewers cannot rely solely on accuracy metrics and producer statements on this issue. It is generally inadvisable to blindly trust claims made by developers because they can be incomplete or misleading.[88] One concrete example is that raw accuracy metrics do not guarantee data-shift robustness and only reflect performance on training and test instances.[89] Only a global explanation of the

---

[82] See Sect. 3.2.

[83] See e.g. Department of Defense (2015), para 6.7.1.

[84] Lawand (2006), p. 928; Bothe et al. (2013), p. 231; Department of Defense (2015), para 6.6.3.4.

[85] Sandoz et al. (1987), para 1466.

[86] Sandoz et al. (1987), para 1402; Parks (2005), p. 133.

[87] Davison (2017), p. 12.

[88] Sandoz et al. (1987), para 1473.

[89] Ribeiro et al. (2016), p. 1.

algorithm can provide this abstract understanding, which requires XAI. Freitas remarks that understanding a model "might give us more confidence that the model is really capturing the correct patterns in the target domain (rather than patterns valid in past data that would not be valid in "future" data)."[90] Thus:

$$X \text{ must allow } \textit{ex ante} \text{ general determination of appropriate circumstances of use, approximate performance in these circumstances, and datashift robustness} \tag{2}$$

This criterion only requires that the evaluation *can be* made; it is a minimum benchmark. It is, however, a crucial one, as this X value also indirectly impacts the possibility to make a P-evaluation. If X is insufficient, no reliable statements on performance can be made. The *substantive* evaluation of P, however, is done in more direct relation with the principles of indiscriminateness and superfluous harm.

For indiscriminateness, it is required to establish that the weapon is not indiscriminate in the intended circumstances of use. For conventional weapons, this usually involves analysing technical details such as speed, accuracy, reliability, failure rates, test results, and error circular probable.[91] For AIWS, the AI's performance measure (P) would form part of this analysis. Because of the many factors involved and the fact that IHL provides no proscribed mechanism to States for conducting these reviews,[92] it is impossible to define strict mathematical minimum benchmarks for P to determine 'indiscriminateness'. What is certain is that so-called 'ultimate reliability' is not the standard. Speaking generally, Fenrick remarks that "one can predict that a certain percentage of any weapon will malfunction and hit the wrong object".[93] This unavoidable failure rate has never caused weapons to be labelled 'indiscriminate', as there is no such thing as a perfect weapon.[94] Nevertheless, it is evident that some P-values will be undeniably insufficient: if the accuracy is so low that the weapon cannot reliably make the distinctions it is required to perform during operations, there would be good reason to regard it as an 'indiscriminate weapon'.[95] Thus:

$$P \text{ must allow the weapon to reliably make the necessary decisions within its intended task domain and environment} \tag{3}$$

[90] Freitas (2014), p. 2.
[91] Boohtby (2016), para 19.5.5.
[92] Parks (2005), p. 107.
[93] Fenrick (2001), p. 500.
[94] Boohtby (2016), para 6.1.2.
[95] Switzerland (2016), para 8.

Finally, we consider superfluous harm, or "a harm greater than that unavoidable to achieve legitimate military objectives".[96] The superfluous harm rule is relatively unimportant for our current discussion. Historically, superfluous harm has primarily concerned a weapon's effects rather than its accuracy or decision-making method. Schmitt explains that "the rule addresses a weapon system's effect on the targeted individual, not the manner of engagement".[97] When applying this rule, emphasis is usually placed on the weapon's munition (e.g. exploding bullets, fragmenting projectiles and incendiary weapons) or damage mechanism (e.g. chemical weapons, serrated edges and blinding laser weapons). There is broad consensus that the superfluous harm rule is generally not relevant for discussions concerning AI in weapons.[98] Of course, AI can be installed into a weapon that fires exploding bullets, but in that case, the weapon would be rendered illegal not by its performance metrics or opacity, but by its type of projectile. As such, we can conclude that this rule does not impact our *P* vs. *X* evaluation in any way.

In sum, for the Adoption Phase, we have formalised two minimum requirements of *P* and *X*. Let us refer to these benchmarks as *min(P)* and *min(X)*, i.e., minimum values for each variable below which the weapon would not be IHL-compliant. (2) and (3) are cumulative rules and both must be fulfilled to pass the Adoption stage. While these provide a useful indicator as to the minimum criteria that should be set for *P* and *X* in terms of design, they do not answer what should happen *after* these benchmarks are reached. At the moment, IHL thus seems indifferent as to whether to prioritise *P* or *X* as long as *min(P)* and *min(X)* are fulfilled.

4.3 Operational Phase

A shift from Adoption to Operation does not bring forth many substantial changes with regard to (3). Commanders must still ensure to not employ a means of combat which is indiscriminate.[99] As during review, this requires the decision-maker to predict and foresee the approximate behaviour of the AIWS, suggesting a need for a global understanding (i.e., "how it will make decisions in all circumstances").[100] Explainability is also necessary for proportionality calculations. This principle requires commanders to refrain from launching attacks which would result in excessive civilian harm vis-à-vis the concrete anticipated military advantage.[101] This necessitates a robust understanding of how much civilian harm the AIWS's use would likely cause. This confirms the applicability of (2), namely that the AIWS

[96] ICJ (1996), paras 78-79.

[97] Schmitt (2013), p. 9.

[98] Schmitt (2013), p. 9; Thurnher (2014), p. 220.

[99] Additional Protocol I (1977), Art. 51(4)(b).

[100] Doshi-Velez et al. (2017).

[101] Additional Protocol I (1977), Art. 57(2)(a)(iii).

(s) under consideration must be equipped with sufficient *X* to make this global determination possible, including reasonable guarantees of data-shift robustness. As such, the *min(X)* criterion is maintained. Because commanders must reject the use of AIWS which cannot function in a sufficiently discriminating fashion in the expected operating environment, the concept of *min(P)* is also maintained, below which the weapon would be illegal to use.

Unlike the Adoption phase, however, obligations during operations stretch further than merely (2) and (3). This is due to the precautionary rule which requires commanders to "take all feasible precautions in the choice of means and methods of attack with a view to avoiding, and in any event to minimizing, incidental loss of civilian life, injury to civilians and damage to civilian objects".[102] This 'minimisation rule' primarily involves weighing available options: "If there is a choice of weapons or methods of attack available, a commander should select those which are most likely to avoid, or at least minimize, incidental damage."[103] Here, 'methods' refers to altering the method or logistics of attack, such as attacking at night.[104] 'Weapons', in contrast, refers to weaponeering, i.e., selecting the option from all feasible alternatives which leads to the lowest harm to civilians. Considering our current discussion, we will focus on the latter.

The minimisation rule involves a comparison prevalent in IHL, namely that between the utility of a weapon (in terms of the military benefit provided by its use) vis-à-vis the harm it will likely cause to the civilian population.[105] Let us note the first factor as *U* ('utility') and harm as *H*. Comparing two weapons (*w*) on the basis of *U* and *H*, the minimisation rule can be expressed as:[106]

$$\mathit{If}\ \frac{U_a}{H_a} > \frac{U_b}{H_b}\ \mathit{then}\ \text{obligation to use}\ w_a,\ \mathit{else}\ \text{use}\ w_b \tag{4}$$

Thus, given a choice and all other factors being equal, it would be required to choose the weapon with the "least damaging course of action compatible with military success".[107] For example, when choosing between an inaccurate gravity bomb and a more precise laser-guided bomb ($U_a \approx U_b$, $H_a > H_b$), the rule would require the use of the latter.[108]

For our discussion, we shall assume a 'pure' comparison between two weapons which have identical damage mechanisms and functions. This is important as a perimeter defence turret will provide an entirely different form of military utility to a

[102] Additional Protocol I (1977), Art. 57(2)(a)(ii).

[103] ICTY (2001), para 21.

[104] Sandoz et al. (1987), para 2200

[105] Sandoz et al. (1987), para 1428.

[106] If there are more than 2 feasible options to choose from, the rule can simply be applied iteratively.

[107] Rogers (2000), p. 177.

[108] Belt (2000), p. 149.

loitering drone—the overall *U*-values of the weapons would be too strongly influenced by this subjective and contextual determination. Instead, let us take two AIWS, w_1 and w_2, whose only difference lies in that w_1 is less accurate but more explainable than w_2 ($P_1<P_2$, $X_1>X_2$). What does IHL mandate us to do? To answer this question, we must consider how *P* and *X* factor into the variables of *U* and *H*.

Increasing the performance of a weapon fulfils a dual purpose. First, increased accuracy reduces a system's false positives, i.e., "when a machine mistakenly identifies a subject as possessing an attribute, when in fact the attribute is absent".[109] In context, this would reduce the instances of civilian targets being misclassified as a valid target, reducing *H*. It is almost universally given as an example of (4) that, *ceteris paribus*, higher-accuracy weapons should be chosen because such weapons offer "the best prospects of avoiding, or minimising, incidental injury or collateral damage".[110] One commentary to API explains that the rule is an "injunction to promote the maximum feasible accuracy", because this lowers *H*.[111] However, improved *P* also can reduce false negatives (i.e. legitimate targets are misclassified as no-strike objects).[112] These failures may not negatively impact civilians, but do reduce the weapon's *U* (from the user's perspective) as they are less effective, flexible, reliable or efficient. In either case, improving *P* positively impacts *U*/*H* (by maximising the weapon's military utility or minimising civilian harm caused). We can thus conclude:

$$\text{Maximise } P \text{ whenever possible} \tag{5}$$

(5) may at first glance seem evident or redundant as a mere reaffirmation of one part of the P/X dilemma: obviously we want to maximise both *P* and *X*, as both are important, but we cannot do so due to the P/X trade-off. However, remember that (2) and (3) reflect baseline criteria, while in contrast, (5) makes a statement about the relative value of *P* past this minimum point. Unlike the indiscriminateness rule which does not capture the value of 'more' discrimination beyond what is necessary to render the weapon non-indiscriminate (*min(P)*), the comparative nature of *U*/*H* found in (4) has no ceiling: more *P* is *always* better.

In contrast, *X* does not contribute significantly to minimisation beyond *min(X)*, reflecting the minimum level of explainability enabling substantive evaluations and predictions of the weapon's performance. This is not to say that zero additional value is generated when moving *X* past *min(X)*. Consider, for example, w_1 and w_2 respectively representing a linear regression model and an opaque model supplemented with a XAI surrogate. As w_1 uses an inherent solution, we can assume it provides a higher level of explainability than the post-hoc solution of w_2.[113] The

[109] Margulies (2017), p. 416.

[110] McLaughlin (2014), p. 235.

[111] Bothe et al. (2013), p. 406.

[112] Margulies (2017), p. 416.

[113] See Rudin (2018), for an extensive analysis for why this is necessarily the case.

increased explanatory power of w_1 would allow commanders to even more meticulously predict the exact behaviour of the system compared to w_2. Remember however that according to Fig. 2, a shift from w_2 to w_1 necessarily entails a reduction in *P*. As long as both AIWS have passed *min(X)*, we would argue that increasing *P* has a greater relative value than increasing *X*. Further increasing *X* only provides marginal benefits in the form of more accurate behaviour determinations, and may even have a ceiling (once an inherent model is fully understood, it cannot be made even more 'explainable' irrespective of how much further we reduce *P*). In contrast, increasing *P* has the continuous and significant benefit of improving *U/H* and reducing relative harm, fully in line with the spirit of the precautionary rule in IHL. As such, we can refine (5) into:

$$\text{After } (min(P), min(X)), P \text{ has more relative value than } X \qquad (5')$$

Representing our analysis thus far graphically, we obtain (Fig. 3):

Where *y* is the function representing discrete *P*-to-*X* trade-off options, *min(X)* and *min(P)* are the minimum respective values for legal use (reflecting (2) and (3)), *RV* is the relative *P*-to-*X* value (reflecting (5')) and options in the orange areas reflect insufficient *P* or *X* values (and are illegal per se). The *RV* curve favouring *P* indicates that between legal options w_1 and w_2, *P* should be prioritised over *X*.

One final factor not present during the Adoption Phase is the obligation to respect and ensure respect.[114] To address failures after the fact, XAI is needed as a way to analyse an instance in detail, i.e., to provide "the ability to audit a prediction or decision trail in detail, particularly if something goes wrong".[115] In contrast to previous requirements for *X* as captured in (2), this requires local understanding.[116] As such, it is important to amend (2) to include this criterion, as an AIWS whose opacity frustrates prevention, reparation and the assignment of responsibility would not be in line with IHL requirements.[117] In addition, while the duty to address violations only triggers *ex post* (after a failure occurred) and was therefore not discussed during our analysis at the Adoption Phase, it seems both intuitive and efficient to require *X* to fulfil this requirement as well during Adoption, if only to ensure that commanders always have AIWS available which fulfil our amended *min (X)*. Thus, for both Phases, we arrive at the following revision:

X must allow *ex ante* general determination of appropriate circumstances of use, approximate performance in these circumstances, and datashift robustness; and *ex post* local interpretation (2')

[114] See Sect. 3.2.

[115] Weller (2017), p. 25.

[116] Hoffman et al. (2018), p. 4.

[117] Kwik and Van Engers (2021), pp. 56–58.

Fig. 3 Minimum and relative values of P versus X

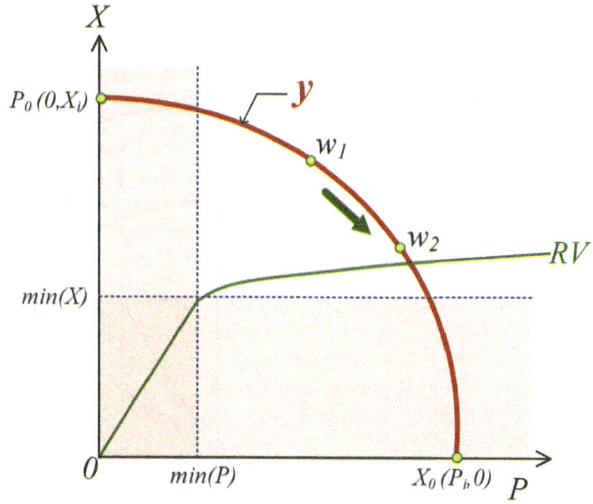

P does not factor into the obligation to respect and ensure respect in any way.

5 Applying the Tenets in Practice

Combining our findings in (1), (2'), (3) and (5') into concrete guidelines for decision-makers to follow, we arrive at the following two-step process:

1. *If* $X < min(X)$ or $P < min(P)$, *then* weapon is illegal; *else*
2. Prioritise *P* over *X*

As discussed previously, it is for each decision-maker or institution to determine the appropriate values for *min(X)* and *min(P)* taking into consideration the intended circumstances of use and, during the Operational Phase, to take all feasible measures to obtain any concrete information relevant to this analysis.

Applying these guidelines to more specific XAI solutions with varying P/X Ratios, we can determine under what circumstances resort to inherent solutions would be mandated by IHL, and otherwise when post-hoc solutions are sufficient to fulfil IHL obligations (and should thus be chosen because they provide higher *P*). Suppose in Fig. 4 below that for each *y*, the purple part represents inherent solutions and the red part post-hoc solutions:[118]

For y_1, past *min(X)*, there is the option of choosing either an inherent or post-hoc solution. The *RV* curve's preference for *P* over *X* past (*min(P)*,*min(X)*) would suggest

[118]For a sample spectrum of where specific XAI solutions would be placed on *y*, see for example Barredo Arrieta et al. (2020), p. 100.

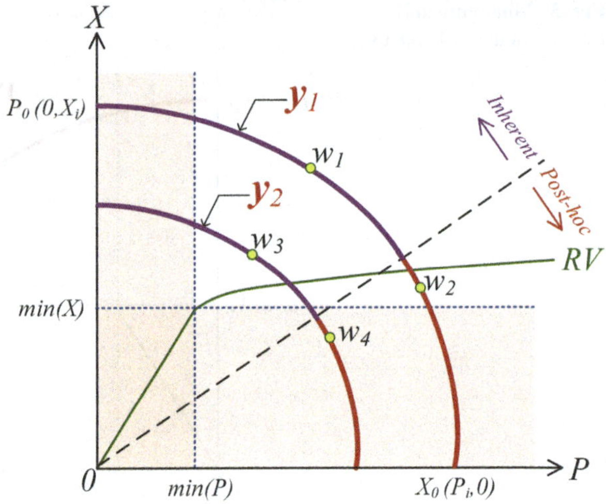

Fig. 4 Comparing XAI options

that resort to a post-hoc solution at approximately the intersection point (w_2) would be optimal for adherence to IHL. This could, for example, be a tree ensemble coupled with a simplified surrogate for explainability.[119] However, consider y_2, representing a domain or task of higher complexity. In this situation, while more accurate, the available post-hoc option (w_4) is unable to attain the minimum requirements of explainability to fulfil (2'). In this situation, there is no other choice than to adopt an inherent solution (w_3) despite the significant drop in performance. Once again, the *RV* curve intersection with y_2 confirms this.

To illustrate this more concretely, let us return to the scenario sketched in Sect. 4.3. To recall, in that instance we considered w_1 and w_2, respectively representing an intrinsic model and an opaque model with a XAI surrogate. Let us assume that the systems in question are antipersonnel active protection systems designed to guard a military convoy traversing an open field, tasked with neutralising any attackers. To do this, the system calculates the attacker's position from the incoming projectile's trajectory, identifies the person with sensors, and fires a counterround (a defence sometimes called 'shooting the archer').[120] It was argued that in this case the commander should select w_2, the opaque model, because it provides better accuracy (see Step 2). While the surrogate XAI may not provide intricate details on how exactly the system accounts for range, ballistic trajectory, the shooter's movement and other factors it takes into consideration, it provides the commander a sufficient general understanding of how the system will operate, and thus sacrificing *P* for w_1's intrinsic explainability would not be recommended.

However, let us now take y_2 representing an altered operational domain, that of urban areas. Because urban areas are sprawling, irregular and feature many agents,

[119] See Barredo Arrieta et al. (2020), p. 94.

[120] Kline (2018).

the AI designers had to include more complex features into its architecture. w_4 represents their best efforts in doing this, boasting an impressive accuracy rating (a higher P than w_1, the intrinsic model used in open fields, in fact). However, this P-level could only be obtained through an opaque model. When examining the surrogate XAI's explanations, the commander is not satisfied that they understand the system well enough to foresee how it would perform if the shooter is running through a crowd, hiding behind a counter, or firing from a rooftop ($X_4 < min(X)$). Thus, following Step 1, they must discard this weapon as an option. Their alternative, w_3, has a much lower but still acceptable accuracy rating ($P_3 > min(P)$), and, as an intrinsic system, provides sufficient understanding on how it would react to the above scenarios. Therefore, they would select w_3 in this situation.

6 Concluding Remarks and Future Research

In this article, we examined how to translate the principled norms in IHL related to the use of weapons into practical guidelines when decision-makers are faced with the dilemma of adopting more explainability or more performance, in light of the performance-explainability trade-off. By operationalising IHL norms in the form of X and P, we derived tenets which can guide decision-makers into avoiding inherently illegal alternatives and, amongst the legal options, to determine the optimum P/X Ratio to fulfil obligations related to distinction, proportionality, necessity and precautions. We graphically illustrated how these tenets would inform the decision in practice and answered the question of when recourse to inherent solutions is mandatory vis-à-vis post-hoc solutions. Keeping the recommendations in this article in mind, decision-makers will be better able to make an informed holistic analysis of the many factors that ultimately determine the legal use of a weapon, the P/X Ratio being one of them.

A few matters still remain unresolved. First, it remains a significant challenge to quantify these elements; 'explainability' still lacks a uniform measurement system and legal concepts such as *U, H* and even 'intended circumstances of use' are highly qualitative, casuistic and may even be subject to different interpretations.[121] One commentator in fact relents and simply accepts that "[i]nevitably, the assessment will be subjective".[122] Despite the foreseeable difficulty in doing so, the authors would greatly appreciate attempts to formulate more concrete guidelines for these issues.

Second, it is valid to question what methods to use to determine, in practice, if *min(X)* has been achieved as required by (2'). Evidently, not all explanations are equally good. Many authors have written about how to evaluate the quality of XAI

[121] Sandoz et al. (1987), para 1439.

[122] Bothe et al. (2013), p. 226.

and how to compare their *X*-values,[123] although ultimately, "there is little consensus on what interpretability in machine learning *is* and how to *evaluate* it for benchmarking".[124] More research in this area will enable a more concrete formulation of (2').

References

Abaimov S, Martellini M (2020) Artificial intelligence in autonomous weapon systems. In: Martellini M, Ralf T (eds) 21st century prometheus managing CBRN safety and security affected by cutting-edge technologies. Springer Nature Switzerland AG, Cham, pp 141–177

Adadi A, Berrada M (2018) Peeking inside the black-box: a survey on explainable artificial intelligence (XAI). IEEE Access 6:52138–52160. https://doi.org/10.1109/ACCESS.2018.2870052

Barredo Arrieta A, Díaz-Rodríguez N, Del Ser J et al (2020) Explainable artificial intelligence (XAI): concepts, taxonomies, opportunities and challenges toward responsible AI. Inf Fusion 58:82–115. https://doi.org/10.1016/j.inffus.2019.12.012

Bastani O, Kim C, Bastani H (2017) Interpreting Blackbox Models via Model Extraction. arXiv:1705.08504 (cs)

Bathaee Y (2018) The artificial intelligence black box and the failure of intent and causation. Harv J L Technol 31:889–938

Belt SW (2000) Missiles over Kosovo: emergence, lex Lata, of a customary norm requiring the use of precision munitions in Urban areas. Nav Law Rev 47:115

Biran O, Cotton C (2017) Explanation and justification in machine learning: a survey. In: IJCAI 2017 Workshop on Explainable Artificial Intelligence (XAI). pp 8–13

Boothby WH (2016) Weapons and the law of armed conflict, 2nd edn. Oxford University Press, Oxford

Bothe M, Partsch KJ, Solf WA (eds) (2013) New rules for victims of armed conflict: commentary on the two 1977 protocols additional to the Geneva Conventions of 1949, 2nd edn. Martinus Nijhoff, Leiden

Boulanin V (2016) Mapping the development of autonomy in weapon systems: a primer on autonomy. Stockholm International Peace Research Institute, Stockholm

Chakraborty S, Tomsett R, Raghavendra R, et al (2017) Interpretability of deep learning models: a survey of results. In: 2017 IEEE SmartWorld, Ubiquitous Intelligence & Computing, Advanced & Trusted Computed, Scalable Computing & Communications, Cloud & Big Data Computing, Internet of People and Smart City Innovation (SmartWorld/SCALCOM/UIC/ATC/CBDCom/IOP/SCI). IEEE, pp 1–6

Cummings ML (2018) Artificial intelligence and the future of warfare. In: Cummings ML, Roff HM, Cukier K et al (eds) Artificial intelligence and international affairs: disruption anticipated. Chatham House, London, pp 7–18

DARPA (2016) Broad Agency Announcement: Explainable Artificial Intelligence (XAI), DARPA-BAA-16-53

Davison N (2017) A legal perspective: autonomous weapon systems under international humanitarian law. In: UNODA Occasional Papers No. 30, New York, pp 5–18

Deng B (2015) The Robot's Dilemma: working out how to build ethical robots is one of the thorniest challenges in artificial intelligence. Nature 523:25–27

---

[123] See Guidotti et al. (2018), pp. 6–7; Mueller et al. (2019), p. 69.

[124] Doshi-Velez and Kim (2017), p. 1 (emphasis in original).

Department of Defense (2015) Law of War Manual, Updated December 2016

Doshi-Velez F, Kim B (2017) Towards A Rigorous Science of Interpretable Machine Learning. arXiv:1702.08608 (stat)

Doshi-Velez F, Kortz M, Budish R, et al (2017) Accountability of AI Under the Law: The Role of Explanation. arXiv:1711.01134 (cs)

Doswald-Beck L (1997) International humanitarian law and the advisory opinion of the International Court of Justice on the threat or use of nuclear weapons. Int Rev Red Cross 316:35–55

Engstrom L, Tran B, Tsipras D, et al (2019) A Rotation and a Translation Suffice: Fooling CNNs with Simple Transformations. Proceedings of the 36th International Conference on Machine Learning 97:1802–1811

Fenrick WJ (2001) Targeting and proportionality during the NATO bombing campaign against Yugoslavia. Eur J Int Law 12:489–502

Fleck D (ed) (2013) The handbook of international humanitarian law, 3rd edn. Oxford University Press, Oxford

Freitas AA (2014) Comprehensible classification models. ACM SIGKDD Explor Newsl 15:1–10. https://doi.org/10.1145/2594473.2594475

Gill TD, Fleck D (eds) (2010) The handbook of the international law of military operations. Oxford University Press, Oxford

Gillespie T (2014) Algorithm [draft] [#digitalkeywords]. In: Culture Digitally. culturedigitally.org/2014/06/algorithm-draft-digitalkeyword

Guidotti R, Monreale A, Ruggieri S, et al. (2018) A survey of methods for explaining black box models. ACM Computing Surveys 51, Article 93

Hansen LK, Rieger L (2019) Interpretability in intelligent systems – a new concept? In: Samek W, Montavon G, Vedaldi A et al (eds) Explainable AI: interpreting, explaining and visualizing deep learning. Springer Nature Switzerland, Cham, pp 41–49

Hoffman RR, Mueller ST, Klein G, Litman J (2018) Metrics for Explainable AI: Challenges and Prospects. arXiv:1812.04608.

Hofman L (2020) De nieuwste wapenwedloop gaat niet om bommen, maar om algoritmes (en hoe die te foppen). Available via de Correspondent. https://decorrespondent.nl/11511/de-nieuwste-wapenwedloop-gaat-niet-om-bommen-maar-om-algoritmes-en-hoe-die-te-foppen/826075404-95eb7eba.

House of Lords (2018) Select Committee on Artificial Intelligence, Report of Session 2017-19, AI in the UK: Ready, Willing, and Able?, HL Paper 100

ICRC (2019a) 'Statement of the International Committee of the Red Cross (ICRC) under agenda item 5(b)', Convention on Certain Conventional Weapons (CCW), Group of Governmental Experts on Lethal Autonomous Weapons Systems (Geneva, 25-29 March 2019)

ICRC (2019b) Artificial intelligence and machine learning in armed conflict: a human-centred approach. ICRC, Geneva

ICTY (2001) Final Report to the Prosecutor by the Committee Established to Review the NATO Bombing Campaign Against the Federal Republic of Yugoslavia

Karim A, Mishra A, Newton MH, Sattar A (2018) Machine learning interpretability: a science rather than a tool. arxiv.org/abs/1807.06722

Kellenberger J (2010) Strengthening legal protection for victims of armed conflicts. Int Rev Red Cross 879:799–804

Kline J (2018) Countertargeting: offense enabler and defense enhancer. In: US Nav Inst Blog blog. usni.org/posts/2018/03/27/countertargeting-offense-enabler-and-defense-enhancer

Knight W (2019) Military artificial intelligence can be easily and dangerously fooled. In: MIT Tech Rev. www.technologyreview.com/2019/10/21/132277/military-artificial-intelligence-can-be-easily-and-dangerously-fooled

Kuang C (2017) Can A.I. be taught to explain itself? New York Times.. https://www.nytimes.com/2017/11/21/magazine/can-ai-be-taught-to-explain-itself.html

Kwik J, Van Engers T (2021) Algorithmic fog of war: when lack of transparency violates the law of armed conflict. J Future Robot Life 2:43–66. https://doi.org/10.3233/FRL-200019

Lawand K (2006) Reviewing the legality of new weapons, means and methods of warfare. Int Rev Red Cross 88:925–930
Lipton ZC (2016) The Mythos of Model Interpretability. arXiv:1606.03490 (cs)
Margulies P (2017) Making autonomous weapons accountable: command responsibility for computer-guided lethal force in armed conflicts. In: Ohlin JD (ed) Research handbook on remote warfare. Edward Elgar, Cheltenham, pp 405–442
McLaughlin R (2014) Unmanned naval vehicles and the law of naval warfare. In: Nasu H, McLaughlin R (eds) New technologies and the law of armed conflict. T.M.C. Asser Press, The Hague, pp 229–246
Molnar C (2019) Interpretable machine learning: a guide for making black box models explainable. Lean Publishing
Mueller ST, Hoffman RR, Clancey W, et al (2019) Explanation in Human-AI Systems: A Literature Meta-Review Synopsis of Key Ideas and Publications and Bibliography for Explainable AI. DARPA XAI Program, Arlington
Nguyen A, Yosinski J, Clune J (2014) Deep Neural Networks are Easily Fooled: High Confidence Predictions for Unrecognizable Images. arXiv:1412.1897 (cs)
Pamp O, Thurner PW (2017) Trading arms and the demand for military expenditures: empirical explorations using new SIPRI-data. Def Peace Econ 28:457–472. https://doi.org/10.1080/10242694.2016.1277452
Parks WH (2005) Conventional weapons and weapons reviews. Yearb Int Humanit Law 8:55–142
Ribeiro MT, Singh S, Guestrin C (2016) Why Should I Trust You?: Explaining the predictions of any classifier. In: Proceedings of the 22nd ACM SIGKDD International Conference on Knowledge Discovery and Data Mining. Association for Computing Machinery, New York, pp 1135–1144
Rogers APV (2000) Zero-casuality warfare. Int Rev Red Cross 837:165–181
Rosenberg M, Markoff J (2016) At Heart of U.S. Strategy, Weapons That Can Think. New York Times A1
Rudin C (2018) Stop Explaining Black Box Machine Learning Models for High Stakes Decisions and Use Interpretable Models Instead. arXiv:1811.10154 (stat).
Russell SJ, Norvig P (2010) artificial intelligence: a modern approach, 3rd edn. Pearson, New Jersey
Samek W, Müller K-R (2019) Towards explainable artificial intelligence. In: Samek W, Montavon G, Vedaldi A et al (eds) Explainable AI: interpreting, explaining and visualizing deep learning. Springer Nature Switzerland, Cham, pp 5–22
Sandoz Y, Swinarski C, Zimmerman B (1987) Commentary on the Additional Protocols of 8 June 1977 to the Geneva Conventions of 12 August 1949. Martinus Nijhoff, Geneva
Sassoli M (2014) Autonomous weapons and international humanitarian law: advantages, open technical questions and legal issues to be clarified. Int Law Stud 90:308–340
Schmitt MN (2013) Autonomous weapon systems and international humanitarian law: a reply to the critics. Harv Natl Secur J, pp 1–37
Schwartzenberg C, van Engers T, Li Y (2020) The fidelity of global surrogates in interpretable Machine Learning. In: BNAIC/BeneLearn 2020 Proceedings, Leiden University, Leiden, 19-20 November 2020
Singer P (2009) Wired for War: The Robotics Revolution and Conflict in the 21st Century. Penguin Press, London
SIPRI (2017) Literature review for the Policy and Operations Evaluations Department of the Dutch Ministry of Foreign Affairs, Final Report. SIPRI, Solna
Switzerland (2016) Towards a "compliance-based" approach to LAWS. In: CCW Informal Meeting of Experts on Lethal Autonomous Weapon Systems, Geneva, 11–15 Apr. 2016. Geneva
Theunissen E, Suarez B (2015) Choosing the level of autonomy: options and constraints. In: Williams AP, Scharre PD (eds) Autonomous systems: issues for defence policymakers. NATO, The Hague, pp 169–195

Thurnher JS (2014) Examining autonomous weapon systems from a law of armed conflict perspective. In: Nasu H, McLaughlin R (eds) New technologies and the law of armed conflict. T.M.C. Asser Press, The Hague, pp 213–228
Tolk A (2015) Merging two worlds: agent-based simulation methods for autonomous systems. In: Williams AP, Scharre PD (eds) Autonomous systems: issues for defence policymakers. NATO, The Hague, pp 291–317
Weller A (2017) Transparency: motivations and challenges
Wilson C (2020) Artificial intelligence and warfare. In: Martellini M, Trapp R (eds) 21st century Prometheus managing CBRN safety and security affected by cutting-edge technologies. Springer Nature Switzerland AG, Cham, pp 141–177

The manufacturer's authorised representative in the EU is Springer
Nature Customer Service Centre GmbH, Europaplatz 3, 69115 Heidelberg,
Germany. If you have any concerns regarding our products, please
contact ProductSafety@springernature.com

Printed and bound by CPI Group (UK) Ltd, Croydon, CR0 4YY
28/09/2026
02224075-0010